toring, but spits at Ben when he tries to play into there, which is very rude and ill-tempered. He is black & she is orange-coloured.

P.S. With love and New Year's wishes to all of you.

from yours affly

Macaulay.

Rose Macaulay

By the same author

In the Chinks of the World Machine:
Feminism and Science Fiction

Rose Macaulay

SARAH LEFANU

Virago

A *Virago* Book

First published by Virago Press 2003

Copyright © Sarah LeFanu 2003

The moral right of the author has been asserted.

A CIP catalogue record for this book is
available from the British Library.

ISBN 1 86049 945 7

*Endpapers show a letter from Rose Macaulay to
eight-year-old Mary O'Donovan, 1926*

Typeset in Caslon by M Rules
Printed and bound in Great Britain by
Clays Ltd, St Ives plc

Virago Press
an imprint of
Time Warner Books UK
Brettenham House
Lancaster Place
London WC2E 7EN

www.virago.co.uk

For J. N. and M. B. R.

Contents

Rose Macaulay

INTRODUCTION

Rose Macaulay was born Emilie Rose Macaulay at Rugby on 1
August 1881, the second of the seven children of George
Campbell Macaulay, then an assistant master at the school, and
of Grace Mary Conybeare, George's second cousin once
removed. Grace's father was the Reverend William Conybeare.
Her mother Eliza was the daughter of the Reverend Joseph Rose
and the great-granddaughter of the Reverend John Macaulay,
George's great-grandfather. Both sides of the family had produced generations of clergymen and academics, few of whom,
said Rose Macaulay, 'had denied themselves the indulgence of
breaking into print'.

Rose was a family surname on the Conybeare side, but was used
as if it were a Christian name in the Macaulay household. As a
small child, Rose Macaulay was Rosie. As a schoolgirl in her teens,
she was Emilie or Emily. At Oxford she was Miss Macaulay to
begin with, then Emily, and to some friends Rozemly; she was the
poet E. R. Macaulay in the pages of the *Saturday Westminster* in the
1900s, and she was R. Macaulay, or to her amusement Mr
Macaulay, when her first novels were being published between
1906 and the outbreak of war in 1914. In the last year of her life
she was Dame Rose Macaulay, amusing herself by pretending to be
a wise woman with black cat and herb garden.

She found it useful to be able to be either Emily or Rose Macaulay. Emily was what her sister Jean called her 'police name'. It was Emily Macaulay who picked up the driving offences, of which there were many, for Rose's passion for driving did not include a great concern for the rules of the road; and the same unknown Emily Macaulay could be called upon if necessary during the course of Rose's secret love affair with the novelist Gerald O'Donovan. The way that her names could be interpreted in different ways: a surname for a Christian name, a man's name for a woman, seems singularly appropriate for a writer whose fictional creations often slide between the masculine and the feminine, and whose work is so concerned with questions of ambivalence and secrecy. Through the pages of all Rose Macaulay's novels stroll heroines with boys' names: John, Cecil, Neville, Rome, Stanley, Denham, Carey, Julian and Laurie, who are variously adventurous, restless, and intellectually curious; and their counterparts and companions, who are sensitive, generous boys and men with names like Margery, Ruth, Jayne and Vere.

Rose Macaulay was one of the few women of the first half of the twentieth century to earn her living entirely through her writing. Throughout the 1920s, 1930s and 1940s she was close to the heart of literary and political life in Britain, observing, participating in and satirising it. She was friends with Ivy Compton-Burnett, Elizabeth Bowen (who was first published through her recommendation), Rosamond Lehmann, and Virginia Woolf, with whom she enjoyed a scratchy and rivalrous relationship. She was friends with Rupert Brooke, with E. M. Forster (writing the first full-length critical book on his work), Walter de la Mare and T. S. Eliot. She sat on committees (the NCCL, the Peace Pledge Union) with Forster, Storm Jameson and Stephen Spender, and was one of the thirty-nine witnesses for the defence at the trial for obscenity of the lesbian writer Radclyffe Hall's *The Well of Loneliness* in 1928. She wrote for the *Spectator*, *Time and Tide*, the *New Statesman* and for John Lehmann's *New Writing*. She broadcast regularly for the BBC from its inception in the early 1920s through to the 1950s, and under the chairmanship of George Bernard Shaw was a member of the BBC Standing Committee on Spoken English.

Wherever you turn, in any decade in the first half of the twentieth century, there is Rose Macaulay. But she is in no one place centrally, nor for long. 'Forever in transit', Rosamond Lehmann said of her, 'physically, intellectually, spiritually'.

A woman of contradictions and complexities, Rose Macaulay was gregarious but intensely private, warm-hearted but secretive, sharp-tongued but easily provoked to laughter, highly intellectual but retaining a delight in childlike physical activity, passionate about literature but constantly mocking and satirising those caught up in literary endeavour. She gave the impression of being sexually uninterested in men ('Poor dear Rose, judging from her works, is a Eunuch', said Virginia Woolf, who did not take kindly to her own books being less popular than Rose's), while for a quarter of a century she was passionately and, according to her own criteria, sinfully in love with a married man. The relationship ended only with his death in 1942. When Daisy, in Rose Macaulay's 1928 novel *Keeping Up Appearances*, reflects on people's 'queer hidden selves', she could be thinking about Rose Macaulay herself.

In a writing career that covered the first fifty years of the twentieth century, Rose Macaulay produced twenty-three novels (three of which won major literary prizes), six books of essays and criticism, four books of travel and history, two collections of poetry, and left behind a large correspondence, from which three volumes of letters have been published. Her fiction alone shows an enormous range: from explorations of intense family relationships, through mystical quests, to the brilliantly funny social satires of the 1920s. The novels that came out of the years of the First World War, *Non-Combatants and Others*, *What Not* and *Potterism*, all engage in different ways (as does her war poetry) with the issues surrounding war well in advance of the works that have since become the canonical prose works of the period. *Non-Combatants*, published in 1916, was one of the first anti-war novels to appear, and remains one of the most powerful. In the novels set in the febrile years of the 1920s Rose Macaulay began to make formal experiments with structure and voice, and to play with thematic concerns that came to be associated with the modernist movement, that is, notions of time, identity and consciousness; these novels, which include *Dangerous Ages*, *Told by an Idiot*, *Crewe Train*, *Orphan Island*, and *Keeping Up Appearances*, were hugely successful.

In the 1930s Rose Macaulay turned to history and biography with an acclaimed historical novel, *They Were Defeated*, set in the seventeenth century, and a book on John Milton. Her explorations of the past became a way of understanding the restless times she lived in, and also a way of understanding her divided self. Throughout her life, in her written journalism and her radio work, she was a sharp and vigorous commentator on matters of public and popular interest. She was always an intrepid traveller and in the 1940s and 1950s became a stylish and engaging travel writer. After ten years' silence as a novelist she returned triumphantly to fiction in 1950, publishing first *The World My Wilderness*, set in a ruined London after the Blitz, and six years later her final book, *The Towers of Trebizond*.

'Does Ancestry Matter?' This was the question that Rose Macaulay replied to in 1928 in an article in the *Daily Express*. She went back to Macaulay beginnings: 'I can meditate on that Danish Olaf who came long ago to raid the Highland coasts, settled in the Hebrides, and there bred a line of MacOlafs, or Macaulays, who doubtless lived largely on the fish they caught. (I like fish.) They developed into a warlike and turbulent little clan, with a spurred riding boot for crest and a valiant boast of intrepidity in their motto < *Dulce periculum* >. They lived largely on sheep raided from other clans: in the family records there is mention of at least one who was captured and hanged by his enemies for this theft. (I, too, like mutton.) They concurred in the slight alteration in British religion that occurred in the sixteenth century, and early in the eighteenth century one of them so far departed from the martial traditions of his family as to become a minister of the Scottish church.'

This scion was the Reverend Aulay Macaulay of Harris, whose two sons John and Kenneth (Presbyterian ministers respectively of Inveraray and Calder) met and were insulted by Samuel Johnson on his tour of the Western Isles. Rose Macaulay's ancestors then became 'addicted to preaching, reading and writing, instead of to raiding and fighting'. Her great-grandfather left the Church of Scotland to become an Anglican. She was related through both Conybeares and Macaulays to the historian Thomas Babington (Lord) Macaulay, in whose footsteps she followed with her biography of John Milton.

'I'm a mere battlefield of opposite people – my ancestors,' Rose told Virginia Woolf one evening at a party in the 1930s. 'Take this as a simple illustration: I want to walk all day alone: but I also want to drive my car.' Woolf recorded in her diary how they all laughed at what Rose called her 'battling lizards'.

Besides the writing and reading, the Anglicanism and the mutton-eating, Rose Macaulay also claimed the influence of heredity on her passion for swimming, which was conceived in childhood days in the warm Mediterranean and never later relinquished. She claimed that perhaps 'some Conybeare rector in Devonshire once married a mermaid', and that that was how she came to be 'vaguely ichthyous and mer'. As a child she dreamed of being the captain of a ship; her paternal grandfather had been at sea before turning to the Church. Ancestry did matter to Rose, but it was never straightforward. These ancestors that she looked back to were men, and it is hard not to see the androgynous figures that appear in so many of her novels as having a part of their source in a sense of conflict between herself and her male ancestors.

As well as providing an image for her pulling and pushing ancestors, the battling lizards were also the embodiment of conflicts she felt in her own writing, particularly in the inter-war years: between populism and intellectualism, and between journalism and scholarship.

Rose Macaulay's work is important and influential and intriguing, and within the work is visible the complex struggle of a self-reflective woman writer who constantly questioned the value of her work and its place in relation to that of her contemporaries. Yet since her death in 1958 there has been barely a handful of critics, amongst them Alice Bensen, Alice Crawford and Jeanette Passty, and her two biographers Constance Babington Smith and Jane Emery, who have read Rose Macaulay in depth and written of the importance of her place within twentieth-century letters.

For a writer so prolific and so successful in her own lifetime it is curious that she should have been so systematically marginalised by literary and cultural critics. Perhaps it is because she was never long enough in one place, never long enough with one group. The place that Rose Macaulay holds within twentieth-century English literature is a shifting, uncertain place, and one that is reflected in the recurring theme of dual identity that she explored in much of her fiction.

Among her friends and contemporaries she was perhaps most like Ivy Compton-Burnett in eschewing the conventional life, but she was less eccentric than Ivy, more mercurial, and where Ivy was the centre of her own circle, Rose was the centre of none, but passed through many. And her voice speaks in a tone that is sceptical, questioning, and full of doubts not only about the world outside but about her own right to be recreating it through language. It sounds peculiarly modern.

At times she can be exasperating: in her obsessiveness, in her neurotic-sounding over-diffidence, in the sometimes unquestioned assumptions of her class background, and in the pedantry of the churchiness of her later years. But these are rare moments, to be offset against the intriguing nature of a writer who lived in a different age but whose complicated feelings and expressions of unbelonging and exile – and it is possible to read her final and triumphant novel of love and loss, *The Towers of Trebizond*, as an extended metaphor for the unbelonging which she always felt – whisper in our ears across the intervening years.

The picture of Rose Macaulay in this biography is a composite portrait that has been built up from her work and her letters and incorporates bits of the different selves she presented to the world. It draws on descriptions by her contemporaries and by her previous biographers and on the interpretations of those who have written about her work. Everyone's picture, including any self-portrait by Rose, is, of course, subjective. It is like opening a series of boxes: in one box, beneath the layers of tissue paper you will uncover one Rose Macaulay; in another box there will be another Rose, not very different perhaps, but seen from a different angle, profile, perhaps, rather than full-face. This biography is another in that series of boxes.

A box features in the publisher Victor Gollancz's picture of Rose Macaulay. Rose had a treasured bird-in-the-box, and Victor Gollancz describes her delight in the revelation of what is hidden within the box, the glory of the bird springing out and singing. His Rose was a generous, party-loving, sociable Rose, whose 'dry little spasms of mocking laughter . . . so lovably revealed part of her character' (note that careful 'part'). To Victor Gollancz she was mistress of 'that prettiest element in punctuation, the colon'; while to Virginia Woolf she was 'very erudite' on the subject of commas. For Noel Annan, Rose was 'a fox' that he started and chased back to what he called the 'intellectual aristocracy' of the nineteenth-century liberal families to whom she was variously related. For Gerard Irvine, a young Anglican priest Rose met and became friends with in her seventies, she was like St Rose of Viterbo: tough, curly-haired, and loquacious.

Five months after Rose Macaulay's death in 1958 *Encounter* published a collection of tributes from some of her friends. Choosing different aspects of her personality to highlight (although her recklessness behind a steering wheel features in

most of them), they all comment on what Harold Nicolson iden-
tifies as her 'combination of opposites': her fierceness and her
generosity; her appearance of frailty and her wiry strength; her
delight in solitude and her capacity for friendship; her asceticism
and her pleasure in the world.

And then besides the Rose Macaulay of contemporaries,
friends and critics, there are the Roses of her previous biographers. Constance Babington Smith was Rose Macaulay's first
biographer and a distant cousin. Some years before she died, she
gave to the Wren Library, Trinity College, Cambridge, all Rose's
family papers in her possession, and her own research notes.
Rose's handwriting is not easy to decipher. Early in her career she
developed an idiosyncratic form of shorthand, which makes leg-
ibility even harder; nor would she ever let a train journey pass
without taking the opportunity to scribble a letter or two (one
soon recognises these, even before one reaches the inevitable 'plse
excse hndwrtg, am on trn'). Constance heroically transcribed
copies of almost all the letters she had gathered for her own
work on Rose. The two women had met late in Rose Macaulay's
life after her return to the Church of England, and Constance's
picture of Rose was coloured by her own connection with her,
that is, a friendship informed by their shared religious practices,
and by her close friendship with Rose's surviving sister Jean, also
a devout Anglican; and it was circumscribed by Gerald
O'Donovan's widow being still alive. Jane Emery's Rose
Macaulay, sixteen years later, is a more solid and more literary
Rose. By then both Jean Macaulay and Beryl O'Donovan had
died. Besides the scholarship and literary analysis that Jane
Emery brings to bear on Rose Macaulay there is also a new light-
hearted Rose whom she discovered through Muriel Thomas,
who had been married to Gerald's son Dermod, and one of
whose daughters was Rose's godchild.

On the publication of the third volume of letters in 1964, six
years after Rose had died, V. S. Pritchett wrote of her: 'As she
grew old, she may have looked like a jolly skeleton but she did

not fall back upon the resources so often drawn upon by distinguished English maiden ladies: dottiness, vagary, awful composure or annihilating egotism. She was as lively as a needle. She remained the discreet, learned and intrepid spinster of irreverent eye and rapid, muttering wit, always on the go, always out and about, always working. Startling as a bicyclist, terrifying as a car-driver, she must have been eye-opening to passers-by in Spain, Portugal, Italy, Greece and Turkey, when they saw that the elderly, frail and relentless enquirer into their antiquities had also on her programme a determination to get a swim in before settling down to a sandwich lunch on the lonely roadside. Activity was her principle, asking questions her ironical pleasure.'

For my own portrait of Rose Macaulay in these pages I have drawn on these biographers and critics, and on published and unpublished letters and memoirs and reminiscences. My own feelings about Rose Macaulay, my Rose Macaulay, have changed and varied during the course of the book, as emotions in any close relationship must fluctuate. I was originally attracted by the 'queer hidden selves' of her writing life, the way her fiction coexists with biography and travel, her scholarly seriousness with her comedy. I was also attracted by the secrets in her own life, for I believe that writers thrive on secrets; and I was interested by the way that she was able to so organise the life of her heart that her love affair was protected and she herself was free to write; it seemed, and still seems to me, unusual for a woman to carve out for herself the emotional space within which she can pursue her art without sacrificing love or friendships. Rose Macaulay would pay a high price for this, in the eight or nine years of loneliness after her lover's death.

Alice Crawford described Rose Macaulay's writing as 'one of the great barometers of twentieth-century English fiction', in the way that it both registers and forecasts 'shifts in cultural pressure'. Rose Macaulay recorded with wit, imagination and intelligence the events of a period of profound upheaval that included two world wars, the end of Empire, and the emancipation of women. She was born a late Victorian, and observed the birth of the modern world. I hope that the picture I have drawn of this clever, complex, secretive and generous woman, whose life intersected with the lives of a great number of those who were writing in England between 1910 and 1950, will encourage readers to turn to her books: to her novels and essays, and to her biographies, travel books and histories.

CHAPTER ONE

The Gs

'If you and Father hadn't married,' we used to ask my mother, 'which
of your children should we be?' 'Neither of us, of course,' my mother
replied. 'You would have been quite different people.'

Letters to a Friend

'This has been almost my happiest year, I think,' Grace
Conybeare wrote in her diary at the end of 1867, the year she
turned twelve. She wrote about family visits, carriages, servants,
churchgoing, ponies and her two cousins Ellie and Amy who had
been taken in by Grace's widowed mother Eliza Conybeare when
their own mother died. At the end of every year Grace received
a volume of Pettitt's *Annual Diary* from her brother Edward. He
was 'about 14 years older than my mother,' his niece Rose
Macaulay wrote, 'so we always looked on him, with his patriarchal beard, as an old man'. He made Grace learn Greek as a
child, Rose reported, 'because he said she would have to talk it in
heaven, it being the language of that country'. Diary-keeping
was viewed in the same vein; it encouraged the disciplines of
self-analysis and reflective thought, and provided a stimulus for
meditation on behaviour in this life in relation to the life here-
after.

On her twelfth birthday Grace received a 'beautifully bound' copy of *Hymns Ancient and Modern* from Edward, a pair of skates from her mother, and from Ellie some rosettes for her beloved pony, Bow. She was as enthusiastic about books as she was about ponies. That year she read *Mary Barton*, *Eric, or Little by Little*, and *David Copperfeild* [sic], and 'Mama' regularly read aloud to all three girls. That year, 1867, they listened to *Guy Mannering*, *A Winter's Tale*, *Henry VIII*, *Heartsease* and *The Antiquary*. These were the books that Rose and her brothers and sisters would, in turn, read and have read to them.

On the inside covers of Grace's girlhood diaries are fashion sketches of the kind that twelve- and thirteen-year-old girls still draw: ink doodlings of women with tiny waists, full sweeping skirts, and hair swept up from willowy necks. Also on the inside covers of the diaries are keys to the ciphers that Grace used, worked out in these early years with Edward's help. She used the cipher for the anniversaries of deaths, such as those of her father, the Reverend William J. Conybeare, who had died when Grace was two, and of her brother Bruce, who had died before she was born; she used it to record catching sight of nice-looking boys in church or at evening parties in her uncle's rectory; and to note, when Edward was married, news of his wife Frances's pregnancies. Edward too used a cipher in his diaries when writing of sex and of death.

Edward kept a diary for seventy years, from 1854, the year he turned twelve – the age Grace was when he presented her with her first diary – to 1925, the year of Grace's death. He was an Anglican vicar for over thirty years and then, late in life, he converted to Roman Catholicism and was, Rose wrote later, 'at last content'. The sixty or so volumes of his diaries are crammed in tiny, neat handwriting with observations, opinions and reflections on his own family, on parish matters, and on Grace and George, whom he referred to as 'G and G', or simply 'the Gs', and their family.

Edward had grown up in the knowledge that writing and

reflecting were not just a part of his duties as a country vicar but an integral part of any educated man's life. When he took Holy Orders he could expect the vicarage he would live in to have a library and a study, and he would expect to have time every day to spend in them.

Not so his sister Grace. Grace had no formal education that would encourage her in the self-discipline of regular diary-keeping; nor, when she married and set up house, could she expect either the physical space or the time in which to reflect on her experience and to write about it. A married woman's time was not her own. Grace struggled for the first few years of marriage and babies to keep up the diaries, but they soon became only a record of coughs and colds, whooping cough and chickenpox. She abandoned them in the 1890s in favour of the anniversary book which she had kept from the time of her marriage and would keep until the year of her death, in which she recorded births, deaths and family events. Unlike a diary, whose blank pages challenge the keeper to create their own subjects for meditation, the anniversary book, which was called *Morning Light*, provided subjects for reflection with a poem and Bible extract printed on each day's page.

But in her teenage years Grace had been an enthusiastic diary keeper, and her writing provides a lively picture of the girl who would grow into Rose's mother, of Rose's father George Macaulay when he was a young man, and of the two of them together, Grace and George, in the days of their courtship when they enthusiastically confided in each other their hopes and dreams for the future.

There are intimations in the diaries of the woman Grace would become, glimpses of the kind of person she would be to her own children. As she grew older she made fewer references to ponies and dogs, and more to visiting the poor of the parish and the instruction of village girls. She began teaching a Sunday class of girls, and soon extended it to a Friday evening. Sometimes she would read to them as they worked at their sewing; at other times she would make them memorise their catechism. 'I have such a capital plan now,' she wrote in 1871, when she was fifteen: 'every Friday the child who has done best comes up after the rest have gone, and dusts my little room. They enjoy it very much, and it keeps my room beautifully clean.'

She was already bossy, controlling and brimful of pedagogic energy. Her children, variously, benefited and suffered, or both, and in later years in Great Shelford, when all had left home save her second daughter Rose, Grace would be gathering together another generation of village girls and indulging in more 'capital plans' for their religious and moral instruction.

At fifteen Grace felt she was nearly grown up. In April, when Eliza had to fill in the 1871 Census form, Grace 'got mother to put "unmarried" after me, instead of "young child". I do wonder what we shall all put down in the next census. So much happens in ten years.' In ten years she would be married to George Macaulay, mother of one child and pregnant with Rose.

George Campbell Macaulay was the eldest son of the Reverend Samuel Herrick Macaulay, vicar of Hodnet in Shropshire, and his second wife Georgiana Anne Ferguson. Samuel Herrick Macaulay died in 1873, when George was twenty-one. There were five boys and two younger sisters, Anne and Mary, the latter (seen as a 'termagant' by Rose and her sisters) fifteen years younger than George. George had been, according to Rose, 'one of those sons of the parsonage who read Darwin as they grew up and suffered Doubt, which remained with him thro' life'.

Grace Conybeare first met George Macaulay in 1874 over tea in the rooms in King's College, Cambridge of her (and his) cousin James Smith. He looked 'very clever and intensely sarcastic', and she didn't like him 'half so much as William', George's brother, whom she had first met a few weeks before at her mother's childhood home, Rothley Temple, in Leicestershire. At the end of that year, just nineteen, she concluded her diary with: 'It has been a wonderfully happy year to us – really the happiest

I have ever had – that is getting "same" to say at the end of every diary, but it is always true.'

During the next three years Grace left her mother's house in Weybridge to spend increasing amounts of time at the Vicarage in Barrington, a few miles outside Cambridge, where Edward Conybeare had taken a living in 1871. Edward and his wife Frances were benign overseers of the attentions paid to Grace and her cousin Emily Rose, who was often staying there with them, by their young cousins William and George Macaulay and James and Walter Smith, who were undergraduates at King's College and at Trinity College. Edward, not usually noted for his sense of humour, characterised Grace, Emily and even his own wife Frances as early Christians, and the young men as prowling lions and tigers.

Soon the two widows, Mrs Conybeare and Mrs Macaulay, were exchanging invitations, and Grace met the other Macaulay boys, Kenneth, Harry, and Reginald who was still a schoolboy. There was a holiday in Scotland when Grace and Harry alarmed the rest of the party by getting lost on the slopes of Ben Lomond as darkness fell, and there were visits from all the brothers to Weybridge, with parties, dances and skating. When Grace went to stay at Barrington she would be rowed up and down the river by one Macaulay or another, and there was talk and 'chaff' late into the night about marriage, platonic love, friendship, and the ideals of a good life. Grace, it seems, was in love with all of them.

However, by the end of the second summer of acquaintance with the Macaulays a strong sexual attraction had developed between Grace and George, although Grace continued to talk about him only as a cousin. In September 1875 she wrote to her cousin Emily Rose to keep her up to date on developments with the lions and tigers, that 'George is more charming than I ever saw him before. He and I thoroughly got into cousinship together and talked and quarrelled and chaffed to our hearts content.' They visited Petworth with her mother Eliza, and she, according to Grace, thought George 'in face and form more beautiful' than any of the Greek statues they admired. Grace concurred: 'I longed for some artist worthy of the subject to sculpture him as a young Greek demi-God . . .' Then in a flurry of denial that doubtless fooled her cousin as little as herself Grace added a postscript: 'I think it well to add I am really still fonder of W than of G Macaulay.'

George was handsome and sensitive and admired for his oratorical skills. He was 'brilliant' at reciting poetry; he had been coached by Alfred, Lord Tennyson himself, whose sons were friends of his, in how best to declaim Tennyson's verse. At this point his preference was for Shelley, whose passionate republicanism appealed to him, but Tennyson's lessons were not forgotten. Every New Year's Eve in Italy, when the children were little, he would declaim 'Ring out, wild bells' from *In Memoriam*.

In April 1876 George left Cambridge with a first-class degree in classics, having been ranked fourth in his Tripos. He began a course of lectures to working men at Shoreditch Town Hall. Grace attended one, probably the first, along with her mother, William and Kenneth Macaulay, and James Smith. 'The audience tremendously radical, as was George himself,' wrote Grace in her diary, with a touch of pride, although her mother 'was a little taken aback sometimes by his "radicalism"'. He did not get regular work until the autumn, when he took a temporary teaching post at Marlborough College, but he was not happy there and left after only one term, at Christmas 1876. He failed in his attempts to get an appointment as assistant master at his own old school, Eton, and in December 1877 was turned down by Harrow School. He had got into trouble in his second year at Trinity for some scurrilous Latin verses on the subject of an undergraduate, a prostitute and a senior proctor. Perhaps that was held against him, or it may have been reports of the 'radicalism' of his lectures to the working men at Shoreditch that put off the headmasters who interviewed him. Or perhaps he was too open in his admiration for Mr Gladstone and the Liberals, and their support for Home Rule for Ireland. A desire to broadcast his views – there was a rousing poem in the *Spectator* on the Serbian/Turkish conflict, and a letter in *The Times* about the Indian famine, which argued that 'Conquest is a luxury' and that the English people should pay for such a luxury through taxation – may not have inspired confidence in his suitability as a schoolmaster.

Meanwhile he was courting Grace. When she was in Weybridge he stayed nearby in Putney with James Smith; when she was in Barrington he followed her there. He copied out poetry for her: Swinburne's 'Ode on the French Republic', Walt Whitman and, as always, Shelley. There was some tutoring, but he did not have a salaried job.

In October 1877 George went in for the Lamb Fellowship at Trinity and failed to get it. It was not uncommon to fail on the first attempt at a fellowship, but George took it hard. He wrote Grace a sonnet which gracefully suggested a cause for his disappointment and copied it into her diary. It began:

> I do confess I longed that this might be,
> Not chiefly that the prize itself was sweet,
> But for a gift to lay before thy feet,
> Which might commend my worthless love to thee.

Five days later, on 15 October, they became officially engaged. For her twenty-second birthday a fortnight later George gave Grace a copy of the poems of Elizabeth Barrett Browning.

That year Kenneth, the third Macaulay boy, after two years of study in London, went to Birmingham to begin a career in glass manufacturing, and William, closest to George in age, was on the brink of a lifelong academic career at King's College, Cambridge. George had to get a job. As a single man he may have lived off poetry and passion, but as a married man he would require a steady income. After nearly two years without regular work, George was finally appointed assistant master at Rugby School by the headmaster Dr Jex-Blake at Easter 1878, on a salary of about £120 per annum, with special responsibility for coaching the boys for entrance to Trinity and King's.

Grace had visited Newnham, one of the women's colleges at Cambridge, where she was shown over by two 'most charming and ladylike and refined girls'. She wrote in her diary: 'I longed to be there.' But Grace could only have got there with dedication and self-discipline, and then there would have been no time for the delightful round of social visiting that took up so much of her and her mother's year, nor would there have been time for all the chaff and chat about love and marriage and platonic friendships that she so enjoyed.

Grace was clever and opinionated, and a match in both witty and intimate conversation for her handsome, moody, sharp-tongued George. When she became the mother of small children she would pass on to them her passion for stories, for adventure and for high emotion; but her lack of intellectual training would leave her with very little to fall back on in later years, when her children were growing up and struggling for their independence.

George did achieve the fellowship the following year, although he gave up its rights and privileges immediately, in order to marry. But he appears to have been haunted by his first, early, failure. Perhaps the solitary nature of the scholarship of his work on the Greek historian Herodotus and, later on, on the medieval poet John Gower seemed to him of less significance than the public recognition by peers and mentors that an academic appointment brings. He was to suffer another two disappoint-ments within the next ten years, when he lost the Clark Lectureship to Edmund Gosse in 1886 and the following year failed to get a post he had applied for in Sydney, Australia. Nonetheless he remained engaged in the kind of scholarship for which he had been trained and he was able, later on, to re-enter the academic world.

The differences between George's education, aspirations and expectations of life and those of Grace were the differences that divided middle-class men from women, and already, in late Victorian England, those differences were beginning to be eroded. All their daughters and sons would have professions, and their second daughter Rose would not just 'long to be' at a university but would actually be there. But for George and Grace those differences, at base differences in temperament but confirmed by circumstance and convention, would lead to an increasingly marked divergence. Grace would make difficult emotional demands on her family, while George would withdraw further and further into a private world of scholarly research. This is not to say that they were spectacularly unhappy, but it was not a model marriage that inspired any of their children to emulate it.

They were married on 19 December 1878, when George was twenty-six and Grace twenty-three, and after a honeymoon in Italy they settled in 11 Hillmorton Road in Rugby, a terraced house five minutes' walk from the school. Grace became pregnant almost immediately, but miscarried in February and was in bed for ten days. Over the next few months there were a series of 'disappointments', but by the end of July she was pregnant again and feeling too sick to move. At the beginning of October the doctor insisted that she get up and take exercise, and prescribed an anti-nausea potion. 'Half-living on blessed stuff called Konmiss,' she wrote, 'which prevents my being sick.'

Grace and George's first child, Margaret Campbell Macaulay, was born at 2 a.m. on 23 March 1880. Grace could not attend the christening five weeks later for she was too ill to get out of bed. She had a 'gathered breast', that is, an abscess, and a high fever. Throughout May, she could sleep at night only with the help of chloral. Margaret was weaned early as Grace could not feed her for the pain, so she would have been suffering simultaneously from the pain of breasts swollen hard with milk. On 24 May the breast abscess was lanced under chloroform, and was lanced again the following day. An injection of morphine gave 'wonderful relief'. But the relief was short-lived, and two weeks later the abscess had to be lanced yet again. It was not until well into June that Grace began to recover.

On 21 July came news of the death from cancer, after six

months of pain, of Grace's cousin Emily Rose. She was twenty-nine. Coded entries in Grace's brother Edward's diary suggest that Grace may have been pregnant again and again suffered a miscarriage; whether this was the case or not (there is nothing about it in Grace's diaries), she was pregnant again by the end of the year and hoping for a boy. When a second girl was born, on 1 August 1881, she was named Emilie Rose after Grace's cousin. Grace held strong dislikes, some of which, her daughter Rose claimed, she passed on to her; she disliked sewing, mustard and cats, and also confessed to an antipathy towards 'very recently born infants'. By the end of 1884, Grace would be the mother of five children under the age of five. One can reflect that a liking for newborn infants might have made up for the physical toll inflicted on Grace by the whole business of producing them.

Rose was born to parents who were discovering the hard way the rigours and exhaustion of parenthood. Of their first child, Edward was to write a few months later, 'Margaret a unique child very clever and good in nursery, but a tremendous handful requiring the *undivided* attention of *both* her parents continuously.' Even allowing for Edward's tendency to exaggerate, it seems that Grace and George were already struggling with their first child.

But there were advantages to Rose in these unpropitious circumstances. Grace's desire for a boy possibly fed her second daughter's later ambivalence about her own femininity; whatever its origins, this ambivalence was an important source of creativity. And to be born to parents whose hands are already full with a first child is not an unmixed disadvantage, especially if you are clever, dreamy, imaginative, and like to be left alone. Another girl, Jean, was born just under a year after Rose, giving Rose the opportunity to be a 'twin' for one week every year. After the three girls came the much-longed-for son, Aulay, in 1883, and the following year another boy, Will.

At the beginning Grace and George were still riding high on

the pleasures of love and youth. Grace managed to be astonishingly active despite her repeated pregnancies. In the summer of 1880 she and George rode around the Isle of Wight on hired tricycles, and so enjoyed it that they were determined to acquire a double tricycle, which, for £12, they duly did on their return. Instead of driving a carriage like other masters and their wives, the young Macaulays rode around Rugby on this tricycle. They were unconventional in other ways, being much more closely involved with their children than was common amongst middle-class parents. Grace wrote to her mother: 'Yesterday I did a thing of which I know you would approve: put the big round bath in the playroom with lots of salt water in it, and let Margaret and Rose splash there to their hearts' content for nearly half an hour. They did make a mess – we shut them in quite alone! . . . George is eager for their next bathe that he may turn on the hose through the back garden door upon them! . . . I am making them bathing caps.' As Constance Babington Smith says, quoting this letter, such a breakdown of nursery protocol may well account for the rapid turnover of nurses, noted by Edward in 1884: 'Grace seeking her sixth nurse in the twelvemonth!' – which is a more generous view than that Grace was a difficult and demanding employer.

Grace's mother and George's brothers were frequent visitors to Hillmorton Road, and there was support for the young mother from a cook and housemaid as well as the string of nurses. But as the babies relentlessly appeared, so Grace's health deteriorated. She was not just being worn down by pregnancy and the demands of childbirth and lactation, but by having to cope with a seemingly endless series of children's illnesses. In May 1886 Edward wrote in his diary, 'anxious news of Grace, overdone with nursing Aulay through bronchitis', and a few weeks later, 'Gs both cruelly worn down with work from 5.30 a.m. to midnight daily.'

For some time the Macaulays had been thinking of leaving England for a warmer climate. Grace had been diagnosed as having a tubercular throat, and as her father had died of tuberculosis at the age of forty-one it was thought – mistakenly, as it turned out – that she was under threat of an early death. By the next year Grace's throat was 'in constant haemorrhage' and she had taken to a bath chair for much of the time. Nonetheless she was pregnant again, and this time she really did not want to be. Eleanor Grace, born on 15 June 1887, Grace and George's sixth child, was never to overcome her mother's dislike of her.

They had decided on Italy, where it would be warm, cheap and not too far away for Eliza Conybeare and the Macaulay brothers to visit, and George resigned his post at Rugby at the end of the summer term.

'. . . [T]hey all leave Sept 15 for empty space,' wrote Edward dramatically. They may not have gone off into empty space, but it was a step into the unknown. George was giving up a dull but steady teaching job for the uncertainties of independent scholarship in a place far from his brothers and from his Cambridge friends. Grace was leaving behind a mother who had always been her strongest support, a brother who was, if annoying, at least reliable, and a network of friends made at Rugby. But for Grace it proved to be a wonderful move, and for Rose and her four closest sisters and brothers, it was a move to Paradise.

CHAPTER TWO

Amphibious Days

On wet sands now the stars are gray,
What do the brown nets hold for keeping?
Will you these from the rock-green bay?

Sweeter to breathe than flowers in May
Is the silver the nets are heaping
On wet sands, now the stars are gray.

Surely now I have heard you say
You love the little bianchetti leaping:
Will you these from the rock-green bay?

And seven tunnies enmeshed at play
Dance, because of my water-sweeping,
On wet sands, now the stars are gray.

This is my wooing and this my way:
Will you garner my night's sea-reaping?
Will you these from the rock-green bay?

Small bianchetti my vows shall pay –
Silver things between meshes peeping,
On wet sands, now the stars are gray.
Will you these from the rock-green bay?

'A Ligurian Valentine', from
The Two Blind Countries

'There is a shore,' wrote Rose Macaulay of the Italian Ligure de
Ponente, where she lived from the age of six to the age of thirteen, 'along which the world flowers, one long sweet garden

strip, between the olive-grey hills and the very blue sea.' The Macaulays left England and arrived in Genoa in September 1887, installed themselves in the Smith Hotel, and set about looking for somewhere to live. They decided on a small seaside town called Varazze on the Ligurian coast about twenty minutes by train west of Genoa. It was not only a fishing port but also a popular holiday resort, with elegant hotels, a promenade and beach huts.

Those seven childhood years by the edge of the sea in Italy furnished Rose Macaulay with a vision of a paradise that she was to recreate in her fiction over and over throughout her life, representing it variously as a retreat from the outside world, a sanctuary in which forbidden love could blossom, and a lost Eden. Her description of it as 'one long sweet garden strip' appears in her 1912 novel *The Lee Shore*, where she imagines 'vagabonds' on the road looking through an open door in a garden wall and seeing 'an Eden, unimaginably sweet, aflame with oleanders and pomegranate blossom, and white like snow with tall lilies'.

For the first three years in Varazze the Macaulays lived near the town centre in the upper floors of a house off the via San Ambrogio. The dining room opened out on to a balcony, and there was a terrace below planted with orange trees. Grace would take two or three of the children shopping with her in the mornings and Rose later remembered the pleasure of 'hanging about the dark little shops, with their sacks of coloured beans, long wands of macaroni, and lovely plaster madonnas, saints and cattle'. It is not so different now. In the via San Ambrogio there are florists, pasta shops and hat shops, much as there must have been in the 1880s; goods are displayed temptingly on stands outside doorways, making the narrow *carrugi* even narrower. A fishmonger displays tables of octopus, squid and anchovies, freshly caught from the sea. Every so often a scooter noses its way down the *carrugi*, weaving in and out of the groups of shoppers, walkers and talkers. Along with the electric lighting inside the shops, this is perhaps the only difference that a hundred years or so has brought.

There is still a smell of drains, mixed in with the fish, coffee, flower and cake smells that enrich the air, and it was a concern with the drains, and the part they played in George's severe attack of typhoid in the summer of 1890, that persuaded the Macaulays they must move. Grace, as was her habit every summer, had taken the older children back to England, leaving George in Italy. His illness brought out four separate doctors and all the available Macaulay brothers. Already George and Grace had seen a house that they desired, a square red house on the eastern edge of the town, and called for that reason – it being on the eastern, or rising side – the Villa Levante. In January that year they had looked over it. Now it seemed imperative to move for health reasons, and the next year, in May 1891, with financial assistance of £1,000 from Grace's mother Eliza, they bought and moved into what became known as the Villa Macolai. It had an *orto*, a walled garden, 'full of oranges and lemons, eucalyptus and figs, and behind rose steep terraced hills, clad with pines, olives, myrtle and juniper, with stony paths winding up them'. A terrace with wrought iron gates opened directly on to the beach, and when there was a high sea the water 'would occasionally rush into the garden and through the basement windows, making a miniature subterranean ocean that could be pleasurably navigated on boards'.

With the sea at their front door Rose could endlessly daydream about her future as a naval captain, and although that was a dream that she would be obliged to abandon in later girlhood, the sea flooded her imagination and stayed there for ever. Looking back in later years on the 'peculiar qualities and pleasures' of swimming, she described bathing off the Italian coast as being 'in the top class':

The Mediterranean lay curved about our little town, on a sandy shore, practically tideless, of course, and on fine summer days as

smooth as silk and of that incredibly pure bright blue that you
don't ever see off our British coasts. The shore shelved steeply
down at the sea's edge, so that a few steps took you out of your
depth, and there you were, swimming in the blue, clear, warm
stuff, diving to the bottom to pick up stones and shells, floating
on your back, with your eyes shut against the burning sun and
flipping yourself lazily along with your hands, treading water
upright, racing arm over arm to a rock that jutted up just below
the surface a hundred feet from shore; or perhaps we would
paddle out in the canoe, and drop into the sea from its end; and
if it tipped over we would sit on its keel and paddle it about
upside down . . . The great thing was to be as far out to sea as
possible when one was summoned in, so as to have a long swim
back.

More than half a century later Rose claimed that the day they
were given their canoe, which they named the *Argo*, 'returns to
me still in dreams'. None of the children managed to match the
stamina of George who, 'to the admiration of the whole town',
swam the three miles or so from the Villa Macolai across the bay
to the western promontory.

Rose and her two sisters Margaret and Jean, and the two
boys, Aulay and Will, were brought up together: the girls did
what the boys did, whether it was swimming, riding and running, or reading, learning Latin and playing cricket. Perhaps it
was this lack of distinction in the way the Macaulay girls and
boys were brought up, even more than the physical freedom, that
distinguished Rose's life as a girl in Italy from that of her contemporaries in England.

It wasn't that Rose wanted to be a boy, it was that she didn't
recognise what it meant to be a girl. Later, when they returned
to England and were living in gloomy Oxford, and her father
told her that she would have to stop her nonsense about wanting to be a naval captain, it was, in a sense, too late for her to
learn this lesson. She had already started her apprenticeship as a

writer, with novels that invariably started: ' "Man the lifeboats," shouted the captain, "because we have struck a rock and are sinking fast." '

Rose Macaulay was to return throughout her life to the idea of a world in which there was no demarcation between the sexes, from her early novels, *The Furnace* (1907), and *The Valley Captives* (1911), in which the central characters are a brother and sister, a girl–boy pair, through to her very last book, *The Towers of Trebizond* (1956), in which, notoriously, the narrator's gender is deliberately unassigned.

The warm climate of Italy was conducive to life outdoors, and the lack of English 'society' in Varazze meant that the Macaulay children were unburdened by many of the restrictions suffered by most middle-class children in England. They ran around barelegged and barefoot on the terrace and there were picnics and swimming from April throughout the summer. The girls wore sailor frocks designed by Grace. What could be more ideal for the carrying of an incubating duck egg? 'There it lay, in that repository designed by heaven for carrying about oranges, books, rabbits and kittens, so that the wearing of sailor suits, male and female, made a family inclined to thinness bulge in front as if they had been reared on some rich health food.'

This description of carrying an egg in a pouch is as much a picture of an imaginative as it is of a physical freedom. The eggs never hatched, they were probably unfertilised anyway, but that didn't stop Rose imagining the full life that lay ahead of her with her 'dandling', her 'nestlechick', her loving pet. The rabbits, dogs, goat and pony, the ducks and chickens, hatched and unhatched, of the Villa Macolai played their part in the imagination of the dreamy Rose as much as the pirates and explorers of the Victorian tales of derring-do – *Coral Island, Masterman Ready, The Swiss Family Robinson* – that she read perched in the branches of a tree or on the top of the orchard wall.

Years later she wrote nostalgically of 'sitting alone in an olive tree up the hill or in an ivy clump on the top of the *orto* wall, reading or writing poetry or stories . . . or spinning one's private interminable tales of perilous and heroic adventure by land and sea, while the mule carts jingled along the shore road, and the fishermen hauled in their heavy nets with loud cries of expectation and hope, and the hot sweet tang of the hillside above mingled with that of the sea below'.

George worked on his translation of Herodotus and coached the children in Latin, Italian, maths and botany, while Grace supervised reading and writing lessons, and led the family in nursery songs, and hymns, and tear-jerking Italian songs such as 'Sono Orfanella', which appealed to the sentimental streak in Grace's character. At the age of fifteen she had composed a long narrative poem about two orphan girls who die of cold on Christmas Eve as they crouch outside a church listening to the organ playing. They read massively: Dickens, George Eliot, Scott, *Robinson Crusoe*, *Lorna Doone*, *The Three Musketeers*, and the novels of Charlotte Yonge, which Grace had read and re-read when she was a girl. Yonge's *The Daisy Chain*, the story of a huge family of brothers and sisters who are left motherless as a result of their father's reckless driving of the carriage, was a great favourite, as was her story of virtue tested and triumphant, *The Heir of Redclyffe*, which Grace read to Margaret when she was ill with scarlet fever in 1889. Of the noble, misunderstood hero of *The Heir of Redclyffe*, Sir Guy Morville, Rose later wrote: 'It is impossible, probably, for a later and less hero-worshipping generation to imagine the impassioned devotion that I and the sister a year above me [Margaret] poured at the feet of this young baronet, with his Morville temper, his flashing hazel eye, his lip bitten in rage till it bled, his noble self-conquests.' In her late sixties, she confessed, 'I cannot even now recall Guy, or type his name, without emotion . . .'

Rose discovered poetry: she was given Tennyson (then Poet Laureate) when she was eight, and an illustrated Shelley the following year. Much of the Shelley, and of the Browning, whom she was also reading, was 'above my intellectual grasp, but my pleasure in it was ecstatic'. To John Lehmann years later she claimed to have been a Shelleyan 'since I was given the Poems on my 9th birthday (in Italy) – and when I was unhappy or in disgrace I used to chant to myself the first 8 lines of "Many a green isle needs must be" – a great solace.' The incantatory pleasures of poetry are strongly present in the poetry that she herself wrote.

Scrupulous accounts of the children's pocket money and gifts of money from the uncles were kept. At Christmas 1887 Uncle Regi sent the five eldest children £2 each, and £1 15s. for six-month-old Eleanor. Out of her share Rose bought a paintbox, presents for Margaret and Jean (totalling sixpence), and, most expensively, a desk for 15s. 6d. For the three years 1892, 1893 and 1894, Rose's expenses were £11 1s. 9½d., which included roller skates, a share in a goat, and a share in a bicycle. Her income was £13 12s. 1d. By then she was reading Thomas à Kempis, whose *Imitation of Christ* she received as a thirteenth birthday present. 'I remember sitting in the top branches of trees and reading about how I ought not to dispute about the Trinity, and how it was vanity to hunt after honours . . . and that I should withdraw my heart from the love of visible things . . .' With great sense Grace 'threw cold water' on many of these admonitions.

One of the great advantages of growing up abroad was that the young Macaulays were spared the dreariness of the social life that went with middle-class respectability in late Victorian England, for there were only a few neighbours in Varazze of sufficiently high standing to warrant being called on. Perhaps this fed Rose's impatience with the social round when it was inflicted on her later on. There was a Signora Massari and her husband the General, and to instil some social graces into them Grace would take Margaret, Rose and Jean with her in turn. Sometimes the Italian ladies would try to kiss the children, which they did not very much like. Little Will, 'il piccolo cherubino', was a particular favourite. Nor was there any of that dismal Sunday churchgoing which their peers in England suffered. Indeed later Rose recalled that they had been brought up 'to use Sunday as a day for unrestricted license and liberty and riotous living'.

The family's emotional and cultural self-sufficiency was extraordinarily important in Rose Macaulay's development as a writer. The few visitors were mainly family: the Macaulay uncles. There was William, who encouraged his friend and colleague from King's, Roger Fry, to stay with the Macaulays on his way to Rome, saying 'there are no other English people there', and reassuring him that George's wife Grace was 'singularly unlike' her brother Edward; Kenneth, who was wonderfully practical and made rigging and hatches for the *Argo*, as well as repairing Margaret's cooking range after it had caught fire and consumed her best velvet coat; generous Reginald, on holiday from his business in Bombay, with presents from India and regular gifts of money to the children, and charming feckless Harry. Grace's mother Eliza Conybeare was a regular visitor, and occasionally some Smith cousins, Daisy and her father Henry.

Through the end of the 1880s and the beginning of the 1890s they would hear of Jack the Ripper, of the endless struggles in Parliament over Home Rule for Ireland, of the beginnings of women's suffrage, of George Bernard Shaw and the Webbs and their new socialist manifesto, of safety bicycles and the Shop Hours Act, but none of these featured large in the world of the Macaulay children, a world that was bounded by the olive-grey hills rising steeply behind and the blue line of sea that formed the horizon.

Life in Italy was very active, and included canoeing, bathing, walking in the hills, star-gazing, and night-time expeditions every midsummer eve in pursuit of fireflies. There was the endless trying out of broken-down old cabhorses to find a suitable steed – one of them fell to its knees with brave Margaret on its back, clinging to its mane – before Uncle Regi stepped in and provided a decent pony for them – Pintz – along with its keep. Grace threw off her incipient invalidism and embraced the outdoor life. It was Grace who rode Pintz from his previous owner in San Remo, along the rough tracks over the hills, laughing at the local people who were shocked 'to see phenomenon of a lady on horseback'. She recorded with delight the first swim of the season, and George providing her with a cork raft to float on.

Alongside this was intellectual activity: the older children sat examination papers sent over from England by Uncle Edward Conybeare; Grace accompanied George to Genoa where he gave a series of lectures on Frederick II, the philosopher-king. Grace was as thrilled as her husband by the arrival of advance copies of *Herodotus* by G. C. Macaulay. On long walks in the moonlight George recited Dante to Grace and the children. For the first few years in Italy Grace and George seemed to recover the lively amiability of their courtship days. 'G shaved off beard and got new evening shoes!!' is a typical entry in Grace's diary, for February 1890.

There was, too, heightened emotion, in this 'largish, self-sufficing, and somewhat neurotic community herded together on a Mediterranean shore'. Rose described it as 'passionate and ecstatic like a wilderness of monkeys, pleasure and pain being, both by parents and children, very sharply felt as ecstasy and anguish'.

And there was the whole gorgeous business of Italian Catholicism with richly coloured tapers brought into the house every Candlemas and processions with clouds of incense and 'great simpering wax saints' being carried through the narrow streets. When, after many years of estrangement, Rose returned to the Anglican Church in the last years of her life, she would remember with joy the Catholic festivals of her Italian childhood: Candlemas, when the children bought tiny candles of twisted and coiled coloured wax, that burned with flames like tulips; All Souls' Night, when the Italians lit the graves in the cemetery with little lamps, 'to cheer "*nostri cari defunti*"', and of course Christmas, with 'the lovely plaster sheep and cows and angels in the Cribs in the dark little shops in the piazza arcades, and the harsh bells clanging out from the 14th century church among them, and the orange and lemon trees shining on the terraces of the hills above the town'.

Santa Caterina, the patron saint of the Ligurian coast, who drove out the plague in 1376, came to occupy a special place in Rose's imagination. On her feast day, 30 April, crowds would gather in the piazza San Ambrogio, beneath a small statue of the scourge-wielding Saint Ambrose set into a niche in the piazza wall, outside the church where, at other times, Grace would lead her girls to kneel and say their prayers in the incense-filled darkness. The little Macaulays in their sailor frocks and suits were there to watch as Santa Caterina was carried out from the church on a bed of white marigolds and borne through the town, surrounded by swaying crucifixes decorated with gold and silver flowers, bearing Christs adorned with flowers and jewels and cherubs carrying cups of gold in which to catch the precious blood. The Macaulays would follow the procession to the Chiesa di Santa Caterina, on the eastern edge of town, just short of the Villa Macolai. As it wound its way through the narrow alleyways towards the church on the sea front, the people sang, and still sing, more than a hundred years later, the 'plaintive hymn' that Rose has her characters Betty and Tommy Crevequer sing in *The Furnace* and in *Views and Vagabonds* (1912), the prayer to Santa Caterina for protection:

> 'Difendi, o Caterina
> da peste, fame e guerra,
> Il popol di Casteleto
> In mare e in terra . . .
> . . . Difendi, o Caterina,

Da Guerra e terremoto
Il popol di Varazze
A Te devoto'

George Macaulay was the only one to disapprove of this rampant Catholicism. Rose described his reaction to an invitation from the parish priest to her little brother Will:

> The *parroco* wanted one of my brothers, a beautiful child with curly hair and large, thoughtful, misleadingly innocent blue eyes, to be little St John the Baptist and lead an unruly lamb in the annual procession of Santa Caterina da Siena, the town's patron saint. My brother, I think, was for doing this; he thought it would be fun to lead the lamb. His brothers and sisters were certainly for it; we thought it would be fun to see the lamb leading him. Our mother was for it; she thought it would be friendly to accept. Our nurse was for it; she thought he would look sweet. But my father, the only member of the household who had been to a public school, was not for it; he thought it would look silly, and vetoed it.

This is one of the few veiled criticisms of her father that Rose Macaulay ever made in print. Not that it is much of a criticism; but it suggests obliquely that the masculine privilege of a public school education demands a sacrifice or at least curtailment of the life of the imagination. Throughout her life as a writer, Rose was to hold ambivalent feelings about the relative value of the imagination and rationality, which were expressed most clearly when she was asked to talk or write about her own work. Usually she spoke of her father in adulatory terms: 'I doted on my father,' she wrote. 'As children we endorsed what our Italian servant said of him – "*proprio come il Signor' Iddio – sa tutto, tutto!*"' [sic] ['Just like the Lord our God – he knows everything, everything!'] Yet through the pages of Rose Macaulay's novels stalks a succession of fathers who are neglectful of their children, who

shirk their domestic responsibilities, and who stand accused of
nothing less than cruelty. Looking back at their childhood after
Rose's death in 1958, her sister Jean said, with an odd use of the
personal pronoun: 'Rose was very close to her father'. Jean did
not feel close to their father. The picture of the happy family
conjured up in Rose's reminiscences was not shared by all.

Jean later told Rose's biographer Constance Babington Smith
that Grace never concealed her preference for some members of
the family over others. 'You never knew whether she would
praise you or blame you,' said Jean. She described how she and
Rose 'invented a game called "Families" in which both of them
acted the part of a mother, with twelve or thirteen children
apiece. Each of the "children" had a definite personality, and the
two "mothers" compiled periodical "Charm Lists", in which they
graded their families in order of current preference.'

Margaret, according to Jean, was their mother's favourite
among the girls. She was passionate and sensitive. In the photographs she looks clever and intense and pretty, with long dark
curls and – like Will – a mischievous smile. Jean lacked confidence and was nervous of her mother's uncertain temper. Rose,
the second eldest, was considered to be the 'good' one. This was
probably how her self-sufficiency was interpreted. She was
'good' because she was elsewhere, rehearsing stories over and
over in her mind – a writer's first apprenticeship – neither in
conflict with nor in fear of adult authority. When Margaret
rebelled against authority and Jean quietly submitted to it, Rose
simply ignored it. Aulay, the first-born son, was doted on by
Grace. He was a bright, clever boy and, in Grace's eyes at least,
early on responded to his responsibilities towards his mother.
When Grace, worried about the uselessness of the household
servants (they did have to sack one of the Italian nannies for
being carried home dead drunk by the police), thinks that one of
them, Teresina, might have swept up and thrown away some
dropped jewellery, she is reassured by Aulay: 'You needn't be
afraid Mother: I always examine the dustpan before I let it go

downstairs every day.' The youngest of the five was Will, he of the blue eyes and golden curls and winning smile, naughty Will who wasn't quick at his lessons like his older brother, '*il piccolo cherubino*' who would have looked so sweet leading the lamb in the church procession, Will who was adored and protected by his big sister Rose.

Grace found it easier to get on with older children. When Margaret for her ninth birthday was given a black puppy called Laddie, Grace recorded her asking 'in accents of incredulous rapture': 'Is it really my own dog? My very own live dog?' and commented: 'It is delightful to have a child of nine.' Alas, Margaret's accounts for February 1892 – only three years later – show an expenditure of 3s. 10d. for Laddie's gravestone.

But although Jean felt that she was not one of the preferred ones, it was Eleanor, the youngest surviving daughter, who bore the brunt of her mother's prejudice and what Rose later called euphemistically her 'temperament'.

Born after a pregnancy during which Grace had been ill and exhausted, perhaps Eleanor was doomed to appear plain and unlovely. In Italy Grace was soon pregnant again, and the seventh child, Gertrude, was born in 1888 golden-haired and generally acknowledged to be beautiful. 'Baby pretty and healthy,' Grace noted in her diary, and proudly, 'Italian midwife astounded by no swaddling and at other English arrangements of the event.'

Into one of the back pages of Grace's 1890 diary are fastened locks of hair from each of her children, with the names and ages written carefully beside them by the older ones. Margaret and Rose aged ten and a half and nine and a half, have the darkest curls. Jean and Aulay, aged eight and a half and seven, have hair that is chestnut brown with a golden tinge. Will's curl, at six, is paler. Of them all Eleanor's lock of hair, at three and a half, is the mousiest, while Gertrude's, aged two, is, without question, pale gold.

The two youngest were treated, not unreasonably, as 'the

babies', with a nursemaid to look after them, and the 'eldest five' as Grace refers to them in her diaries soon became 'the Five' to their mother and father. In *Personal Pleasures* (1935) Rose remembered 'the Five' at nursery tea:

> . . . a nurse presides, feeding us with bread and butter. One eats the crumb; one arranges the bitten crusts in a circle under one's saucer, out, so one hopes, of sight. One tilts one's chair back on its hind legs, rocking to and fro.
> 'Now then, Miss R., don't tilt your chair.'
> 'But A. is tilting his. May A. tilt his chair?'
> Telling tales. We do not tell tales of one another now . . .
> Some one is licking the treacle from her bread.
> 'Now then, Miss J., that's not pretty. How often have I told you? . . . *Master W.!*
> Master W., in mood of ill-timed levity, has flung his bread and treacle at the ceiling. To our delight, it sticks there for a moment, before falling down. It leaves on the ceiling a sticky golden-brown smudge. Master W. is in trouble.

The accounts of Rose's childhood that she began to publish in the 1930s consistently present a charming picture of a happy family of five children. The opening of her essay 'Villa Macolai' is typical: 'When I think of my childhood, I see, as background to its various episodes, its glorious dreams of imagined adventure, and inglorious actual escapades, a smooth, warm, blue sea curving round a fishing bay . . . And, putting out on it, a Rob Roy canoe containing five children, three in the middle and one astride on each end. For thus, on a fine summer evening, the Macaulay family was used to embark on its daily nautical adventure to the jut of rocks half a mile up the shore. Arrived at these rocks, the crew would turn pirates, maroon one another, find islands and treasure, fight for life, fling one another into the sea, overturn the craft and sit on its backside, and finally voyage home as wet as it was possible to be.' These accounts regularly fail to mention the two youngest siblings, Eleanor and Gertrude.

Grace in these years showed indulgence towards tiny misdemeanours of all the children except Eleanor. Eleanor at the age of two and a half had already acquired a reputation as being greedy and dishonest, characteristics initially assigned to her by her mother.

While Eleanor, along with Gertrude, was one of 'the babies', Grace tolerated her least favourite child. But in April 1892, when Rose was ten, less than a year after the move to the healthy house on the edge of the town, golden-haired Gertrude caught meningitis and within a few days was dead. Whatever was the upset and the grief suffered by mother, father and siblings, the real tragedy was Eleanor's. Not quite five years old, no longer one of 'the babies', and never to be one of 'the Five', she would now never belong. She was picked on fiercely by Grace, left undefended by her father, and excluded by her five siblings, who followed their mother's lead and made no effort to incorporate the youngest sister into their charmed circle.

Eleanor was left out of the flurry of activity attendant on Gertrude's death. Grace's mother whisked Grace and the three older girls away to Venice to take their minds off the tragedy. Eleanor was left behind. On their return Rose, Margaret and Jean were enrolled in the local convent school. They spent only six months there, a 'rather strange six months', according to Rose, although there is no hint in her account of it that this, their first step outside the family circle, took place immediately after Gertrude's sudden death. Those six months must have been just as strange for Eleanor, the little girl suddenly left alone at home.

There is a photograph of the Macaulay family on holiday from Varazze in 1892, at Uncle Kenneth's house at Clent in Worcestershire, a few months after Gertrude's death. George (who has grown his beard again) stands in the background wearing a black band around the left arm of his tweed jacket. Next to him is Uncle Willie. Grace is in black, sitting next to her sister-in-law, Mary Macaulay. Mary is next to her brother Kenneth, who sits in the centre looking sporty in moustache and tweed cap with a dog on his knee. The children are all in dark mourning clothes, Aulay sprawling confidently next to Uncle Kenneth. Margaret, holding a cricket bat, looks at the grown-ups, as does Jean, who sits demurely on the ground. Rose is also sitting on the ground, cricket ball in her lap, waiting to get on with the game, and sweet Will dandles a toy gun. There is no Eleanor. The next year, too, 1893, the Macaulays holidayed in England without Eleanor.

Edward Conybeare noted his sister's harsh treatment of Eleanor, and always spoke kindly of her in his diaries. His daughter Dorothea also commented on it: the Macaulays 'in flagrant sin', she wrote to her father of yet another photograph of the '5 elder Macaulays without a trace of Eleanor', taken in Savona in 1897.

Rose never referred to Gertrude in the accounts of her childhood that she published, but the memory of Gertrude was kept alive within the family, and Rose and Margaret would return to Varazze and visit her grave long into adulthood. Gertrude's expenses, listed alongside the other children's in the back pages of Grace's diary, in the last year of her life from 1891 to her death in April 1892 amounted to 13s. 4d., while her income, from Uncle Regi and Grandmama, was £3 5s., leaving, as was carefully noted, £2 11s. 8d. 'Remainder spent on lockets for the other children, New Years Day 1893,' is simply recorded.

When they were grown up Eleanor lived in India, translating the Bible into local languages and working for the Society for the Propagation of the Gospel among the 'untouchables', the irony of which could hardly have escaped someone as alive to language as Rose was. She made regular, if infrequent, trips to England from India. Rose at least came to be haunted by the memory of how badly Eleanor had been treated by the rest of the family in Varazze.

Two days before Rose died she wrote to her cousin Dorothea Conybeare, in answer to a question Dorothea had raised about life after death, a recollection of how Gertrude's death had affected the family and in particular how it had affected Eleanor's place within it:

> Yes, Mother did begin to think of it a great deal after Gertrude died. It was an agonising loss. It is quite true that she was a most adorable child – much the nicest of us. Beautiful, unselfish, amusing, imaginative, very intelligent, *and tidy*, which in our family is unique! She used to pick up litter from the floor and tidy it away, to the amusement of Fanny, our dear nurse, who was no tidier than our parents were.

It is hard to believe that this paragon of Rose's imagination is a child of two or three years old. She went on:

> We all petted and adored her; and it *was* a pity she didn't live her life. Of course poor Eleanor suffered by contrast. Mother could never really *love* her much, and showed it much too plainly. And she was divided by years from the rest of us, who were all, so to speak, in one gang. So she was rather lonely, and I think it was that which made her take to stealing things. (I mean jam from cupboards etc, nothing serious, though once or twice she did take money). When she went away to school and got under the influence of mistresses who were religious and were kind to her, she developed excellently and became extremely good and religious and did splendid work. I always feel remorseful that we elder children didn't take more notice of her, but a gap of nearly three years at that age is difficult to bridge. And she lacked the gift of *charm*, which Gertrude had so abundantly.

What, at this stage, motivated Rose to write of her sister that as a child she had stolen money 'once or twice', and why try to disguise the unpleasantness of the accusation behind the evasive

and dishonest 'nothing serious . . .'? This is so untypically disingenuous of Rose that it is difficult to resist the idea that her own
feelings about Eleanor remained unresolved.

With Gertrude's death the paradise of Varazze was touched
with grief and loss. The year after, Uncle Harry died. Like his
younger brother Reginald he had been a brilliant athlete, but he
had left Oxford with unpaid debts and fled to America.
Reginald had found him work with Wallace & Company in
Bombay, but it hadn't lasted. He was thirty-six when he died in
Siam. Harry, lacking a public life, was denied a public death. He
vanished from the family picture just as Eleanor did, although
later a plaque was erected in his memory in the outer wall of St
Luke's Church in Hodnet, beneath the plaques to his mother
and father. A death that is somehow not quite right, a death that
can't be dealt with by the survivors in a straightforward public
way, is something that recurs in Rose Macaulay's fiction, in
Non-Combatants and Others (1916), in *Potterism* (1920) and
again in *Told by an Idiot* (1923). The emotional unease gener-
ated by the deaths of characters in these novels perhaps echoes
the unease that Rose felt at the death of her Uncle Harry, an
uncle she loved and for whom she was not allowed to mourn.

Rose was thirteen when the Macaulay family returned to
England in 1894, although they continued to spend winter holidays in Varazze until Rose was a young woman. George had
begun to feel increasingly trapped by the small world of family,
and once his edition of Herodotus was done he came to experience living abroad as a state of cultural and political exile. And
it was felt that the children would benefit from some conventional education. So they returned: to Oxford High School for
the three older girls and the Oxford Preparatory School for the
boys, 'and pretty dim it seemed, after our libertine and barelegged scrambling about our Italian shore and hills, complete
with canoe and pony'.

The landscape of Rose's Italian childhood was touched with

agony as well as with ecstasy, but as she returned to it again and again in her imagination she tried to banish from it the memories of loss, death and cruelty. She recreated it as a world in which there was no separation between landscape and the inner life, and in which the ever present sea offered endless opportunities for the dissolution of the self. In her 1912 novel *The Lee Shore*, she presented it as a haven for people broken by the world, a paradise blessed by the Gran Protettrice Santa Caterina. Then again in 1919 she went back in *What Not: A Prophetic Comedy*, a novel about forbidden love, written just after Rose herself had fallen deeply and permanently in forbidden love. In *What Not* the lovers, Kitty and Chester, flee to Italy on a secret honeymoon, to Cogoleto, 'a tiny fishing town fifteen miles up the coast from Genoa, shut in a little bay between the olive hills and the sea'. They walk, they talk, and they swim. They pass 'amphibious days' moving from sea to land and back again, just as the young Macaulays did: 'Chester and Kitty would swim out for a mile, then lie on their backs and float, gazing up into the sea-blue sky, before the sun had climbed high enough to burn and blind. Then they would swim back and return to the inn and put on a very few clothes and have their morning coffee, and then walk up the coast, taking lunch, to some little lonely cove in the shadow of rocks, where they would spend the heat of the day in and out of the sea.' Later the two lovers climb the hills behind and 'look down over hills and sea bathed in evening light, and see to the east the white gleam of Genoa shimmering like a pearl, like a ghost, between transparent sea and sky, to the west the point of Savona jutting dark against a flood of fire'.

These were the hills and the sea that Rose Macaulay shared with those she loved most in the world, and in adulthood she visited them again with her lover Gerald O'Donovan. Ghosts and fire are glimpsed in the distance to east and west, but the bay itself, the bay of her childhood, is guarded by the hills. Varazze provided for the older Rose memories of an Eden that nourished her vision; it also fed her strong desire for self-sufficiency and the positioning of herself, as a writer, on the edges of the worlds she described. In all Rose Macaulay's work there are echoes of those childhood ecstasies and anguishes, of yearning for that perfect, no longer attainable world of companionship and emotional freedom.

Chapter Three

Edwardian

... those brief ten years we call Edwardian seem now like a short spring day. They were a gay and yet an earnest time. A time of social reform on the one hand, and social brilliance on the other ... A queer time! Perhaps a transition time; for that matter, this is one of the things times always are.

Told by an Idiot

i

'Startling news of Macaulays having taken house at Oxford!' wrote Edward Conybeare in his diary on 18 August 1894. How Edward would have loved Grace and her family to have returned to Cambridge. She had seen her brother for brief visits now and again when they were back on holiday from Italy. Now the last thing Grace wanted was to live close enough for him to start interfering, as she saw it, in her life. When Margaret, Rose and Jean were registered at Oxford High School in September, George described himself as being a former Fellow of Trinity College, Cambridge and Assistant Master at Rugby, 'now engaged in literary work'. He needed a library. If Grace couldn't live in Cambridge because of her bossy brother's propinquity, then Oxford, with the Bodleian, was the obvious place to settle.

Rose recognised the symbolic importance of the change in circumstances on their return from Italy, and wrote out a will. 'My dog Fido' would go to little Will, who needed protection now that he was to be separated from his big sister. 'All my dolls', unsuitable, according to Grace, for a girl of Rose's age, went to seven-year-old Eleanor. Other members of the family would receive various treasures: a diamond ring, 'all my knives', a Venetian mirror, a swing, a stamp album, a moonstone brooch, a Burne-Jones picture, stilts and wooden skates. This was the solemn end of childhood, and childish things had to be put away. Rose was no longer 'Rosie', but entered Oxford High School as 'Emily'.

They moved into 3 Clarendon Villas, Park Town, just north of the centre of Oxford, with the High School on the Banbury Road on one side, and on the other the Oxford Preparatory School (later the Dragon School) where the boys would start in 1895. No more ponies and goats and rabbits, no more scrambling up and down the hills and going out at night to the hilltops to catch fireflies or down to the beach to look at the stars. The 'literary work' on which George was engaged was not backed, as it was for others of his class, by a comfortable private inheritance, so now, although Eliza Conybeare helped out, it was a dreary life of scrimping and saving. The girls were dressed in brown corduroy which Grace managed to get cheap in a shop in south Oxford and, back in the real world with a vengeance, George Macaulay informed his second daughter that the navy was closed to girls. The difference between girls and boys was made brutally clear to Rose.

By the time she was fourteen Rose had grown beyond her passion for the asceticism and anti-sensuality of Thomas à Kempis, whose *Imitation of Christ* she had read and taken to heart the previous year. She now moved on to the pragmatism of John Stuart Mill, and indeed had gone so far as to lose her faith, although she was too shy to admit this to the vicar who was preparing them all for confirmation. But à Kempis had offered her a way, however negative, of interpreting the sensual world. Rose did not want to grow towards womanhood. Twelve-year-old Cary Folyot in *Keeping Up Appearances* (1928) is sickened and horrified by what she discovers about sex, and determines to become a nun so as to avoid the 'beastly' business, which she has learned about through a secret reading of Freud's *The Interpretation of Dreams*. Although the circumstances do not exactly reflect Rose's (*The Interpretation of Dreams* was not published in Britain until Rose was in her twenties), Cary is not the only child in Rose's fiction to be frightened and distressed by sexual knowledge, and the tenderness and empathy with which these girls' states of minds are described suggests that Rose understood such feelings very well. Her boyish fantasies could no longer be articulated (although they were not very deeply hidden, and would continue to erupt well into adulthood, particularly whenever Rose went near a boat). Meanwhile she dug herself more firmly than ever into family, flanked by her sisters.

'George today discovered in Varsity Library Gowers lost work Speculum Homines!' exclaimed Edward in his diary in April 1895. George's discovery seems to have passed into family history as a serendipitous stumbling over a musty old manuscript in a dusty corner. Whether it was a stroke of luck or the result of meticulous scholarly searching or whether, as is perhaps most likely, it was a combination of the two, the finding of this lost manuscript of John Gower's, the *Mirour de l'Omme*, or *Speculum Meditantis*, was important for George Macaulay. He worked on the manuscript for the next four years, bringing out an edition ('a huge work with lovely bits imbedded', said Edward), with the Clarendon Press in the last month of 1899. It would take him back into the mainstream of academic life, leading first to a professorship at the University of Wales in Aberystwyth, and then eventually back to Cambridge, where his academic career had got off to such a shaky start with his Latin verses about proctors and prostitutes.

Meanwhile the family moved further out of town to 350

Banbury Road, in the more countrified air of Summertown. It was a comfortably sized brick house with a covered veranda and, in suburban style, a name: Thule. 'Rightly,' commented Edward. Margaret, Rose and Jean continued at the High School where they were trained, in the words of the headmistress Lucy Soulsby, in 'true religion, good manners, and sound learning, in that order'.

The girls did not shine as pupils, but Rose adored her history teacher, Bertha Browne, and found in her an inspiration that would stay with her for the rest of her life. Margaret left aged sixteen. Rose and Jean stayed on but their attendance was patchy. For long periods and especially in the winter months Rose and her sisters returned to Varazze with their mother.

In December 1898 Rose, as E. Macaulay of Form VI, had her first publication, a poem called 'The Sea', which she had entered for a prize competition in the school magazine. It was a four-stanza poem in the style of Tennyson, who had died in 1892 after more than forty years as Poet Laureate, and was awarded the prize for being 'distinctly the best, both in form and conception'. It starts:

> Sunny and calm and bright,
> >Ocean, great ocean,
> Lit with the sky's blue light,
> >Fathomless ocean!
> No movement stirs thy silent smiling deep,
> No playful breeze disturbs thy peaceful sleep,
> >But far on the distant land
> The ripples dance upon the yellow sand,
> >Ocean,
> Upon the shingly sand.

The other three stanzas apostrophise Ocean as 'shimmering', 'terrible' and 'furious'. Here the sea, a central image in all Rose's work, appears as a symbol of changeability, and although the poem is not especially original, we can see how interested she already is in the pliability of language, and how she pushes at the rhythm and the metre. It is not a bad try for a seventeen-year-old.

Despite the financial strictures there were plenty of family outings and holidays during the Oxford years. In July 1895 the Macaulays and the Conybeares visited the India Exhibition together and went on the Great Wheel. For Rose's fourteenth birthday in August they went to the Crystal Palace. There were holidays spent at Uncle Kenneth's house in Clent in Worcestershire, where they rode ponies and played cricket, and as far as they were able recreated the life of 'the Five'. They trooped to the village shop and bought Woodbines 'and smoked them sitting in a row on the pig-sty roof', they played pirates in the barn and found grassy slopes and rolled down them like barrels over and over until they were sick. They had seaside holidays at Red Wharfe Bay on the Isle of Anglesey.

But inevitably the five were being scattered. Aulay and Will spent two – interrupted – years together at the Oxford Preparatory School before Aulay won a scholarship in Mathematics to Clifton College, a school set up along the same lines as Rugby on the pleasant hills outside Bristol. Clifton College had a reputation for being more liberal and less corrupt than some of the other public schools, and was the only one to accommodate Jewish boys, with a house, then as now, especially for them. In the previous decade Roger Fry had found Clifton's high-mindedness a relief after the sleaziness of his preparatory school, where one of his loathed responsibilities as top of the school had been to hold down the smaller boys while they were flogged by the headmaster.

Only one of Aulay's letters home from Clifton survives. It describes to his father with unconcealed excitement the drama of the suicide of the corps sergeant in the school armoury: 'I didn't see him after he had done it but someone who saw him said that he was quite unrecognisable and the top of his head was blown off. The bullet went right through his head, the ceiling above, and then through the roof . . .'

Aulay retained his scholarship throughout his time at Clifton, and left when he was nearly seventeen to go to the Royal Military Academy at Woolwich, from which he would join the Royal Engineers and be posted to the North-West Frontier. Will was sent to Marlborough, where he struggled up the school, managing to reach halfway before leaving at eighteen.

Just before her eighteenth birthday Rose left the Oxford High School. Despite the lack of money, the girls were not pushed into getting work. Teaching was one of the most popular professions for women in the early 1900s but of all four Macaulay girls it was only Eleanor who became a teacher, working in a school in Lahore before she became a missionary. Grace was happy for Eleanor to leave and pursue an independent career, but she wanted her other girls at home. Both Margaret and Jean had to struggle hard to be allowed to leave.

Uncle Reginald, whose estate in Scotland they used to visit in the summer, and who kept the Macaulay family provided with snipe and pheasant, recognised and responded to Rose's intellectual potential. Just as he had come to the rescue with funds for a pony in Italy, now he saved Rose from shouldering the role of daughter-at-home. He offered George the money for her to go to university. She had passed the Oxford and Cambridge Joint Board Higher Certificate Examination in History, French, German and Elementary Mathematics, and had achieved a distinction in History, her chosen subject. In October 1900 she took up a place at Somerville College to read History. Margaret became their mother's companion and confidante.

Somerville had been Walton Manor, a grey stone house built in 1826 in three acres of land between Woodstock Road and Walton Street, five minutes' walk from St Giles's, the heart of the town and the university. When Rose arrived in 1900 it was still quite rural, with a buttercup field and old farm buildings, although the farm pony had recently departed and was not replaced. The fees, for board, lodging, tuition and lectures, were about £30 a term for the best rooms.

It had opened twenty-one years earlier as a non-denominational hall of residence, with thirteen students, choosing as its model a scientist, Mary Somerville, rather than a saint or a patron of the Church as the other women's colleges did. The ethos of religious independence suited Rose Macaulay, who thought of herself now, like her father, as an Anglo-agnostic. Whereas in Lady Margaret Hall the life of the students was modelled on 'that of a Christian family', in Somerville it was modelled on 'that of an English family'. By the time Rose was at Oxford the presence at lectures of a lady chaperone, armed with white cotton knitting, had been pronounced no longer necessary; but girls still had to sit apart from boys at lectures, and all social occasions where men were present required a chaperone.

For the first time Rose made friends outside her immediate family circle. There was Margerie Venables Taylor, who read History with Rose under Miss Beatrice Lees, and went on to become a Romano-British archaeologist. And, two years their senior, there was Olive Willis, who later founded the girls' public school, Downe House.

One of the freedoms offered by Somerville and the other women's colleges was time to read, to write, to think, or just to be alone. For young women in late Victorian England solitude was the rarest prize; unmarried women without a profession had to be doing things, and had to be seen to be doing things: charity, domestic tasks, or the dreary social round of morning visits and tea-parties. It was from this that Rose escaped for the three years of her time at university.

Somerville had the largest library of all the women's colleges, and was unusual in allowing its undergraduate students access to all its books. The History course began with the Anglo-Saxons, but Rose's chosen special period was the seventeenth century, and she immersed herself in this. She loved it. Political science and

political economy were part of the course, and she was also reading Dante and the nineteenth-century poets and philosophers
whose ideas would influence her first novels. Two lines from
Dante furnished the epigraph for *Abbots Verney* (1906), her first
novel; the symbolist poet and philosopher Maurice Maeterlinck
provided her with the epigraph – and central symbol of a purify-
ing fire – for her second novel, *The Furnace*, and the idealist
philosophy of Hermann Lotze nourished her third novel, *The
Secret River* (1909).

'I liked Oxford,' she wrote years later, 'the river, work, people,
Oxford itself, even hockey, at which I was good.'

Hockey remained a favourite game of Rose's for the next ten
years. In the early 1900s blouses with a collar and tie were worn
for games and although hockey skirts had crept up from ankle
length to six or seven inches from the ground they remained
tight waisted. At that length the skirts were considered inde-
cently short for cycling, so another skirt had to be worn over the
hockey skirt for the ride to the playing field.

Rose and Margerie Venables Taylor spent a great deal of time
on the river, either in a punt or in one of the Somerville boats
that were kept in the newly built boathouse. It was like a recreation of childhood days of solitary reading, interspersed with
vigorous games and playing around in boats. But despite the
good friendships and the pleasures of intellectual endeavour, and
despite the hockey and the rowing and punting and the hours of
quiet, uninterrupted reading, Rose was not happy.

Every year the young women of Somerville College who had
just taken their final exams staged a 'going-down play' for the
other members of the college. In June 1903 it was a pageant: each
young woman dressed up as her 'totem' animal, the creature that
was most illustrative of her personal characteristics, and was presented to the audience with a humorous introduction. Miss E. R.
Macaulay chose to represent herself as a caterpillar, standing out
from the others, which included a frog, a monkey, a rabbit, an old
grey sheep and a peacock, as the only one that had the potential

to turn into a different incarnation. The anonymous description is in three parts:

The Caterpillar is a long and wriggly creature often found in the garden. It has been conjectured that this animal feeds upon leaves and grass but the shyness of its habits in this matter have hitherto defeated the attempts of the most scientific enquirers to discover the kind and quantity of its food, and the usual hours at which it feeds. One fact alone is certain; the caterpillar is not carnivorous. It has been known upon one occasion to consume a whole banana, but this can only be taken as an exceptional case, for the animal eat [*sic*] nothing during the twenty four hours preceding and following this phenomenal meal.

Its other habits lend themselves more satisfactorily to accurate observation, in that they are apparent to the naked eye. The caterpillar is extremely agile and nimble being totally unburdened by a memory. It may frequently seen [*sic*] looping its way to Keble at 11, in the touching hope of arriving in time for a 10 o'clock lecture at Queens. It has been observed clinging to a punt-pole, and is often to be found in a rowing-boat (preferably an Outrig) adhering fixedly with its foremost parts to the handle of an oar, whilst its other extremity from time to time lightly touches the stretcher.

Its favourite place for weaving its cocoon is the Admiralty Office, and it will answer any questions concerning Training-ships with promptness and ambiguity. Its language however is peculiar to itself, and those who are unaccustomed to it occasionally have some difficulty in understanding the answer when it has been given. Its celebrated speech upon 'Privilege of Parliament' will ever live in the memory of those who heard it. The Caterpillar has an aspiring nature, and is apt to forget that its wings are as yet undeveloped – a neglect which sometimes leads to disastrous results.

Later on in life Rose Macaulay became sufficiently self-assured to make comedy out of her ambivalence about food. In 'Eating and Drinking' she described how the discovery of fire and cooking 'was to prove an ever growing burden' to man and womankind, and recommended to those who were not 'slaves to baked-meats' and who were fortunate enough not to be compelled to prepare food for others, the eating of 'such objects as are sold in a form ready for the mouth, such as cheese, bread, butter, fruit, sweets, dough-nuts, macaroons, meringues and everything that comes (if you have a tin-opener) out of tins'. But her refusal to eat didn't strike her friends as comic when she was at Somerville.

'She was entirely obstinate about college meals,' wrote Olive Willis, 'and would go without food rather than sit through a college dinner'. The food on offer, like all institutional food in those days, was unappetising. Rose's contemporary Margaret Thomas (later Lady Rhondda, editor of *Time and Tide*), couldn't stand the discomforts of Somerville for longer than two terms, saying later how much she 'disliked the food, and, more still, the way in which it was served'. But Rose's reluctance to eat went further than a dislike of the cooking would warrant. Olive Willis remembered trying to tempt Rose to eat bread and milk in her room, and having it refused.

She refused to eat in public. She barely ate in private. Yet she was far from shy and silent. She suddenly found a voice and was willing to speak in public debates in the junior common room, but she spoke so hurriedly that her audience found her difficult to understand. Her friends were struck by the change from an adolescent girl so painfully shy and unaccustomed to company that she was able only to relax with her siblings, to a young woman from whom speech poured in a torrent. Olive Willis found little sign in the undergraduate Rose of the successful public figure she would become: 'She looked like an unfledged bird, a young eaglet perhaps, but in that thin defenceless form, it wasn't easy to realise future development. In the almost unintelligible torrent of words, it wasn't possible to recognise a master of language.'

But someone had caught a glimpse of a later Rose. The anonymous writer, or writers – and perhaps Rose herself was involved – of the description of the caterpillar offer not just her eccentricities: an aversion to food, absent-mindedness, a mad passion for the navy and all things to do with boats, and a mode of speaking that distances the audience from the speaker; they also give us the caterpillar's 'aspiring nature'. Rose was ambitious. In the past Rose's intellectual ambitions had been sustained and nurtured at home. In a household with a father who was a published scholar and where both parents valued literary culture, Rose had been the most bookish of the children, the one in whom her parents' literary aspirations were most clearly expressed. At school, securely supported by a sister on either side, she had found an inspiring teacher. But at Somerville, as intellectually hungry as ever, she was for the first time outside the security of the family circle.

Perhaps Rose's self-starvation and her sudden garrulousness were attempts to ward off the frightening reality of being on her own. Having moulded herself in the image of her doubting, self-questioning, intellectually scrupulous father, she was now cast adrift from him. One hundred years later Rose would very likely be diagnosed as anorexic. But while anorexia is associated with anxiety and conflict about sexual maturity and the social and cultural meanings of femininity, it is also, at a basic level, indicative of a hopeless wish to keep the body in a childlike state. It is concerned with the desire not to grow up.

In Rose Macaulay's fiction a variety of young women who are active, flat-chested and boyish try to escape this destiny. Some of them see obscurely, others more clearly, that the price exacted by adulthood is a curtailment of their ambition and aspiration.

Perhaps the scene between thirteen-year-old Imogen ('I myself was Imogen, roughly speaking,' Rose suggested later) and her cousin Billy in *Told by an Idiot* offers an insight into Rose Macaulay's state of mind. Regarding the facts of life Imogen has been kept by her mother 'in the ignorance . . . suitable to her years'.

Billy says:

'I know something you don't. I know how babies come.'

'Don't care how they come,' Imogen returned, astride on a higher bough of the aspen tree than her cousin could attain to. 'They're no use anyhow, the little fools. Who wants babies?'

Billy, having meditated on this unanswerable question, amended his vaunt. 'Well, I know how puppies come, too. So there.'

Imogen was stumped. You can't say that puppies are no use. She could think of no retort but the ancient one of sex insult. 'Boys are always bothering about stupid things like how babies come. As if it mattered. I'd rather know the displacement and horsepower and knots of all the battleships and first-class cruisers.'

'You don't.'

'I do.'

'Bet you a bulls-eye you don't.'

'Done. A pink one. Ask any one you like.'

'Well what's the Terrible?'

'14,200 tons; 25,000 horsepower; 22.4 knots. That's an easy one.'

'The Powerful.'

'Same, of course. No, she only makes 22.1 knots. Stupid to ask me twins.'

Billy considered. He did not like to own it, but he could not remember at the moment any other ships of His Majesty's fleet.

After further taunting, Imogen 'collapsed into sudden good temper':

'Don't let's rot. Why did the gooseberry fool?'

To change the subject further, she swung herself backwards and hung from the branch by her knees, her short mop of curls swinging upside down, the blood singing in her head. Billy, a nice but not very clever little boy, said, 'Because the raspberry syrup,' and truce was signed. Who, as Imogen had asked, cared how babies came?

But not caring how babies come is different at thirteen from at twenty, twenty-one and twenty-two. In childhood it is not something that you need to know, but as an adult it is: it could not have failed to strike Rose, at a women's college, being taught by single, independent women, that babies are the enemy of promise. Her own mother was a prime example.

Later Rose discovered a way of being grown up, of moving outside the family circle and loving someone else, while still pursuing her ambition and her need to write, but at Somerville the way was not clear.

Nobody seems to have thought, then, that Rose was struggling with deep difficulties. Perhaps she was odd and eccentric, but in 1900 any woman who dared to go to Oxford University and dared to claim the same educational rights as her father and uncles and brothers was considered a bit odd. Her contemporaries were aware of her anxieties about failure, but they would not necessarily have recognised Rose's eccentricities, so accurately described through the figure of the caterpillar, as indicative of profound disturbance. Olive Willis saw some of the tensions in the young Rose: 'Perhaps the most curious trait in her character when she was young was her great diffidence, a sense of failure and inadequacy, combined with a confidence in her own opinion . . . As she became famous this diffidence left her and she spoke deliberately and firmly, without that engaging hesitation which used to trip her up in her most vehement and absurd arguments . . . Her strange eyes never altered, grey as glass and often unseeing as though she realised the world through other senses and other ways.' (In later years Vera Brittain would accuse Rose of pretending not to see her.)

In the book of the going-down pageant some of the animals are given their own mottoes. The motto given to Margerie

Venables Taylor, the frog ('a bright little animal of aquatic
habits'), was 'Mirth with thee I mean to live.' Most, like the
frog's, are unexceptional. The one ascribed to the caterpillar, however, illustrates a state of inner tension and conflict. It adds to the
judgement passed already about Rose's 'aspiring nature' and hints
at an anxiety that is its corollary. The motto is: 'Fain would I
climb but fear to fall.'

None of her friends realised that Rose's peculiar behaviour
was symptomatic of an approaching nervous collapse.

Rose Macaulay failed to sit her final examinations. Instead,
with the backing of the Vice-Principal of the college and her
tutor, Miss Lees, she applied for and was granted an *aegrotat*,
which confers a degree but without ranking. It is not clear to
what extent this was Rose's decision. Margerie Venables Taylor
later wrote: 'ERM applied for an aegrotat or was persuaded to
apply – by the Vice-Principal [Miss Bruce] and her tutor, Miss
Lees'. Soon after the exams Rose herself suggested that Miss
Lees was the agent of it. She sent a pencil drawing to Margerie.
Entitled 'The Flamingo and the Hedgehogs: A Story of
Schools', it shows Rose and Margerie as two hedgehogs in a
game of *Alice in Wonderland*-style croquet, with Miss Lees as the
flamingo. Margerie is rolled into a ball ready to be hit through
the croquet hoops, but the Rose hedgehog is blocked from doing
so by the flamingo's beak.

Olive Willis later proposed that Rose had reached some kind
of intellectual crisis, offering 'a dislike of formal questions and
answers when there seemed so much more to say on every subject' as a reason for her failing to sit the exams. It sounds as if
Rose was paralysed by a fear of failure, and if applying for an
aegrotat was a suggestion that came from Miss Lees, then she
probably saw it as the only way that her eccentric, tomboyish
student would get a degree at all.

Like the college she attended, Rose Macaulay was struggling
to find her own identity and to make a place for herself in the
world. But Somerville, while determined to keep its sense of

itself as different, independent and non-denominational, nonetheless strived to belong to the university, and it finally succeeded. Somerville's oblique relationship to the university was not unlike Rose's own relationship both to the academic world and to the Church. She felt ambivalent and managed to place herself on the edge, wanting to belong and yet not being able to. Perhaps this was why, in the end, she left Oxford without a ranked degree. But even had she had a ranked degree, that degree, because she was a woman, would not have been fully recognised by the university. She yearned to be inside, but at the same time she couldn't bear to be. Perhaps, for Rose Macaulay, that was the place most conducive to creativity.

Her early novels are concerned with the anguish of yearnings and fears about belonging and exclusion, about freedom and about being trapped. Later she transformed this ambivalence towards the institutions on whose peripheries she placed herself into the sharp irony of the novels she wrote between the wars, when as author she danced dangerously on the edges of an establishment world and anatomised it from there.

But in 1903 she was still the caterpillar, its wings as yet undeveloped. She was not yet the butterfly.

ii

Eliza Conybeare died at the end of 1902 and left all her money
to Grace (causing a certain coolness between Grace and her
brother Edward). This legacy of over £7,000, with George's regular salary, meant that there was no necessity for the girls to seek
employment, although Jean was already making plans to do so.
When Rose left Somerville in June 1903 she went home. Since
the autumn of 1901 the Macaulays had been living in a house
called Ty-Issa, or Ty-Isaf, The Lower House, in the valley of the
River Ystwyth three or four miles south of Aberystwyth, where
George Macaulay was Professor of English Language and
Literature. Ty-Issa is just along the river from Llanfarian, a clus-
ter of Nash-designed houses that belonged to the University of
Wales at Aberystwyth. These were reserved for professors and
their families. Ty-Issa belonged to this group of houses but stood
apart from the rest of them, further inland along a short stretch
of the river, and about a mile by narrow winding lane. The houses
of Llanfarian lie on the south side of the River Ystwyth; Ty-Issa
is on the north bank, round a bend in the river and out of sight
of the rest. It is a square white-painted house, tucked under a
steeply rising bank, with a sprawl of farm buildings beside it. It
looks out over sloping fields down to the river.

On a bright day the house gleams charmingly. Friesian cows
graze by the banks of the glinting silver river. In autumn the
bank that rises behind Ty-Issa is a riot of gold and red. But it is
not difficult to imagine what it would look like on a grey
winter's day. Then the sides of the valley crowd in upon the
house, and there is nothing to see from the windows but sodden
muddy cows standing in sodden muddy fields. The nearest
company for the Macaulay girls were the daughters of other

professors, and even they were out of sight round the bend in the river.

'A very pleasing abode,' wrote Uncle Edward Conybeare, delighted as always with other people's fortune, and went on to describe the 'fairy woodland ravine' that was close by. Perhaps closer to Rose's feelings about Ty-Issa was his phrase 'extraordinarily out of the world'. George had written to his friend Francis Jenkinson, University Librarian at Cambridge: 'Our house is well-sheltered by hills and surrounded with woods, a very pretty place, and a paradise for birds and probably also insects.' Which is all very well for a man who goes out to the Department of English at the university every day, but the paradise for birds and insects did not hold quite the same charm for his clever, restless daughter Rose.

Every day began with family prayers, which according to cousin Dorothea were 'most painful musically', with Aunt Grace consistently playing wrong notes on the piano and Uncle George able to sing only three notes. 'The oddness of those Macaulay family prayers can hardly be exaggerated,' wrote Dorothea. Rose had just spent three years in a vigorously non-denominational institution. She considered herself an agnostic, and was temperamentally unsympathetic to religious enthusiasm of any form.

She had also become temperamentally unsympathetic to her mother. Margaret kept a diary for some of the time that they lived at Ty-Issa, and the minor tiffs between Rose and her mother that she recorded suggest a strong frustration on Rose's part. Margaret describes a typical afternoon: 'After tea . . . played an exciting game of croquet with Father, Rose helping with advice to "hit the post" when she had done disagreeing with Mother, up in the wood, about whether larch trees are nicest straight or crooked.'

From 1904, with Aulay already in India, Jean training to be a nurse and Eleanor, who was at boarding-school, back only for holidays, Rose and Margaret were much in each other's company. They would walk to Llanfarian, and then home along the riverbank. On hot days they would bathe in the pool below the bridge, hiding under the bridge when the 4.45 train passed by. It was now that Rose once more forged a closeness with her elder sister Margaret which was to last, despite the divergence of their interests and their lives, until Margaret's death during the Second World War.

Grace would have been happy for her girls to marry, and pushed Margaret in the direction of Dick Brooke, elder brother of the more famous Rupert. The Macaulays had kept in touch with William Parker Brooke and Mary Brooke and their three sons since Rugby days, when the Brookes lived in number 3 Hillmorton Road, just a few doors down from George and Grace. Margaret's diary entry for 21 July 1906 records 'wet day' (a variation on the more common 'wet all day'), 'Dick Brooke came in evening,' and then tantalisingly, 'just the same as he always was'. As Margaret's 1906 diary is the only one of hers that has survived, we will never know how, to Margaret and Rose, Dick 'always was'. It was fortunate that nothing came of Grace's plans, for poor Dick became alcoholic and was dead at the age of twenty-six. Perhaps it was partly Grace's pushing that put Margaret off the idea; as a child she had been the one most resistant to her mother's authority. When Margaret decided to enter a religious order and become a deaconess some years later, one wonders whether perhaps this was a way to escape from Grace.

Margaret later wrote a novel, *The Sentence Absolute* (1914), which is set in a Welsh seaport town called Aberyrfon, where Gwen Powell and her sister Peggy live in a house up the valley with a larch wood rising behind, its 'light plumes of luminous green against the deep blue sky'. It is a novel about marriage and morals: Gwen thinks she doesn't want to marry, but loses her heart to handsome Tony Venning, who has his heart in the right place but is weak-willed, and in order to get out of debt accepts a bribe. Gwen believes him to be 'absolutely straight' and is horrified when she finds out what he has done. The lovers part, each of them being too proud to say what they feel. Gwen can be seen as a mixture of Margaret herself and her sister Rose, and handsome Tony's weakness surely has parallels with Dick Brooke's. In the end the lovers are reunited, having both learned through suffering, and through an acceptance of God, to suspend, in Robert Browning's words, the 'sentence absolute for light or shade'.

Like her protagonist, Gwen, Margaret enjoyed the tennis parties, the dances, the church bazaars and the general round of country social life in which the Macaulays were invited to participate. But Rose was restless, feeling trapped within the confining valley walls. Wales seemed to oppress her, even if she was away from the house and her mother. She and Margaret went on a farewell bicycling jaunt with Will before he set off for Canada in the spring of 1906. Margaret wrote down odd snatches of Will's conversation, many of which concerned Rose's moods: 'Rose is simply furious,' Margaret records him saying, and then, 'Look at Rose, white to the lips with rage because she's missed her bath.' In *The Valley Captives* Rose wrote: 'It seemed that the rain never ceased, nor the desolate surging of the wind. Always, night and day, it ground bare boughs together till the wet woods grieved dismally like the grey sea . . .'

But there were breaks from the gloom. There were still holidays in Varazze, and the Macaulay uncles, William and Kenneth, better appreciated what life was like for their nieces in the foggy Welsh valley than Uncle Edward Conybeare with his fairy ravines, taking them to Italy in the spring of 1905, first to Rome and then to Naples. This trip with the Macaulay uncles proved a turning point for Rose, for it introduced her to an adult Italy, an Italy of art and culture and history and antiquity, which was different from her familiar childhood Italy of ponies and canoes and barelegged freedom.

When she and Margaret returned to Wales Rose, aged twenty-three, started work on her first novel. She was already a published poet. Since leaving Oxford she had been submitting work to the *Saturday Westminster*, and the family were used to scanning its competition pages every week to see if E. R. Macaulay had won a prize with a poem or pastiche. But this was the first time since childhood story-writing that she had attempted a sustained fictional narrative. As writing was a valued activity in the Macaulay household Rose was able to shut herself away and wrestle with the particular problems that confront a novice writer of fiction. Later she told her Somerville friend Olive Willis: 'I tried to put some bit of you, very clumsily, into my first novel'. She used her as a model for one of the minor characters, Jane Gerard, who has 'excellent brains, an immense fund of common sense, a rather fine face, and an overweening sense of the ridiculous'. Rose was never confident about her ability to create credible characters. To Olive she went on: 'And of course one doesn't put people whole into books – one alters and twists to suit the mergencies of the story – at least I do. And often mix up two people together, or invent half and copy half.'

Rose borrowed elements of the plot of *Abbots Verney* from the early and mid-Victorian novels by Walter Scott and by Charlotte M. Yonge of her childhood reading: themes of inheritance of property, inheritance of moral traits and, one she would return to in later novels, the drama of an unjust accusation. But her treatment of the themes is very different from the earlier novels. In her childhood reading, the heroes would be well-born but misplaced in society. Virtue and breeding would go hand in hand; the virtuous, after struggle, could rightly claim the material prize that both their virtue and their background merited. But Verney Ruth, in *Abbots Verney*, is involved in a bitter and suffocating family entanglement. Verney's father is a cheat, and Verney's own virtue is called into question by his grandfather, who has brought him up and hopes to save him from the corrupting influence of Verney's father, his own son. The young man and the old man are caught up in complex interplay of pride and self-denial. Verney in his lonely stubbornness is like another modern hero, the working-

class poet Savage Keith Rickman in May Sinclair's 1904 novel
The Divine Fire.

Unlike the novels Rose Macaulay looked back to, there is a
resolutely anti-heroic theme to *Abbots Verney*, articulated by
Rosamund Ilbert, the central female character: 'One thinks one
will never forget,' Rosamund tells Verney, 'and one tries in vain to
forgive people; but in the end we forgive them through no merit
of our own, but simply because life carries us on and forces us to.
Oh, it's no good trying to be too heroic; all we need do is to trust
to life to slur things over for us – in time.' Later, in the sullen days
when Verney is back with his grandfather, unforgiven and unforgiving, watching the old man deteriorate towards death, he
remembers something that Rosamund has said, that it was 'the
business of the young to make life possible to the old'. The novel
explores the uncertainties and the compromises of family ties
and responsibilities; nothing is predictable.

As original as the anti-heroic tone of the story, is Rose's
reimagining of the concept of 'abroad'. She wrote to Margerie
Venables Taylor about how she had enjoyed writing the book,
saying, 'Specially the Roman part I loved doing; it was just like
being there again, you know, & walking abt the streets . . .' Later
in the same letter, chatting about some mutual friends who had
just got married: 'how very nice for them to be starting by going
to Italy; marriage would have its points, you know! Fancy spending from April to June there; I wonder where they'll go. Are
they both fond of travelling abt? What I love to do is to do those
things on the cheap, and avoid the big hotels full of bloated
English & Americans & go to little tiny places.'

But the Rome she presents is a more complicated and darker
place than she implies in her correspondence, and its darkness is
what makes it so interesting as a representation of liberation.
There is a world of Romes in *Abbots Verney*: there is the Rome of
the rich *inglesi*, with their carriages and their afternoon calls and
their dinner parties. This is the Rome that turns its back on
Verney after his father has sponged off it, and then cheated it at

cards. Then there is the tourist Rome. Verney earns a little money painting postcards of Roman scenes to sell to tourists. The Rome that they want to see, and that he is obliged to provide, always has a sprig of peach blossom overhanging the view of the Colosseum, irrespective of the season; Verney learns the other necessary components of this particular Rome: 'the string of scarlet seminarists crossing the piazza, the man in sombrero and the girl in laced-up bodice and folded handkerchief, the gay wine-cart, the vividly-hued garments hung on clothes-lines across the narrow streets'. This is a Rome idealised for commercial purposes; as Verney creates it, so he loses his innocence. And as he paints these sentimental pictures Rome becomes increasingly ugly and hostile; the air is filled with the smells of overripe cheese and decaying fish and the Tiber becomes a scummy trickle through a stinking fever-ridden city. This is the death-dealing fever-inducing Rome like Henry James's Rome in *Daisy Miller*, the Rome of high summer, deserted by the English, with 'stale yellow foam' and piles of rubbish along the shores of the Tiber. In the hot squalid streets Verney converses with anarchists and swears at the beggars who can't believe that an Englishman has no money. This is a dangerous Rome, and it almost kills Verney.

Whereas E. M. Forster, writing at the same time of Italy and the English in Italy, offered the Italian people as a life-affirming contrast to the gloom of English conventionality, Rose Macaulay offers the place itself, with all its darknesses, its dangerous fevers, its lies and illusions, as a liberating alternative to England. In a striking reversal of the expectations of Victorian melodrama, Verney at the end of *Abbots Verney* is disinherited by his grandfather. 'He had lost Abbots Verney; but Rome and the cities of the world were his – a wide heritage.' The last line was uncompromising: 'Verney went down to Rome.'

Rose finished the novel in the spring of 1906, and submitted it to the publisher John Murray, who had been a contemporary of her father's at Eton. Perhaps to take her mind off the waiting Rose volunteered to help out at a settlement for factory girls in Chesterfield, run by the sister of her Oxford friend, Olive Willis.

Back in Ty-Issa in July, Rose heard from John Murray that he would like to publish her novel. He asked her however to make the ending less bleak. Not only was the hero disinherited and leaving England, but the reader was offered no hope that Verney might, eventually, find happiness with Rosamund Ilbert. 'Publishers of course have you altogether in their grip,' Rose wrote to Margerie Venables Taylor, showing a quick understanding of the relationship between writer and publisher: 'if they say you must do a thing you jolly well have got to do it.' She agreed to introduce a 'note of hope' or in John Murray's words 'a gleam of light' by writing an epilogue. He 'even particularized his gleam into an engagement', she told Margerie, 'so imagine me sitting down with set teeth to manufacture it for him. I made it as vague and indefinite a gleam as I decently could, and sent it to him saying Will this do?' It satisfied John Murray, but you have to be a very careful reader to detect the hint of the 'engagement' that Rose wrote with her teeth set. The epilogue provides a rather fine example of Rose's more obscure prose, and the gleam of hope carries small chance of being detected.

Although publishing a novel was considered praiseworthy within the family, Rose was anxious about revealing herself to the public at large. 'I have not published a novel before,' she wrote to John Murray. 'I should not wish to publish it under my name, but anonymously.' Murray demurred, and it came out under the name R. Macaulay. Rose explained to Margerie: 'It was to have been anonymous, you know, but Murray said it would be better not – sell better, he no doubt meant, & I suppose he's right.' It was generally assumed that R. Macaulay was a man. Rose was amused by this: 'I now, it seems, go under the name of Mr. R Macaulay; so in future address me so. The reviewers nearly all do!'

This was a time of transition for Rose Macaulay. She made jokes about being a writer. To Margerie's – surely facetious – suggestion of a biography, she responded, 'if you will write mine, in a bright & popular & yet scholarly style, I will write yours . . .' Nonetheless, she was now a proper writer. She had found what she wanted to do.

Rose was twenty-five when *Abbots Verney* was published in December 1906. Although she had spent considerably more time abroad than was common for Edwardian girls, it was always with the protection of older family members. Apart from the three years at a women's college in Oxford she had hardly been away from home and family at all. Yet in *Abbots Verney* she was already questioning the conformations of family and class and exploring the possibilities of a wider world. It is resolutely modern. Yet it rarely appears in discussions of novels of the early 1900s.

There are at least two reasons for this. The title is misleading. Rose called it *Abbots Verney* after her original title, 'The Aftermath', was rejected by John Murray because there had recently been another novel of that name. Abbots Verney is a place, a family, a property and an inheritance, but the novel calls all these things into question. (Compare *Abbots Verney* with E. M. Forster's cleverly entitled *Howards End.* That too is a place, a property and an inheritance. The word 'End' makes all the difference.) Rose herself made it difficult for people to read the book for themselves to see what it was like by regularly refusing permission for extracts to appear in anthologies, and by demanding that it be removed, along with her other pre-Great War novels, from the shelves of the London Library.

The reviewers called it 'a fine novel', 'a novel of great promise', 'a clever book – unusually so; a thoughtful, judicious, well-developed book, full of interesting people', 'a remarkable novel', 'an unusually capable book', and 'far above the common run of novels'. Yet Rose was, and remained, diffident about it. 'I don't fancy it circulating in college, somehow,' she wrote to Margerie

Venables Taylor, in the first of a lifelong series of attempts to disown her works of fiction: 'It's too trivial and unacademic to be smiled on there, and also it's too private – sentimental, serious, I don't know what – for me to like the idea of people I know reading it; I never can get used to it, somehow, it makes me feel so shy.'

On publication, John Murray told her that the *Sunday Chronicle* had decided not to serialise it as it would go over the heads of their readers, and offered the courteous and gallant comment: 'This is no doubt a compliment, but I think their heads must be pretty low.' Rose replied to his letter, 'I was afraid they might find the book bored them rather on closer inspection.' It was just the first of many instances of Rose castigating her work as 'boring'.

This was not false modesty, but an expression of a quite profound uncertainty about the worth of her work. Possibly it was a necessary disguise, or even a necessary self-deception. Perhaps such deprecation allowed her to do the things she wanted to do; serious, difficult things, like her exploration of cruelty and humiliation in her early 'Edwardian' novels; ground-breaking things like the series of novels in the 1920s in which she employed unreliable narrators, characters with multiple personalities, fragmented narratives, and all of them resolutely popular, resolutely rejecting the elitism of modernism. Perhaps, in other words, she needed to dismiss the importance, and the difficulty, of her work in order to be able to undertake it.

In a self-portrait Rose wrote as an 'auto-obituary' in middle age she described her writing career thus: 'She wrote from her earliest infancy, with the greatest zest, and began to publish the sprouts of her fancy at a young age. Descended on both sides from long lines of eloquent and well-informed clergymen, few of whom had denied themselves the indulgence of breaking into print, she busily wrote down from her earliest days those little thoughts that occurred to her childish fancy.' She harboured an anxiety that the writing of fiction in particular was an 'indulgence', and that anxiety is expressed in the figures of the writers and the readers who throng the pages of her novels. In *Told by an Idiot* Rome Garden refuses to write books because it is an undertaking 'she regarded as rather common, like getting married, or standing for Parliament'. Rose became adept at self-deprecating jokes about writing (and indeed about getting married), but the diffidence was real and so was the anxiety about the quality of her writing, as she expressed it over and again in letters to publishers and friends. Thirty years after her first novel came out she was writing to Frank Swinnerton, who was putting together a literary anthology: 'Oh dear oh dear. Must you really quote from that absurd, juvenile, & (I hope) forgotten book, Abbots Verney?'

iii

Abbots Verney came out two months after the Macaulays had left the Ystwyth valley and moved to Great Shelford just outside Cambridge, where George had taken up a post in the newly created discipline of English. For £1,800 they bought a solid, square, handsome brick house called Southernwood, built in the 1890s and standing in two acres of land.

The move to Great Shelford was a step away from childhood and back towards the world. It was a small village, characterised by Rose in a later novel as 'rather intelligent . . . many of its inhabitants are leisured, and will readily, if advised, form study circles, and read recommended literature'. She was even more mocking in a letter to her friend Margerie: 'There are at least three mountains in our neighbourhood quite 6 ft high . . . the natives regard them as young Alps. We mistook them for molehills at first. We have to be very guarded in our language on the subject when we converse with the inhabitants.' Still, it was only a few miles from Cambridge. George was finally back at Trinity after years in the wilderness; Uncle William was Senior Tutor at King's; after twelve years of struggle Edward Conybeare had finally yielded to Rome, given up the living at Barrington, and had moved into Cambridge with Frances and their youngest child, Dorothea, the same age as Rose; here he was writing and publishing books on local history.

There was Cambridge in one direction, and London in another, where Rose had a publisher whom she visited for the first time, in the elegant eighteenth-century building at 50 Albemarle Street, just off Piccadilly, and where Lord Byron and Sir Walter Scott, both successfully published by John Murray II, the grandfather of Rose's John Murray, had met each other for the first time in 1815.

In April after the move Rose and Margaret went on another trip to Italy with the two uncles, William and Kenneth, this time to Venice, proving to Rose once again that you didn't have to be married to go to Italy. She wrote on a postcard to Will, 'I should be a gondolier if I was a man', showing that although she was now, at the age of twenty-five, aware of the limitations imposed by her gender, dreams of captaining a boat were still with her, a gondola doing as well as a battleship.

She had already begun work on a second novel, set in Naples and in Varazze. *The Furnace* is deeply nostalgic for Rose's childhood world of 'the red house beyond the town' and the brothers and sisters who 'navigate the white canoe'. It is dedicated to those siblings, already 'scattered laboriously over three continents'. The novel features a brother/sister pair, Tommy and Betty Crevequer, who return to their childhood home of Santa Caterina (it had been called Varazze but was changed at Rose's request when the manuscript was already at the printer's) after surviving a firestorm in Naples consequent on the eruption of Mount Vesuvius. The firestorm is a metaphor for their cataclysmic meeting with the outside world. Like *Abbots Verney* it shows the influence of Henry James, whom she was reading 'with fascination' at the time. But it celebrates retreat and isolation, and is written in a prose that manages to be both cerebral and clotted, reflecting a lack of forward drive to the narrative. John Murray admitted that he didn't rate this novel 'quite so high as its predecessor'.

Betty and Tommy Crevequer are less brother and sister than female and male expressions of the same person, introduced to the reader as being almost indistinguishable: 'There did not seem to be any particular difference between them, externally. The boy might have been twenty-three and the girl twenty-two; or it was quite equally likely to be the other way about.' They both have melancholy eyes, both of them stutter, they finish off each other's sentences, and each understands what the other one is thinking without having to articulate it.

By the end of the novel their need for each other, their essential indistinguishability, has been validated by experience. Each has only the other one. This could have been a portrait of a passionately intense sibling love, but it does not succeed. Their reversion to childhood self-sufficiency manages to sound nauseatingly smug and affectedly childish: 'I'm thinking, Tommy,' Betty says at the end, when the two have retreated to Santa Caterina, 'that you're very lucky to have me to play with you, and that I'm rather lucky to have you to play with me.'

Rose was made deeply anxious by the scattering of her siblings and the fragmentation of her childhood world, but her anxiety seems to be at work unconsciously in the novel, to its detriment. 'I did my best to make it appeal to the general public,' she wrote to John Murray, going on to make the quite incorrect claim that it was 'practically a love story'.

In September 1907 the Macaulays added to the land they owned by buying a large tranche on the western edge of the Southernwood garden, two separate plots next to each other, that stretched all the way from the main street of Great Shelford down to the River Cam. That month Rose won a prize in the *Westminster Gazette* with some sonnets 'in the style of Rossetti'. *The Furnace* came out in November. Like *Abbots Verney*, it was published on a profit-sharing basis. *Abbots Verney* earned £16 each for author and publisher, and *The Furnace*, despite John Murray's reservations, £53 each.

Early in 1908 Jean, having finished her training at Guy's Hospital, started work in a hospital in Southampton. Rose began her third novel. In April she and Margaret went off to Italy again, this time on a bicycling holiday with their father and Uncle William. Soon after their return William provided the family with what Uncle Edward described in his diary as a 'magnificent boathouse' on the bank of the river, with a 'cunning device for concealment of key'. Here Rose finished *The Secret River*, alternating writing with swimming 'in a slow, winding Cambridgeshire river, among water lilies and water fowl and weeds and mud, drifting down the gentle current or swimming against it, holding on to drooping willow boughs and being swayed softly about with the stream, slippery water lily stems stroking one's body'. There is a watery sensuousness in this novel that is more pronounced than in any of her others. Her reminiscence continues: 'Which reminds me that if one is so fortunate as to find a place and a time when one can bathe without a bathing suit, it enormously increases the pleasure of a bathe. The feeling of water, even river water, against one's bare skin is delightful.' Sometimes she slept out in the boathouse. It must have been safe enough from others' eyes for naked swimming in the river.

When Rose delivered the manuscript to John Murray she included a photograph of the river. Only the very edge of the boathouse roof is visible, one corner pillar and the end of the veranda between pillar and wall. At the corner, and a foot or so below floor level a precarious-looking wooden stepladder leads down into the water, and next to it a tree leans out over the water at an angle of forty-five degrees. The river, clear and smooth as glass, and reflecting roof, pillar, steps and leaning tree, takes up half the photograph. 'The slumbrous afternoon was on the slow green river,' she wrote underneath, 'like the burden of a dream.' The photograph appeared as a frontispiece to the novel.

The protagonist of *The Secret River* is a poet called Michael Travis, who has embarked on a journey both physical – along the river – and metaphysical, through and around the ideas of philosophers and poets from Plato, through Dante, to the *fin-de-siècle* Celtic poet 'Fiona Macleod', taking in Maeterlinck, W.B. Yeats, Paul Verlaine, Hilaire Belloc, the Earl of Surrey, John Bunyan, St John Fisher and Sir Thomas Browne. Each chapter opens with a lengthy metaphysical epigraph.

Michael swims, or lies on the riverbank, and while transforming metaphysics into poetry his own senses become more and more finely tuned to the music of the natural world, which is played by 'the hidden people' of the river. His poetry is a recording of this music. This is about seeking and finding the essential unity at the heart of things, and Michael is led, at this stage, to 'the Rose at the World's End', where 'he lay at its heart, and its petals flamed and covered him, and he had no more need of music'.

So far, so slumbrous; readers nowadays would probably agree with the Somervillian who accused Rose in the college magazine of neglecting her vocation as a novelist in favour of 'this new genre of prose rhapsody'.

Then suddenly the novel takes off in quite another direction. For Michael has not always been alone in his universe. He had loved a woman, Cecilia, who abandoned him in favour of his best friend, as a result of which his soul shrivelled and he lost his poetic powers. Now Cecilia reappears and we seem to be in quite a different novel. For the final two chapters, before Michael slides into the 'cool, dim waters' of his inevitable release through death, Rose Macaulay provides us with a sharp, economical and bleakly humorous portrait of a marital misalliance.

The Secret River becomes a novel about the Marriage Question, a recurring Edwardian theme, appearing in novels contemporary with *The Secret River*, such as May Sinclair's *The*

Divine Fire (1904), and E. M. Forster's *The Longest Journey* (1907). Both Sinclair and Forster draw, too, on the literary, mystical imagery that Rose put at the heart of *The Secret River*.

Michael Travis is less man than Pan, that popular Edwardian fantasy figure: a natural creature with human characteristics, half man, half god; half boy, half man. Michael can be seen as a development of the girl/boy sibling pair, Betty and Tommy Crevequer of her previous novel, themselves caught in a timeless world between childhood and adulthood. Through Michael's immersion in the secret river he embraces nature and the sensory world and rejects the binary distinctions of human/animal, adult/child, and male/female. Travis combines the brother/sister qualities of the Crevequers in *The Furnace*, prefiguring a long line of androgynous figures in Rose Macaulay's fiction.

'Picturesque Platonism,' said Uncle Edward Conybeare of *The Secret River*, describing the first half and ignoring the portrait of a marriage. If *The Secret River*, its picturesque Platonism aside, is at least partly a portrait of the tragedy of a marriage based on mid-Victorian laws, what personal feelings fed the darkness of that portrait, the trajectory of it that leads to death, and not just individual death, but the death of the vision and the music? Portraits of marriages are rare in Rose Macaulay's fiction. There is one in *Crewe Train*, but only at the end of the novel are the doors slammed shut and the bolts drawn. There is a marriage in *Dangerous Ages*, in which the wife, shallow-minded, querulous Mrs Hilary, is more of a trial to her children than to her husband, who has relinquished responsibility and shuffled it on to his children. Both Mrs Hilary and Cecilia are destructive of other people's creativity. Their philistinism sucks out and feeds off others' intellectual and creative energies. Curious, then, that Rose should have chosen to dedicate to her mother the only two of her novels that feature philistine destructive wives. Perhaps she was in some conflict over the appropriateness of this dedication, for it was the cause of a muddle with John Murray. When Rose received advance copies she saw that the dedication to her mother had been omitted. She sent a telegraph to enquire why, and learned that no dedication had been received. She asked him not to send out any copies. Both then apologised to each other, and eventually the book was published with the dedication 'To my mother' inserted. It was beautifully produced, with four blue flowers on the front growing out of a green vine that twists its way up the spine of the book.

But by then the publication of Rose's third novel had been completely eclipsed by other events.

On 11 February 1909, three weeks before *The Secret River* was due out, news came that Aulay, due home on leave from India after five years' absence, had been killed. At first the circumstances of his death were not clear, and awful rumours that he had been kidnapped and tortured before being murdered trickled back to England. It was only when a letter arrived from his colonel some weeks later that the Macaulays discovered what had happened. He had been taking some weekly wages by bicycle to the members of a work gang building a road, had been set upon by four men who stole the money, blindfolded him, tied his arms behind his back, and shot him in the chest. 'The crime was non-political,' Reuters reported, 'the officer having been murdered for the sake of a sum of 1,500 rupees which he was believed to be carrying. Most of the money, however, had been sent by train.'

This was hardly better than the rumours of torture. It was devastating news, from which Grace never fully recovered. Rose herself found it almost impossible to reconcile herself to the realisation that 'the Five', those 'other citizens of Santa Caterina, Varazze' would never now 'inhabit again the red house beyond the town and navigate the white canoe'.

She returned to and replayed the hideous confusion and uncertainty surrounding the circumstances of Aulay's death in later novels. In *The Making of a Bigot* (1914) Arnold falls to an accidental death beneath the feet of an angry crowd; in *Non-Combatants and Others* (1916) Alix's anguish at the death of her soldier brother, no more than a boy, is intensified when she discovers that rather than having been killed in action, as she had thought, he has died from a self-inflicted wound; Mr Jayne in *Told by an Idiot* (1923) is murdered when he is mistaken for someone else. These are all reprises of Aulay's untimely death.

CHAPTER FOUR

Georgian

The first Georgian years, the years between 1910 and 1914, are now commonly thought of as gay, as very happy, hectic, whirling, butterfly years, punctuated, indeed, by the too exciting doings of dock and transport strikers, Ulstermen, suffragists, the *Titanic*, and Mr. Lloyd George, but, all the same, gay years. Like other general-isations about periods, this is a delusion. Those years only seem especially gay to us because, since July 1914, the years have not been gay at all . . .

Told by an Idiot

i

In 1905 a poem entitled 'Song of Prosper the King' by E. Rose Macaulay was published in the *Saturday Westminster Gazette:*

Sweet, like the smell of the wine in a fishing city,
   – (A small stone city, set round a blue-washed bay) –
Keen, like the breath of the sea over wide peat-bog land,
   Young, like the odorous blowing of winds in May,
Brave, like the birth of a poet's most high desiring,
   My lady Yvaine, sang Prosper, did pass this way.

It was the beginning of a long and important relationship with Naomi Royde-Smith, literary editor of the *Westminster Gazette,* who ran a weekly competition in the *Saturday Westminster*. That year Rose was twenty-four. Looking back to that time, she later wrote: 'Most of us, whatever we may do about it later, write poetry in our twenties. Such an activity is, at the least or at the most (as the case may be) a vent for our subliminal selves; into it we discharge our ghost-consciousness.'

'Song of Prosper the King', with its images of the sea, the wind and the seasons, and its lofty diction, is typical of her early poetry. Later she was critical of what she identified in *Catchwords and Claptrap* as the 'verbal haloes' of some late nineteenth- and early twentieth-century verse, which were created by 'the repetition of certain words and phrases' such as 'purple, pale, dim, strange-coloured, opaline, cristalline, chrysoprase, shimmering, glimmering, shadowy, grey, blind, swooning, orchard, honey-coloured moon . . .' Her own early poetry was not free from these verbal haloes. As in the prose of *The Secret River*, her imagery tended towards the Neoplatonic and the mystic, with an abundance of roses, altars, gates and veils. Yearning, loss and revelation were favourite themes. From 'Peace and the Builder' there is, 'The bitter dust, the broken stones of hope/(They shine like fallen stars in the moon's blaze)'; from 'Trinity Sunday': 'So veil beyond veil illimitably lifted:/And I saw the world's naked face'; from an untitled poem: 'The porter of the Temple of the West/Flings gold gates wide and shows/The Altar of the Rose,/Blooming for him, for him; and well he knows/That in him now his holy of holies glows.'

Walter de la Mare is a hovering presence in these *Saturday Westminster* poems, many of which appeared in her first collection in 1914, *The Two Blind Countries*. The title of the collection comes from 'The Alien', a poem whose final verse contains two of the adjectives from her list: 'On either side of a gray barrier/The two blind countries lie;/But he knew not which held him prisoner,/Nor yet know I.'

Walter de la Mare reviewed *The Two Blind Countries* for the *Times Literary Supplement* on 9 April 1914, calling his review

'On the Borderland'. 'She has the second sight,' he wrote (anonymously, as all *TLS* reviews were), 'the odd quick nerve that carries to consciousness news of the unheard, unseen.' Some of the poems he found too obscure, but he recognised an 'imaginative truth' in her work. 'We know that the world is imperceptibly tumbling into ruin – which is only exaggerated change,' he wrote, with a prescient sensitiveness to themes that are only half formed in this early work of Rose Macaulay's, but which were more fully explored by her in later years. 'Our very faces are ever exquisitely slowly fading and dying and being renewed. These queer, crazyish, often far too obscure poems tell that kind of truth.'

The poet Edward Thomas also noted the influence of Walter de la Mare on Rose Macaulay, and compared the two of them in his review of *The Two Blind Countries*, suggesting that Rose's poetry was 'more intellectual and less sensuous' than de la Mare's. The *Spectator* review said: 'Out of familiar things she contrives to draw a magic which sets all our definitions tottering.'

Rose had been winning prizes in Naomi Royde-Smith's competitions in the *Saturday Westminster* for well over a year before the appearance of Rupert Brooke's name. The competitions were for serious and for light verse and prose, for pastiches, parodies, and language games. Nowadays the literary competitions in the back pages of the *Spectator* and the *New Statesman* provide the same opportunities for showing off cleverness and facility with form. Then, as now, established writers and unknowns rub shoulders on the page. K. T. Stephenson gives an extract from the diary of Jane Eyre when she takes up a post in Islington and becomes involved in a complicated plot about her employers' stuffed canary. M. N. Keynes provides a list of schoolboy howlers, including, under 'languages', 'hors d'oeuvre: out of work' and 'pas de deux: father of twins'. The most common poetry pastiches are of Browning, Byron, Chaucer and Pope, and there are 'modern' nursery rhymes. 'Eggy-peggy,' goes one post-Boer War rhyme, 'Tommy's got a wooden leggy/Now he'll have to beggy-weggy.' A. A. Milne provides a Rudyard Kipling pastiche, 'Sing a Song of Sixpence: The Song of the Tanner'. But not all the contributions are comic or satiric. Walter de la Mare's 'A Ballad of Christmas' is a sinister poem about the three 'traitors' Herod, Pilate and Judas, who appear as ghosts, 'dark/with death each orbless eye'. Rose Macaulay's poems tend on the whole to be serious attempts at whatever formal challenge has been set: such as an 'alliterative verse' on 'October', which starts, not very alliteratively: 'Strong the prince's hands are, yet wondrous in tenderness . . .'

Rupert Brooke's name is first mentioned in 1907. His poems are clever and confident. This is his 'Mary Had a Little Lamb, after Ben Jonson':

> Shepherdess of one fair sheep . . .
> Say what magic spell doth keep
> By thy side thy one fair sheep? . . .
> Leave unbarrèd stall and fold,
> Love requireth no constraining . . .

Another of his prize-winning poems, 'The Little Dog's Day', has a dog speaking in dog Latin and doing every wicked thing it has ever dreamed of doing: 'He took sinewy lumps from the shins of old frumps,/And mangled the errand-boys – when he could get 'em./He shammed furious rabies, and bit all the babies,/And followed the cats up the trees, and then eat 'em.' Brooke's prose contributions include accomplished and witty parodies of Dickens, Carlyle, Milton, Ruskin and Pater.

Women and men were represented even-handedly in the pages of Naomi Royde-Smith's *Saturday Westminster* literary competitions, in contrast to the total exclusion of women ten years later from the pages of the Georgian Poets anthologies edited by Rupert Brooke's friend and, after Brooke's early death, memoirist, Edward Marsh. Of the seven named contributors who had five or more prize-winning poems in the first *Saturday*

Westminster compilation in 1908, one was Rupert Brooke, with five poems, and another was E. R. Macaulay, with six. 'I hate it,' he said of it, 'in spite of the pleasant fact that the book is almost entirely written by Rose Macaulay, Lord Curzon and myself.'

Rupert's brother Dick died in January 1907, soon after the Macaulays moved to Great Shelford. By then Rupert was at King's College, where his uncle Alan Brooke was Dean and where Rose's uncle W. H. Macaulay was a Senior Tutor. George Macaulay became Rupert Brooke's English tutor, and it was on his advice that in June 1909 Rupert moved out to Grantchester. It was highly unusual for undergraduates to live outside their college, let alone outside Cambridge; George was concerned that this promising young man, eldest surviving son of old family friends, showed signs of falling victim to the distractions of Cambridge social life.

In Grantchester, two miles downriver from Great Shelford, where the Macaulays were still reeling from the loss of Aulay four months before, Rupert Brooke took rooms in a house called The Orchard. Rose and Rupert began to spend some time together, either in Southernwood, with its garden now planted by Grace with poplar and chestnut, or in the meadows of Grantchester, where they walked and talked of poetry and writing. After Rupert Brooke's death in 1915 Rose wrote to Walter de la Mare and described her memories of 'paddling in the Grantchester meadows' with him, on one occasion talking of de la Mare's poetry: 'it was rather like versicle and response, and you would have been amused if you had been there no doubt'. But thin, shy Rose Macaulay, six years older than Rupert Brooke, was not part of the Brooke crowd. The young women of that set included the Olivier girls, daughters of a diplomat, and the Darwin girls, Gwen and her cousin Frances, who as children of Cambridge academic families had had the advantage of being brought up on the sidelines of what social convention and fashion dictated, and in a milieu of intellectual freedom. The Macaulay girls were different. Their childhood abroad had isolated them and thrown them back on to their own family resources, rather than giving them the sophistication that the Olivier girls appeared to have; and while George's struggles with Doubt had influenced his second daughter in her intellectual voyaging, the dominant emotional force in the household had always been Grace. After Aulay's death Rose retreated into the Church, groping in her grief for some kind of Christian meaning or consolation. That summer she went on the first of a series of retreats with Grace, Margaret and Jean. Compared to the Oliviers and the Darwins and clever Ka Cox from Newnham, who was to have a disastrous love affair with Rupert Brooke, the Macaulay girls, with their church connections, their good works (Rose retained her connection with the Chesterfield settlement after the move from Wales) and their longstanding acquaintance with Rupert's own mother, must have seemed straitlaced and, probably, a bit Victorian. Rupert Brooke had written to his mother as soon as he heard of Aulay's murder, saying that he wanted to offer condolences to the Macaulays, especially as they had been so kind to him at the time of Dick's death. 'I don't want to worry them or harass Mrs Macaulay, but don't you think I might write, to Margaret or Rose, at least?'

When Rupert Brooke saw the Macaulays after his move to Grantchester, Rose was in the grip of depression. That month she wrote to Margerie Venables Taylor, explaining that a visit to her in Oxford would need 'more pulling of oneself together than I feel capable of'. She went on:

I have come to the conclusion that my besetting sin is Accidie . . . consequently I sit at home & feel like a toad under a stone. I'm afraid I don't do anything these days, which is very feeble. I don't even write books . . . I am so stodgy these days. I haven't an idea in my head or a word to bestow on anyone – total vacuousness & inertia. Thank you very much for your sympathy. One of the minor troubles of a thing like that is that it seems to take all the object out of life & makes it difficult to feel it worth while to do anything of any sort – but that again is Accidie, I feel sure, & shld be discouraged.

In the same letter she described her writing of *The Secret River*: 'I loved writing it – it kept me amused through last summer when I was playing down by the river & sleeping out – it is so nice down there, & we have a nice little hut to play in & its so far away from everything that you can pretend you didn't hear the bells for meals.' There is something determinedly childlike in the 'playing' and the 'nice little hut' and ignoring the summons to family meals, which is like the determination of Betty and Tommy Crevequer from *The Furnace* to turn their backs on the outside – adult – world and be playmates for each other for ever more. Such a determination to appear light-hearted and unconcerned did not fool the University Mission to Central Africa, to whom she applied in desperation for something to do to relieve her grief. They rejected her as being too unstable. Late in the year she overcame her inertia and started another novel, for which John Murray offered her an advance of £50 against royalties. In it were distilled the feelings of impotence and frustration that she had experienced in family life in Wales, and anguish and rage at the loss of one of the Five.

The Valley Captives is an intense and terrifying novel about the physical and mental violence inflicted on a boy called Tudor Vallon by his stepbrother Philip Bodger, and the reluctance of any adult to step in and protect him. Tudor is sent from his home in Wales to a public school in England, which, his father hopes, will make a man of this frail, sensitive boy. The bullying stepbrother Philip is already at the school, with a 'coterie of large friends'. We learn that for Tudor, 'the fear of what they would do with him was a sharper anguish than what they proceeded to do. What they did, varied according to mood and opportunity, from mere rough teasing that a stronger and tougher-fibred victim might have taken with indifference, to the infliction of the acutest bodily anguish. Sometimes they merely made him smoke himself sick; at other times he had to drink himself intoxicated; but these were the lesser evils . . .'

There is a striking similarity between the descriptions of Tudor being bullied and the descriptions of twelve-year-old Charles Bampton and his little friend Sapper being bullied in *Perversion*, the three-volume novel by Rose's grandfather J. W. Conybeare, published half a century earlier: 'One favourite entertainment was to set him and Sapper side by side upon a bed and force them each to smoke a cigar. As they had neither of them ever smoked before, of course this made them very sick. They were then ordered to represent coffee-house politicians, discussing the affairs of the nation over their cigars, and to stimulate their ingenuity they were branded on the cheeks with the red-hot end of the cigar from time to time.' Charles is then made to dance naked in the dormitory in front of an audience of the bully and his cronies: a depiction of sexual bullying that is hinted at in the unspecified greater evils of Rose's novel.

Perversion, 'a slight and brief novel about family life', as Rose described it in a private joke, may have been a primary literary source for the school sequences, but whereas in her grandfather's novel the source of corruption is in the school, in *The Valley Captives* the corruption breeds at home, and school features only as an extension of home.

The Valley Captives is primarily about the death of the family. Tudor's father Oliver Vallon prefers not to see what is happening to his son, and his passivity and 'nervous egotism' make him reluctant to act to protect him. Tudor's sister John (the first of Rose Macaulay's many heroines who masquerade under a boy's name) is too young to protect or save him. Their mutual sibling love is painfully twisted by John being forced into the role of voyeur to Tudor's pain and humiliation. Father and sister make up Tudor's immediate family, and both of them fail him.

The novel shows an obsessive concern with pain and motiveless violence. Philip Bodger commits acts of violence as casually as he eats or drinks or lounges around the house. He is like a force of nature, or mythical creature, against which ordinary life has no power. But – and again, as in *Abbots Verney*, this is a response to the novels of Rose Macaulay's childhood reading in which virtue is finally rewarded – there is no redemption through suffering. Instead Rose chooses to explore a psychology that makes the victim embrace the perpetrator of his abuse.

Some of the torture takes place in a house with yard and sta-bles and pigsty and wash-house, 'all with climbable roofs', where they go to stay for holidays. For this Rose drew on the topography of Uncle Kenneth's house at Clent, where the Five had spent many happy holidays. The adults amuse themselves with croquet; behind the garden wall Tudor and John are thrown into a hole in the wash-house floor, where Philip and his sister throw pieces of burning paper down on to them until they agree to say; 'We're little donkeys. We're little funks. We're little beasts. We wish our name was Bodger.' Then one day Philip Bodger goes 'rather too far'. Tudor, terrified and alone in the dark pit, tries to climb up to the grating in the floor above, and falls. His right arm is broken and mends crooked, and he damages his spine, and always afterwards walks with a slight limp. These are outward signs of an inner fear that dominates Tudor's life, that checks the swiftness of his mind and blurs the brightness of his imagination. This is a portrait of a child who is without protection. His father has turned his back on him; no teachers at his boarding school step forward to protect him from Philip and his gang of bullies. The reader asks: what has this child done to be so abandoned? The novel offers no answer.

This was the first novel Rose wrote after Aulay's death. The uncertainty surrounding the motives for and the manner of his death were all in her mind as she wrote it. And there was another child, still at home while Rose was writing *The Valley Captives*, who, after years of mistreatment and neglect, was about to leave the Macaulay family home for ever. In September

1910 Eleanor started her training as a teacher: she only ever reappeared, briefly and infrequently, as a visitor. For Rose *The Valley Captives* was a vent for her subliminal self, a work into which, as well as into her poetry, she discharged her 'ghost-consciousness'.

Two curious aspects surround the publication of this novel. The first is that she chose to dedicate to her father a book that contains an unforgiving portrait of a father who fails his only son. It is impossible to say to what extent the distant and emotionally disengaged Oliver Vallon is a deliberate portrait of George Macaulay; but such a gesture shows at least an ambivalence of feeling about him which echoes the ambivalence behind Rose's dedications to her mother of *The Secret River* and *Dangerous Ages*. Edward Conybeare noted in his diary: 'Rose's new book out The Valley Captives. Sad.' It is more than sad: it is tragic, like Aulay's early death, and like Eleanor's childhood.

In the year that Rose Macaulay was writing this novel there were three men who exerted an intellectual influence over her. As well as her father, there was P. N. Waggett, a charismatic Cowley Father whom she had first encountered while she was an undergraduate, and whose sermons she had been attending since Aulay's death. Waggett provided one of the three epigraphs for *The Valley Captives*, the gnomic 'There is need, then, to emphasise the prudence of adventure', and he also provided one for her next novel, *The Lee Shore*. And there was her fellow-poet Rupert Brooke. Their relationship provides the reader of *The Valley Captives* with the second curiosity.

'Black wings of fear' and shadows that darken the light are recurring and dominant images in the novel. On two occasions the shadows depart: one is when Tudor swims in a deep pool at a bend in the river, which he experiences, in a way reminiscent of Michael Travis in Rose's previous novel, as a 'cool rose of peace'; and the other is when he sometimes manages to escape the horrors of school to visit a kind old cousin. In her house and

garden 'peace wrapped him round – a warm, sunlit peace ema-
nating from the very bricks of the old wall, absorbed with
mouthfuls of honey and bread, gently suffusing the shadows
with tinted light, till at last it triumphed wholly and swept
them back to wait their hour'. Later, in desperation, he flees the
Welsh valley and goes in search of the remembered sanctuary of
'fire, and bread and honey for tea'. Honey has become for him
the symbol of the safe childhood that was denied him in his
own home. He finds his cousin, not in her town house but with
her servant and companion Susan in her cottage in the woods,
in 'a murmurous place, full of the humming of bees and the
sighing of ancient trees'. His first question is: 'And will there be
honey for tea, please, Susan?' The honey provides a moment of
safety for Tudor Vallon, but it is no more than a brief moment
snatched from a life of pain and fear. He leaves the sanctuary of
the cottage in the woods to return to the Welsh valley, and to
his death.

The Valley Captives was published in January 1911. Travelling
in Germany the next year Rupert Brooke wrote the first draft of
a poem he called 'The Sentimental Exile', a lively, witty, self-
mocking version of home thoughts from abroad, which
concludes, after its excoriation of the various types of English
people to be found in the villages of Cambridgeshire, including
the Shelfordians with their 'twisted lips and twisted hearts', with
the now famous line: 'And is there honey still for tea?'

Was Brooke quoting Rose Macaulay's Tudor Vallon? That
summer the King's College magazine, the *Basileion*, printed
'Fragments from a poem to be entitled "The Sentimental
Exile"'. A few months later, in October 1912 it was published
in the first volume of *Georgian Poetry* under the title 'The Old
Vicarage, Grantchester', and appeared again in November in
Harold Monro's *Poetry Review*. The new title gives an early
indication of the way that readings of the poem would drift
away from its original mocking tone, so that in later years the
final two and a half lines would be decontextualised, and

quoted, separately from the preceding eighty or so lines, as an unironic evocation of a period now lost for ever: a period that nostalgia has recreated as the perpetual summer of pre-war England. In the various drafts that Brooke made of the poem he shifted around the words of the penultimate line and a half: '... oh yet/Stands the church clock at half past three ...' and '... and still/Stands the church clock at ten to three ...', but the final line − 'And is there honey still for tea?' − never changed. It is a better line than Rose Macaulay's; it is a novel-ist's line of dialogue transformed into poetry. And there is another difference: Rupert Brooke makes his sentimental exile expect the answer 'yes' to his question, while Rose's tragic hero expects the answer 'no'.

Between 1909 and 1912 Rose Macaulay and Rupert Brooke, on the occasions when they were together at Southernwood, or at The Orchard, or at The Old Vicarage, where Rupert had moved in the early summer of 1911, must have shared honey for tea. Indeed The Old Vicarage was famous for the honey from its hives. As two working writers it is unlikely that they would not have discussed the symbolism of honey in relation to childhood and the past. It is possible however that they did not talk about it; that they were, separately, transforming a common experi-ence, and an experience they held in common, into metaphor. There is no record of either of them referring to it. When the poem was published in the *Basileion* it may not have seemed very striking − after all, what is a shared metaphor between friends, when it appears, on the one hand, in a novel by a young female writer, and on the other, in a poem by a young man in a college magazine? *The Valley Captives* was the first of Rose's novels to be published in the United States, by Henry Holt. But that was nothing compared to Rupert Brooke's posthumous fame.

Did Brooke feel uneasy about it at the time? It has always seemed odd that he did not invite Rose Macaulay to contribute to the first anthology of Georgian poetry. He thought her important enough to receive a copy of it, but not, it seems, to be a contributor, although the Christian/pantheistic tendency of her poetry at the time was very much in tune with the literary taste of his co-editor Edward Marsh. Perhaps he really did not rate her poetry highly; but her best poems are comparable to those of Walter de la Mare, who was a major contributor to the first and all subsequent volumes. Perhaps there was a more personal reason. Perhaps the honey for tea – shared, borrowed, or taken – created an awkwardness in their professional relationship, a bond between them that he would have liked to sever.

We never quite trusted Rupert, said Rose's sister Jean to Constance Babington Smith after Rose's death. But Jean wasn't specific, offering the suggestion only that Rupert had cheated at games they had played as children. But the Macaulays didn't see much of Rupert in the games-playing days of childhood, and he was Eleanor's age, considerably younger than Rose, Margaret and Jean; they only got to know him again in the poetry-writing days of early adulthood. 'I often wonder what Rupert would have turned into if he'd lived,' wrote Rose many years later. 'An outmoded elderly poet? Or would he have left poetry and been a scholar-don? He was a charming creature.'

Perhaps Rupert Brooke gave no more than a passing thought to his and Rose's use of honey for tea, for how was he to know how famous those lines would become? In the same way he could not have foretold the consequences of his remark to the actress Cathleen Nesbitt on returning from taking tea with Walter de la Mare in his child-infested home: Rupert light-heartedly asked Cathleen if he should leave his 'future wealth' to her or 'to some poets so that they may have time to write good poems'. His, and Cathleen's, impulsive generosity changed the lives of Walter de la Mare, Lascelles Abercrombie and Wilfrid Gibson.

ii

In February 1911, just after the publication of *The Valley Captives*, Rose and Rupert shared a *Saturday Westminster* prize for a poem addressed to a living poet, and each won a guinea. In those days Rupert used to spend time in London, staying at Eddie Marsh's flat in Gray's Inn. 'He is a delightful person to stay with,' he wrote to Rose; 'he is so much away.' Rose remembered the days of visiting Rupert Brooke in London in the anthology *Coming to London*:

> I sometimes went up to meet Rupert for lunch or dinner and plays, and his friends, who were apt to be poets, such as Edward Thomas and Wilfrid Gibson and Ralph Hodgson and others, sometimes came to lunch too, usually at the Moulin d'Or. I was envious of Rupert, who walked about the streets without a map, often with a plaid rug over his shoulders, as if he was Tennyson, which seemed to me a very good idea and gave him prestige, and people turned to look at him as he strolled through Soho with his golden hair and his rug, and I was proud to be with him.

Rose had been brought up by George Macaulay to see Tennyson as a lion to be adored and emulated (Tennyson's sons, Lionel and Hallam, had been guests at George and Grace's wedding), and by associating Rupert Brooke with Tennyson Rose is recreating the awe she felt; but it was awe at his social and sexual and urban confidence, awe at his golden hair and his easy ownership of the streets of London; as for his poetry, the association with Tennyson places Brooke in the past. Tennyson had been dead for nearly two decades, and had come to stand for Victorianism, for the old values against the new, for England and imperialism against Europe. It was Alfred, Lord Tennyson who had spoken of 'the poisonous honey spread from France'. Brooke and the Georgian poets may have had youth as their currency, but it was never translated into modernity. It was other poets, the

Americans Eliot and Pound, and H. D., who looked abroad for the ideas that would come to define modernism.

Rose went on to describe their friendship with Naomi Royde-Smith: 'Rupert and I used to go in for the Saturday Westminster Problems, which were usually writing poems, and we both won quite a lot of prizes for this. This Problems page was edited by Naomi Royde-Smith, and we both wanted to meet her; Rupert had heard that she was "frightfully amusing". I forget which one of us met her first, but I met her sometime between 1910 and 1912, and was dazzled, for she was amusing and interesting and brilliant, and had beauty, and almost more charm than anyone else. She was very kind to me.' Naomi would be kind to Rupert, too, providing an escape for him after his breakdown in 1913 by arranging for him to be commissioned to travel to America for the *Westminster Gazette*, on a trip with all expenses paid and four guineas for each of a series of articles.

Naomi Royde-Smith introduced Rose to Walter de la Mare, with whom Naomi herself at that time had an intense and passionate friendship. 'He was very beautiful, and had a fantastic wit and funniness, and his poetry was exquisite and full of ghosts and shadows and dreams . . . His mind and the cadences of his verse had a delicate, reticent wildness that no other poet has exactly had.'

Rose was dazzled not just by Naomi Royde-Smith and Walter de la Mare but by everyone she met: 'I wished that I too lived in London, with whose inhabitants I had fallen collectively in love.'

Those inhabitants were not restricted to poets and other writers. There was the Ballet Russe, which 'really was something to go mad about'. 'London blazed with stars,' she said: Diaghilev, Nijinsky and Pavlova, Caruso and Melba at Covent Garden, and Chaliapin singing in Beecham's Russian Opera season at Drury Lane. The artistic ferment of those years had as its initial symbol the first Post-Impressionist exhibition put on by Roger Fry at the Grafton Gallery. Virginia Woolf would later claim that this was the point – December 1910 – at which human character changed. It represented the incursion of ideas that were both modern and foreign into an England that was little used to them and did not know how to react. Arnold Bennett's was a lonely voice in praise of the new painting, as it was in praise of Dostoevsky, who, with Turgenev and Chekhov, was now being translated by Constance Garnett. Others jeered.

In January 1913 Harold and Alida Monro opened their Poetry Bookshop in Devonshire Street. Rose went regularly. There she heard Walter de la Mare, who read his poetry 'deplorably', and the incantatory W. B. Yeats, who was 'fascinating, peculiar, and eventually soporific'. There was a 'kind of poetry intoxication', and a blossoming of literary magazines: Ford Madox Hueffer's *English Review*, Middleton Murry and Katherine Mansfield's *Blue Review* and *Rhythm*, and, 'more detonating and flashy', Wyndham Lewis's *Blast*, which published Marinetti, whose 'vehemence when he lectured was alarming'.

Rose Macaulay was an observer rather than a participant. As well as closely observing the literary and artistic turmoil of pre-war London, she was also listening to the voices of people calling for social and political change. She had already started work on what would be her first prize-winning novel, *The Lee Shore*, but she put it aside in the spring of 1911 to write *Views and Vagabonds*. In 1909, after the publication of Sidney and Beatrice Webb's Minority Report of the Poor Law Commission, Rupert Brooke had become an enthusiastic Fabian. *Views and Vagabonds* was a satire on his romanticisation of the rural working class.

In the opening scene we are introduced to a handsome hardworking radical young blacksmith, who, we are led to believe, is of gentle birth, one Benjamin Bunter, second son of Lady Lettice and Lord Mervyn, prospective Tory candidate for Norfolk. Benjie has been through Eton and Cambridge and is now dedicating his life to the moral and cultural improvement of the working classes. To that end he is living and working amongst them and, to the horror of his parents, is about to marry one of them, a local mill-hand called Louisa – Louie – Robinson. Benjie's views are shared enthusiastically by his cousin Cecil, an undergraduate at Cambridge, one of those garrulous, clever young women for whom Rose Macaulay always had a soft spot, their wrong-headedness usually being excused on the grounds of their youthfulness. Cecil is determined to be a friend to Louie and to draw her into the life of the intellect and pro-gressive politics, into secularism, republicanism and female suffrage. Louie is steadfastly uninterested. Meanwhile Cecil accompanies Benjie on a caravanning tour campaigning to raise the political consciousness of the oppressed rural poor in the southern counties.

The previous year, in the summer of 1910, Rupert Brooke and his friend Dudley Ward toured the New Forest in a horse-drawn caravan campaigning for Fabianism. Neither of them recorded whether, as they exhorted the rural poor on village greens, they were stoned for their pains, as happens in *Views and Vagabonds*. It is reasonable to suggest that priggish, moralistic Benjie is loosely modelled on Rupert Brooke.

But there is another, more flattering, Brooke figure (as Rose said about her writing of *Abbots Verney*, she often mixed up people together, or invented half and copied half) in Benjie's younger brother Jerry, who is an artist and poet, and can see straight, says Anne Vickery, who is one of those detached, ironic women who recur in Rose Macaulay's fiction, and who is Cecil's friend and contemporary at Cambridge. Jerry is associated with Grantchester, offering to Benjie, battle-scarred in his struggles with the working classes who he has discovered are annoyingly deaf to his exhortations for self-improvement, the healing powers of the River Cam and Grantchester. 'So they rowed up a slow, weedy river, between foaming billows of meadowsweet, and landed and bathed beneath a weir, and lay in a field, and had a large tea, with muffins, at the Orchard.'

That same summer, before Rupert Brooke and Dudley Ward went off together, while Rose was finishing *The Valley Captives*,

Rupert had invited her to go on a caravanning tour with him. Rose would have liked to, but her father forbade it. It has been suggested that Rose, coming up to the age of thirty, resented George exercising his paternal authority. In the novel, Cecil leaves Benjie in the caravan every evening to spend the night respectably in a local inn. The two loudly insist on their cousinship as the most important aspect of their relationship, and profess scorn for old-fashioned notions of propriety, but Louie sees through their apparent innocence to the threat posed by Cecil to her marriage. It is uneducated, unsophisticated Louie who understands that Cecil's constant stream of talk with Benjie is an expression of her sexual desire. Rose was aware of her own propensity for garrulousness. This novel suggests that she was aware of it as a form of sexual display and disguise.

Although Rose Macaulay condescendingly peppers Louie's speech with dropped aitches and bad grammar, it is Louie who has the clear moral vision, not the Cambridge-educated Cecil. She is given a degree of profundity that contrasts with the shallow emotions of some of the other characters. In the end the reader can't help but be pleased that Louie gets the husband and the baby she so desires. And there is an element of *schadenfreude* in the transformation of Benjie the upper-class radical into a respectable husband and father and pillar of lower middle-class gentility.

Despite the fierceness of Rose Macaulay's attack in this novel on people who base their lives and their morality on abstract ideals rather than on pragmatic reality, what is striking about it is the sense that at last she is having fun with her writing. The *Spectator* called it 'a curious, clever book . . . a vivid if somewhat fantastic sketch of the difficulties which confront our young intellectuals when they are involved in the intricacies of practice'. It is as if she has firmly turned her back on the dank imprisoning valleys of Wales and is returning to the landscape of *The Secret River*, flat, watery and willowed, with affection and with considerably more humour. There is a new relaxation in the writing. She has discovered she has a satiric gift and there are potential targets for it all around. Benjie's mother, Lady Lettice, is a fine comic creation, with her wide-ranging prejudices – socialist vicars, vets, tax collectors included – and her love of generalisations. 'Socialism should be left to the upper classes,' she declares.

The Crevequer twins reappear, making mayhem of the niceties of English social distinction. The Crevequers, English by nationality but Italian born and nurtured, stand for what E. M. Forster's Italians stand for in his early novels, that is, for democracy, for a different kind of civilisation, for a life force that is unstoppable, shocking but attractive. The novel has a distinctly period feel in its obsession with class, and the melodramatic revelation of the secret of Benjie's birth has an Edwardian or even Victorian flavour. Rose came back to some of the themes when her comic style was more assured: Louie being 'taken up' in London is a precursor of Denham Dobie's being thrust into the civilised world in *Crewe Train*. And Mrs Venables the narrow-minded, dangerously gossipy popular novelist, seen before in *The Furnace*, reappears in various forms.

Views and Vagabonds came out in February 1912. Six months later *The Lee Shore*, which Rose had returned to after finishing *Views and Vagabonds*, was published. Without telling her publisher John Murray, she had entered it for a fiction prize offered by Hodder & Stoughton, and won the first prize of £600. 'I am extremely delighted to have so much money all at once,' she wrote to S. C. Roberts, an old family friend and head of Cambridge University Press, thanking him for his congratulations. John Murray, the publisher of her first five novels, was hurt at her secrecy, but graciously relinquished all rights after an exchange of letters. Rose had doubtless not allowed herself to think that she might win the prize; in which case there would have been no point in informing John Murray of her flirtation with another publisher. One of her comments to S. C. Roberts was characteristic: 'The book is very poor, but I can only suppose that the judges' taste in fiction was poor also, so all was well.' The *Daily Chronicle* had reported incorrectly that the prize won by the 'Young Lady Novelist' was worth £1,000. Rose corrected this, allowing the pleasure and excitement to overcome her natural diffidence: '. . . I'm afraid the Young Lady Novelist didn't win a £1000, but only £600. £400 of the thousand that ought by good rights to have been mine (I am sure I deserved both the 1st & 2nd prizes) went to another, which was a shame.' The novelist Beatrice Harraden was one of the judges, and described *The Lee Shore* as 'in a class by itself above any other work sent in'.

Running through *The Lee Shore* is the refrain: 'from him that hath not shall be taken away even that which he hath'. The novel explores the social as well as the religio-philosophical implications of this. 'That division,' runs the epigraph from her mentor Father Waggett, 'the division of those who have and those who have not, runs so deep as almost to run to the bottom.' The mouthpiece in the novel for this deterministic view of social destiny is Rodney, 'an apostle, a vegetarian, a fine football player, an ex-Fabian, and a few other things', who embraces the Have-Nots and is instrumental in dissuading Peter from running away with someone else's wife. In such a world view Peter can't Have (someone else's wife), because he is by nature one of the Have-Nots.

Peter Margerison is known affectionately to his male friends as Margery. He takes his place amongst Rose's other male characters who have feminine-sounding names, nicknames or surnames: Kay, Vere, Jayne, Ruth. Someone says of Peter that he 'might be a young lady'. Described variously as brittle, frail and delicate, he is introduced in the first scene of the book being injured on the school playing field and being carried inside, pale and fainting, in the strong arms of a godlike and masculine older boy. Peter has a loving heart, a characteristic that the book suggests is a part of his frailty, his delicacy, his femininity.

Like *Views and Vagabonds*, which she was writing at the same time, *The Lee Shore* explores the clash of opposing ideas. Rose

Macaulay felt, with some reason, that she wasn't very good at breathing life into characters who are mouthpieces for a collection of views and opinions. Peter, for example, who loves the thingness of things in the material world, wonders, 'What was spirit apart from form?' whereas the renunciating Rodney maintains that 'the reality that shone always behind the shadow foreground dropped the shadows like a veil and emerged in clean and bare translucence of truth'. This wrangling of philosophies, as if Hegel, Moore and Lowes Dickinson are characters in the story, echoes the opening scenes of Forster's *The Longest Journey* where Rickie and Ansell discuss 'the existence of objects' and whether the cow is there, or not.

Where *Views and Vagabonds* was a response to Fabianism, *The Lee Shore* was a response to the arguments that were still going on throughout the reigns of Edward VII and George V with the legacy of a previous era, with the materialism of late Victorianism. The countless sects and groupings that sprang up in the 1890s were variously concerned with alternatives to the materialist life in all its manifestations. The Haves and Have-Nots and the ascetics and dissolutes of *The Lee Shore* provide some replies to these questions.

Rose Macaulay loved ideas. She was an intellectual. But she was also struggling to be a novelist. The conflicting desires to create credible characters who are rooted in a recognisably real world, and on the other hand to explore ideas and opinions through those fictional characters reflect the conflict within herself between the intellect and the imagination. In this novel, more than in *Views and Vagabonds* which is kept sharp by Rose's newly discovered comic tone, the Platonism constantly threatens to overwhelm the story. Here Rose is expressing her love for the Idea of ideas.

And yet – and this is why she continued to write fiction despite her doubts about it – she finally comes down on the side of the real. In the final scene Peter/Margery is alone with his baby on the lee shore, a lone madonna in Italy. The baby is not a particularly convincing baby, being more an Idea of a baby than a real baby, but nonetheless Peter is left with a future and a new life to nurture, unlike Rose's earlier androgynous Pan-figure, Michael Travis.

Peter ends up wandering along the Ligurian coast from Varazze to Cogoleto and back. This is what he is left with after he has renounced the world. The difficulty here is that Rose Macaulay herself, whatever the drift of her argument, does not see the Ligurian coast as a place of loss. On the contrary, it is 'an Eden, unimaginably sweet', and she herself is the vagabond peering in through an open door in one of the walls, at the ole-anders and the pomegranate blossom. Loss, for the writer Rose Macaulay, is precisely what is presented in the pages of this novel as acquisition and possession, that is, the life of middle-class respectability and stability that Peter has renounced. That was what Rose herself had had to give up Eden for when the Macaulays returned to Oxford from Italy in the mid-1890s. It is not surprising that *The Lee Shore* is a puzzling book to read; for if Rose Macaulay cannot convince herself of her own argument, what hope then is there for the reader to be convinced? She admitted as much in a letter to Hugh Walpole the following year, writing to him about his novel *Fortitude*, which he had said had similarites to *The Lee Shore*, and whose hero is also called Peter: 'And your Peter had a much worse time than mine really; mine was at least allowed to keep his infant & to end in a warm place in sunshine with a donkey, & liking life; instead of on a cold hill in a world without so much as a dog, & liking nothing.'

The Lee Shore is a novel of inconsistencies and contradictions, possibly because Rose was uncertain how to reclaim imagina-tively her childhood world, especially as she was already beginning to experiment with an authorial position – first adopted in *Views and Vagabonds* – that placed her as an observer on the edge, a position that she continued to hold in her next novel and in her work of the post-war decade. But a pleasing irony of *The Lee Shore* is that while its theme is of loss and of self-denial, this was the novel that released Rose Macaulay from the self-denial of home life by allowing her to see herself, and be seen by others, as a professional writer. The lee shore may be a haven for the sick, the sad, the frail and the unfortunate, but it provided Rose Macaulay with £600 and the possibility of a life as a professional writer. 'Money *is* nice to have,' she admitted to Katharine Tynan, who had written to congratulate her.

The Lee Shore was published in August 1912. At the end of that month Uncle Edward Conybeare visited Southernwood and found Rose and Margaret 'up tree in their new grove'. There is something charming, but curious, in this picture of two sisters in their early thirties, dressed in cumbersome pre-war long skirts, one a successful writer and the other a novice deaconess, climbing trees at the family home. Middle-aged Nan in *Dangerous Ages* climbs a tree on her fortieth birthday, before going off for a solitary swim in the river. Nan is escaping from the pressures of domestic life, from a husband and two grown-up children, when she climbs her tree. Neither Rose nor Margaret had husband and children to escape from. Perhaps they were escaping from Grace – or, indeed, from the visiting Uncle Edward himself?

The previous year, on one of her regular visits with a Shelford friend to the mission house of the East London Deaconesses in Bethnal Green, Margaret had asked to be taken on as a novice and was accepted for a trial period of a month. She had not dared tell her mother herself, so had asked Rose to do it for her. On hearing the news Grace had fainted, and on coming round from the faint, had a fit of hysterics. Margaret passed the trial period, and was now on a two-year novitiate. Later, Grace talked proudly of her eldest daughter the Deaconess, but during these two years she expressed her distress so forcefully that Margaret was given special dispensation for regular and frequent visits home. In the photographs taken in the years after Aulay's death Grace looks like an old woman. The tubercular throat seems not to have developed, but there were bouts of non-specific illness. However, in between the spells in bed or bath chair, the so-called 'rest cures' with no visitors allowed, Grace was her usual busy self, organising the village girls and demanding attention from any daughter at home. Margaret had had hopes of becoming a writer. A retelling of Chaucer for schoolchildren, *Stories from Chaucer*, had been published by Cambridge University Press, but *The Sentence Absolute* had not yet been accepted for publication. Perhaps she felt that with Rose already a successful writer there was no room for her to do the same. Now in her thirties, it was too late to train as a nurse, as Jean had done, or, like Eleanor, as a teacher. The religious life was an alternative to accepting the unwelcome fate of unmarried daughter at home. She was ordained by the Bishop of Stepney in June 1913.

During these years Rose was partly at home in Great Shelford and partly in London. She had lost her agnosticism after Aulay's death and was now a regular churchgoer. Rose went to the neighbouring village of Sawston, perhaps to avoid attending church with her mother, perhaps to avoid having to spend time in front of the inappropriately militaristic memorial triptych to her brother Aulay in the chantry chapel, and partly because she liked the High Church vicar at Sawston. After Aulay's death Grace reverted energetically to her old passion for instructing village girls on matters religious and improving. As one of the villagers remembered: 'Mrs Macaulay led her daughters a dreadful life but she was exceedingly kind to the girls who came to her weekly Bible class, and, for those who stayed for the whole of morning worship, there was an invitation to tea on Sunday afternoon.' Grace always sat in the back pew in the Church of St Mary the Virgin so that all were under her gaze. Those who fidgeted, giggled, whispered and generally misbehaved did not receive an invitation to tea.

The Bible classes were held in a shed built on the land adjoining the Southernwood garden. Grace sometimes slept there, until driven out by fleas, which she blamed on their neighbour

Mr Pearce's hens. George too ran classes, for boys, and with Rose would take the boys out on the river, a delight that was not on offer to Grace's girls.

Grace was querulous and difficult, but every so often Rose escaped with her father. In April 1912 they went together on a cruise around the Greek islands, and the following year on a bicycling tour of the New Forest. The Hellenic cruise was a decidedly high-minded affair: other travellers included Jane Harrison the Newnham classicist, Dr Edward Lyttelton the headmaster of Eton, the Irish judge Sir John Ross and his son Ronald Ross, at whose house in Dunmoyle Rose spent some time that summer, and Logan Pearsall Smith, who would become a friend of hers in post-war London. This trip provided the inspiration for a short story called 'The Empty Berth', the first of only three stories Rose ever published. It is a ghost story, about a young schoolmaster called Shipley on a Greek cruise, whose eyes are opened to the Greece of Apollo and Artemis and radiant youth by the genial, wine-drinking, life-loving ghost of the man who was to share his cabin, one H. Cottar. In this story Greece represents life, democracy and sexuality, while respectability, propriety and the narrow morality of the English middle classes are satirised, especially through the figure of Mr Steele, the headmaster of Shipley's school. It is a story of life and liberation, told with grace and lightness. Quite what Dr Lyttelton thought of it one can only imagine.

Rose was now in a position to disburse some of her earnings. In October that year she assumed responsibility for the upkeep and education of an orphan called Arthur, who was lodged with a couple in the village and who was referred to by the rest of the family as Rose's 'waif'.

In 1913 Uncle Regi provided a London flat for Rose, in Southampton Buildings off Chancery Lane. Naomi Royde-Smith, Walter de la Mare and Rupert Brooke were amongst the guests at the flat-warming party. This could have been an escape route for Rose from the intensity of Grace's emotions, yet she continued to spend considerable amounts of time at home. She was now the only child available to her parents, for Will was in Canada, Margaret and Jean were working in London, and Eleanor, since September 1912, was working as a mission teacher in Lahore. The core of the family, the family that was still so important to Rose, now consisted of her two ageing parents. As the only daughter left she felt a strong sense of duty towards them. But equally important was what they offered her: an excuse for her reluctance to embrace wholeheartedly the literary and cultural ferment of London life, and a vantage point from which she could observe, at a distance, and write about in her fiction, the independent life she both longed for and feared.

In March 1914 Rose published a novel that provided a portrait of this febrile pre-war metropolitan world. *The Making of a Bigot* is set in a society so crammed full of causes and beliefs that no one belief has any claim to be taken more seriously than any other. Through the protagonist, Eddy Oliver, Rose Macaulay gives us one of her first workings out of what would become a recurrent theme: the intellectual and emotional difficulty of prioritising values. Eddy sees the virtues of all things: socialism, pacifism, Christianity and national service; he edits a newspaper called *Unity*, which supports tariff reform, referendums, the minimum wage, Prayer Book revision, Home Rule, Unionism, Liberalism and Toryism. It lasts for three months. Eddy's friends the Denisons want 'Votes for Women, and Liberty for Distressed Russians, and spinning-looms for everyone'. Eddy takes young men from an East End working men's club to see Granville Barker's Shakespeare, to Roger Fry's Post-Impressionist show, to a talk by a church socialist, and to a National Service League speaker, who lectures on 'The Path of Duty is the Path of Safety'.

This is a *roman-à-clef* of pre-war London, where tall, handsome 'promising young poet' Billy Raymond gives a reading 'all to himself' at the Poetry Bookshop, where the fashionable artistic world flocks to Cecil de Moines's play *Squibs*, where Jane

Dawn, who has a 'chaste, elfin quality', draws and makes prints like Gwen Darwin and has 'two new Duncan Grants and a Muirhead Bone' hanging on the walls of her flat. Watching all this is Bridget Hogan, who, like Rose Macaulay, is a few years older than the others. She is thirty-four, and has 'ironic eyes, and a slight stutter'. 'One is sure that the characters are drawn from life,' said the *Saturday Review*. 'The artistic set of London which fluctuates between Chelsea and Soho is well described.'

Rose Macaulay is having fun here; at the expense of all the London people with whom she had fallen collectively in love; at the expense of herself, unable to commit to a course of action, or to an emotional tie; at the expense of a too-fine philosophy that sees too clearly and can act on nothing. But while a system of moral and artistic relativity is the butt of good-natured satire, Rose Macaulay shows up the limits of that relativity. For this brave new liberal world retains its cruelty towards women who dare to step outside the limits of conventional sexual morality. Rose Macaulay once again explores the imprisonment of a marriage that cannot be dissolved.

And like a dark thread woven through the chat and the laughter, through the modernness of all these young people with their paintings and their poetry and their plays and their scorn for the Tory-voting fuddy-duddies and members of the artistic establishment who are 'not even Edwardian' but 'late Victorian', running beneath Eddie's attempts to encompass all and to embrace the whole world, is the shocking fact of violent conflict.

Conflict is there, conflict is real; and at the end of the novel Arnold Denison, who is clever, and cynical, and truthful, becomes caught up in a confrontation at London docks between strikers and anti-strikers, goes down in the crowd and is trampled to death.

'Very clever and amusing,' wrote Eddie Marsh to Rupert Brooke of *The Making of a Bigot*.

Although Rose Macaulay herself, unlike many other writers, was not engaged in the maelstrom of struggle for political reform, the repercussions of revolution and repression break through the witty amusing surface of the novel. 'Behind all the talking and the writing and the ballet and the theatres and the poetry,' she wrote of the Georgian years in London, 'there were a few quite uncivilised noises off, from Ireland, and from the Balkans, and from strikers and suffragettes. Not being politically minded, I do not think that I attended very closely.' Nonetheless the noises off can be heard as Arnold Denison falls to his death beneath the feet of the crowd in *The Making of a Bigot*.

CHAPTER FIVE

Non-Combatants

Alix lay awake. Her forehead was hot and her feet were cold. She was tense, and on the brink of shivering. Staring into the dark she saw things happening across the seas: dreadful things, ugly, jarring horrifying things. War – war – war. It pressed round her; there was no escape from it. Every one talked it, breathed it, lived in it. Aunt Eleanor, with her committees, and her terrible refugees; Mademoiselle Verstigel, with her round robin's eyes that had looked horror in the face so near; Uncle Gerald, with his paper and his intelligent city rumours; Dorothy and Margot with their soldiers, who kept coming to tea, cheerful, charming and maimed; John, damaged and stammering, with his nervous eyes and his quiet, humorous trench talk; Basil, writing from his dug-out of Boche and shells . . . little Paul out there in the dark . . . they were all up against the monster, being strangled . . .

Non-Combatants and Others, 1916

Germany invaded Belgium at the beginning of August 1914, and on the 4th of that month Britain declared war. Rose Macaulay had just turned thirty-three. She was in Canada with her father George, visiting Will in the clapboard farmhouse he had built on the high prairies of Alberta. They managed to get a passage home aboard the *Laconia*, a British liner sailing under Dutch colours, and were back in Great Shelford by the end of September. Will stayed in Canada to bring in his harvest, and then followed his sister and father to England. As a schoolboy at

Marlborough shooting had been the only activity in which Will had excelled. Now he would join the King's Royal Rifles. By then Jean had signed up with the French Red Cross and was nursing in France. Rose did not involve herself in the war until well into 1915.

An initial romanticisation of the war, shared by a great number of those who were not on active service, was in Rose's case fed by her envy of masculine freedom. Rose could be a tomboy and climb trees, but she could not go and fight. Yearning for the heroism of war in her poem 'Many Sisters to Many Brothers', she recalls childhood games with toy soldiers and bathroom battle-ships, when sister and brother were evenly matched. And when games gave way to fights, 'Your black eye matched my bleeding nose'. She asks, 'Was there a scrap or ploy in which you, the boy,/Could better me?' Now the boy is at the Front, and his sister bemoans the unfairness of sex distinction that sends him to battle and leaves her to knit socks:

> Oh, it's you that have the luck, out there in blood and muck:
> > You were born beneath a kindly star;
> All we dreamt, I and you, you can really go and do,
> > And I can't, the way things are.
> In a trench you are sitting, while I am knitting
> > A hopeless sock that never gets done.
> Well, here's luck, my dear; – and you've got it, no fear;
> > But for me . . . a war is poor fun.

Many women yearned to be in the front line, some for romantic reasons, some for altruistic reasons, and many for a mixture of both. A lot of women went as nurses, VADs and ambulance drivers, working in the 'blood and muck' like Rose's sister Jean Macaulay and finding it rather less glamorous than Rose, at that stage, imagined it to be. 'Many Sisters to Many Brothers' was quickly anthologised in a volume published to raise money for Belgian refugees, entitled *Pro Patria et Rege*: the title gives a fair indication of orthodox feeling in the first months of the war. The great majority believed that the war was being fought for King, for Country and for the God of King and Country. A minority believed that it would thoroughly shake out the last vestiges of Victorianism and would bring about a new, livelier and better world. The romanticism in both views, with hindsight, seems astonishing. But no one knew then how the Great War would be so unlike all previous wars. Neither view – the preservation of old values or the inauguration of new ones – challenged a belief in progress that had its roots in the mid-nineteenth century. Whichever way you looked at it, the war could only make things better. While Rose Macaulay herself had already developed an ironic attitude towards such an amelioristic philosophy (an attitude which had probably been formed by her seventeenth-century studies at Oxford and which would find its most trenchant expression in her 1923 'history' of Britain, *Told by an Idiot*), she was nonetheless, in the early months of the war, in line with most of the rest of the population in believing that the war was right, was noble, and would be over very soon.

Another poem, 'The Garden', offers a specifically Christian consolation for the sacrifices the soldiers are making:

> . . . Have they lost all,
> They who fell dumb in the spring-time of age?
> Have their still bodies only sleep for wage?
>   Nay, see how they have won
> For their drifting dust a goodly heritage –
> A garden, full of flowers and the sun.

Gardens and flowers and suns were recurring images of England and home in early war poetry, appearing in Rupert Brooke's 'War Sonnets', two of which, 'The Dead' and 'The Soldier', appeared alongside 'Many Sisters to Many Brothers' in the 1915 collection *Poems of Today*. Rose's 'drifting dust' in 'The Garden' echoes

Brooke's more famous and specifically English 'richer dust' in 'The Soldier' ('. . . There shall be/In that rich earth a richer dust concealed . . .'). Rose would not be able to write again anything so optimistic and so much a part of a well-established pastoral-religious consolatory tradition. This was the end of her innocent, naïve glorification of military life. The longing to be out there in the trenches, fighting alongside the men, was transformed in her later war poetry into something altogether darker and more sinister.

In May 1915 Rose signed on as a VAD (Voluntary Aid Detachment) at Mount Blow, a large house in Great Shelford which had just been converted into a military convalescent home. To say, as one of the villagers did, that Rose 'was not very successful with scrubbing floors and other menial tasks' was to put it politely. She was useless. She failed to move the boots off the floors she was scrubbing, she failed to tie her skirt up out of the way of the scummy water, she probably scrubbed herself into a corner rather than out of an open door, as if in a comic film about the hopelessness of the middle classes who have always had servants to do their dirty work. But Rose was not averse to physical labour. Her inefficiency was an expression of deep distress. Rose's sister Jean thought that it was 'a mad choice' of Rose's to work as a VAD, for she 'was hyper-sensitive to physical pain and also uncontrollably squeamish; she tended to vomit or faint at the sight of blood or the mere mention of horrors'. A photograph shows her hunched and miserable on the steps of the hospital.

Her experiences of war now unleashed for Rose Macaulay a nightmare vision. She had written earlier of the other worlds hidden by the veneer of civilisation, of 'the wild things from without' and the 'blind bog-beasts', and how those visions had left her 'reeling and baffled and blind'. Now the nightmare was not of ancient monsters invading the civilised world, but of dismembered bodies and shattered minds bearing witness to a civilisation that preferred not to hear their testament.

Rose began work on another novel. *Non-Combatants and Others*, published in the spring of 1916, was one of the first novels of the Great War, if not the very first, to deal with the reality of war rather than the fantasy of it. In it she explored the deleterious effects of war not just on survivors from the Front, but on the non-combatants at home. The protagonist is a sensitive, nervy art student called Alix Sandomir whose younger brother Paul, aged eighteen and a half, is out in France. Alix hates and fears all thoughts of war.

The novel opens with Alix discovering her cousin John, wounded in the head and recently released from hospital, walking in his sleep, sobbing and moaning, and turning towards her eyes that are 'wide and wet, and full of a horror beyond speech'. Alix's reaction, like Rose's own, is to vomit from fear and dread. John's efficient VAD sister leads him back to bed and soothes him, and says to Alix: 'You'll never be any use if you don't forget yourself, Alix. You couldn't possibly nurse if you were always giving in to your own nerves. After all, what they can bear to go through, we ought to be able to bear to hear about . . .' Alix can't accept this. 'What they can bear to go through . . . But they can't, they can't, they can't . . . we can bear to hear about . . . but we can't, we can't, we can't . . .'

The novel is crammed with images of dismembered and broken bodies: 'What was it John had said on the balcony – something about a leg . . . the leg of a friend . . . pulling it out of the chaos of earth and mud and stones which had been a trench . . . thinking it led on to the entire friend . . .'

This was Rose's experience of Mount Blow. The reality of death and injury was almost overwhelming. She could no longer believe that soldiers were 'born under a lucky star', that war was any kind of 'fun', or that on the other side of death lay a flower-filled sunny garden.

In the novel news comes that Paul has been killed. People try to comfort Alix: 'He died a noble death . . . serving his country in her need,' says one woman. 'He has begun to live now, dear, for ever and ever,' says another. The truth, as Alix soon discovers, is that Paul's nerve had gone, after seeing his best friend 'cut to pieces by a bit of shell before his eyes'. He had started taking risks, hoping to get hit, and having failed at that, he had shot himself in the shoulder and died lingeringly of the wound. One of Paul's fellow-soldiers says: 'The thing is not to think. Not to imagine. Not to remember . . . It's over, don't you see, for Paul. He's clean out of it . . . It's a score for him really, as he . . . did mind so much.' But Alix can't agree: 'It isn't a score for him to lose all the rest of his life, that he might have had afterwards.'

For soldiers to deliberately put themselves in the way of enemy fire, either in the hope of a wound that would guarantee them being sent home, or in the hope of a quick way out of the horror, was not uncommon. Neither were self-inflicted wounds, fatal or otherwise. Officers and men were routinely presented as heroes in the narratives of their deaths sent to relatives at home, as Vera Brittain realised and sets out in her war memoir *Testament of Youth* in 1933. She describes being told by his colonel that her brother Edward had been killed by a shot to the head: 'I looked at him in silent reproach, for I frankly did not believe him. At that late stage of the War – as I had realised only too well from the agitated efforts of Army Sisters to mitigate truth with compassion in letters describing the last moments of men who had died in hospital – the colonels and company commanders on the various fronts were so weary of writing gruesome details to sorrowing relatives, that the number of officers who were instantaneously and painlessly shot through the head or the heart passed far beyond the bounds of probability.' The irony of the gap between the real manner of death and the representation of the death to grieving relatives is pointed up in Siegfried Sassoon's poem 'The Hero', written in August 1916.

News of the manner of Paul's death marks a turning point for Alix. With aching head, hands 'as cold as fishes', and vomiting uncontrollably, she realises that flight from the horror of war is futile. Driven by his death to try to make sense of the concept of God and God's relation to humanity, Alix tries various churches. None provides an answer to the hideous puzzle of war, although she is sympathetic to a clergyman friend, who articulates the 'embittering and demoralising' plight of the non-combatant, saying: 'To have one's friends in danger, and not to be in danger oneself – it fills one with futile rage.' Finally Alix becomes aware that there are three possible courses of action for non-combatants: to be for the war, to ignore the war, or – her choice – to fight against the war. Overcoming her earlier fastidiousness and solitariness, Alix now throws in her lot with her mother, an effective campaigner for the Society for Promoting Permanent Peace. Rose herself was to act similarly after the war when she enthusiastically promoted the work of the League of Nations Union.

When *Non-Combatants and Others* came out in 1916 it was not well received. The *Englishwoman* accused Rose Macaulay of 'belittling those who fight' by giving us a protagonist whose misery blots out 'all that is splendid or pitiful in life or death'. The *Times Literary Supplement* was lukewarm. The reviewer had difficulty with Rose Macaulay's 'note' and 'style': 'impossible as it is to exaggerate the misery and horror of these times, we feel that her note is, somehow, forced, and that her very style, with its careful elimination of sentimentality, contributes towards a general effect of exaggeration'. The cool authorial voice that Rose Macaulay was beginning to use with increasing confidence was well suited to her exploration of the dreadful ironies of the Great War. The contradiction between the statement that the horror of war cannot be exaggerated, and the statement that Rose Macaulay does exaggerate it, shows the reviewer's ambivalence towards Rose's at times ironic treatment of such a dangerous subject. The reviewer equates sentimentality with truthfulness. Soon after the publication of the book, and in between the appearance of these two reviews, that is, between May and

August 1916, the débâcle of the Somme offensive had taken place. Sixty thousand men were killed or wounded on the first day alone. Perhaps sentimentality was needed to soften the awful facts.

But Rose couldn't afford to be sentimental. She needed to eliminate sentimentality in order to bring all her passion for the truth to bear on her subject, for in *Non-Combatants*, as well as writing about the widespread horrors of war, she was also writing her way out of her own horrors, as she had done before with *The Valley Captives*.

Two deaths preceded the writing of *Non-Combatants*. The first was that of her fellow-poet and sparring partner Rupert Brooke. Rupert Brooke had joined the Royal Navy, and in April 1915 was sailing through the Aegean towards the Dardanelles. He was bitten on the lip by a mosquito while on board ship, and suffered a severe reaction to the bite. He developed blood poisoning and within a matter of hours he died. On 23 April he was buried on the island of Skyros. Rose's recorded response was entirely conventional; writing to Walter de la Mare in praise of his obituary of Rupert she said: 'It seems all alive with his humour and aliveness, and the most inside self that I should not think very many people even who knew him well understood.' But it is possible that she considered this to be another of those accidental deaths like that of Aulay, and that Rupert Brooke's death too is echoed in the way that Paul dies in *Non-Combatants*. And it may also have played a part in the change in Rose's attitude towards the war. At first she had held herself aloof and romanticised it from a distance. Very soon after receiving news of Rupert Brooke's death, she signed on at Mount Blow and at once began a radical revision of her thoughts.

The second death came only two months later. George Macaulay suffered a sudden stroke at the end of June and died a few days later. Rose had been her father's closest, best child. He had been her adored father, a model for her beliefs, her aspirations and her conduct. But of the immediate family only Margaret and Jean (on compassionate leave from France) attended the funeral. Rose and her mother Grace were both too stricken even to appear at the funeral. There are no more details of Rose's incapacity. It is impossible to say how much she was affected by her mother's grief, how much by her experiences of the sick and wounded at the military hospital, and how much by her father's death following so closely after news of the death of Rupert Brooke. To be unable to attend the funeral suggests that Rose was truly stricken. Was this another breakdown, like the one six years earlier after Aulay's murder, and the one six years before that, when she was at Oxford? Save for the breakdown in 1909, which Rose referred to obliquely in correspondence with Margerie Venables Taylor, there is no written reference to these episodes, only what Rose's sister Jean mentioned later. It seems that they were infrequent, but curiously regular. Each time Rose recovered through writing: her first novel *Abbots Verney* after the Oxford breakdown, the rage-filled *The Valley Captives* after Aulay's death, and out of the horrors of the mass destruction of war and her own private griefs, *Non-Combatants and Others*.

On Christmas Day 1915 Rose wrote to Katharine Tynan to express thanks for her poetry collection *Flower of Youth:* 'I first came across it when I was feeling rather unhappy about the death at the war of several intimate friends of mine – Rupert Brooke was one – the sort of people who just can't be spared – & it gave me a feeling of comfort that nothing had before.' She went on, 'Xmas, of course, is an especially sad time for everyone this year. We've not only a brother in Serbia, as well, of course, as all the friends and relations killed that everyone must have, but my father has also died in the last few months; & I think there are times when one's father seems a greater loss than any other could be.' In February 1916, while still part-time at Mount Blow, Rose started work as a land girl on a local farm, for 3d. an hour. 'Rose M now spreading manure!!' wrote Uncle

Edward Conybeare in his diary, aghast. But despite having to be outside in the biting dawn winds of Cambridgeshire, Rose found the work much more congenial than cleaning the wards of the sick and wounded soldiers. Being outside in the open air gave her – as always – a sense of emotional freedom. From her work as a land girl she produced a clutch of five poems called 'On the Land, 1916', comprising 'Driving Sheep', 'Burning Twitch', 'Hoeing the Wheat', 'Spreading Manure' (not only could she spread manure, she could even write a poem about it) and 'Lunch Hour'. They are generally cheerful and celebratory in tone. Edward's daughter Dorothea, a great taker of photographs, took a picture of Rose with the other land girls. They stand in skirts and hats, holding hoes and pitchforks, grinning at Rose as she swigs from a bottle. 'We lay in the shadowed ditch,' she writes in 'Lunch Hour', 'a peaceful circle/Of food, drink, smoke, and mirth.' Even as she enjoyed the egalitarian camaraderie and appreciated the freedom of working on the land, she continued to explore the ambivalence of her own feelings as a non-combatant. In 'Spreading Manure' she wrote of the bitter cold of that spring:

> I think no soldier is as cold as we,
> Sitting in the Flanders mud.
> I wish I was out there, for it might be
> A shell would burst, to heat my blood . . .

After the unflinching realism of *Non-Combatants* this seems a strangely inappropriate response to the horrors of the trenches. But as the poem continues we see that it is partly at least the expression of a death-wish:

> I wish I was out there, for I should creep
> In my dug-out, and hide my head.
> I should feel no cold when they laid me deep
> To sleep in a six-foot bed.

At home Rose, seen by the villagers as 'a slave to her mother', bore the brunt of Grace's grief for George, and her constant need for attention. Rose had been infuriated by Grace's domestic small talk back in the Welsh valley days ten years before. Now a permanent semi-invalid (at times more semi- than at others), Grace was even more demanding. It was at this point, on one of the retreats that Rose and Grace regularly attended, that Rose met Father Hamilton Johnson of the Cowley Fathers, who was to play a significant role in the last few years of her life. Many years later he recalled discussing with Rose 'how a young lady living with her family might most suitably conduct herself'. This memory is tantalisingly uninformative: did she confess to being driven to distraction by her mother, and ask for his advice on how to deal with it? He remembered looking out into the garden from the parlour where he was hearing confessions and seeing her 'pacing up and down very gravely and slowly' in the steadily drizzling rain in a dark tweed suit, 'tall and grave and thoughtful'.

She had slipped into *Non-Combatants and Others* a brazen conjunction of her mother Grace with a dim, cliché-bound woman who is married to an Oxford professor, lives in Summertown in a house called Thule and keeps cats. 'A kind little mediocrity . . .' says Alix's mother of this woman, who had been kind to Alix while her mother was away. Alix tries feebly to defend the woman on the grounds that she is 'very nice and kind'. But this cuts no ice with her clever mother.

'"Oh – all that." Daphne waved it aside. "Of course. But too stupid to be tolerable, even as a background to your day's work, no doubt . . ."'

In the spring of 1916 Grace decided it was time to leave Great Shelford. Moving closer to London would make it easier for Margaret to visit and would be welcomed by Rose, who had given up her London flat at the beginning of the war. A register of university women had just been compiled to enable the Civil Service to call on women graduates for war work.

Being closer to London would mean Rose could get a Civil Service job, as well as pick up the literary contacts sundered by the war. They found a house on the west side of London (not particularly convenient for Margaret, who was still in the East End) at Hedgerley near Beaconsfield in Buckinghamshire. Grace arranged for Southernwood to be let, and they moved in at the end of the year. In January 1917 Rose started work as a junior administrative assistant in the War Office, in the department that dealt with exemptions from military service and with conscientious objectors. She worked a ten-hour day, but at weekends there were long walks in the Buckinghamshire countryside and through Burnham Beeches, and she sometimes stayed with Naomi Royde-Smith at her cottage in Holmbury on the North Downs in Surrey. Naomi was still in love with Walter de la Mare, and Rose wrote to him urging him to visit, describing Hurt Wood, near Holmbury, as 'the peacefullest and silentest and sweetest-smelling place anywhere'. But it was only like that when the guns in France were silent, as Rose was only too aware.

Hurt Wood was the setting for her poem 'Picnic, July 1917', in which she explored further the painful position of the non-combatant and the attempt to build defences against the horror of knowledge. The poem is in three parts. It starts:

> We lay and ate sweet hurt-berries
> In the bracken of Hurt Wood.
> Like a quire of singers singing low
> The dark pines stood.

The pines are like angels blessing the land, which is 'drowsy and quiet and sweet'. The picnickers, in a stuporous dream, 'drowsily' hear the great guns beat up the wind and refuse to respond to what the guns are telling them. The final verse of the first part shows what in Freudian terms might be called this lack of affect:

We did not shake with pity and pain,
Or sicken and blanch white.
We said, 'If the wind's from over there
There'll be rain tonight'.

The second part of the poem explains the listeners' refusal to engage: they have peered 'Through the gates of hell' and now have built up walls around themselves against the pity, rage and pain that they once felt. The guns they hear are 'muffled and far away/Dreams within dreams'. They have distanced the war that the guns tell of: 'And far and far are Flanders mud,/And the pain of Picardy . . .' But in the final three verses of the poem the poet is forced to admit that the walls are not as secure as she might hope, and she begs the guns to be still and the wind to stop blowing so that the listeners can go back to sleep again. Like a child terrified at night, she thinks that if she lies very still the monster will go away:

Oh, we'll lie quite still, nor listen nor look,
While the earth's bounds reel and shake . . .

She knows how fragile the defences are. And once those go, there will be no protection for the fragile, vulnerable human inside:

Lest, battered too long, our walls and we
Should break . . . should break . . .

Rose was thirty-seven when the war ended. In 1919 her second collection of poetry, *Three Days*, was published. It contained a number of poems about the war and was dedicated to her friend and one-time publisher Naomi Royde-Smith, in whose company she would take her first steps in the post-war literary world. It was reviewed in the *Times Literary Supplement* by Walter de la Mare, under the interestingly ambiguous title 'On the Threshold'. (Perhaps it is only with hindsight that 1919 appears as a threshold, a stepping-place between two worlds; de la Mare's title referred to the 'otherwhere' setting of the poems.) He suggested that her work as a novelist, as 'a clear and close observer of "the normal"', would make a difference to the reception of her poetry. He praised her as a writer of imagination but characterised her as not primarily a poet. 'Her poetry,' he wrote, 'is an emanation from her work, and, at its best, is as lovely an emanation as her personality is faithful, courageous, and, to use a fine old word that is now a little tarnished with neglect, amiable.'

The poems in *Three Days* were divided into three sections. The war poems – including 'Picnic, July 1917', the five poems of 'On the Land, 1916', 'New Year 1918', which would become a regular on BBC broadcasts, and 'The Shadow' – appeared in the section 'Yesterday' of the three days of the title. The other two sections were 'Today', that is, immediately post-war, and 'Any Day'. This was Rose's final collection of poetry. In the mid-1920s she featured in Humbert Wolfe's Augustan series, but only with already published poetry. In his introduction to the volume in which her work was featured Wolfe wrote: 'The dark lantern is a true image to apply to her work, because those who like it best have always been aware of something held back, some quality in reserve. They believe she will someday bring that quality into play, and they believe that it will prove to have in it as much of tears as laughter.' The reserve, or reticence, which Humbert Wolfe, himself a poet, and a friend of Rose's, recognised in her was integral to her sense of self. But the hidden quality in her work, that he believed would have sadness as well as laughter, was never expressed in her poetry. When she came back to writing poetry in her sixties she had left it unpractised for too long.

The final entry in Rose's manuscript poetry book, in which she kept fair copies in black ink of all her poems, is dated 12 January 1919. It is, significantly, a poem called 'Nostalgia', and it is about the Italian landscapes of her childhood.

Three Days was highly praised on publication. 'Miss Macaulay is one of the most interesting of contemporary poets,' said the *Athenaeum*. 'She always has something to say, something intelligent and original . . . [she is] a very accomplished metrist.' But for Rose the poetry that she loved, the poetry that explored in lilting rhyme and metre the strange otherworlds that lurked in the corners of her imagination, could only exist in the past.

Towards the end of *Non-Combatants and Others* there is a scene where Alix is waiting, alone. 'She had been having tea, and was reading *Peacock Pie*. She preferred this poetry to any written since August 1914, which had killed fairies.' Alix is speaking for Rose Macaulay as well as for herself. Walter de la Mare's *Peacock Pie* was published in 1913. The Great War, Rose believed, had killed de la Mare's fairies, just as it had destroyed the world that could accommodate the benign ghost of Rose's sun-drenched Hellenic journey in her 1913 story 'The Empty Berth'. There were too many real ghosts now crowding the world.

Resolutely she turned her face forward and began to reinvent herself from poet to novelist of and commentator on the post-war world. This literary role would be launched with *Potterism*, her bestselling novel about the epitome of the modern world, a creation of the Great War itself – the popular press. Victorian girl, Edwardian novelist and Georgian poet were now behind her.

Rose was to write of E. M. Forster in the 1930s, that 'today we are realists'; that realism began in the 1920s, after the vanishing into darkness of 'the imaginative twilight of the British classic-nurtured mind'. The world had been shaken and 'Pan, perhaps gun-shy since the four years of war, has retired from the English scene.' It was not only Forster's romantically faun-haunted English scene that didn't survive the war; the mists and veils and dim glimmerings of other worlds that were characteristic of Walter de la Mare's poetry, and that had been so influential on

Emilie Rose Macaulay, aged three

Grace Conybeare at eighteen

George Macaulay in the 1890s

Bridesmaids in 1886: Rose (left), aged five;
Jean (centre) and Margaret

Varazze, 1880s: Procession on 30 April, the feast day of Santa Caterina

Villa Macolai, Varazze

The Macaulays (without Eleanor) at Clent in 1892, wearing mourning for Gertrude. *Standing*: Uncle William, George. *Sitting*: Grace, Aunt Mary, Uncle Kenneth, Aulay, Margaret. *On the ground*: Rose, Will, Jean

Thule in Summertown, Oxford, 1890s

Rose at fifteen or sixteen, c. 1897

Aulay, aged sixteen or seventeen, in the OTC, Clifton, c. 1900

'The Caterpillar is often to be found in a rowing boat . . .': Rose Macaulay as seen by her contemporaries at Somerville

Ty-Issa, near Aberystwyth, early 1900s

Rupert Brooke, 1913

MISS ROSE MACAULAY,

Who has won the first prize in Hodder and Stoughton's competition.

Rose in 1912, on publication of *The Lee Shore*: 'The Daily Chronicle portrait is certainly remarkably like me!'

The Macaulays at Southernwood, Great Shelford, c. 1913: (*l. to r.*) George, Grace, Jean, Rose, the dog Tom, Margaret

Walter de la Mare, 1916

Naomi Royde Smith, c. 1910

Books by Rose Macaulay

MILTON
ROSE MACAULAY

2/-
net

ROSE
MACAULAY
Pleasure of Ruins

BLED SHORE
Rose Macaulay

THEY WENT
TO PORTUGAL

Rose Mac

Hogarth Essays

Second Series

They were defeated

Rose Macaulay

Nursing staff and patients at Mount Blow Red Cross Auxiliary Hospital, Shelford, 1915.
Rose is sitting far left

'a peaceful circle': Rose (*centre, drinking from bottle*) as a land girl, 1916

Rose's own early poetry, didn't survive either. Or perhaps they did survive, translated into the cheesecloth and ectoplasm of countless seances attended by people desperate to get a glimpse, however obscure, of that other world into which their sons and husbands and brothers had vanished.

CHAPTER SIX

Gerald

It's queer, isn't it, how strong it is, this odd, desperate wanting of one person out of all the world.

Kitty Grammont, in *What Not*

At the beginning of 1918 Rose was transferred from the War Office to the Ministry of Information, newly set up by Lloyd George. Beaverbrook was the minister of information and another press baron, Lord Northcliffe, was director of the department of enemy propaganda. Because of her knowledge of Italian Rose was posted to the Italian section of this department, which was run by Gerald O'Donovan, an Irishman living in exile from his homeland, a novelist, a reformer and an ex-priest.

When Rose met him, Gerald O'Donovan was forty-six and the author of two novels, *Father Ralph* and *Waiting*. *Father Ralph*, published in 1913, tells the story of an idealistic young Irish priest whose attempts to reform the daily lives of his parishioners and to transform the quality of their spiritual lives are blocked at every move by an entrenched church hierarchy whose commitment is to retaining their own power rather than working on behalf of the people. The clergy in the novel are, variously, drunken, lecherous, self-serving and pig-ignorant. Eventually

Father Ralph leaves the priesthood. (Much later John Betjeman wrote to Gerald O'Donovan to ask where he might find a copy of that 'first-class novel', *Father Ralph*, so that he could give it to his wife to read before they went to Ireland, as he couldn't think of a surer way to nip in the bud her pro-Romanist tendencies.)

Waiting was published the following year, 1914. The story concerns the struggle in Ireland over the Church's control of the schools, dramatised in a conflict between a rural schoolteacher, Maurice Blake, and his corrupt parish priest Father Mahon; it is also about the cruelty of the Church towards people in mixed marriages, like the Catholic Maurice and his Protestant wife, Alice. Story aside, it is, like *Father Ralph*, 'a bitter and . . . deadly attack on the priesthood', as Walter de la Mare wrote in his review of it for the *Times Literary Supplement*. De la Mare singled out one scene, a supper with Father Mahon and neighbouring priests, as 'a piece of satirical bludgeoning not unworthy of Swift'.

Meeting Gerald O'Donovan was the turning point in Rose Macaulay's life. He was the love of the rest of her life, and influenced all the work that was to come: from the clever, confident, successful novels of the next decade and a half, through to what she wrote in the years after Gerald's death in 1942, when she explored in different ways the subjective experience of loss and loneliness and the perception of change and decay, and her final novel, *The Towers of Trebizond*.

But Gerald was a married man. For the sake of Gerald, Rose would sacrifice the Church that had sustained her through periods of grief and despair; she would sacrifice intimacy with her sisters Margaret and Jean; she would sacrifice the public acknowledgement of her beloved partner. But there was a lot that she would gain. After all, she was a novelist and skilled at making things up, and it may have been precisely the need to dissimulate that was part of the appeal of the relationship. And how much did the opinion of the outside world matter? Her childhood years in Italy, when family had provided all that was needed to feed her emotions, her intellect and her imagination, had inculcated in her a disregard for the opinion of the outside world. Now, in adulthood, not only did Rose Macaulay not need to fit in, but she flourished in the position she had chosen for herself on the edge of things. It provided a vantage point for her writing from which she could look at the world obliquely and ironically. There were practical advantages too: by choosing a married lover Rose could have love and companionship, and yet continue to work and to write. She would escape the domestic and emotional drudgery of wifehood.

Gerald had been a priest until the age of thirty-eight. By the time Rose Macaulay met him in the last year of the Great War he had moved a long way from his early life. He had thoroughly reinvented himself, although he was exploring in his fiction, and would continue to explore in another four novels, the world he had left behind. If the significant moment in Rose's life was her meeting with Gerald, his significant moment had occurred years earlier, in 1904, when, known then as Father Jeremiah O'Donovan, he had left the parish of Loughrea in Co. Galway, in the west of Ireland.

The seven years of his curacy at Loughrea at the turn of the century, however partial and piecemeal must be their reconstruction, hold the key to an understanding of Gerald O'Donovan, for it was in those years that he flexed his first ambitions, and was defeated.

While elements of Gerald O'Donovan's first novel, *Father Ralph*, are strongly autobiographical and the picture in it of life in the Catholic Church is written 'in deadly earnest and with extraordinarily intimate knowledge', there are key differences between the author's experiences and those of his protagonist. Jeremiah O'Donovan was born in Kilkeel, Co. Down in 1871. His grandfather had been a tenant farmer, and his father was a building contractor and minor government official. O'Donovan's character Ralph comes from the minor gentry. An upgrading of his own social status was something that O'Donovan would become noted for, and would regularly be a cause for resentment amongst colleagues and acquaintances. Ralph is an only child. Jeremiah was the sixth of eight children. Much later Gerald O'Donovan's eldest daughter Brigid would talk of her father's affectionate nature, and accounted for it as the result of the large happy family in which he grew up; yet when he left Ireland for good in 1910 all ties with his family were severed. There is no record of whether he made the break with them, or they with him. In the novel when Ralph leaves the Church he is rejected by his mother, who sides with the Bishop against him: 'He searched her face anxiously for some sign of softness, for the motherly feeling that used to co-exist side by side with her narrow, religious views. All was hard, cold, repellent. He longed to throw himself at her feet, to lay his head in her lap, to feel her arms around him and her warm kisses on his head.' It is to no avail. When he tells her he acted according to his conscience, he sees a 'look of horror' come into her eyes and she accuses him of blasphemy.

Like his fictional creation, Jeremiah O'Donovan flirted briefly with the Jesuits before finishing his studies at Maynooth, the 'nursery of all the priests of Ireland'. There, for the first time, he fell foul of the Church: there was a row over some unsuitable books that he had ordered and that he was obliged by his superiors to return. Falling foul of the authorities would be a recurring event in O'Donovan's later career.

But in 1895, when he was ordained for Clonfert diocese and became Father Jeremiah O'Donovan, his future must have seemed full of possibilities. In 1897 he arrived as second curate for the parish of Loughrea, a small country town in Co. Galway, where he was the protégé of the Bishop of the diocese, the forward-looking John Healy, and where a new cathedral was being built.

St Brendan's Cathedral at Loughrea became a showpiece for the Celtic revival in the arts, financed with the help of Edward Martyn, a local landowner, playwright, and friend of Lady Gregory and the Yeats family, and through money raised by Father O'Donovan, as secretary of the Building Committee, on lecture tours in America. It was O'Donovan who put the suggestions of the committee into practice, and commissioned Irish artists to work on Irish motifs. This was at a time when Irishness was associated with backwardness, and when the convention for church decoration was imported bad reproductions of Italian images of the saints.

Father O'Donovan commissioned stained glass windows for the Cathedral from the An Túr Gloine workshop, which had just been set up by Sarah Purser. She was a successful portrait painter who had worked in England, where she made large sums of money – 'I went through the British aristocracy like the measles,' she said later – which she shrewdly invested in Guinness when it became a public company in 1886. English artists came over to work under her auspices: A. E. Child would continue to work on windows for St Brendan's for another thirty years. His first three were installed behind the altar in 1903. Sarah Purser's windows include in the west porch a richly coloured and detailed St Brendan the Navigator in his boat, which is matched in the east porch by a window installed fifty years later, a muted and abstract St Brigid by Patrick Pye.

While part of the energy of the Celtic revival came from the internationalist outlook of many of the artists and practitioners, equally important was the value placed on local crafts and local materials. Local craftsmen were employed to carve the woodwork alongside sculptors from Dublin and England. But perhaps what Father O'Donovan most deserves to be remembered for are the twenty-four banners of Irish saints that he commissioned, designed by Jack Yeats, his wife Mary Cottenham, and Pamela Coleman Smith, and embroidered in silk and wool on Irish linen by Jack's sisters Lily and Lolly Yeats and the craftswomen of their newly set up co-operative, the Dun Emer Guild. Some of those banners are now in the National Gallery in Dublin, but the loveliest are still in Loughrea, kept in the museum next to the Cathedral rather than on display, so the reds and blues and purples and greens are as bright as when they were first woven.

Most of the banners had been completed by the early 1920s, and St Brigid was the last window to be installed, in 1953, but in other parts of St Brendan's the work that was initiated by Jeremiah O'Donovan still goes on, over a hundred years after the first commissions. In later life Gerald O'Donovan never came back to Loughrea. When he left, the leaving was final.

Nowadays visitors come from all over the world to admire the artwork of St Brendan's Cathedral, but despite his championing of that work O'Donovan was alive to the bitter contradictions of it. This was perhaps one of the reasons that he never returned. For all its glory the art was the symbol of what was wrong with the Catholic Church in turn of the century Ireland. In *Father Ralph* the young priest looks down on the town of Bunnahone from a cliff at the sea's edge and thinks how beautiful it looks with the sun striking the convent windows and the roof of the Cathedral, but he is challenged by his companion, a freethinker called John Byrne, as to what he can really see. 'The Cathedral, the two convents, the monastery, the asylum, the workhouse, the bishop's palace, the parochial house and, I think, the Emporium . . .' he replies. 'That's the history of the town in a nutshell,' says Byrne. 'All that's left of the people after the Church has got her divide is the workhouse or the asylum. There's the Emporium, of course, and the other big shops. They wouldn't be long in it if they didn't pay up too. Instead of doing all the bleeding direct, the Church lets Hinnissey and his like bleed the people and then the priests bleed Hinnissey. My neighbours go without a roof to the houses that they're paying Hinnissey for. Hinnissey gave a thousand pounds to the new Cathedral.' At a mass in the Cathedral the following Sunday, where the Bishop has announced the building of a new seminary, Father Ralph sees 'the blood of the poor' in the 'muddy red of a stained glass window'.

The economic basis of God's glorification could be seen in the wretched hovels that straggled along the muddy Main Street outside the Cathedral, the grim habitations of men and women who were kept in poverty by the publicans and shopkeepers and kept in ignorance by a church hierarchy that was more interested in amassing riches than in the material, let alone spiritual, welfare of its people.

This was the other side of Father O'Donovan's life in Loughrea, the seven years that he spent struggling to improve the quality of daily life for his parishioners. Chronic drunkenness was a major cause of the destitution and degradation of the majority of the poor people. O'Donovan founded the Total Abstinence Society and negotiated the lease of a military barracks from the British War Office, which he opened as a temperance hall. The Total Abstinence Society had a membership of 200 men in 1900, and 300 by the following year. It had a library, a gymnasium, and held weekly general meetings, from which proposals were put forward to the town commissioners on matters such as public sanitation and street lighting. The Society was involved in the work of language revival from the outset. One of the first talks was given by Douglas Hyde, who had founded the Gaelic League in 1893. Father O'Donovan was active in the Gaelic League and was elected to its governing body in 1903. He also served on the committee of Horace Plunkett's Irish Agricultural Organisation Society and agitated for an industrial revival through technical schools in the rural areas, especially for girls, who he believed were particularly in need of education and training in crafts that would be useful to them. He wrote a devastating attack on convents and the wastefulness and cruelty of keeping girls shut up in them, a prey to the unbridled desires of corrupt priests, in *Vocations* (1919). Men's use of women as units of economic exchange is a theme that runs through all O'Donovan's novels. In *Vocations* one of the young women rebels against 'being bought and sold like a bundle of cloth' and Ann, the heroine of his last novel, *The Holy Tree*, talks of being 'sold like a pig'. Father O'Donovan antagonised the Catholic hierarchy further both by encouraging the involvement of Catholic lay-people in social affairs, and by calling for state control of secular education. His ideas on the social benefits of co-operation were, as his biographer John Ryan puts it, 'almost utopian'. John Ryan quotes him on co-operation saying:

> It is the bringing together of all classes, high and low, rich and poor, educated and uneducated, on terms of equality, for the common good. It is a levelling up and a levelling down. It is the raising of the poor and uneducated to the level of the rich and educated, and it is the bringing down of these from the exclusive position of isolation they hitherto occupied in Ireland.

It would be possible to see Father O'Donovan simply as an idealistic and passionate priest who had the interests of his parishioners close to his heart, who wanted them to flourish both materially through education and industry, and also spiritually through involvement with and contemplation of an Irish aesthetic which looked back to tradition and outwards to a wider world; a man whose very breadth of ambitions for others would lead him into conflict with the conservative institution of which he was a part. But the story is more complicated than that. The more stories that are told, the clearer it becomes that O'Donovan was not simply 'the good priest' but was a man driven by his own inner conflicts and desires. Loughrea a hundred years on still remembers Father O'Donovan, and remembers him in a variety of ways. The question of why he left Loughrea in 1904 has not been answered definitively.

His critics from within the Church have pointed to his commitment to extra-parochial affairs — the fund-raising lecture tours in America, the trips to Dublin and elsewhere for conferences and annual meetings of the various organisations he was in — as coming into conflict with his duties as a parish priest. He stands accused of being too fond of spending time with the rich and influential figures of the Celtic revival movement, who gathered in Edward Martyn's house or with Lady Gregory at neighbouring Coole Park. He was not there for much of the daily grind of the parish. Others, it is said, had to shoulder his share of the baptisms and marriages and funerals, and this made him unpopular. His energetic work as president of the Total Abstinence Society belies this; he may not have performed as many baptisms as the other clergy, but he may well have felt his time was better spent working for the amelioration of material conditions for the babies once born, so that they would actually survive the first few years of infancy.

Bishop Healy promoted Father O'Donovan to the post of parochial administrator, but in the spring of 1904 Healy was himself promoted to be Archbishop of Tuam. Six months later Bishop Thomas O'Dea was appointed to the diocese of Clonfert. He was a different kind of man from Bishop Healy. This was the Bishop O'Dea to whom Augustus John attributed the celebrated phrase 'the degrading passion of love', and who stipulated, when Augustus John rented a house in Galway from some nuns, that he should not 'paint the nude'. O'Dea, story tells, demanded that O'Donovan spend more time in the parish; more likely he demanded O'Donovan spend more time on conventional parish duties. Horace Plunkett noted in his diary in September 1904 that O'Donovan had clashed with his Bishop who had 'no knowledge of life whatever', and the following month that O'Donovan had gone to London 'to live by his wits (they being too enlightened for the ministry under Maynooth)'. O'Dea left no official account of the departure of his difficult, wayward administrator, but in two letters that he wrote to Father O'Donovan in the days just before he left Loughrea, he expressed only regret that O'Donovan's mind was made up, thanked him for his 'valuable services' and assured him that 'no wish or prayer for your welfare can be more sincere or earnest'. Perhaps the bitterness towards O'Donovan expressed by the local clergy came later, after he had started publishing his novels. Photographs of all the parish administrators from the late nineteenth century to the present day are displayed in the Cathedral Museum; all, that is, save Father O'Donovan.

The town turned out *en masse* in October 1904 to wave him off at the railway station, behind the Railway – now O'Dea's – Hotel. The departure from Loughrea of Father Jeremiah O'Donovan was reported in the *Western News*:

> Long before the train started the platform and the road leading from the town were crammed with young and old, anxious to get his blessing before he left, and several knelt on the ground to receive it, and as the train steamed from the station cheer after cheer was raised for the good *soggarth* who was severing his connection with them. Father O'Donovan appeared deeply affected, and kept waving his hat until the train was out of sight.

This was O'Donovan's turning point: the twist of the road between one life and another. In *Father Ralph* the decision to leave the parish and the priesthood takes place at the same time, and Ralph knows that it will probably mean physical exile from Ireland. It is a painful moment: 'Cut off by his family, by his Church, by his country – the voice of the train dinned in his ears in a rapid, ceaseless refrain. The sounds mocked him. The mountain, in the pale, watery sunlight, seemed to wear a sneer. He sat down again, hunched in a corner, oppressed by a sense of overwhelming defeat and failure. Gone, gone, gone, family, Church, country, gone, gone, gone . . . seemed to pierce his brain and sear it . . .'

There had been a marked physical change in Father O'Donovan during his seven years in Loughrea. Photographs of him at the time of his ordination – one still hangs, unlabelled, in a back room in the Temperance Hall – show a handsome clear-eyed young man. But in a photograph taken only six or seven years later, when he was thirty-one or thirty-two, he seems to have aged by twenty years. Already his gaze is haunted and his mouth tight-lipped; his face has the closed look that would be apparent in all later photographs of him. Ten years on Jack Yeats painted a series of portraits of types from Irish life. Jack Yeats's priest does not look typical: he is neither coarse peasant nor plump hedonist, but a visionary who sees his vision curtailed. Father Jeremiah O'Donovan might have been in Yeats's mind's eye.

The review of *Father Ralph* in the *Times Literary Supplement* was headed 'A Modernist in Ireland'. The Papal Encyclical against Modernism, which anathematised both scientific and historical interrogations of the Bible and of Catholic dogma and reaffirmed the centrality of unquestioning faith, was what pushed the novelist Gerald O'Donovan's Father Ralph from the Church. He finds the textbook on ecclesiastical history that he studies at Maynooth to be 'illiterate' and asks himself: 'Was the writer merely stupid and incompetent, or was he dishonest?' He goes on, 'No thinking mind could accept the reasoning of the philosophy and theology schools with their puerile major premises assuming things as proved that bristled with difficulties. Scripture teaching was a series of evasions.' The encyclical, published in 1907, was undoubtedly one of the factors in Father Jeremiah O'Donovan's decision to leave the Church. By the time of the encyclical, which condemned rational enquiry as a sin, O'Donovan had been for three years a priest without a parish, and a reformer without a cause. Now, with the Encyclical against Modernism, he would be an intellectual without an intellectual system that he could any longer believe in.

John Ryan characterises Gerald O'Donovan as 'a versatile and sensitive man' who was cut adrift when he left Ireland, and spent the rest of his life failing to find a cause to replace what he had left, leading a life of relative isolation and of 'disappointed hopes and unfulfilled promise'.

For the following six years he drifted between Dublin, America and London. Men like George Russell and Horace Plunkett, with both of whom he had worked in the Irish Agricultural Organisation Society, and writers he knew such as George Moore, offered him work, contacts and friendship, but he couldn't stick at anything, and offers of money invariably soured the friendships.

There was a short-lived attempt at being a literary agent in America for Horace Plunkett. It is not clear at what stage he cut all ties with his family, nor is it clear exactly when he left the priesthood, but it seems to have been some time late in 1908 or early 1909. Horace Plunkett records him as being bankrupt and thinking of unfrocking himself in 1908. By then he was based in London, but returning every so often to Ireland.

In the summer of 1910 he was staying at the country house of Hugh Law, MP, in Co. Donegal, when twenty-four-year-old Beryl Verschoyle arrived as another house guest. Gerald O'Donovan, no longer Father Jeremiah, proposed marriage to her within five days, 'in so determined and authoritative a manner', recorded Beryl, 'I could only say "yes".' Gerald was square-jawed and handsome, and although at five foot eight he was two inches shorter than Beryl, he had a dominating physical presence. 'His keen blue eyes,' Beryl wrote, were shadowed by 'thick, heavy eyebrows', and while H. G. Wells's description of 'his eye like a rifle barrel through a bush' indicates, perhaps unconsciously, the hostile or combative impression he was capable of making, especially on men, it is also revealing of his powerful charisma.

A year later, when O'Donovan's first paid job as a married man had come to a premature end, Horace Plunkett noted drily, 'O'Donovan without a job, but with wife with money.' Plunkett's cynicism is surely not unrelated to O'Donovan's having rejected his own offers of help and their consequent falling out; but while he was not necessarily wrong in imputing financial motives to Gerald's choice of wife, there were, as in any marriage, all sorts of other factors. Beryl herself gave a fuller picture in her memoir when she wrote: 'Gerald was considerably older, and exceedingly brilliant intellectually. Nobody thought me at all up to his standard, which was true, and I was humbly aware of it. He loved me for what I was, gay, young and enthusiastic.'

He had had a seminary education and had then lived a vigorously argumentative intellectual life, whereas Beryl had been a privileged Edwardian girl. Beryl and her sister Gladys, Bay and Glay as they were known, had been brought up by two sets of grandparents, moving back and forth from an Irish country rectory to an apartment in Rome, a social centre of Italian aristocratic life, with a spell at a school in Brussels which was claimed, romantically, to be the original of Lucy Snowe's school in Charlotte Brontë's *Villette*. In Rome the girls had partied vigorously with a stream of Italian counts and princes and dukes; they had been guests at one country estate after another; when high society had been swept by the craze for hot air ballooning Beryl had been the first girl to go up in one, to show the aristocratic wives and daughters that it was quite safe for a woman to do so. At twenty-four Beryl was worldly, but in a narrow sense of the word. She was also innocent, untried and uneducated.

And after all those years of struggle with the church hierarchy, years of living in and running away from an impoverished and backward country town, followed by five or six years of wandering homeless, penniless and alone, it is surely no surprise that Gerald fell for a 'gay, young, enthusiastic' and very pretty young woman like Beryl, who was more than willing to love and revere him. He had just released himself from his vows of celibacy. No wonder it took him only five days to propose marriage. The daily letters that he wrote to Beryl before their marriage, page after page of passion and longing, leave no doubt about his being desperately in love with her.

Gerald and Beryl were married in London in October 1910, and moved into the Lodge of Toynbee Hall, the Universities Settlement in Whitechapel in east London, where Gerald had been appointed sub-warden. One imagines such a job would have suited Gerald well; Toynbee Hall was not just a centre for practical social reform but it attracted a wide range of radicals and intellectuals. Unfortunately for Gerald, Beryl couldn't stand it. There was a brewery nearby, and a dust destructor; Beryl complained of the sickening smell in the air after rain, and of the slime on the pavements. As the only woman in a building where thirty-five men lived she was expected to organise the house-keeping, a task in which she had no experience whatsoever, and also to be the lady of the house amongst a group of men who could hardly have been more different from the Italian aristocrats with whom she was accustomed to socialising. Her statement that life in Toynbee Hall was 'a curious and violent contrast to the life I had always lived' seems admirably understated. They left. The excuse was Beryl's 'ill-health'. In fact she was pregnant with her first child. But perhaps her pregnancy and dislike of the surroundings was no more significant than Gerald's restlessness.

They moved to a house in west London where Beryl had the baby, a girl they named Brigid, and Gerald wrote his first novel. 'The new book and our first child brought us great happiness,' Beryl wrote later. She went on to reveal more of a feeling of insecurity than perhaps she intended. 'I myself felt secure and wanted, no longer an "amusing" visitor, but the very centre of our dearly loved home.' Dermod, their son, was born two years later and in 1913 they moved out of London to the Norfolk coast, where they hoped to live more cheaply and in surroundings more congenial to a growing family. Gerald was forty-three when war was declared. He signed up in May 1915, and was posted to Hull in the Service Corps, where he managed to rationalise food distribution, reduce the rent paid for billets, and also to get on the wrong side of his superior officers. By October that year he was 'invalided out'. Six months later he had a job with the Ministry of Munitions but that went the same way: a radical critique of the status quo from Gerald O'Donovan followed by his swift removal. He was to retell these experiences in his third novel, *How They Did It*, published in 1920. It is a powerful satire on war profiteering in which the spiritual and moral bankruptcy of those who arrange to stay at home and get rewarded with wealth and honours is contrasted with the courage and self-sacrifice of the soldiers, both men and officers, at the Front.

In 1917 Gerald became London agent and editor for the Glasgow-based publishing house, William Collins. This too was

short-lived, for when a London office was opened Gerald clashed
with the person appointed to run it, Godfrey Collins. However,
he returned as reader after the war, and was responsible for seeing
through to press Rose Macaulay's novels of the 1920s. It was in
the course of his work for William Collins in 1917 that Gerald
first met Marjorie Grant Cook, who had written a novel, *Verdun
Days in Paris* (published under the name of Marjorie Grant),
about her experiences of wartime work in France, which was
published by Collins in 1918. Marjorie would become, like Rose,
a lifelong friend to Gerald's children, like Rose a godmother to
one of his granddaughters in years to come, and like Rose she
would be devoted to Gerald and accepted into the O'Donovan
household by Beryl as a 'family friend'. Tellingly however,
although the names of both Marjorie and Rose appear with some
frequency in Beryl's pocket diaries, neither of them features at all
in her memoir.

Later that year Gerald – despite all his experiences with government wartime bureaucracy – got a job in the Ministry of
Information in Crewe House in London. The place was thick
with writers: Arnold Bennett was director of the French and
H. G. Wells of the German section. It was probably on the
latter's recommendation that O'Donovan was appointed to run
the Italian section. A few months later Rose Macaulay was transferred into his department.

Years later Rose's sister Jean was to maintain stoutly that when
Rose fell in love with Gerald she didn't know that he was married; it was Gerald, therefore, who carried the blame for
precipitating an adulterous relationship. Perhaps this was the
case. There is no evidence to prove or disprove it. Jean herself was
working in France throughout most of the first year of Rose and
Gerald's relationship, and was not on hand to receive confidences
of this nature from her sister, had they been forthcoming. But
had Rose thought Gerald to be an unmarried man at first, she
might easily have mentioned this to Grace. While some kind of
agreement was reached later on between Rose, Margaret and

Jean that the subject of Gerald was not something that they could share, their mother Grace liked him. Gerald's birthday was one of the few non-family birthdays that Grace marked in her anniversary book *Morning Light*, and if it meant that she had to pretend that her daughter's relationship with this man was not a sexual one, then she pretended it.

In *Told by an Idiot*, published five years after they met, and seen through to press by Gerald, Rome Garden falls in love with Mr Jayne not knowing that he has a wife and two fair-haired children tucked away in Russia. This is how Mr Jayne's confession is described: 'By June, 1890, they were in love; a state of mind unusual in both. They did not mention it, but in July he mentioned to her, what he mentioned to few people, that he had a Russian wife . . .' They are rowing up the Thames together. They try at first to pretend, as neither has admitted they love the other, that this is of no consequence: 'So cool and well-bred were Miss Garden and Mr Jayne that you never would have divined that the latter, eating sandwiches, was crying within his soul, "My dearest Rome, I dislike my wife. We make each other sick with *ennui* when we meet. We married in a moment's mania. It is you I want. Don't you know it? Won't you let me tell you?" or that the former, sipping cider, was saying silently, "You have told me this at last because you know that we have fallen in love. Why not months ago? And what now?"'

The fact that Rose Macaulay described the beginning of an affair like this in a novel is no proof that this is how her relationship with Gerald started. Indeed the rumours that she didn't at first know he was married may well have started as a result of the piece of fiction. The love affair was worked over in different ways in her books throughout the rest of her life; it is there as a haunting presence in all her later work. The events in her novels cannot be read as an undistorted reflection of her life. However, to say that we cannot read directly from the work back to the life is not to say that the life is not there in the work. Rome and Mr Jayne behave in a civilised fashion for precisely four months, pretending there is nothing between them, and then in November, while taking tea together, Mr Jayne breaks, and says 'I love you.' And that's it: 'He drew her up from her chair and looked into her face, and that was the defeat of their civilisation, for at their mutual touch it broke in disorder and fled. He kissed her mouth and face and hands, and passion rose about them like a sea in which they drowned.'

Perhaps Rose and Gerald were inextricably in love before he told her he was married, perhaps not. When they did admit that they loved each other, and when Gerald told Rose that he was married, the question must have been, as with Rome Garden and Mr Jayne, 'And what now?'

Marriage was not the only significant factor in Gerald's life in the spring of 1918. He was about to become a father for the third time. Mary was born in Norfolk on 8 April 1918. In June, when the baby was only two months old, Gerald asked his wife Beryl to accompany him as interpreter on an official trip to Italy, leaving all three children at home. The trip was a near disaster. The future of the southern Slav states was under debate in the Rome Congress, and all O'Donovan's passion to promote self-determination for small nation states came to the fore. Beryl recorded the trip as a successful series of important negotiations conducted by Gerald with high-ranking officials. Others took a less glowing view of his activities. He managed to antagonise almost every party involved: the Embassy, British Military Intelligence in Rome, the Vatican and the Catholic hierarchy. He was answerable to no one except Lord Northcliffe. Harold Nicolson at the Foreign Office wrote of him: 'The energy and enthusiasm which made him so valuable a propagandist rendered him somewhat dangerous as a diplomat'. Some months later the British Ambassador to Italy, in a letter to the Foreign Office, described all the activities of the Italian section of the Department of Propaganda as 'disastrous'.

It sounds as if Gerald O'Donovan was trying to organise single-handedly the whole of post-war Europe. A determination to do things on his own, or an inability to co-operate with other people, or a mixture of both seems to have dictated his mode of behaviour in Italy. But why did he dash off so quickly, and why take Beryl with him? There must have been other Italian speakers around who could have acted as interpreter. What was he running from? From having fallen in love with Rose, or from Rose having fallen in love with him? Was it this that drove him to such frantic activity?

Meanwhile back in England Rose Macaulay was writing a novel about illicit love called *What Not: A Prophetic Comedy*. The heroine is a young woman called Kitty Grammont who works in a government office and falls so deeply in love with her boss Nicholas Chester that even to be in his vicinity is enough to make her lose consciousness and fall to the floor. Nicholas is 'long and lean and sallow, with black brows bent over deep, keen, dreaming eyes' and lips that carry a 'queer suggestion of tragedy and comedy'. The two of them marry in secret and spend a bliss-ful and secret honeymoon in Cogoleto, the neighbouring village to Rose Macaulay's beloved Varazze.

The illicitness of the love in *What Not* is based on a concern that harks back to a pre-war social anxiety about the inheritance of intelligence. In the novel the population is classified in A to C grades according to intelligence, and those at the lower end of the scale are not allowed to marry and reproduce. As this is a comic novel the consequences of such a social regulation of sexuality are seen as absurd and laughable. But the novel also suggests, in a way that links the pre-war enthusiasm for eugenics with a con-temporary anti-war sentiment, that if only the general level of intelligence in the population could be raised, then there need never be another war.

What Not is a strange novel that presents two particular dif-ficulties to the reader. The first is that Nicholas Chester, who is the Minister of Brains, is simultaneously a ludicrous and a seri-ous character. His absurd policies of social interference are consistently mocked throughout the novel, but the reader is asked to take him seriously for the profound and passionate love that he inspires in Kitty Grammont, through whose eyes we view him.

The second difficulty for the reader comes from being asked to accept marriage as a metaphor for forbidden love, or in other words, marriage as a metaphor for adultery. Nicholas Chester is himself 'uncertificated' for marriage by his own rulings, for he has a sister and a brother who are classified as 'imbeciles'.

In real life Rose couldn't marry Gerald, the man she loved, because he was already married. In *What Not* Kitty Grammont can't marry Nicholas Chester because he is obliged by law to remain unmarried, so that the moral implications of embarking on an adulterous affair are sidestepped by making marriage itself the forbidden fruit. When their secret marriage is discovered Nicholas is criticised by the press for a betrayal of principle. But this fictional betrayal is rather different from the betrayal of another person that is the betrayal of adultery. Kitty finds it very easy to forgive him; and so indeed does the reader, for it was not a real principle, and so not a real dilemma, in the first place.

Rose Macaulay wanted to examine in this novel the consequences of illicit love, but avoided a far-reaching examination by presenting the illicitness as not serious; in *Told by an Idiot* the moral consequences of the illicit love between Rome Garden and Mr Jayne are avoided by his sudden and shocking murder.

Rose boldly chose a futuristic setting for this semi-satirical novel about social control and the conflict between private desire and the public good; her 'brave new world' pre-dates Huxley's version by well over a decade. But the folly and danger of scientific control over human beings is the background rather than the focus of this novel; the focus is overwhelmingly on physical heterosexual love and the fruits of that love. The pages are scattered with references to the abandoned babies that are both the representation and the consequence of forbidden unions. Countless babies are left in ditches, or if they're lucky are dropped off at vicarage doors. There is only one loved, wanted and happy baby in the whole story, and he is the illegitimate child of an adulterous union.

We may speculate on a variety of desires and fears that this plethora of fictional babies represents. For the first time in her life Rose Macaulay was in love with a man who loved her. He was married to someone else and, within a few months of meeting Rose, had become a father for the third time. There is no evidence that Rose became pregnant, but it is inconceivable that pregnancy and giving birth to a child was not at least an imaginative possibility for a thirty-six-year-old woman engaged in her first passionate sexual relationship.

What Not was published by Constable, who the same year brought out her poetry collection *Three Days*. Sidgwick & Jackson, who had published her earlier collection, were taken aback to be informed she had gone elsewhere. 'We could wish you had offered us the novel also,' wrote the disappointed Mr Sidgwick, pained but polite, 'as we find it very difficult to obtain good fiction at present. An abundance of inferior work is sent to us, but we do not care to publish this.' *What Not* came out in March 1919. Two months later, in May, Rose had another nervous breakdown. It has been suggested that this was the result of illness, anxiety over her brother Will, who had been wounded in battle only two months before the Armistice and was undergoing a series of operations on his right arm, as well as being the result of Rose's struggle with herself over whether to continue the relationship with Gerald. But the typical pattern of breakdowns is that they occur post-crisis so it is possible that the breakdown in the early summer of 1919 was a consequence of events of the previous year, when Rose was writing so passionately about illegitimate sex and illegitimate babies and when the object of her love had fled precipitately from her.

The abandoned babies of *What Not* were not the only fictional babies to make an appearance at around this time in novels by close friends of Gerald O'Donovan. Marjorie Grant Cook's novel *Latchkey Ladies*, published in 1921, is set in London in 1917, in the world of war work in government offices and single working women. The heroine Anne Carey is, like her author, a Canadian. She and many of the other women in the novel hate office work and get little satisfaction from their independent lives. The latchkey, symbol of autonomy, is a 'metal seal of liberty to eat and live and die unregarded'. While the title ostensibly refers to the wartime phenomenon of single working women, it also draws attention to the possibilities of the novel as a *roman-à-clef*. Anne has a love affair with a playwright and poet called Philip Dampier, a married man whose marriage is explained thus: 'Dampier was forty-one, and he loved his wife, but he had never been in love with her. She had fallen in love with him, and they had been married. It is not only women who marry for a home.' Like other married men such as Beryl O'Donovan's Gerald or Rose Macaulay's Nicholas Chester, Philip has penetrating eyes and a striking face that is at once 'sad and eager'. Anne becomes pregnant, and has the child, a daughter, whom she loves passionately, but who dies while still a baby. She does not tell Dampier, and reflects later that he 'gave up nothing for me'.

Between 1918 and 1920 both Rose Macaulay and Marjorie Grant Cook were writing novels about love, sex, adultery and babies. Fiction may be an unreliable guide to the events of people's lives, but that is not to say that it is an unreliable guide to the desires of the heart. It is hard to believe that Marjorie Grant Cook was not, also, in love with Gerald O'Donovan.

Babies, it seems, were on everybody's minds. It was perhaps an unpropitious time for the only real baby, Mary O'Donovan, to have been born, only a month or two after Rose and Gerald met.

On their return to England after the wild and hysterical tour of Italy, the O'Donovans moved from Norfolk, which they could no longer afford, to a cottage in Dorset, where Beryl spent a miserable winter with a leaking roof, an outside lavatory, and a husband who was dedicating all his time to writing and did not appreciate the interruptions of domestic life and three small children.

Between 1920 and 1922 he published another four novels. In 1920, the same year as *How They Did It*, he brought out *Conquest*. *Conquest* is an exploration of Irish nationalism, and is interesting both for its crossing of categories (the two central characters are, respectively, a Protestant Irish nationalist and an English-educated Catholic) and for O'Donovan's portrayal of a woman as the central revolutionary character who is prepared to sacrifice love for a political cause. A concern with the lives of ordinary Irish people lies at its heart. It ends powerfully with one of the characters in the trenches in France unwrapping his dinner from a scrap of newspaper and reading there that his only son has been shot by the English for his part in the Easter Rising.

Vocations followed in 1921, and in 1922 the last novel that Gerald wrote, *The Holy Tree*. The story unfolds through the mind of the heroine, an Irish village girl called Ann, who has been 'sold like a pig' to a man she doesn't love. Much of it is written as a stream of consciousness, following the twists and turns of her contradictory and conflicting thoughts and emotions as she struggles in the grip of an overwhelming sexual passion for an itinerant revolutionary nationalist.

Much later Rose Macaulay talked about Gerald's novels in a letter to Rosamond Lehmann: 'To me his real work, the one I love, is The Holy Tree, that he wrote in 1922, for me. In it he puts his whole philosophy of love, through the medium of Irish peasants – all the things he would say to me about love and life, all he felt about me, all we both knew. He wrote at the beginning of my copy the lines from Yeats about the holy tree. It was burnt up with my other books [Rose lost all her books when her flat was bombed in May 1941], but he gave it me again and inscribed it, so at least I have that, and can hear his voice talking to me through it.'

What is most extraordinary about the novel is Gerald O'Donovan's conflation of sexual and religious passion, expressed not just in the religio-erotic imagery but in the prayer-like rhythms of the prose. After Ann and her lover kiss for the first time, she feels that nothing has ever 'brought her closer to God'. It was 'like as if the soul of him had passed into her through his lips, and took some time to steady itself'. And, like a prayer of imprecation, 'His strength was in her limbs and in her mind and in her heart.' But Ann goes beyond identifying his strength as Christ-like. She jettisons similes in favour of a total identification of her lover with Christ. She experiences a fusion with him by a divine spark, 'the pattern of which, may God forgive her, she could find only in the Son of God Himself'.

The Holy Tree has perhaps not been accorded the critical interest it merits because of its Irishness; it might have seemed to critics too parochial in its concerns (the position of women in rural Ireland and the role of the Catholic Church in maintaining it) and too awkwardly naturalistic in its representation of Irish speech patterns. But of all Gerald O'Donovan's novels it is the most formally risk-taking, and the fractured stream-of-consciousness prose captures wonderfully the flighty, fractured nature of the protagonist's thought processes and the violence – the almost physical violence – of her emotions.

The year after *The Holy Tree* came out Heinemann published Marjorie Grant Cook's *Another Way of Love*. In this, her third novel, she painted a grim picture of rural French Canada at the turn of the century, and used it as the setting for a powerfully emotional story of unfulfilled maternal love which ends in bleak madness. And then Marjorie Grant Cook stopped writing novels. She seemed to have slipped altogether out of literary circles for more than a decade, before reappearing in 1934 with the first of a further five novels published under the name Caroline Seaford. However the opening up of the *Times Literary Supplement* archives revealed that although she had stopped writing novels she had not stopped writing altogether. The introduction to the *TLS Centenary Archive* opens with a paragraph on new contributors to the paper in the 1920s:

Among the most prolific of those who first began writing for the *TLS* in this period was Marjorie Grant Cook, who reviewed more than 1200 books in the 1920s and 30s, including work by many of the leading women writers of the day both in Britain and the USA. Cook was an early advocate of Willa Cather, wrote discriminatingly about the first novels of Rosamond Lehmann, and also reviewed books by Radclyffe Hall, Storm Jameson, Naomi Mitchison, Vita Sackville-West, Edith Wharton and Rebecca West. Her tastes were catholic: she also covered the work of popular authors such as Richmal Crompton and May Sinclair, and was the person who introduced Tolkien's *The Hobbit* – 'one long enchantment' – to readers of the *TLS*.

With more than sixty books a year to read and review, perhaps it is not so surprising that for more than a decade she produced no novels. Nonetheless, it is curious that both she and Gerald gave up writing fiction when they did. In the five years 1918–23 Rose, Marjorie and Gerald had, together, achieved an output of twelve novels. Then there was silence from Marjorie and Gerald, while Rose was already on the way to becoming one of the most prolific and successful novelists of the 1920s.

Why, after the achievement of *The Holy Tree*, did Gerald O'Donovan stop writing? Perhaps he felt he had exhausted Ireland as a topic, and that he had written out his pain and his passion. Or perhaps he simply had to sacrifice something: and that between Rose Macaulay, his hard-won family life and his writing, it was only his writing that he could do without.

CHAPTER SEVEN

An Earnest, Grown-up Working Woman

Thomas, the wind sings up the lane,
And Easter Day comes back again,
With the palm breaking to silver bud,
And lilting bells, and wet, brown, mud . . .

It may be dogs and men must part
Upon the edge of fairyland,
Wherein you run, whereout I stand.
If I should enter now with you,
And play there all this Easter through,
I might forget the world's a place
Where I must run a strenuous race,
And make my mark, and use my wit,
And earn my bread and do my bit.
I might forget that I am human,
An earnest, grown-up, working woman,
Writing books and reading news
Thinking thoughts and holding views,
Meeting friends and talking sense . . .

'To Thomas – An Easter Address' (*Three Days*)

i

Rose too paid a price. Gerald O'Donovan went for a year to
Italy with his wife and three children, and when he returned in

1921 Rose, after long struggle, admitted her love and committed herself to it. The price was her spiritual life within the Anglican communion. She felt herself, henceforth, outcast. The price was intimacy with her sisters Margaret and Jean and her cousin Dorothea Conybeare, who unanimously viewed her choice as 'a sad tragedy'. But for her life as a writer it was a price worth paying. Paradisal retreats continued to feature in her fiction of the 1920s, but Rose herself had chosen reality: the real thing, love, the body. It gave her writing a depth and a confidence that it had not had before.

'The twenties were, as decades go, a good decade,' she would write of this period in *Life Among the English* (1942); 'gay, decorative, intelligent, extravagant, cultured. There were booms in photography, Sunday film and theatre clubs, surrealism, steel furniture, faintly obscure poetry. Proust, James Joyce, dancing, rink skating, large paintings on walls of rooms.'

In 1922 T. S. Eliot's *The Waste Land* was published in the first issue of *Criterion*. Rose's later description of the recognition with which she read *The Waste Land* casts it as a de la Mare-style poem, as the kind of poetry that she herself had always liked and emulated: 'Here was the landscape one knew, had always known, sometimes without knowing it; here were the ruins of the soul; the shadowy dreams that lurked tenebriously in the cellars of consciousness; in the mysterious corridors and arcades of dreams, the wilderness that stretches not without but within . . .' But there are other kinds of images in *The Waste Land*: the images of a fragmented London, of broken bits of history surfacing, of London as shifting layers revealing a mosaic of a resolutely urban world. Images of sterility, of brokenness and lack of continuity: these form the underbelly of a decade that was gay, extravagant and cultured.

Rose analysed *The Waste Land* in terms of her own beliefs in the universality of event and emotion, saying, 'our generation has no monopoly, no increase, as has sometimes been proudly claimed, of complexity, or of waste lands'. She concluded provisionally that,

'T. S. Eliot's poetry is not characteristic of our age.' Then, uncomfortable with such a categorical statement, she modified it: 'except insofar as it has shaped the age's poetic expression'.

While *The Waste Land* describes the 'wilderness . . . within', the comedy of life that we see in Rose Macaulay's work of the 1920s is – as was suggested about her 1925 collection of essays *A Casual Commentary* – 'life deliberately seen from the outside only'. Or partly. The same reviewer wondered about that, concluding that 'perhaps she is not as cold and as detached as she would like to be'. In her work of the 1920s Rose perfected the role of detached observer, but at the same time there are hints of an inwardness that arise from the creative tensions and conflicts that she felt about her work: between its populism and its intellectualism, and between making money and serving art.

On the brink of this 'good decade', she offers us a self-portrait of the woman she wishes to become; characteristically self-mocking, and in the form that she was about to abandon as being unsuited to the new age's poetic expression:

> An earnest, grown-up, working woman,
> Writing books and reading news
> Thinking thoughts and holding views,
> Meeting friends and talking sense . . .

Like many grown-ups, and particularly like those who have led an intensely imaginative childhood life, she found it hard to believe that she was indeed an earnest, grown-up, working woman. Not that she was earnest, ever, but during the 1920s she became a successful novelist, journalist and what would come to be called a cultural critic. She grasped the post-war world and satirised it. The seven novels she published, from *Potterism* to *Keeping Up Appearances*, show a dazzling range of style, structure and tone; they manage to be serious as well as funny, accurate as well as fantastic, as certain in their creation of the absurd as in their representation of the poignant and the painful. And if, as

Alice Bensen says, she 'found the world full of subjects for raillery, she also found it full of occasions for delight'.

Virginia Woolf met Rose Macaulay for the first time in 1921 and wrote of her:

> Rose Macaulay dined here last week – something like a lean sheep dog in appearance – harum scarum – humble – too much of a professional, yet just on the intellectual side of the border. Might be religious though: mystical perhaps. Not at all dominating or impressive: I daresay she observes more than one thinks for. Clear pale mystical eyes. A kind of faded moon of beauty: oh & badly dressed. I don't suppose we shall ever meet for she lives with Royd Smith [*sic*], & somehow won't come to grips with us.

Rose would probably have agreed with Virginia Woolf that she was badly dressed – in those days she tended to favour patterned jumpers and was not exactly chic. She described her eyes as greeny-grey. A photograph taken in 1922 by Instead, was, she said, 'usually considered the only one I have which is at all like me'. While she may not have been fashionable she looks strikingly modern in comparison with many of the women writers whose faces look out from the pages of contemporary literary journals, with her short hair, bare neck and clear gaze rather than the frills and furs and elaborately styled hats.

Rose's relationship with the Woolfs and with the Hogarth Press was never entirely easy, despite the striking parallels between herself and Virginia Stephen. Both had been intelligent young women brought up in late Victorian intellectual households. Both had fathers who were writers and scholars. (Virginia's father was always referred to by Rose's parents as 'poor Leslie Stephen', because he had lost his faith.) Both had had passionate relationships with much-loved siblings. Both, indeed, had family secrets. Both had had the mish-mash of education that was the middle-class girl's portion at the time, while funds were provided to send brothers to public schools. Virginia's adored Thoby was at Clifton, unhappily, a year or two after Rose's adored Aulay had left. Rose had achieved Oxford, but left without taking a degree and had then turned her back on academic life. In young womanhood the paths of their lives diverged: Rose, while writing her first novels, remained, partly resentful but not openly rebellious, sheltered by the parental home; she was a long time growing up. Virginia Stephen lost her mother, her maternal half-sister and then her father and grew up much quicker. She was at the centre of the anti-establishment cultural avant-garde that was to become known as the Bloomsbury Circle, an artistic and literary group whose members such as Roger Fry and Lytton Strachey would be instrumental in dismantling the late Victorian and Edwardian ideology that tenaciously hung on in the face of the upheavals of the First World War. However, her own importance in the development of twentieth-century writing was not recognised until well after her death. In the early 1920s, when she and Rose met, Rose Macaulay was already a successful, fêted writer, whereas Virginia Woolf was almost unknown outside her own circle. But she had something that Rose Macaulay felt she herself lacked: intellectual gravitas. Virginia Woolf scorned the literary circles in which Rose moved when they first met, 'the riff-raff of South Kensington culture' who used to come to Naomi Royde-Smith's Thursday evening gatherings. Rose felt that scorn. Each, then, had something the other wanted and lacked.

Potterism: A Tragi-farcical Tract had come out in May 1920. It was the first of Rose Macaulay's novels to be published by William Collins, who went on to publish all the rest of her fiction. Though Gerald was one of their chief readers, it is not clear how closely he was involved with Rose's books once they were submitted. His involvement came at an earlier stage. As she said, 'I always talked over my novels with my companion, who stimulated my invention . . .'

Potterism is an attack on the 'Potter Press', loosely based on the press empire of Lords Northcliffe and Beaverbrook, for the untruthful sentimentality of its representation of reality. Potter himself rises to power through the lies propagated by his press during the 'great opportunity' of the war, as 'With energy and wholeheartedness it cheered, comforted and stimulated the people. It never failed to say how well the Allies were getting on, how much ammunition they had, how many men, what indomitable tenacity and cheerful spirits enlivened the trenches. The correspondents it employed wrote home rejoicing; its leading articles were noble hymns of praise.' One of the epigraphs to the book is by Samuel Johnson: 'My dear friend, clear your mind of cant . . . Don't think foolishly.' Potterism goes further, tainting all thought and action, corrupting everyone. The only character in the novel who is uncorrupted, a Jewish journalist called Arthur Gideon, insists everyone is, to a greater or lesser extent, a Potterite: 'Every profiteer,' he says, 'every sentimentalist, every muddler. Every artist directly he thinks of his art as something marketable, something to bring him fame; every scientist or scholar (if there are any) who fakes a fact in the interest of his theory; every fool who talks through his hat without knowing . . .'

A small group set themselves up as an Anti-Potterite League and meet regularly in the 1917 Club (a fashionably radical club of which Rose herself was a member). There are five of them – the Potter twins, Jane and Johnny, clever children of Lord Potter himself and his wife Leila Yorke, writer of bestselling romantic novels – and their three friends Arthur Gideon, a quiet and rational chemist called Katherine Varick, and a well-connected young clergyman called Laurence Juke.

Rose Macaulay experimented with five separate voices to structure the novel: first person accounts from Arthur Gideon, Katherine Varick, Laurence Juke and Leila Yorke, framed by two sections 'Told by R. M.', third person narratives that show Rose's sophisticated playfulness with the role of omniscient author.

Quite as striking as the formal experimentation is the critique that the novel provides of what is presented as widespread anti-Semitism amongst the English middle and literary classes. Rose had explored this before, in a sub-plot of *The Lee Shore*, but here, in a bold move, she makes a favourite plot device of her childhood reading – a wrongful accusation – into a trial of Arthur Gideon's Jewishness. The reviewer in the *Times Literary Supplement* felt that the farcical element was prioritised over the tragical, to the overall detriment of the novel, pointing out that Gideon's tragedy – he is killed in Russia while trying to protect a Jewish family from an anti-Semitic mob – fails to move the reader because we don't see into 'the conflicts of his heart'.

The power of the popular press and of popular fiction to sensationalise and to sentimentalise real life remained a concern over the next few years. Rose increasingly came to question her own part in it; but here in *Potterism* she is sufficiently light-hearted to play around with the conventions of the kind of writing she is satirising. The 'mystery part', Rose wrote, that is, the murder of which Arthur Gideon stands accused, was written 'for my brother, who said "For goodness sake write a book in which they stop talking & commit a murder or something." Stop talking they didn't – but they did manage a kind of semi-murder, of which I am rather proud, though I am told by some reviewers that it oughtn't to be there at all. Reviewers will say that kind of thing, bless them.' And she continues: 'Yes, the world is full of Potters – but, not being Gideon, and, in fact, being really one myself, I don't much mind – at least I do mind, but resignedly and without rancour.'

The criticism in the *Times Literary Supplement* is fair: for *Potterism* is, as its subtitle proclaims, a tract. But it was a tract that touched so cleverly and topically on the post-war excesses of the popular press that it was an immediate success, not just in Britain but also in America.

No wonder Virginia Woolf was cautious in her approach to this bestselling novelist. A later description shows Virginia's mix of perspicacity, jealousy and uneasiness towards Rose, along with a desire to be fair. Again she comments on Rose's leanness and feyness, but this time she allows her an essential writerly core:

> Then Rose – too chattery chittery at first go off; lean as a rake, wispy, & frittered. Some flimsy smartness & taint of the flimsy glittery literary about her: but this was partly nerves, I think; & she felt us alien & observant doubtless . . . After all, she has no humbug about her; is exactly on a par as far as conventions go, I imagine; only frosted & rather cheaply gilt superficially with all that being asked to speak at dinners, to give opinions to newspapers, & so on; lunching at the League of Nations; dining with Iolo Williams, meeting Jack Squire who has grown whiskers & looks like a verger.

They went on to talk about liking people, and liking books, and liking pictures, and Rose, recorded Virginia Woolf, 'showed up rather well in argument, & maintained that a book is a subjective thing; she attacks authority in literature. But people know about painting as it is a more technical art. Then she said (this makes me think she will wish to be called Rose) how she had dreamt she was staying with us in a cottage in Surrey, a 15th century house, full of old beams & candle lit.' Virginia Woolf ends her account of Rose with a generous summing-up: 'In some light she has the beautiful eyes of all us distinguished women writers; the refinement; the clearness of cut; the patience; & humbleness.' And a final qualification: 'It is her voice & manner that make one edgy.'

Virginia Woolf '. . . had so much fun, and humour, and a kind of genial friendliness', Rose wrote to Hamilton Johnson to correct his opinion of her, 'though also much malicious comment (discreetly *not* published)'. Not published then, in the early 1950s, but published now. Rose would surely have taken in her stride even the cattiest comments that Virginia made about her. Rose's qualities as a writer and as an intellectual went some way to redeem what Virginia Woolf judged to be her poor clothes

sense and her voice and manner. But there was nothing to mitigate Virginia's harsh view of Naomi Royde-Smith, who not only
wore dangling earrings but was too plump; she was the epitome
of flimsy glittery literary and was altogether beyond the Woolfian
pale.

When Rose Macaulay and Virginia Woolf met in 1921, Rose
was spending a night or two each week in London, where she
rented a room from Naomi at 44 Prince's Gardens, a square of
Georgian terraced houses around a tree-filled garden off
Exhibition Road in South Kensington. She and Naomi hosted
regular Thursday evening literary soirées of fifty or sixty people.
Storm Jameson, newly arrived in London from Whitby in the
north of England, was introduced to these events by her publisher at Constable:

> Naomi I found a little formidable with her air of a younger more
> affable Queen Victoria. But Rose Macaulay, who shared the flat
> with her, had been kind on my first evening, and I had no fear of
> her, nor of her salty tongue. She was enchanting to watch, a
> narrow head covered with small curls, like a Greek head in a
> museum, with that way she had of speaking in arpeggios, and the
> lively hands, the small arched nose and pale deep-set eyes . . . One
> Thursday evening, I watched her with Arnold Bennett. He hung
> over her, mouth slightly open, like a great fish mesmerized by the
> flickering tongue of a water-snake.

Like Virginia Woolf, Storm Jameson, too, cast a critical eye.
'None of the currents setting towards the future troubled this
urbane backwater,' she wrote in *Journey from the North* (1969).
'The great figures who sometimes glided through were none of
them rebels – Arnold Bennett but not D. H. Lawrence, Eddie
Marsh, not T. S. Eliot, not even a young Raymond Mortimer . . .',
but her friendship with Rose, begun the evening that Rose was
kind to her, never faltered.

Naomi and Rose were very close in the early 1920s, in the days

when Rose was openly going around with Gerald O'Donovan.
There were weekly lunches hosted by J. Reeve Brooke in his
rooms at the top of Mitre Court in the Temple. Naomi's
Westminster Gazette office was just round the corner; Rose and
Gerald were both regular guests. Reeve Brooke, a cousin of Dick
and Rupert's, was married to Dorothy Lamb, sister of Henry
Lamb the painter, acolyte of Augustus John. Dorothy was hugely
sociable and a great party-goer. Between January and May 1922
she noted in her diary five lunch dates with Rose, two dinners,
and two teas, and a similar number of dates with Naomi.
'Lunched and razzled around with Naomi,' is a typical diary
entry. She and Naomi often went with Rose to visit 'Mrs
Macaulay' in Beaconsfield, and Naomi became so close to Grace
that she referred to herself as Grace's 'imitation daughter'. Gerald
too was a regular visitor to Beaconsfield. Rose wrote to Sylvia
Lynd in 1920 to praise her recently published poetry collection
The Goldfinches, saying 'Jerry O'Donovan was reading it aloud to
my mother and me the weekend before last – he liked it too,
immensely'. At this point, while Gerald was still writing novels,
Rose exerted herself on behalf of his books; Sylvia Lynd and her
husband Robert were powerful figures in the literary world.
Sylvia was a poet and literary critic. Her husband Robert, pro-
Fenian son of a Belfast Nonconformist minister, was literary
editor of the *News Chronicle*, where so heavy was the drinking
amongst the journalists that the proprietor arranged a fire alarm
to ring in his room every time a whisky and soda was ordered
from the canteen. From 1913 to 1945 Robert Lynd wrote a
weekly essay in the *New Statesman* under the sobriquet 'Y.Y.'.

Rose was anxious that Gerald should be well regarded by the
Lynds. At the end of 1921, after Sylvia had reviewed *Vocations*,
Rose urged her to come to one of the soirées at 44 Prince's
Gardens: 'I expect you'll meet Gerald O'Donovan . . . he wants to
meet you, I know. He liked your review of him, but has this bee
in his bonnet about not being thought propagandist or biassed
about anything to do with Catholicism, and is sensitive about it –

it's really merely that he loves the Church still and doesn't like people to think he is up against it. You'll like his next book, I think [*The Holy Tree*]: it is really extraordinarily fine, and even beautiful – and up against nothing.'

The Lynds were extremely hospitable and Rose soon became a regular guest at their house in Keats Grove, Hampstead. It was the beginning of a long and close friendship with Sylvia. Rose's enthusiasm for parties waxed stronger the older she became. She also gave parties: not in her flat, where she carefully guarded her privacy, but by inviting people to dine in restaurants with her. Virginia and Leonard Woolf attended one of these 'pot-house' evenings in 1926, never to repeat the experience. Leonard had just – temporarily – resigned the editorship of the *Nation & Athenaeum*, and Virginia was feeling deeply antagonistic towards the journalists and writers associated with it. She was scathing about the fellow-guests: 'There were 10 second rate writers in second rate dress clothes, Lynds, Goulds, O'Donovan . . .' She described the occasion to Vita Sackville-West as 'a ghastly party', and recorded the unsatisfactory exchange she had had with Gerald: 'in the whirl of meaningless words I thought Mr O'Donovan said Holy Ghost, whereas he said "The Whole Coast" and I asking "Where is the Holy Ghost?" got the reply "Where ever the sea is" "Am I mad, I thought, or is this wit?" "The Holy Ghost?" I repeated. "The Whole Coast" he shouted, and so we went on, in an atmosphere so repellent that it became, like the smell of bad cheese, repulsively fascinating . . .'

This must have been one of the last occasions when Rose and Gerald were seen together in public. Some time in the mid-1920s there was a painful break-up between Rose and Naomi over indiscretion on Naomi's part about Rose and Gerald. There is no record of what the specific indiscretion was, but it seems to have happened around the time of publication of *Crewe Train* in 1926. In the novel Evelyn Gresham, one in a line of romantic novelists who are careless with the truth, stretching back through *Potterism*'s Leila Yorke to Mrs Venables in *The Furnace*, stands accused of malicious invention, nearly breaking up a marriage by spreading rumours about a non-existent adulterous affair and its consequent pregnancy. Naomi suggested that Evelyn Gresham was a portrait of the writer Viola Garvin, a friend of Rose's, to which accusation Rose replied: 'I fear that this means Naomi is telling people it is. It's not a portrait in the least, it only has perhaps, a touch of Mrs Garvin's mannerisms and way of talk . . . As to the scandal-mongering, Naomi does much more of that herself.' Rose was perhaps not entirely innocent; but she goes on to accuse Naomi of indulging in precisely the kind of dangerous gossip shown in the novel. Naomi initiates the subject and then 'what she hears and what she tells are strangely like, I notice, sometimes'.

Naomi had no need to invent an affair between Rose and Gerald: perhaps she spoke of it too freely. It seems unlikely that we will ever know what she did say that caused the rift. But a rift occurred, and Naomi, who began publishing novels in the 1920s, later developed a paranoia that Rose, and Rose's circle of literary friends, were plotting against her and bribing literary editors not to review her books.

From this time Rose became much more careful to protect her relationship with Gerald from the public gaze. But by then a pattern had been established that allowed Rose into Gerald's home life. Throughout the 1920s and 1930s she would have lunch every other Sunday with the O'Donovans at their house in Albury, Surrey. On the Sundays she wasn't there Gerald would spend hours on the phone to her after lunch working out the day's crossword with her. Although Rose's name does not appear in Beryl O'Donovan's formal memoirs, it does appear with some frequency in Beryl's appointment diaries for those years. The same is the case with Marjorie Grant Cook: tea, lunch or supper with 'Miss Macaulay', 'Miss Cook', 'Marjorie' or 'Rose'. Which doesn't exactly fit with the way that Brigid, the eldest O'Donovan child, remembered them. She thought of Rose and Marjorie, she said, as people who were 'fond of him [Gerald], fond of us, and not so fond of my mother'. Gerald and Rose had a lot to talk about, Brigid maintained, as Rose provided the intellectual stimulation for Gerald that was lacking in his own family; she seemed to Brigid as a child to be 'a faithful family friend', which 'indeed she turned out to be'.

While her affair with Gerald created a distance – not a great distance, but a withholding of intimacy – between Rose and her sisters, she gained through it another kind of intimacy. Rose was close to the O'Donovan children throughout their childhoods, and achieved some of the domestic pleasures of family life without having to be a wife.

Brigid always denied that there had been an affair between her father and Rose. Beryl never admitted it. Perhaps welcoming Rose into the family afforded Beryl a sense that she was at least partly in control.

Whatever façade was put on to everyone's satisfaction in the O'Donovan house in Albury, Rose and Gerald were able to be together without pretence on their trips abroad. These, starting in the early 1920s, became more frequent as Rose hid him from her public life in London. Sometimes she would go off on holiday with the Reeve Brookes; sometimes she would accept a working commission – she was a co-lecturer with Gustav Holst on a Lunn tour in Switzerland in 1925 – and, abroad already, would simply go on to meet Gerald.

Gerald needed to make no excuses to his family for his frequent disappearances. He brought up his children in the belief that he was a target for the ire of the powerful Catholic establishment, and that his family must never know what work he was engaged on for fear they would 'let it out' – which seems a remarkably convenient position for a man who wants to be away from home with no questions asked. And there were other excuses for him to be away: the Italian contacts he had made after the war, and later on, in the 1930s, his work for Czech refugees. Beryl probably preferred not to know the details of his travels abroad.

Rose's postcards home to Margaret and Jean, and to publishers and editors, reveal her itineraries with no mention of Gerald. But she recalled some of the places they visited on their 'secret stolen travels' in an elegiac story she wrote in 1942, when she knew that Gerald was dying. In 'Miss Anstruther's Letters' Miss Anstruther has lost her lover and all the letters he wrote to her. She tries to recreate the past through memory:

> The balcony where they dined at the Foix inn, leaning over the green river, eating trout just caught in it. The little wild strawberries at Andorra la Vieja, the mountain pass that ran down to it from Ax, the winding road down into Seo d'Urgel and Spain. Lerida, Zaragoza, little mountain towns in the Pyrenees, Jaca, Saint Jean Pied-du-Port, the little harbour at Collioure, with its painted boats, morning coffee out of red cups at Villefranche, tramping about France in a hot July; truffles in the *place* at Périgueux, the stream that rushed steeply down the village street at Florac, the frogs croaking in the hills about it, the gorges of the Tarn, Rodez with its spacious *place* and plane trees, the little walled town of Cordes with the inn courtyard a jumble of sculptures, altar-pieces from churches, and ornaments from châteaux; Lisieux, with ancient crazy-floored inn, huge four-poster, and preposterous little saint (before the grandiose white temple in her honour had arisen on the hill outside the town), villages in the Haute-Savoie, jumbled among mountain rocks over brawling streams, the motor bus over the Alps down into Susa and Italy . . .

These are the places that Rose and Gerald went to together.

For Rose the regular trips abroad were not only a way of being happily with Gerald out of the way of gossips and away from the constraints of being a 'faithful family friend'. Abroad had always been an important part of her fiction, but whereas before it had been tinged with nostalgia for a childhood world, now the warmth and the colours and the sunshine of the Mediterranean countries fed the vision of the South Sea islands of which her imagination was so fond, and became the counterpart to the chattery-chittery metropolitan post-war world that she anatomised.

Meanwhile it had become essential for Rose to have the privacy of a flat of her own. She was briefly at an address in the Edgware Road and then moved to St Andrews Mansions in Dorset Street, just south of the Marylebone Road and west of Baker Street, a quiet flat looking out on to a quadrangle. She would remain in the W1 postal code for the rest of her life, a truly central Londoner.

Settled in London, beginning to make a name for herself, Rose Macaulay at the outset of her post-war career was generous with her encouragement of the younger women writers coming up behind her.

'The beginning of my life as the greater part of it has been since,' wrote Elizabeth Bowen in *Coming to London*, 'was when I was asked to tea to meet Rose Macaulay at the University Women's Club: this I owed to her friend, my headmistress, Olive Willis. In youth, and I suppose always, it is kindness with a touch of imaginative genius that one rates most highly: this I had from Rose. She lit up a confidence I had never had: having written stories, I showed them to her.' Rose introduced Elizabeth Bowen to Naomi Royde-Smith, who bought her first story and published it in the *Saturday Westminster*. She described the 'memorable' Thursday evening parties, showing none of Storm Jameson's intellectual discrimination: 'Inconceivably, I found myself in the same room as Edith Sitwell, Walter de la Mare, Aldous Huxley . . .' When there were enough of Bowen's stories Rose commended them to Sidgwick & Jackson: *Encounters* was published in the summer of 1923. Later on there was trouble with Sidgwick & Jackson, who turned down *The Hotel*, but demanded the right to retain options in Elizabeth Bowen's next two novels (perhaps having learned the hard way from their experience with Rose). This elicited a flurry of advice from Rose. 'I have been talking to my most trusted friend about it today; he used to publish, and knows all about publishing ethics.' Three pages counselling the use of cool reason and persuasion are followed by: 'My friend says, "If it was me, I should probably say to Sidgwick, Go to hell; anyhow I am going to Constable's." But you might, if you preferred them, use gentler methods . . .' The friendship between the two women survived Gerald's hot-headed advice. When Constable brought out *The Hotel* in 1927 Rose replied to Elizabeth's anxiety that it was too 'gushing': 'I doubt if the writer of your books could gush, even if they tried hard. That is partly the quality which is so attractive in them – their detached restraint and humour, I mean – so civilized and refreshing!' Writing of *The Death of the Heart* in 1938 Rose told her it was 'a book that gets under the skin', and a decade later praised the 'texture of the writing' in *The Heat of the Day*, 'which I suppose I really care for more than any other quality in a book'.

Vera Brittain was another young woman encouraged and helped by Rose at the beginning of her career, although the friendship, unlike that with Elizabeth Bowen, did not survive. They met in December 1921. Rose had offered to run a bookstall at a fund-raising bazaar at the University Women's Club for her old college, Somerville. Vera, ambitious and halfway through writing her first novel, volunteered for this stall. She wrote to her friend Winifred Holtby that she was 'terrified' of meeting Rose. But, 'In the end the bazaar proved much less alarming than I had feared.' Always supremely conscious of dress, Vera described herself as 'painstakingly and elaborately dressed in brown marocain and a brown velvet picture hat with a flame-coloured "glycerine" feather trailing over the edge'. Her sartorial judgement of Rose, 'far more appropriately clad in a neat blue coat-frock', differed from Virginia Woolf's. She went on:

> I stood entranced and watched Rose Macaulay casually convers-
> ing with the half-legendary gods of literary London. John

Buchan was there, brisk and unpretentious, and the bluff and cordial Hugh Walpole, over whose new novel, *The Cathedral*, I was to laugh and weep so rapturously in the next few months. It was too wonderful, too incredible, actually to stand within speaking distance of these Olympian presences. But best of all, perhaps, was the quiet, fatigued moment in which, as we were clearing up the stall, Miss Macaulay asked me what I meant to do with myself now that I'd gone down from Oxford, and I answered, breathlessly daring, that I was trying to be a writer and was half-way through an Oxford novel entitled *The Dark Tide*.

The next year, reading that *Dangerous Ages* had won the Prix Femina-Vie Heureuse (the prize was 1,000 French francs), Vera wrote to congratulate Rose, and received almost by return a note asking after the progress of *The Dark Tide*. It had been turned down by two publishing houses. Rose wrote to J. D. Beresford, chief editor at William Collins, on Vera's behalf, and when it was turned down by him she invited Vera round to discuss his response.

What she really thought of the raw crudities which even a cursory glance revealed, I now shudder to imagine, but she was too considerate, and too wise, to suggest those fundamental reconstructions which maturity and literary experience alone can make. Her advice enabled me to make numerous improvements in such details of style and syntax as were capable of amendment, and I carried away a glowing memory of hot crumpets and brisk, incisive conversation upon which I relied exclusively for stimulus in the disheartening months that followed . . . But for Rose Macaulay I might well have given up . . .

Their friendship did not survive the publication of *Testament of Youth* in 1933. According to Vera, Rose was cold and hostile and referred to the book, and all autobiographies, as 'vulgar', taking particular exception to the account of her kindness to Vera over *The Dark Tide*. The account in *Testament of Youth* shows Rose as a professional writer rather than in any personal light, but by then Rose's reticence about anything remotely personal had become almost neurotic ('why should we tell one another about ourselves?' she asked). Perhaps she had a more general criticism of Vera Brittain's rhetoric in *Testament* passing as 'truth'; or perhaps their relationship couldn't develop beyond the stage of mentor and younger woman. Vera Brittain was notorious for the difficulty she had in sustaining friendships with other women, except for Winifred Holtby.

Their paths continued to cross. In the late 1930s Vera would complain of Rose Macaulay cutting her at Peace Pledge Union meetings, staring through and beyond her with those mystical eyes that Virginia Woolf had noted.

Dangerous Ages, the novel that won the Prix Femina-Vie Heureuse, opens with Neville on her forty-third birthday getting up at dawn to swim in the river, then climb a tree and take stock of her life. Rose Macaulay was forty when *Dangerous Ages* was published in 1921. It was not so very long ago that Uncle Edward had come visiting Southernwood and found Rose and Margaret in the treetops. She had years of swimming ahead of her, in rivers, lakes, seas, ponds, with other people – a sister, a lover, a friend – or, just as happily, alone. But there the identification ends, for Neville is a woman who sacrificed her own life for marriage. Twenty years previously she gave up her medical training to marry charming Rodney and bring up charming Kay and Gerda. Charm does not count for nothing in Rose Macaulay's novels; but nor does it count for quite enough. There is something very clear-eyed about the angle at which this marriage is viewed: Rodney has sacrificed nothing, Neville has sacrificed everything. She decides, now that her charming children are grown, to take up her studies where she left off, but the realist Macaulay knows that women, even in fiction, can't have everything. Neville fails in her endeavours.

Potterism featured a sister/brother pair, similar to the pairs or doubles of Rose Macaulay's pre-war novels such as *The Valley Captives*; in *Dangerous Ages* there are three sisters, and there is something, a little bit at least, of Rose herself in each of them. Closest perhaps to the author's life is that of Nan. She is a writer and is unmarried; the two are not unrelated. She is both physically and emotionally reckless, and sets the pace for the younger generation, for Neville's children. After losing the man she thinks she loves to her niece Gerda she goes off to Rome with her married lover, an artist. The third sister, Pamela, chooses to live in what is described in the novel as a 'mothering' relationship with her close friend Frances.

Pamela and Frances get on quietly and competently with their careers, providing each other with companionship, support and – although it is not stated as such – love. Pamela is allowed the last word in the novel, musing on life, and a very Rose-ish word it is: 'I certainly don't see quite what all the fuss is about.' This is the persona that Rose projected all the years that she was secretly loving Gerald, and so successful was it that it fooled many of her contemporaries. To say that it was a projected persona is not to say that it was simply put on in order to deceive; it was a part of Rose, and it appears over and over again in the sympathetic, intelligent, amused middle-aged women in her fiction. As Rose's love affair with Gerald became an ever more closely guarded secret, so she was able to hide her own feminine self from herself. She no longer had to bother with it. She could concentrate instead on being a writer.

The three sisters in *Dangerous Ages* illustrate different possibilities for middle-class women, and with each sister the reader is made aware of the losses concomitant with their choices as well as the gains. There is a generalised anxiety running through the book which reflects the post-war anxiety about women that was expressed in endless newspaper articles about 'the new woman' and 'the woman question', and which informed such novels as Marjorie Grant Cook's *Latchkey Ladies*. Women's lives were no more shaken up by the war than men's lives, but they were shaken up differently. A whole generation of men had been wiped out; a generation of women were left alone and independent whether they wanted to be or not. Questions about marriage, independence, work, love and sex are explored in *Dangerous Ages*. There are no happy endings because after the war there were no happy endings; there were some things, simply, that worked better than others.

When we see Neville comparing looking at her mother to the medieval memento mori of the skull, we realise that it is less a fear of ageing than a realisation that she has made the same choices as her mother has. But her sisters Nan and Pamela are the first of many strong women of middle age who stride through the pages of Rose Macaulay's fiction.

Despite the anxiety about marriage there is something high-spirited about this novel. Rose was working on it in the autumn of 1920, when Gerald and his family were living in Italy and he was making frequent trips on his own back to England. Rose may not, yet, have made her mind up irrevocably about Gerald, but in this novel it is as if she had decided on the course her life would take. Rose knew what she wanted: writing, independence, and love without domesticity. Nan makes a choice in *Dangerous Ages*. It is a choice not so much for an adulterous affair as a choice against marriage and motherhood. Perhaps Rose's decision to embrace rather than to deny her love for Gerald was also a way of keeping herself safe from marriage.

The literary success of *Dangerous Ages*, which competed with Katherine Mansfield's *Bliss, and Other Stories* for the Prix Femina-Vie Heureuse, built on the commercial success of *Potterism*. There were three novels in the next three years. In September 1921, just after the publication of *Dangerous Ages*, Rose went to Geneva to report for *Time and Tide* on the meeting of the League of Nations. She was and remained a passionate supporter of the aims and ideals of the League, describing it in 1920 as 'one of the few hopes for this troublesome world', and, like Vera Brittain, spoke and wrote on its behalf and on behalf of the support group the League of Nations Union. She used the Geneva conference for the setting of *Mystery at Geneva*, a parodic detective thriller, in which the delegates to a meeting of the League of Nations disappear at an alarming rate. The mystery is not just about what is happening to them all; it also concerns the narrator, a journalist on the *British Bolshevist*, who turns out to be not what he/she seems. The *Times Literary Supplement* commended Rose's accurate evocation of the atmosphere of conferences, of her playing around with national types and characteristics saying, 'the delight of the book lies in her comic wit playing over the surface of these things, hitting off here an Irishman, there a Turk, here a band of Latin-Americans, there a Rumanian lady, here a stenographer, there a journalist . . .'

Mystery came out in 1922, followed in 1923 by *Told by an Idiot*, her picture of forty years of English social, political and religious history embodied in the fortunes of the Garden family, whose head, 'poor papa', is constantly losing and finding his faith. The *New Republic* thought that, flippancies aside, it 'might be used as a textbook in modern social history'. It was Marjorie Grant Cook who reviewed this for the *Times Literary Supplement*: 'a sympathetic as well as a brilliant book,' she wrote. She went on to make some general points about Rose Macaulay's fiction: 'The same men and women recur in all Miss Macaulay's books, strongly marked types rather than individuals. They are now older and more sophisticated, cooler and wittier than the charm-ing young things who vagabonded through Italy before the war . . . The Gardens, talkative, truthful, are familiar Macaulay characters, not warm-blooded, highly entertaining. They matter less than the scenes through which they move, less than their projector's sayings about them, her gay disquisitions, her enchanting excursions into woods and fields, the sea, and, rarely, the secret places of the heart.' This is a perspicacious analysis of Rose Macaulay's relationship as author with the characters she creates, and her brief glimpses into 'the secret places of the heart', but there are two characters in *Told by an Idiot* who do 'matter' as much as the scenes through which they move. There is Rome Garden, who, as Alice Bensen puts it, 'represents the spirit of detachment, the ironic eye, the latest form taken in Rose Macaulay's fiction by that aspect of her own personality that was first projected in Rosamund Ilbert'. And there is the child Imogen, the author's child-self. At the end of *Told by an Idiot*, Imogen sails away on a P & O liner to spend a year in the Pacific Islands.

It is the time of 'Debris', as the section is called in the novel, at the end of the war. Europe is in chaos. Old certainties have been smashed. Imogen is fleeing the broken world she was brought up in, and also the broken pieces of her heart. She is leaving behind her a London where 'all values and all meanings were fluid, were as windy clouds, drifting and dissolving into strange shapes'. But she is also fleeing the mess of personal relationships, a life in which they were 'too tangled; clear thought was drowned in desire'. Imogen, like her author, loves where she should not.

Imogen sails away to a paradise island to escape drowning in desire. But as England is left behind, the island's attractions become meaningless. 'Parrakeets? Bread-fruit? Lagoons and coral reefs? Oh, God, she cared for none of them.' She replays her beloved's voice in her mind: 'To leave me for so long . . . you can't mean to do it . . .'

Orphan Island, Rose's sixth novel in six years, came out in 1924 and is set on the South Sea island to which Imogen sails at the end of *Told by an Idiot*, where a group of orphans had been shipwrecked seventy years previously. The survivors and their offspring have evolved a class-based society under the rigid if alcohol-fuelled reign of Miss Charlotte Smith, a mid-Victorian governess. D. L. Murray, editor of the *Times Literary Supplement*, described the 'philosophic motive' in the novel as '. . . to see how far the postulates of the Victorian social order would hold good, if put to the stark challenge of nature'. He felt it didn't work because of the 'fatuous' nature of Miss Smith's regime. But it can be read as a satire on the prejudices and mores of post-war England as much as on the heyday of Empire. It wasn't just the mid-Victorians who believed in Great Britain as the 'world's hub, peculiarly chosen by the Deity as the centre of his beneficent purposes towards his universe'. Rose later told Hamilton Johnson: 'It was the one of my novels I enjoyed writing most (except *They Were Defeated*), because I indulged in it my morbid passion for coral islands, lagoons, bread-fruit and coconut trees, and island fauna and flora.' One of the pleasantries she allowed herself was to have the black slaves called Zacharies, after her abolitionist great-great-uncle.

Six very different novels in six years; she was pushing at the form, experimenting with this and that, but remaining in touch with her readers. Her fictional output was considerable, and there was even a play, *Bunkum*, ('bunkum' covers most things, according to the heroine Molly: women's journalism, political journalism, book reviewing, differences between girls and men). 'What else would one do with one's thoughts?' Rose said to Virginia Woolf, who was struggling with her 'python' of a book – *To the Lighthouse* – and wondering aloud why she let herself in for such a struggle. But fiction-writing wasn't enough for the woman thinking thoughts and holding views: the thoughts and views were expressed in articles and essays as well.

For all her mockery of the popular press, Rose Macaulay wrote extensively in the inter-war years for the daily papers as well as for the *Spectator*, *Time and Tide* and other literary and political journals. Like many writers she found that working in different forms provided a creative cross-fertilisation; the subjects that inspired, amused and intrigued her appear in her essays and journalism as well as in her novels.

Her first collection of essays was published by Methuen in the autumn of 1925 as *A Casual Commentary*. The wealth of religions from which the thinking – or doubting – person can choose provides the theme of 'How to Choose a Religion', one of the two introductory essays. And the theme of the other essay, 'New

Years', parallels a theme, or melody, that runs through *Told by an Idiot*: an 'infinite variety in sameness'.

'How to Choose a Religion' provides fertile ground for Rose Macaulay's comic gift. She runs through the various branches of Christianity, weighing up their attractions or otherwise. The Roman Catholic branch knows the truth and tells it to you, which, she points out, many people like, but 'a good deal of attendance at services is expected'. The Orthodox has, like the Catholic branch, tradition and dignity but 'its clergy do not always look what our novelists call well-groomed'; they keep Easter 'with great enthusiasm, but at the wrong time'. As Calvinists believe in 'severe, prolonged, and inevitable punishment after death for nearly everyone', then if you are unlucky enough to be one you should try hard to believe you're one of the few exceptions to this rule. 'Many Calvinists,' Rose concludes, 'succeed in believing this.' Her own prejudices are for the Anglican Church, and for Quakers. The drawback of the latter is having to busy oneself with good causes: 'you start funds for the distressed and food centres for the hungry (particularly in Central Europe and specially for those with whom your country has recently had differences), and try to get laws altered'. But, 'Quakers make the best chocolate.'

The introductory essays, 'New Years' and 'How to Choose a Religion', lead on to a section, 'Some Other Problems of Life'. In 'Problems of Social Life' Rose asks: how can a hostess get one of a married couple to come to dinner without the other, boring one? You might think she was sailing close to the wind there, with a wife-free Gerald attending dinner parties with her. Her suggested remedy for an unwanted wife owes much to P. G. Wodehouse, whose characters are forever sending themselves telegrams in order to get them out of sticky scrapes involving aunts, girls or members of Parliament: a 'decoy' telegram is to be dispatched: 'come at once, your mother (or other known relative) dying'. Or, less Wodehousian because less innocent, a drugged cocktail to be offered on arrival, so that the wife spends the evening asleep.

Housekeeping is only one of the many problems of a woman's life: 'At the worst, a house unkept cannot be so distressing as a life unlived.' There's also beauty (how to acquire it and how to retain it), sartorial problems, the chief of these, for women, being 'how to dress well on expenditure insufficient for that purpose'. Rose Macaulay's sharpness of observation is well illustrated in her pursuit of this subject. 'You must either dress badly,' she writes, 'or spend more money than you wish to – in most cases more than you have got. It is a simple alternative, and every woman must make up her own mind which she intends to adopt.' Then the punchline: 'Many women adopt both.'

In these essays Rose Macaulay moves with confidence through her arguments. She is sharp and partial and funny. 'There is a good deal of the eighteenth century poise about her,' said the *Times Literary Supplement* reviewer, whose review was entitled 'The Detached Observer'. It is as if her own detachment from family and Church, and her distance from the conventional married woman's life gave her this poise and assurance. The essays are still fun to read; and indeed some passages make you think that Rose Macaulay was right: there is nothing new under the sun. Consider especially those about cooking and cleaning ('A tradition has now for long been established that cooking and cleaning are woman's work. As these occupations are among the most tiresome which humanity has to endure, this tradition is very unfortunate for women'); about women's magazines ('Why look lined and unlovely? Is your neck too fat? Is it too thin?'); and about letters to the press (divided into those who write admiring letters, beginning, 'Sir, As always, you have taken the only right line on this question,' those who write disagreeable letters, beginning 'Sir, Since the disgraceful article in your last issue, my wife, myself and fifteen others have all given up your paper,' and those who broach some topic other than the rightness or wrongness of the editor, and begin, 'Sir, My small dog has recently taken to whistling between his teeth. I wonder if any of your readers have had a similar experience with their pets' . . .).

Overall the essays provide a vivid picture of metropolitan life in the early 1920s. There is a wonderful fantasy of a day in the life of a Londoner, inspired by one of the 'Sayings of the Week' in the *Observer*: 'The only real crime is not to live life to the full.' Rose Macaulay muses on how her life looks 'a sadly criminal affair', for it is far from lived to the full. She has failed, amongst many other things, to play mah-jong, to dye her hair, to inject cocaine, to make a bead purse or a will, to stand for Parliament, to adopt a child or a pet monkey. To remedy this she plans the perfect crimeless day, starting by consuming coffee, chocolate *and* tea in bed; then she will knock down a policeman and stone the squirrels in Hyde Park, visit an opium den in Limehouse, or a Christian Science Hall, or Scotland Yard with a confession of murder, or Downing Street disguised as a foreign ambassador. What are the lunch opportunities? The Ritz, a little place in Greek Street, or a Lyons soda fountain; then, after lunch, 'I may or may not have a trip in an aeroplane, a cocaine orgie, a matinée, a scene in the street with the police or in the House of Commons with the usher.'

Anxieties about social change, about the impermanence of marriage, about women opting for careers rather than for motherhood feature in these essays. She mocks the barely articulated thoughts and fears behind expressions of anxiety about, for instance, the Sanctity of the Home. Of the Deceased Wife's Sister Act she says: 'That has wrought havoc with the sanctity of the home. But only, presumably, the homes of those who have (a) wives, (b) sisters of wives. One supposes that when the sister-in-law stays with her married sister, she and her brother-in-law have always at the back of their minds, "Ah, if my wife (or my sister) should decease, we two can get married if we like." Such a thought does not make for sanctity.' She pushes at the meanings of articulations of beliefs, and thus reveals irrationalities, complacencies and fears.

At times she seems to have a high-spirited fearlessness in these essays; at other times – and this is noticeable particularly when she charts popular notions about women and their natural roles as wives and mothers – she is ironic, sardonic and satiric. In 'What the Public Wants' she suggests: '. . . bread and circuses . . . money . . . easy death . . . We want success, love and the appreciation of our fellows; and some of us want to reproduce our kind.' And in her meditation on the 'only real crime', she fantasises, after the knocking down of the policeman and stoning the squirrels, kidnapping an infant, 'for it is time I became a mother, since I have heard that no woman's life is really full without the patter of tiny feet and the embrace of little arms'.

There weren't many women writing so fiercely as Rose Macaulay did about women and children in the 1920s. It could be argued that she felt a personal anxiety about questions of independence, of womanhood and motherhood; if she did, then she drew on that feeling to sharpen and enliven her perceptions of and her writing about the wider anxiety of a society that has lost a generation of its young men and the certainties of an earlier age. In 'Some Inquiries' there is one 'Into Human Speech', where 'spinster' appears in a list of words which Rose Macaulay would like incorporated into the Census with a question as to how people would use them. In the same way that 'suggestive' is given a ludicrously negative meaning in common parlance ('Suggestive: indecent or improper. Example: Too many film scenarios are suggestive'), 'spinster', she suggests, is commonly used for 'a disagreeable woman of advanced years, preferably unmarried', with the example: 'Unkind people called her a spinster, but she scarcely deserved this harsh name.' Spinsters were everywhere in the 1920s, sign and symbol of a changed world. Rose was one of them.

The spirit of Rose's Uncle Regi is invoked in the gaiety of much of her 1920s journalism. 'No-one in his company can ever have had a dull moment,' Rose was to write of him in *The Times* when he died in December 1937, 'which seems among the more important epitaphs that a human being can have.' *A Casual*

Commentary is dedicated to this uncle who always supported her desire for independence and encouraged her move to London and into the milieu in which, in the 1920s, she flourished.

ii

By the mid-1920s Rose Macaulay was being advertised by William Collins as 'the wittiest woman writer of the day', but she soon began to chafe at such a label. The tone of her writing darkened in the latter half of the decade, affected at least partly by two events. One was the break-up with Naomi Royde-Smith and her increasingly fiercely guarded secrecy about Gerald; the other was the death of her mother.

Grace Macaulay had had a minor heart attack in April 1924. A year later, at the beginning of May 1925, she had another more serious one. Rose was in France with Gerald and contactable only through poste restante addresses.

She came home as soon as she heard the news and went straight to Beaconsfield, but Grace was already unconscious. She did not recover consciousness, and died three days later, on 5 May. Rose was now forty-four, a grown-up working woman with thoughts and views and friends of her own, but this failure to take leave of her mother on her deathbed haunted her for the rest of her life. It was as if she felt that she had missed the chance for some kind of final resolution to the contradictions of her relationship with her mother: the resentments and difficulties she felt with her, the way she had identified with her father, with his rationality and generous intellect against her mother's domestic pettiness.

The religious community in Bethnal Green in which Margaret was ordained a deaconess was closed down in 1924. Margaret left the religious life, although she would never relinquish her nun's habit, and bought a house in Petersfield in Hampshire. This house, and the house in Liss she moved to soon after, became, after Grace died, the family house. Rose regularly spent week-ends with Margaret; Will and Eleanor would use Margaret's house as a base on their visits from Canada and India. Over the next decade and a half Rose would regain some of the intimacy she had had with Margaret when they were girls.

The change of mood after Grace's death was doubtless as much to do with the sense of an ending as with feelings of regret or remorse. Rose never recovered the creative energy that pro-duced the novel a year of the early 1920s. The change is apparent in her next two novels: *Crewe Train*, her fifteenth, which came out in 1926, and two years after that, *Keeping Up Appearances*.

The heroine of *Crewe Train*, Denham Dobie, has been brought up in Andorra by her reclusive father, a retired English clergyman. He dies suddenly when Denham is twenty-one, and she is translated by her dead mother's relatives, the Greshams, to the busy talkative metropolitan world of publishing, book-writing and partying of Chelsea. 'Oh Mr Porter, whatever shall I do?/I want to get off at Birmingham, but they've sent me on to Crewe,' run the lines of the popular song.

The book is dedicated to 'the Philistines, the Barbarians, the Unsociable, and those who do not care to take any trouble'. That is, to the people like Denham Dobie herself, who cannot see the point of talking about plays (it is enough to see them) or books (read them if you have to); nor the point of having separate courses at meal times, each with a different set of plates and cut-lery; nor the point of cleaning your house as it will only get messed up again.

Denham is in many ways a Rose Macaulay figure, in her love of maps, for example, which give her 'a pleasant feeling of ease' and with which 'you could be merely yourself'; in her love of the sea, and of all wide open spaces; in her dislike of housework and the business of running a house. But at the same time she is a philistine and a barbarian. Although Denham wants to get off the train at Birmingham, Rose herself enjoyed the delights of Crewe, which in this novel we see in the sociable literary world inhabited by the Greshams in Chelsea. One of the funniest scenes is a party given by Evelyn Gresham, graced by some lamas 'fresh from Tibet'. Arnold Chapel, who works in Peter Gresham's publishing house and has just written his first novel, approaches Denham:

> 'Rather wonderful, aren't they,' said Arnold Chapel to Denham, who stood looking big and brown and rather fine in a gold tunic.
>
> Denham turned over the adjective, in her literal way.
>
> 'I don't know . . . I suppose they're quite ordinary where they belong. Just clergymen, aren't they?'

Evelyn surveys her party and sees that it is good:

> This high, happy hum and buzz of people talking on a top note, neither rising, falling, nor pausing, was very musical to her. Nice people chattering together, all in their good clothes, enjoying themselves, refreshing themselves with her well-arranged foods and drinks, looking charming (those who could), talking cleverly (again those who could), chitter chattering like a turning mill stream, greeting one another with ejaculations of pleasure, admiring the lamas in their alcove . . .

We are invited to laugh at the pretension and the shallowness, and at the lamas departing in offended but dignified silence at the arrival of a Sudanese dancing troupe from a Soho cabaret. But parties also are fun and funny, and Rose Macaulay, intensely private like Denham, was a determined and devoted party-goer, attracted not by food or drink but by the endless possibilities for talk. There is another Rose-figure in *Crewe Train*: the crossword-loving Rome Garden, whom we have already met in *Told by an Idiot*; to her, significantly, Denham is a 'sealed book'.

This is what keeps it a comedy, unlike Rose's later novel about a young girl destroyed by the world, *They Were Defeated*: Denham, with her literalness, her selfishness, her childish refusal to do anything for anybody else, is essentially an absurd figure. Denham marries Arnold and has to deal with dinner parties, trying in a puzzled way to follow his advice to engage people in conversation about books she has read. On one occasion she talks about a book on dog diseases. The young man next to her 'thought it was rather a good game, and when she said, "Have you ever had a dog with kidney disease?" he replied, "No, but I have a goldfish with acute neurosis."'

The darkness of vision in both *Crewe Train* and *Keeping Up Appearances* is at its darkest around the subject of writing, an old obsession of Rose's. Denham Dobie, in *Crewe Train*, falls foul of the machinations of novelist Evelyn Gresham (the putative Naomi-figure), and her innocence and honesty offer no protection against the fictions of her novelist husband. Arnold is disappointed when Denham thinks that the heroine of his first novel is a little queer in the head. He believes that the stream of consciousness he has given her is how people think. Denham – little realising that Arnold has in fact based his heroine on her – doesn't agree, but gets straight to the point about the power of novelists: 'You can make people do anything you like; they're not like things, which have to be one way, and every one knows what they're like,' she tells him. And he doesn't even know what things are like. She goes on: 'You've made a mistake about the moon, by the way, on page twenty seven. If it was new, it wouldn't be in the east at ten p.m.' 'Never mind,' is his reply, 'practically all novelists slip up now and then over the moon; it would be rather priggish and pedantic not to. The literary moon doesn't really matter.' The mistake about the moon is a metaphor for Arnold and his friends' inability to see the world as it is, their rearranging through language not just of thoughts but of things. Denham is finally trapped by pregnancy, but that is merely the culmination of the hopelessness of her trying to escape from the world of lies that is the literary metropolitan world of 1920s London. But part of the novel's wit lies in its ambivalence towards this world. Clever, talkative, word-obsessed Arnold Chapel is as surely an aspect of Rose Macaulay herself, as is childlike, literal, sea- and secret-cave-loving Denham Dobie.

'There has always been a sharpness and an angularity about Miss Macaulay's wit,' said the *Times Literary Supplement*. 'Take away the fun from the story and you have underneath the delicate pattern of an unassuming and inarticulate tragedy'.

Not all the reviews of *Crewe Train* were favourable. Rose Macaulay was strongly criticised the following year for the 'extreme frankness' she used to describe Denham's first pregnancy: 'Denham felt, and often was, sick in the mornings.' Rose Macaulay's 'realism is tinged with an obvious pandering to the disgusting license that certain women novelists take such a pernicious delight in exhibiting'. This was not the first time Rose had described morning sickness in her fiction. Jane Potter, in *Potterism* six years earlier, muses on how a baby 'made her feel ill before it came, and would need care and attention afterwards'. Jane is alert to the difference a baby makes to the fulfilment of a woman's ambitions: 'It wasn't fair. If Johnny married and had a baby it wouldn't get in his way, only in its mamma's. It was a handicap, like your frock (however short it was) when you were climbing. You had got round that by taking it off and climbing in knickerbockers, but you couldn't get round a baby.' The difference between Jane and Denham, and perhaps what then makes the difference between the description of morning sickness being acceptable or not acceptable, is that Jane 'wanted the baby too'. Not so Denham, and this surely is what inflames the hyperbole of phrases like 'disgusting license' and 'pernicious delight': for Denham thinks you can get round a baby by simply ignoring it. She continues with her normal life: the childlike round of running, climbing, cycling. As a result she has a miscarriage.

The novel can be read as an examination of the possibility of striking a balance between the unexamined and the over-examined life, between living and the analysis of it. It can be read as a comic dramatisation of the clash of two cultures: one that expresses itself literally, the other metaphorically. But for all its comic brio, it nonetheless ends bleakly for the young woman. At the beginning of the novel we see Denham's Andorran step-mother, who has produced four half-siblings for Denham, as 'a busy, fussing woman', from which the authorial voice generalises: 'the fact being that you cannot, in Andorra or anywhere else, run a house, let alone children, without being busy and fussing, which is an excellent reason for running neither'. The novel ends with Denham pregnant for the second time, installed in a house in Buckinghamshire, receiving advice from her mother-in-law, who concludes her homily on how to be a wife and mother with: '"There needn't really be any empty moments in one's day, if it's properly schemed out. Think of that! Not one empty, idle, useless minute."'

The novel ends: 'Denham thought of it . . .'

Rose Macaulay escaped running house and children, escaped the fate of girls like Denham Dobie whose bodies betray them. She was forty-five when *Crewe Train* came out. She had reached the age when motherhood was no longer a choice that was open to her. In October that year she had a 'small operation' that neces-sitated recovery at Margaret's house in Petersfield. Any conflicts arising from the consequences of her choice to have an affair with a married man, expressed by the young women who yearn for or fear the fruits of their reproductive bodies that appear here and there in the fiction of the early 1920s, were no longer con-flicts for Rose. But there were other, intellectual dilemmas that she faced, that can be seen in the other book that she brought out that same year, *Catchwords and Claptrap*, her first publication with the Hogarth Press.

Cambridge University Press had offered to publish a collection of essays in 1924, but Rose Macaulay had just reached an agree-ment with Methuen. Cambridge would have provided some intellectual cachet to Rose's casual commentary, and possibly alleviated her anxiety about the lack of intellectual rigour in her writing. (Being published by Cambridge might have compro-mised her position – important to her as a writer – of outsider;

acceptance into the scholarly elite of Cambridge, the university of her relations and forebears, the first female Macaulay to be so accepted, would come much later, in the last decade of her life.) The Woolfs' Hogarth Press lacked the antiquity of the university presses but it was attractively high-minded. They would publish two more of her books: *Religious Elements in English Literature* and her critical work on E. M. Forster.

Catchwords and Claptrap was published in 1926 as the fourth title in Leonard and Virginia Woolf's second series of Hogarth Essays. The cover for the series was a woodcut by Virginia's sister Vanessa Bell. *Catchwords* was reviewed alongside two of the previous titles, Gertrude Stein's *Composition as Explanation*, and *Rochester* by Bonamy Dobrée. (*Impenetrability* by Robert Graves was the other title.)

Miss Macaulay, said the *Times Literary Supplement*, 'is at her best when she is most bitter, and it is a pity that she should be writing in a well-bred age which considers, quite wrongly it seems, that all good humour is good-humoured'. The reviewer wished she could be more expressive of her anger at the misuse of language, but it is an intellectual anxiety about her subject matter that she is suppressing rather than anger. An uncertainty of tone is manifest in the clotted style of the opening of the pamphlet. The subject of the first sentence starts off as 'this fantastical currency', meaning language; but it is then kept on hold while the author runs through more than half a dozen sub-clauses, only to abandon it finally in favour of another subject. This is a tendency of Rose Macaulay's: to construct the edifice of a sentence out of a tottering pile of clauses and phrases. Sometimes she does it for intentionally comic effect, but here it seems to express a lack of ease with the abstract argument she is pursuing. Language and its degradation is the subject not just of the first sentence but of the whole pamphlet. She argues against vagueness and on behalf of accuracy in choice of words and phrases. One would expect nothing less from any novelist or poet. But the borderline between linguistic rigour and linguistic snobbery is not always clear. When she castigates the sloppy language of politicians it is Labour politicians who are singled out for disapprobation; she refers to the General Strike of May 1926 and the ensuing coal strike, and suggests that the imprecise language of the workers' spokesmen comes from the emotional nature of what they're talking about, but also, she suggests, from their lack of education. And is there not something slightly snobbish about the title of the pamphlet? *Catchwords and Claptrap*? Does it not imply a pedantic, educated superiority? And is this, too, an expression of anxiety on the novelist's part about the constituency of her readership?

But once she puts behind her the first struggles with the abstract nature of the problem, and then the under-educated Labour politicians, and returns to linguistic detail, she is back on form. She analyses the symbolic and rhetorical use of certain words and phrases: 'women and children', for example: 'They are called in, these unfortunate women and children . . . to do constant duty in emergencies.' On Rudyard Kipling's use of 'Man' in 'If' (the last quatrain: 'If you can fill the unforgiving minute/With sixty seconds' worth of distance run,/Yours is the Earth and everything that's in it, And – which is more – you'll be a Man, my son!'), she imagines some puzzled children asking: 'What would he have turned into if he *hadn't* been able to do all those things in the poem?' As for 'Bolshevism', it 'seems to have lost any accurate connotation, and to imply less a Russian political system than a state of mind . . . usually regarded as undesirable by those who use the word'. The bugbear of Bolshevism appears again in *Keeping Up Appearances*, where young Cary Folyot discovers at some cost that to the English (and especially to English journalists) all Russian revolutionaries are Bolshevists, whatever you say to the contrary.

Keeping Up Appearances, published in 1928 (and in America as *Daisy and Daphne*), offers a different way of exploring Rose's concerns about language and the abuse of power by those for whom it is a professional tool. She moves on from the doubles of her earlier novels, and the double identity of the central character in *Mystery*: the central character in *Keeping Up Appearances* is split into three. There is socially insecure journalist Daisy who writes weekly articles on Women, which she thinks of mockingly as: Should Clever Women Marry Stupid Men? Should Clever Men Marry Stupid Women? Should Women and Men Marry At All? What is the Religion of Women? The Post-War Girl: is she selfish, rude, clever, stupid, drunk, thin, tall, dark, fair? Daphne is her educated, refined alter ego. And the third, more shadowy, is Marjorie Wynne, bestselling author of *Youth at the Prow*, the voice of youth today. *Keeping Up Appearances*, Rose wrote later, 'had its genesis in the reflection how manifold is human nature, and that it might be fun to present one person as two, as far thro' the book as was possible'.

The unreliableness of the narrator becomes the focus of the novel; the lies of fiction spill over, as they do in *Crewe Train*, into lies about life. To suggest that in these two novels Rose was wrestling with her own demons about the morality of writing fiction is not to say that they are not very funny novels. *Crewe Train* in particular has a sharpness and a lack of sentimentality that is similar to the early Evelyn Waugh, whose first novel *Decline and Fall* was published two years later.

Keeping Up Appearances is not entirely successful. The essay-writing style is too obvious in many of Daisy's thoughts, so that it is not Daisy, embarrassed in front of her literary middle-class friends by her large, loud, tipsy mother from East Sheen, that we hear, but Rose Macaulay, holder of opinions on this and that. Daisy is too sharp for her hopelessness and lack of confidence to be convincing. Daisy is an unlikely Rose-figure. But perhaps by now Rose really was beginning to see successful novel-writing in the same way as Daisy views the 'degraded activities' of her novel-writing alter ego Marjorie Wynne: as justified only by the money that such activities generate. Daisy muses on how Marjorie's newest novel, the follow-up to *Youth at the Prow*, will make possible Daphne's marriage to intellectual Raymond Folyot: 'If

Summer's Over and its successors should afford them journeys
abroad, feed and clothe their little ones, pay their income tax,
their gambling debts, their car and wireless licences, and
Daphne's dressmaker, these words would not have been written
in vain.'

Keeping Up Appearances seems to mark a turning point in Rose
Macaulay's development as a writer. One by one, we see glimpses
of the 'queer hidden selves' of all the characters, not just the different personalities of Daisy/Daphne/Marjorie. Rose Macaulay
had committed herself to keeping secret the most important relationship in her life. Perhaps it was living with this that prompted
her, alongside her growing dissatisfaction with the kind of writing she was engaged in, to explore the concept of 'queer hidden
selves' and, perhaps, to try to dramatise, and explore, her own.

Her writing would soon take a different direction, but not
quite yet. She was ever busier as a journalist: in the summer
months of 1928 a stream of articles for the daily papers poured
from her pen: 'Does Ancestry Matter?'; 'Defamation'; 'What
Most Interests You?'; 'If I had My Life to Live Again', and so on.
The year before she had begun a relationship with the British
Broadcasting Corporation that would last until her death. The
radio producer Lance Sieveking first approached her in 1926
and asked her for a short story and when that wasn't forthcoming ('haven't written any,' was her almost truthful reply), for an
extract from a novel. She demurred, on the grounds that an
extract from a novel (her most recently published was *Crewe
Train*) would be 'boring and quite incomprehensible'. She first
had some work broadcast in February 1927. It was 'two short
essays in a lighter vein', from *A Casual Commentary*. Over the
next thirty years Rose Macaulay would give many radio talks
and appear on many panels, representing as she did that combination of braininess and populism that characterised the Home
Service.

She was as hard-working as Daisy in *Keeping Up Appearances*.
Virginia Woolf noted an exchange with Rose about work in

her diary for May of that year: 'About work: "I've got to work tomorrow" I say, excusing myself for not going to Raymond's party. "So have we all" rather sharply. & so on.' This exchange forms part of some sharp speculation on Virginia's part regarding Rose's jealousy of her, and some even sharper speculation, in Virginia Woolf's inimitable way, on how the jealousy may be mutual. They are discussing the Prix Femina-Vie Heureuse, which Virginia had just won for her 'python', *To the Lighthouse*. It starts with: 'Rose Macaulay says "Yes I won the prize" – rather peevishly.' The jealousy, Virginia Woolf believes, 'shows through a dozen little phrases, as we're talking of America, articles &c: she is jealous of me; anxious to compare us: but I may imagine it: & it shows my own jealousy no doubt, as suspicions always do. One cdn't know them if one hadn't got them.'

That year, in November, both Rose Macaulay and Virginia Woolf were, with their mutual friend E. M. Forster, amongst the thirty-nine writers who were prepared to give evidence on behalf of Radclyffe Hall's *The Well of Loneliness*, which was being prosecuted for obscenity. In the end their evidence was disallowed, and the novel was declared obscene.

Rose Macaulay was now part of the London literary establishment. But increasingly she felt the need to escape from the kind of writer into which she had made herself. At the end of *Keeping Up Appearances* Daisy/Daphne, defeated by the forces of propriety and the English class system, flees to America as Marjorie Wynne. Casting off the Marjorie role, Daphne Daisy, no longer split but reborn – temporarily – as one person, plans a final escape from her fractured existence. She dreams of fleeing south, 'down the slender stalk that holds a continent pendant like a great pear, the miraculous isthmus that conducts one into South America as the narrow corridor of death ushers one into paradise'. There, incurable romantic that Rose Macaulay was, she wants her newly born character to see and be amazed by 'Brazilian rivers, forests, armadilloes, and nuts, Bolivian humming-birds, condors and coffee . . . flying squirrels, mysterious Patagonians . . .'

Rose herself attempted a similar escape. She sailed to New York with Margaret in December 1929, then crossed the USA by train to Portland, where they had arranged to meet Will. Rose wrote to Jean: 'Everyone is very much interested in M's clothes; the porters and waiters etc ask what she is. The man who sells candy on the train asked me this morning; he thought we must be coming out to do mission work, and tried to sell us religious books, though I told him we had only come motoring.' Perhaps the eccentric travelling party in *The Towers of Trebizond* a quarter of a century later, and all the mistakes and failures of that mission, sprang from a seed sown here.

They met up with Will and drove with him down the Pacific Highway. 'Here we are,' wrote Rose on one of her many postcards to Sylvia Lynd, 'dashing along the Pacific coast road in warm Californian rain, pine forested mountains on our left and the ocean on our right, marvellously happy. My brother and I drive by turns. I love driving, it is a new and excellent sport. By night we put up in little cabins . . . and cook our own suppers. All very romantic and lovely and funny.' 'Having a hilarious time,' she wrote on another card. And again, 'I love driving.' Will's car was a four-seater Essex – which featured in Rose's South American novel *Staying with Relations* – and they took countless snapshots of each other in the car, beside the car, on the road, and picnicking beside huge cacti. Heading south Rose was reading *The Plumed Serpent*, looking forward to finding out if Lawrence's Mexicans bore any relation to the real ones. But she was disappointed. Just as Daphne Daisy didn't manage it in *Keeping Up Appearances*, so Rose and her siblings were balked of the pleasure in real life: they weren't allowed to cross into revolutionary Mexico because Margaret was dressed as a nun.

The last time Rose had crossed the Atlantic had been with her father, to visit Will just before the outbreak of the war. Now both George and Grace were dead. Of the Five who had played out their adventures together on the beach at Varazze, there were now three adventuring around America. Will was no longer the little boy with curls whom Rose protected, but a man with damaged lungs, a permanently crippled arm and no family of his own. Margaret had been a deaconess. Now her community was closed, but she chose to continue to wear the clothes of the order she had joined. Did she feel they offered some kind of protection? one wonders. Rose, without spouse or children, like her other siblings, was the most successful in terms of a career. This journey provided not just a time for reconsideration of family, but for Rose, who would soon be forty-nine, it provided the chance for a reappraisal of other matters. In May 1929 she had visited a cardiologist. She was diagnosed as having a weak heart. She treated it lightly in a letter to Jean: 'The specialist examined my heart and said it was a poor kind – "a low-grade, C3, tubular heart with a rough patch", probably damaged by past bronchitis. All I can say is that if mine is like that, what must a high-grade, A1, globular heart be like? I should probably, if I had that, be like Grandpa in the Kruschen advertisements, leaping over pianos.' This diagnosis seemed to make no difference to her preferred lifestyle, and she was still swimming happily in the Serpentine over twenty years later. But it coincided with a change in the direction of her work that she was already beginning to make. It was an intimation – a faint one – of mortality. What direction did she want her writing to take? How much time did she have left?

Before she left England she had already started negotia-tions with Leonard Woolf at the Hogarth Press for another book. This would be *Some Religious Elements in English Literature*, the first of her two books for Hogarth in the 1930s. Already she was turning away from fiction. She had explored her own anxieties about novel-writing with sharpness and wit in the two novels she had just published. The next, *Staying with Relations*, is feeble and mannered by comparison, although it has an excellent scene set in ruins in a jungle, an image she would come back to and explore in depth in *Pleasure of Ruins* in the 1950s.

But now, returning from America, it was history and ideas and scholarship that were calling to her.

CHAPTER EIGHT

Histories and Biographies

[This] decade was more serious, less cultured, less aesthetic, more political. The slump blew like a cold draught at its birth, war stormed like forest fire at its close; between these two catastrophes Communists and Fascists battled and preached, and eyes turned apprehensively across the north sea towards the alarming menace which had leaped up like a strident jack-in-the-box from a beer-cellar to more than a throne. Bets were laid on the date of war.

'Twentieth Century' (*Life Among the English*)

'Rose adored parties,' said the publisher Victor Gollancz. 'She was one of the best party-goers in London.' Rose continued to see Gerald as a family friend at weekends, and alone in London, but to parties she went alone. There were regular Friday evening parties at the Lynds' big house in Hampstead, and dinner parties on other evenings. Sylvia described a Sunday evening dinner party from the mid-1930s.

Round the table were Max Beerbohm and his wife, A. P. Herbert, Lionel Hale and Rose Macaulay. Partridges were served. Later they were joined by Margaret Kennedy, author of the bestselling *The Constant Nymph* ('I can't believe it,' Sylvia recorded her saying of its success), and her husband, Ruth Gollancz, Alan Thomas, and the poet Bryan Guinness. Victor Gollancz joined them after midnight. After midnight!

They talked about changing fashions in slang, and the meanings of words like balmy, crackers and squiffy. Rose told them that the only people she ever saw drunk in her childhood in Italy were English sailors 'who were always directed to her father's house in the Italian seaside place where they lived when they had missed their ship and needed their fares home'. (She had forgotten the Italian nursemaid who had been sacked for drunkenness.) They talked about politics; they talked about peace. Victor Gollancz and A. P. Herbert had a loud argument. At 2 a.m. 'Rose rose to go.' Rose had only a week or so before acquired a new car, a one-year-old 10 horsepower Morris. It now refused to start, so everyone went outside to push it down the hill towards town, and in the mêlée A.P. Herbert fell down the area steps, but fortunately was unhurt. Eventually they got it started but couldn't get the lights to work. Gentlemanly Bryan Guinness accompanied Rose home in case she was stopped by a policeman for driving without lights. This was considered exceptionally brave for, according to Victor Gollancz, Rose 'drove at several hundred miles an hour . . . and she could never understand why, when she offered people a lift, they preferred to walk unless positively crippled'.

Rose and Sylvia were very close. For all their complaints about Naomi Royde-Smith's gossip, they themselves spent a good deal of time gossiping. 'London burbles on,' Rose wrote to Sylvia who was in Canada for a few weeks. 'You've missed a bad party at the Botts, a nice one at the Brookes last night, a still uncertain one at the Lows next week. Tomorrow I go sup at the Priestleys.' They had long telephone conversations about the machinations of the Book Society, on whose committee Sylvia sat with J. B. Priestley, Clemence Dane (whom Rose disliked for her 'womanly flutings') and Hugh Walpole, who was the butt of many of their jokes ('Hugh cannot like George Eliot until a highbrow friend tells him he may'). Rose always adored the telephone, and wished that someone would invent a device for when there was no reply, so that 'one can speak a message into the receiver, which is released when it is lifted later at the other end'.

By the 1930s Sylvia Lynd's poetic star was waning. She was a victim of the fierce young men of the post-war generation. Rose was endlessly consoling when Sylvia's books were attacked by 'Grigson and the whole Leavis gang'. And as with the O'Donovans, Rose took a close interest in family: her letters are full of queries about and news of the Lynds' daughters, and later, their grandchildren.

Politics was a passion in this world. It wasn't just the Lynds' links with Irish republicanism – Robert had been a Sinn Fein delegate before the war (although an irregular attender at meetings) and a friend and supporter of Roger Casement, whom he visited in Brixton prison and whose trial he attended – for Rose was familiar with all this through Gerald; what was new to her was the Communist Party, the Left Book Club, the *Daily Worker*. Uninvolved herself, she was central to Victor Gollancz's *Reminiscences of Affection*, his memoirs of that time; his chapter about all the friends who visited Brimpton, their country house near Newbury, is entitled 'Rose Macaulay: And Others'. 'Most people, essaying an estimate of her, would have given first place to her wit. This, in which she abounded, was of the genial kind, or one should perhaps use the word *genialis*, for the full flavour of the Latin original has hardly survived into its English equivalent. Her wit, that is to say, was a welcoming wit, not a rejecting one,' he said of her. Like Sylvia and Robert Lynd, Victor and Ruth Gollancz knew about Rose and Gerald, but Rose always came 'brimping', as she called it, alone, giving a lift as often as not to one of the refugees who passed through the Gollanczs' house in an increasingly steady stream as the 1930s went on. The others who brimped were mostly couples (it made it easier to fit people in, Victor maintained) such as the Lynds, the Brookes, and David Low the political cartoonist and his wife Madeline. Victor wrote of Rose's laughter and gaiety: 'By a lucky chance we have on permanant record the facial expression that went with her laughter. A number of people were down one weekend, and Stefan Lorant, the brilliant photographer of Picture Post, joined us on the Saturday with the idea of taking some pictures. At teatime I started groaning about my weight, and Stefan, I think it was, insisted that in spite of it any four people could lift me high in the air with a finger apiece. I was prepared to risk it, and let my wife, Alan Thomas, Reeve Brooke and Bertie Farjeon have a try. They succeeded, with Rose looking on . . .' The photographs express it well: Rose Macaulay sitting on the edge of the circle, an amused observer.

Victor was a mover and stirrer of people and causes and found Rose unfailingly generous, 'so lavish in her charity that if I asked her for five pounds in some good cause, as I often did, she would usually send fifty'. And she was welcomed into the Gollancz family life as well. She was 'specially fond', Victor recalled, of the youngest of their four daughters, 'ever since our baby was three days old, and Rose had been the first, apart from my wife and the nurse, to take her in her arms'.

Ruth Gollancz designed a book-plate for Rose at her request, based on a favourite story of Rose's in Pliny the Elder's *Natural History* of a boy and a dolphin in the bay of Baiae. The design incorporated a sea-horse and a mermaid, reflecting Rose's ichthyous self-image, with the old Macaulay motto: *Dulce Periculum*.

An idea of Brimpton weekends in the 1930s is given in a thank-you letter of Rose's:

> A line to bless you! What a lovely week-end. I can't forget the garden full of glasses & bottles & toads & music & trees & the moon coming up, and that elf-like child dancing on the sward; and all the lovely day – the garden, & the river, & the tree I sat in, and the onion-potato salad & the chicken & the salmon squash, & the raspberries, and those heavenly tunes playing, and R and V, and everyone . . . so nice, & dancing on the grass, against the background of delphinia.

At the same time as being a part of this circle of energetic, out-going, politically engaged writers and publishers, Rose met and

EX LIBRIS

ROSE MACAULAY

became a part of a quite different circle, amongst whom she made two more close and lasting friendships. The first of these was with Ivy Compton-Burnett. Born in 1884, she was three years younger than Rose. She published one novel before the war, *Dolores*, which she later tried to remove from her *oeuvre* in much the same way as Rose tried to suppress her earliest novels. Her second novel, *Pastors and Masters*, came out in 1925, but it was only when her third one, *Brothers and Sisters*, privately published like the previous two, appeared in 1929 that she began to be noticed. Rose read it, was impressed, and suggested to Ivy that she should go to Rose's own literary agent, Spencer Curtis Brown, and allow him to handle her work. As a result Ivy

Compton-Burnett was contracted by Heinemann for her next three novels. When the Heinemann contract expired after *A House and Its Head* was published in 1935, Rose encouraged Victor Gollancz, whose publishing house was then considered to be one of the most vigorous and forward looking, to take on Ivy, which he duly did.

Rose and Ivy's novels could hardly be more different except in one respect: the way the characters love to talk. Ivy's stagy, mannered, dialogue-dominated novels are all, save one, set in a pre-Great War world of large country houses in which hate-filled and incestuous family members talk each other to death. The 'eager tongues' of the characters, wrote Rose, act as 'several mirrors tilted at different angles'. 'My books won't live,' Rose is said to have said. 'Yours may, Ivy.' But this can be as easily interpreted as typical disparagement of her own novels, as it can be as measured judgement of the lasting quality of Ivy's. After all, Rose was given to such statements. 'I don't take my novels seriously – I only write them to earn money,' she wrote to Hugh Walpole at about this time.

The two writers' personalities and lifestyles were also very different, except, again, in one respect. They were both intensely secretive about their personal lives. Ivy had a whole clutch of family tragedies to hide, including the death of two brothers and the death by suicide of two sisters. When Rose met Ivy she was already living in west London with Margaret Jourdain, an art historian who specialised in furniture, who was, initially, the better-known and more widely published of the two. Rose was a regular visitor for more than twenty years at their flat, first in Linden Gardens, and then, after 1934, in Cornwall Gardens.

Where Rose flitted round London from one party to another, Ivy barely moved from her flat. People came to her. Where Rose had a finger on the pulse of metropolitan life and reviewed it in weekly columns for the *Spectator* and elsewhere, Ivy remained resolutely uninfluenced by the modern world, even in dress and hairstyle, preferring to present herself as a late Victorian. Where

Rose's interest in the preparation and consumption of food was almost non-existent, Ivy and Margaret demanded of their cook elaborately prepared dishes smothered in thick sauces. And where Rose's twenty-year-long love affair was central to her life, Ivy and Margaret considered themselves to be what they called 'neutrals'.

Rose was not alone in being amused by and feeling very much at ease with Ivy and Margaret. They had a wide circle of friends, including the actor Ernest Thesiger who would sit at teatime doing his embroidery; Basil Marsden-Smedley who, like Rose, was a keen bather (he and Margaret Jourdain visited the Ace of Spades on the Kingston bypass when it was opened in the mid-1930s to sample the new pool – Rose must have been abroad with Gerald at the time); James Lees-Milne from the National Trust, whose diaries are dotted with hilarious vignettes of Ivy's bad behaviour; and the novelist Francis King. Ivy's demanding, controlling eccentricity and sharp conversation appealed to Rose's sense of humour.

In the early 1930s Rose introduced her friend Una Pope-Hennessy, the historian and biographer, to Ivy Compton-Burnett and Margaret Jourdain. Una's two sons, John and James, also became part of the Compton-Burnett circle. Ivy cast her net wide and liked to be entertained by the younger generation as well as by her own.

In public Rose presented herself as being alone, showing to the world a very different self from her secret, with-Gerald, self. Perhaps she needed to compartmentalise her life, as the protagonists of her 1920s novels had done, revealing their manifold selves in different places and different circumstances. But while her life remained split between public and private, between different groups of friends, between the relentless heterosexuality of the Gollancz circle and the homosexuality of the Compton-Burnett circle, between politics and writing, between those like Victor Gollancz trying to change the world and those trying like Ivy to keep it as it was, while also dabbling a toe in the waters of

Bloomsbury, Rose's work began to express her interest in an exploration of the more integrated self.

Rose was approaching fifty at the beginning of the decade. She had spent the previous ten years charting contemporary life. Now was the time to look back, to take stock and to consider all that had brought her to the present point. Rose turned to history. The history that she wrote in those years, starting with *Some Religious Elements in English Literature*, including the novel *They Were Defeated*, and her two biographical books on John Milton and E. M. Forster, is full of ghostly whisperings. 'The slump blew like a cold draught at its birth,' she wrote of the 1930s in *Life Among the English*, and 'war stormed like forest fire at its close'; much would be destroyed in that forest fire, but Rose was already attuned to the ghosts' voices speaking out of history.

Leonard Woolf had asked her in July 1929 if she would be interested in writing a short book for the Hogarth 'Lectures on Literature' series, which he himself was co-editing with the King's College don, Dadie Rylands. In *Some Religious Elements in English Literature* the voices she heard started with Cynewulf in eighth-century Northumbria who described the twilight of the old English gods; Rose listened for and heard 'the last shouts of the heathen warriors, the last murmurings of the elf-haunted woods, witch-ridden winds, and storming seas'.

The manuscript was delivered a year later than originally agreed, in March 1931, and Rose promptly went off on holiday with Dorothy and Reeve Brooke to Sicily and then on to Italy with Gerald. There was the usual, necessary, vagueness about the itinerary. The proofs kept on arriving at the wrong place, and when they at last caught up with her she complained to Leonard Woolf: 'Your proofreader has some views about my constructions I do not always share'. Then there was the question of the index. 'I hope you are not wanting that index very quickly,' she wrote in April. As the book was due to be published in May, and in America Harcourt Brace were planning an August publication, the index was wanted very quickly indeed; one imagines that

Rose's request that Leonard Woolf should himself verify the Christian names of all the writers whose names appeared, finally, in the index, might have been the last straw.

Although much of Rose's business was conducted through her agents, Curtis Brown, she was careless about passing things on to them. In her professional correspondence of this period she seems hopelessly disorganised, granting and then withdrawing permission for reprints, for example, or telling one American publisher they could have something when it was already promised to someone else. Demands came at her from all sides, while increasingly she wanted to concentrate on the seventeenth-century material she was rediscovering in her work for the Hogarth book. In November 1930, in the middle of writing *Some Religious Elements*, she had written to Jonathan Cape, turning down his invitation to write a book for him: 'It is not a question of what books I want to write, but of what I shall have time to write. Don't confuse my mind by suggesting new books for me to write just now.' She ends, 'However it is very nice of you to wish to publish a book of mine.'

When *Some Religious Elements* came out in May 1931 it was respectfully received, but it never earned its advance of £50, and five years later Rose was writing to Hogarth offering an idea for another book, on the 'English Heroine', a book she long wanted to write but never did, 'to pay off this unearned balance'.

Meanwhile William Collins, with whom she had a contract for ten novels and who wanted her to continue with the successes of the previous decade, was not best pleased that she was writing for other publishers, nor with her growing interest in subjects historical and scholarly.

But it was her work as a historian that inspired her next novel. One of the chapters in *Some Religious Elements* was on the Anglican/Puritan conflict in the latter part of the seventeenth century, and out of this grew *They Were Defeated*, her novel about passion and principle and about the vulnerability of individuals caught up in the tangle of religion and politics during the years of

Cromwell's rise to power. Published in October 1932, it was the first of three major books of the 1930s in which Rose returned in her imagination to Cambridge, that desired but unattainable place where the ghosts of her past still walked.

Cambridge had been the intellectual terrain of Rose's father and uncles. As a young woman Rose had swum in the secret river and written of the vision it had vouchsafed, but she had felt herself barred from the world of scholarship. Her father George had now been dead for seventeen years; Uncle William had long retired from King's (he would die in 1936), and in 1931 Uncle Edward Conybeare died at the age of eighty-eight. In the Cambridge of Rose's desire – the seventeenth-century Cambridge that she explored in *They Were Defeated* and *Milton*, and the contemporary Cambridge of her book on Forster – the soul and the intellect were united; poetry and scholarship flowered beneath the painted ceilings of the ancient college chapels.

Rose dedicated *They Were Defeated* to her Cambridge uncle, named for the poet who is one of the heroes of the book: 'To my uncle WILLIAM HERRICK MACAULAY this story of Cambridge and of one of our distant relatives'. The novel opens in Dean Prior in Devonshire, which Rose had visited in September 1931. The poet Robert Herrick is rector. He celebrates the simple joys of country life, singing of

> . . . Brooks, of Blossoms, Birds, and Bowers:
> Of April, May, of June and July-Flowers.
> . . . of May-Poles, Hock-carts, Wassails, Wakes,
> Of Bride-grooms, Brides, and of their Bridall-cakes . . .,

but longs for his poetry to achieve a wider critical acclaim.

In the first scene a piglet appears, munching at the harvest fruits and vegetables gathered beneath the pulpit. It is because of the piglet, unseen by parson Herrick sermonising up above, that everyone except for serious Julian Conybeare is giggling; the small creature delights the congregation in much the same way as the lamb skittering down the aisle at Easter in Varazze delighted that congregation. The piglet denotes a time of innocence not just in the symbolism of this novel but also in Rose Macaulay's personal symbolism. When next an animal enters a church in her fiction, the ape in *The Towers of Trebizond*, it will be as symbol of disorder, madness and loss, and a mockery of the concept of Christian communion.

The first part of the book recounts the story of the persecution of an old woman in the village as a witch. Julian's father Dr Conybeare (a character imagined by Rose as 'the son of an Elizabethan schoolmaster who was my ancestor') tries to protect and save her, and when that fails he gives her poison so that she will not suffer the agonies of being tried and condemned. He is suspected by the witchfinder and others and this, together with the reputation he already has for atheistical notions, makes it expedient for him to leave home for a while. He takes Julian to Cambridge to visit her undergraduate brother Kit, accompanied by parson Herrick who is keen to try out his poetry on the sophisticated poets of Cambridge.

But it is a calamitous trip. Fleeing from one danger, Dr Conybeare delivers his daughter into another. All around her Julian sees a ferment of poets and scholars, but all that she is allowed to do is attend a weekly lecture for ladies given by the Platonist Henry More. She is ignored by the poets, until John Cleveland, her brother Kit's tutor, decides to amuse himself with her. Her father fails to recognise this danger, and while he pursues Kit, who has gone off to join the Roman Catholics, Julian is seduced by Cleveland. The scenes where grave, scholarly, serious Julian burns her papers – first the essay on Pythagoras she wrote for Henry More, and then all her poems – are almost unbearably painful to read, not least because of the utter convincingness of her physical, spiritual and intellectual abandonment to the man who has seduced her.

'It is part of her boldness,' said the *Times Literary Supplement* of the plethora of poets stalking the streets of Cambridge in

They Were Defeated, 'that the less familiar names play so large a part. Herrick is, indeed, the principal figure, but Cowley is in the forefront also. If Miss Macaulay were asked, "Who now reads Cowley?" she would certainly reply that she does. But John Cleveland, of whom Mr Saintsbury remarks that everybody interested in him is an everybody not including many bodies, is much more prominent still.' John Suckling, Richard Crashaw and Andrew Marvell appear too, as does, on the sidelines, John Milton, the subject of Rose's next book.

It is Herrick himself, who finds much of the verse he is obliged to listen to sadly tedious and philosophical, and his girl pupil Julian Conybeare who are the poetic heroes of this novel. Julian is a tragic hero. She is killed by a blow to the head when she is knocked to the floor during a fight between Cleveland and her older brother Francis, who is a Puritan, and is driven as much by envy of Cleveland as by the desire to defend his sister's honour. Julian's premature death has echoes in the wider world where the bells of Cambridge are tolling for the execution of Lord Strafford on trumped-up charges. John Cleveland, partial author of Julian's destruction, muses on the defeat of liberty.

'*They Were Defeated* is what it is about,' Rose wrote. 'Every one defeated – Julian Conybeare, Herrick, the Royalists, the Church, etc. . . . It was a lovely century in Cambridge,' she went on, 'or anyhow those immediately pre-civil-war years were. So much poetry, so much flowering of Anglicanism in the middle of Puritanism, so much idealism on both sides.' The synthesis in the novel of character and idea, and the richness and vigour of the language (she went to enormous pains to reproduce authentic seventeenth-century speech, and castigated herself later for an incorrect use of the word 'scientist' when it should have been 'philosopher'), show a profoundly imaginative vision.

Rose was widely praised for having so vividly brought to life a complex period of history, and for integrating the histor-ical characters into the fictional whole. The *Times Literary Supplement* appreciated the risk that she had taken: 'A popular novelist who asks a faithful public to read something entirely new and unexpected deserves credit for boldness; for the public is conservative and inclined to demand from its favourites that to which it is used.' It had been a risk worth taking, the *TLS* decided, for this was 'in many respects a brilliant piece of work'.

They Were Defeated is an imaginative synthesis of fiction and biography. There are also profoundly personal questions being explored. The story of a woman writer and her family in seventeenth-century England perhaps released Rose's writer self from a self-censorship that had manifested itself in her earlier novels in, for example, the ways that her subjects were so often split into pairs or couples. Perhaps in writing about people's desires and dreams and vulnerabilities in the context of a period remote from the modern world she discovered a licence to explore her own obsessions, her own sense of history and her own sense of self. 'Julian's story and end,' she wrote to the historian Helen Waddell, 'were very near my own heart. I feared her death might be too facile an escape and solution – but it seemed inevitable, and that she had already died, and that the blow which killed, therefore, wasn't a bolt from the blue . . .' Always uncertain of her own powers, she added, 'I don't know, though'. *They Were Defeated* is a novel that comes from heart and soul as well as from the intellect.

The year that *They Were Defeated* came out, Rose moved flat again, to number 7 Luxborough House, opposite Marylebone Chapel Gardens, where a huge tree grew outside the windows. 'I've just been distempering the two front room walls primrose-cream,' she told Sylvia Lynd, 'so they are now full of light and grace . . . I do want you to see it, the sunshine & the tree are so wonderful to a cave-dweller. I feel like a troglodyte coming to the surface.' I am 'so happy', she wrote to Jean. Everything was coming together: she had Gerald, she had her friends, and she was wholeheartedly engaged in work she loved. Through her work on English history she was uncovering a sense of herself that was quite different from the ironic, dispassionate self-portraits of her earlier work.

Before she moved on to her next serious project she took time out to have some seventeenth-century fun, writing a preface, at the invitation of the National Smoke Abatement Society, to a new edition of John Evelyn's 1661 campaigning pamphlet about the noxious effects of sea-coal smoke on London and its inhabitants, *Fumifugium: Or the Inconvenience of the Aer, and Smoake of London Dissipated together with some Remedies humbly proposed.*

Rose researched and wrote her biography of John Milton during 1932 and 1933, and it was published in Gerald Duckworth & Co.'s 'Great Lives' series in January 1934. She worked from her father's copy of the *Collected Works*, the fourth edition of 1845, edited by H. J. Todd. At last, in her early fifties, Rose was doing the same kind of work that her father had spent the latter part of his life doing, work of loving scholarship. And there was a connection with an earlier Macaulay scholar: the first published work of Thomas Babington (Lord) Macaulay who, Virginia Woolf pointed out, 'has an odd look of Rose', was an essay on John Milton in the *Edinburgh Review* in 1825.

'As for Mr Milton, I adore him myself,' Rose told Helen Waddell; 'but I did feel that he struck his contemporaries as rather a prig, and even, perhaps *was*, a little'. 'The England which bore John Milton in 1608,' begins the book, 'was, like her distinguished son, a curious paradox, an assembly of unresolved conflicts.' It would not be going too far to suggest that this 'curious paradox' Rose Macaulay defines is a curiously apt description of herself and the England she inhabited in the 1930s. She does not fear the bold brushstroke, and goes on to illustrate by example some of the 'unresolved conflicts' of the period: 'Renaissance ambition and arrogance of learning, Elizabethan splendour of poetry and drama, prose that walked in stiff and rich brocade, prose that floundered and spouted like a whale in the ocean, the stately classical tradition and a spontaneous lyric loveliness peculiarly English, medieval puritanism and scholasticism undispelled by these, with the newer puritanism and scholasticism of the Protestant Reformation overlaying it like a palimpsest; a growing and grumbling sense of personal rights and national liberties, a swelling of that pet vanity of the English, political consciousness, furious convictions expressed in mannerless controversies – these characterised both mother and son.'

This short biography deals with Milton's poetry and drama, his politics and prose, and his marriages. Reading Rose Macaulay's account of the 'odd and disastrous affair' of Milton's first marriage, it is hard not to read into it a sense of her troubled relationship with the marriage of her own parents, two people drawn together by a strong sexual attraction and then finding increasing incompatibility. Milton's first divorce tract of 1643 she calls 'a cry of disappointed pain'. As his tracts multiplied, so his disappointment grew into a disappointment with a body politic that turned a deaf ear to his eminently rational calls for divorce: the new presbyters turn out to be little different from the old priests. There is no villain, maintains the biographer, 'only two victims' of this marriage, which is perhaps what she had sometimes thought of the marriage between her father and her mother.

Perhaps it was writing about the part played by sex in the defeat of Julian Conybeare that freed Rose Macaulay to explore the question of women's sexuality and autonomy in a patriarchal world. In her earlier novel *Crewe Train*, celibacy and solitariness was the desired state for her heroine Denham. But that is not the case for young Julian Conybeare. Nor for John Milton. Celibacy was not unproblematic for Milton as a young man, and he later blamed the misfortunes of his marriage – when he wasn't blaming his wife – on his own lack of sexual experience. Mary Powell left him soon after the marriage, and stayed away for three years before returning. 'What the seven years the two spent together were like to either, we do not know,' Rose Macaulay wrote; 'only that they had four children. To remember Milton's bitter and so recent words about conjugal union when minds are as far as heaven from hell, his contempt for it as only fit for the beasts, is to be faced with a riddle.' Can the act of sexual union between two individuals who hate each other, she is asking, be called sexual love?

'I think he was rather of my father's breed . . .' Rose said; 'I wish one of his wives had been of a mental stature he could have had to take into account – it would have been interesting and might have given a different list to Paradise Lost and Eve. I feel his capacities for love were so immense, and never fully (body and mind together) satisfied.' The importance of historical and personal circumstances to a writer's life is a theme of the biography.

She places *Paradise Lost* within the context of the turbulent times and Milton's personal reactions to them, describing it as

> that most suitable theme for contemplation in a lost and mad world, a world in which it must have seemed to him that all liberty, secular and religious, had gone under. The hanging and quartering of his friends, the disinterring of the dead regicides, one repressive Act after another passed by the Cavalier Parliament, the formidable nets thrown around the Nonconformists, the fettering of the press, the power of the bishops, here was a return into Egypt indeed, for the bitter misoclere, for the proud libertarian whose very garters were shackles to him, for the Republican to whom the Single Person was anathema.

And just as Milton himself becomes every character in the poem, except, needless to say, Eve ('amiable Eve,' Rose calls her, who just wants to get on with the gardening 'without being talked to by her long-winded spouse'), so Rose Macaulay in this biography casts off her Cavalier leanings and becomes a staunchly Miltonic republican.

She hails Milton as a great prose writer, a modernist who seized vernacular language and forged it into something powerful and democratic, quoting with pleasure from the *Areopagitica*, his enthusiastic, idealistic and contradictory tract against censorship;

and despite his being 'behind his days' in the matter of female education (because of his strong bias against all women, including or perhaps especially his own wives and daughters), she admires his pamphlet *Of Education*. When he begins to admonish Cromwell, his erstwhile hero, in the *Defensio Secunda* of 1654, 'It is Milton at his extraordinary best and worst, splendid, exasperating, scurrilous, moving, angry, and grandiose by turns.'

This is a writer's appreciation of a writer. Most of all, perhaps, Rose Macaulay would like to identify herself with Milton the passionate seeker after liberty and as a seeker for the sense of his own place as a writer within English history.

While most critics praised the book for its scholarship and its liveliness, it was panned by Basil de Selincourt in the *Observer*, who described it as being 'in the Strachey style, a little work of art, in its way, but inspired by the dangerous conscientiousness of disillusionment; it is witty, learned, sonorous, devastating; but perhaps not quite detached'. He particularly disliked the analysis of the marriage, calling Rose 'strangely unmerciful'.

Over the next three or four years Rose Macaulay had to define more closely what she meant by liberty; by 1938, when her next biography was published, the shadows of the forthcoming war demanded a definitive resolution of that term. Rose Macaulay in the 1930s was as she had described both Milton and Milton's England: 'a curious paradox, an assembly of unresolved conflicts'. In the three major books she wrote in the 1930s she looked backwards and inwards, and explored both the desired place of union between heart and intellect, and also – through her portrayal of the sexual relationship of Julian Conybeare and John Cleveland, through her account of John Milton's bitterly unhappy (for all parties) marriages, and through her analysis of the failures of representation of heterosexual love in E. M. Forster's novels – the private passions and necessary reticences of sexual love. And as she examined her own relationship to England and to the history of England, she was inevitably drawn into the events that foreshadowed the coming war.

Throughout most of the 1930s Rose was a pacifist, although she could never wholeheartedly follow a party line. Her pacifism grew out of the temperament of the unengaged observer that she had developed so successfully as a writer in the 1920s. She was as ever impatient with the failings of organisations. 'The League of Nations do publish a lot of rather useless stuff, I think,' is the typical tone of a letter to Jean, in December 1934. 'Still, I am sure one ought to support them.' That year, along with 11 million others she signed up to a Peace Ballot, organised by the League of Nations Union. 'I really can't see what harm it can do,' she said: not exactly the sentiments of a committed activist. She believed strongly in freedom of information: ignorance was a vice to be combated. 'I do think it is good for us to be made to think . . . What we all *are* agreed on, of course, is in wanting peace; the rest is just a question of ways of obtaining it, and thousands of people say this is so much a matter for experts that it is a pity the public should even think about it. I can never see this point of view, and think the more we think and say about it the better.'

In 1935 she voted for the Labour candidate in Marylebone, a Dr Elizabeth Jacobs, 'to increase the opposition to the Conservative candidate, who is a safe winner,' she explained. 'I am all for Socialism later, but not yet.'

To Rose, as to many others, the threat of war was not yet real. Her letters are often flippant about world events. 'Will suggests that everyone should draw lots, and the shortest would have to shoot the Duce,' she writes to Jean in September 1935. 'Do you think I ought to go out and have a try, as I feel so strongly about it? I don't feel it would disgrace the family name, but rather honour it. I should have done that which was righteous in the sight of the Lord, also of the nations.' After the announcement of the Hoare–Laval pact two months later, which paved the way for Mussolini's invasion of Abyssinia, Sir Samuel Hoare went holidaying in Switzerland. News came back of a minor accident. 'Everyone is delighted that Hoare has broken his nose skating, and we all hope it hurts,' Rose wrote. The Duce, Mussolini, was a laughable tinpot tyrant in the eyes of the press, and if the invasion of Abyssinia was an embarrassment for the British government, there was strong popular feeling for the emperor in exile, Haile Selassie, in which Rose shared. She attended his press conference in June 1936, and wrote later: 'The Cabinet are now longing for him to go away, he is so embarrassing. Baldwin hasn't seen him, either, and Eden only for 20 minutes. Meanwhile, the King goes to Ascot and all about, and has a good time.' Cold-shouldered by politicians, Haile Selassie was, predictably, given a warm welcome by Victor and Ruth Gollancz at Brimpton.

Rose gave her support not so much to a principle (although the League of Nations was one of those principles) as to individuals she liked and admired: Haile Selassie because he had been forced to flee his country and was now being bullied and humiliated, and Dick Sheppard with his Peace Pledge Union. Dick Sheppard changed Rose from an observer of the 'tale/Told by an idiot' into an activist. She became a sponsor of the Peace Pledge Union in June 1936, and for the next eighteen months spoke and wrote tirelessly on its behalf. With the anthologist Daniel George she was working on a peace anthology called *All in a Maze*. She even, in October 1937, went up to Glasgow to campaign for Dick Sheppard's rectorship of the university, which he was contesting, and won, on a peace platform against Winston Churchill and others.

Earlier that year, in March, Rose Macaulay published *An Open Letter to a Non-Pacifist*, an urgent and intimate argument in favour of non-violent resistance. Pacifism has hardly been tried in the history of the world, she says, but it is nonetheless worth trying. Indeed, 'it is an experiment which no nation or individual who claims and pretends civilisation can afford *not* to try'.

The main point was both a moral and political one: to what extent are citizens obliged to accept the arms policy and the foreign policy of the government from whose protection they benefit? Rose argued for the 'individual inalienable right of conscience', and asked the question that would be asked by thousands only a few years later when Dresden was firebombed, the question that continues to be asked today: 'There have been, surely, State protective measures too barbarous for civilised men and women today to accept. The question is, is organised war among these?'

Her final point answered the claim that war was an inevitable consequence of the universal evils of hate and greed. Against this she urged the proven efficacy of political action: 'So might it have been argued about slave emancipation, that slavery was but one aspect of human disgustingness, and that to abolish it would not end the barbarity which caused it. But did the abolitionists therefore waste their breath? And do we waste ours now in protesting against war?'

Rose sent a copy of the *Letter* to Victor Gollancz. 'I refrained from reading this opus at the time,' he wrote, 'for I was in stays about pacifism and could not have borne to . . .' Gollancz had kept himself closely informed of the developments of National Socialism in Germany, and was well aware of the atrocities already committed in its name. Rose's work in the Department of Propaganda in the previous war may well have made her initially reluctant to believe atrocity stories, but by now Gerald too, who was working with a group organising the placement of Czech refugee children in English schools, was another source of reliable information.

Dick Sheppard died suddenly of a heart attack only a few weeks after he became Rector of Glasgow University. For the next few months Rose continued to support the Peace Pledge Union. She resigned in March 1938, the month the German army moved into Austria.

In May she involved herself in organising a public meeting advertised as 'Writers declare against Fascism'. Hugh Walpole, whom she wanted to speak on 'Freedom', demurred, and she had to reassure him that it was '*not* political'. In the letter she wrote urging him to take part she states her own non-political political position:

... the meeting is of distinguished non-political writers to say what they feel abt dictatorship over freedom of artistic expression & over other forms of liberty – & of course speakers will say anything they like abt *any* dictatorship, left or right. For example 'George Birmingham', who is to speak on Dictatorships & Religion, will certainly refer both to the Nazi and Soviet tyrannies ... And I wld be surprised if Compton Mackenzie confined himself to Fascism, either. Surely, with speakers like these, & Philip Guedalla, Desmond MacCarthy, Liddel Hart, one need not fear bigoted 'Left' politics from the platform. We wanted Jack Priestley also to speak, bt he says he has said in the past what he thinks of Fascism, & tht it wld be silly to go on saying it – one does see this point of view, of course. I myself have no political party – no, I suppose I am a Liberal, actually – I never take part in Communist demonstrations; I hate Communism & Nazism & Fascism, all three. The idea of this meeting is to protest against the fantastic & horrible suppressions of liberty of thought & expression tht Fascism entails, & to emphasise tht freedom is the only soil out of which any decent life, thought, or art, is likely to grow. Is not this sound, & is it really political? Of course attack the Soviet Dictatorship, bt I don't think it shld be singled out for special condemnation, apart from the others, which have done more harm still to liberty, and which are a more present danger in Europe, I suppose.

Rose went on a superb six weeks' holiday, as she described it to Elizabeth Bowen, in August and September. For some of those weeks Gerald was with her. She was in Provence, and in the Pyrenees, and she was in Varazze when Chamberlain and Hitler met at Munich. She had been sending regular postcards to Daniel George who was toiling over *All in a Maze* back in London, giving details of her lotus-eating and of the pleasures of a warm sea and sweet-smelling hills. On 15 September she wrote, 'Our P.M. seems to have saved the world! ... If war is so easily averted as all this, it does seem a pity no P.M. ever thought

of it before'. Germany promptly invaded Czechoslovakia. Britain
was at war with Germany within a year, and this was the last
summer abroad Rose Macaulay ever spent with Gerald.

All in a Maze came out in November 1937, but it had been
overtaken by events. The two thousand years of prose and verse
on the subject of peace, and war, needed less belligerent times to
be savoured. The £25 the editors received as an advance they
split between the International Peace Committee and the Peace
Pledge Union.

At the beginning of 1935 Rose had begun a weekly column,
'Marginal Comments', in the *Spectator*. She covered a wide range
of topics, including Lloyd George on the education of girls,
English smugness, poets and nationalism (with reference to
D'Annunzio and the Italian invasion of Abyssinia), milk ('what
a disgusting drink it is'), Guy Fawkes ('what an ambition to
have'), and passports as a symptom of the general erosion of
individual liberties. Some old favourites appear: the varied pleasures of swimming, for example, and the annoyingness of other
road users, who dazzle you with their lights 'like the eyes of a
tiger or of Signor Mussolini in a rage'. At the end of 1935 she
managed to involve herself and the *Spectator* in a case of dangerous driving. Someone called Lord de Clifford was driving on
the wrong side of the road and crashed into an oncoming car,
killing the driver. He was tried for manslaughter in the House of
Lords, and for dangerous driving in the Central Criminal Court,
and was acquitted on both counts. Rose wrote to her sister Jean:
'what did his counsel mean by saying that driving on the wrong
side of the road was no proof of negligence?' In her *Spectator*
column she wrote: 'It would appear that driving on the wrong
side of the road is considered by the law less dangerous than
other motoring crimes'. She did not say that he had been acquitted because he was a peer, although doubtless her comments on
the 'parade of mummery and pantomime' did not go down well
with the Lord Chief Justice. But she compared de Clifford's
acquittal with the recent case of a woman who had been given a

prison sentence of nine months for taking a corner too fast, and went on to make general remarks about driving on the wrong side of the road being evidence of 'reckless selfishness, stupidity and bad manners'. The Lord took offence, the Lord Chief Justice took offence on behalf of the Lord, and in the ensuing case of libel Rose Macaulay and the *Spectator* were ordered to pay £600 and the costs of the case.

Two days later Rose had to appear again in court to face a charge of 'obstructing the public highway' with her car, and was fined thirty shillings. It was the first of her many parking offences.

Besides the *Spectator* column she was also writing book reviews for the *Times Literary Supplement*, and for the short-lived *Day and Night*, and meanwhile she continued to exert herself on behalf of others. In the mid-1930s she arranged for Brigid O'Donovan, Gerald's daughter, who had just left Oxford, to get a job at Faber & Faber as T. S. Eliot's secretary, and she was trying to get Dermod O'Donovan's articles from Poland – where he was working as a journalist – placed in London papers.

It says something about Rose's frame of mind in this incredibly busy decade of her life that it was the period in which her first two books of 'pleasures' were published, the anthology *The Minor Pleasures of Life* in 1934, followed the next year by a collection of essays, *Personal Pleasures*. Rose was full of joy. Victor Gollancz, describing Rose as someone who had a 'connoisseurship of oddities', was thinking of the odd little objects that she collected and that she gave lovingly to her friends: a 'bird in the box'; a gouache of 'Antient Rome', juxtaposing seven typical monuments; a Victorian glass-painting of Pomona, the goddess of fruit. She was also a connoisseur of literary oddities, which she and Victor Gollancz celebrated together in *The Minor Pleasures of Life*. Rose's book was one of a pair, but, as Anthony Burgess wrote many years later: 'Her *Minor Pleasures* is remembered while, I fear, even the author of the companion volume on *Major Pleasures* is forgotten.'

Minor Pleasures consists of an alphabetically arranged collection of pleasures (or minor pleasures), from Agreeable Encounters to Xenophobia (who else but Rose Macaulay?), with one or more extracts from literature to illustrate each. There are three or four extracts from her father's translation of Herodotus's *History*, including, mischievously, 'Buying Maidens in Babylon' as an example of the pleasure of shopping. The great bulk of the examples come, unsurprisingly, from the seventeenth century: Cowley, Burton, Browne, Herrick, Aubrey and Evelyn, alongside Milton. Pepys appears under 'Parties'. There is also a number of poems by 'Anon'. Rose Macaulay admitted to authorship of just one of these, 'The Chase', and only when later anthologists enquired of her further details of its provenance. It appears under 'Female Pleasures'. 'The fact is,' Rose wrote to John Hayward, 'that I wanted a poem on about [*sic*] women hunting & couldn't lay my hands on one at the moment, so I thought I would write one myself, and it amused me to put it into 17th century garb and date it "c. 1675" (after all, how many years may *circa* cover? I thought perhaps 260 years or so, so dated it thus.)'. John Hayward responded neatly to her disingenuousness about the meaning of *circa* by suggesting that she had dated it too late.

The poem is a celebration of

> the Girles of Artemis,
> Whose traffique was in Woods, whom the wing'd Boy
> Leauguer'd in vain, whom Man would ne're injoy,
> Whose Bed greene Moss beneath the forrest Tree,
> Whose jolly Pleasure all in Liberty,
> To sport with fellow Maids in maiden cheere,
> To swim the Brook, and hollo after Deer.
> Thus, the winds wantoning their flying Curles,
> So rac'd, so chas'd, those most Delightfull Girles.

These girls of Artemis are reminiscent of *Crewe Train*'s Denham Dobie: what they want is the 'Pleasure all in Liberty', to do what they want and not be beholden to others. (The rhyming of the 'flying Curles' with the 'Delightfull Girles' was to cause Rose scholarly anguish later. Or so she claimed.)

A more explicitly erotic poem, which includes voyeurism among the sexual pleasures it hymns, is 'The Private Bathe': 'The Swimming Lady: . . . Being a True Relation of a Coy Lady . . . Swimming in a River near Oxford'. So beautiful is the Lady once undressed that not only do the little fishes swim out to view her, but the Sun himself drops down into the stream:

> Thus was the Rivers Diamond head,
>   with Pearls and Saphir crown'd:
> Her legs did shove, her Arms did move,
>   her Body did rebound: . . .

Once naked and in the river,

> She then did quaff the Juice of Joy,
>   fair Venus Queen of Love
> With Mars did never in more ways,
>   of melting motion move! . . .

Rose never admitted to this 'late 17th c. Anon' vigorously sexual poem on the pleasures of naked bathing; but then perhaps she was never asked about it.

Most surprising of all is the quantity of long extracts from Walt Whitman, almost the only American writer to feature in the anthology. These range from the openly celebratory of male friendship ('A Glimpse' from 'Song of Myself') to the wildly internationalist 'You, whoever you are!' which opens his 'Salut au Monde', and which Rose gives us for the pleasure of Xenophilism.

What was the appeal of Whitman for Rose Macaulay at this point? Perhaps his homosexuality, which positioned him obliquely to the mainstream, and which spoke to the sense that

Rose still had of herself as an observer. Seeing yourself as within the culture and yet outside it: Walt Whitman is the great poet of America and Americanness, while at the same time his celebratory nationalism goes far beyond the boundaries of geography or politics. 'Salut au monde!' he cried out. Perhaps one has to be outside things for the clear vision. Perhaps it was the American exile in the American Walt Whitman that appealed to English Rose Macaulay. Perhaps, too, Whitman spoke to her in the same way that Milton did, in the voice of someone struggling to understand and articulate his own position within history.

Personal Pleasures, the following year, was also published by Victor Gollancz. Here, as well as a number of childhood pleasures from Varazze days, such as Candlemas, Canoeing, Chasing Fireflies, and Hatching Eggs, Rose includes some of her adult pleasures: Driving a Car (of course), and Flying. As a result of the 'enormous bliss' of speeding 'through radiant space' that Rose described in 'Flying', it became widely believed that Rose herself was a pilot.

She covers many of the idiosyncrasies of literary London life in the 1930s, such as the 'boasting' parties that were all the rage and that her friend Logan Pearsall Smith would often host. 'What is that you say you have done? Walked across Jamaica on your hands? That is nothing at all . . . I wrote out "The Ride from Ghent to Aix" backwards. What did you say? You have a certificate of *what*? Signed by the Pope . . . *And* three children . . . Well that was just a mistake, wasn't it; you should have told him . . . You gave ringworm to two archbishops? I really do not see that that is much to boast of. You converted Cherokee Indians when you were six? That is better. And had a tract written about you, called "How Little —— came to Jesus." That is better still . . .'

In the pleasure of 'Reading' Rose gives a picture of the two main London libraries: the London Library, which even then, a good fifty years before its temptations were made famous in the opening pages of A. S. Byatt's bestselling *Possession*, is characterised as 'a notable hunting-ground for thieves'; and the British Library where it is almost impossible to steal the books but where readers lick their fingers to turn the pages and where apparently 'some readers even lick the pages direct with the tongue, but this habit is, I believe, confined to those who have been allowed special access to books not generally accessible, and denotes some peculiar pleasure'.

There are some fine parodies of the work of writers of the 1930s in 'Following the Fashion'. She mocks the style of the little literary magazines and offers some suitable magazine work of her own. A poem '(I call this one "To the Barricades")', with its mixture of lines in Greek, French, Latin and demotic chit-chat, and its rhetorical call to the revolution, nicely marries Auden with Eliot:

> Mr Jiggins goes to the circus.
> (The girls, the hoops, the clowns, the seals, the hoopoes.)
> He has donned his Harrow tie,
> But Borstal was his alma mater true.
> He meets Mrs. Fortescue-Fox,
> With a jade cigarette-holder, long and green like asparagus
>   or a dead woman's fingers
> Or the pale weeds swaying in the duck-pond,
> But never a sprig of rue . . .
> Ohé! Ohé! Mes brave petits! The fat is in the fire! . . .
> Ting-a-ling-a-ling ring the bells of hell; where you bound now?
> Allons, companions, we march to the barricades.
> In the grey dawn of yesterday
> We wipe away all tears: – perhaps.

But there is something formulaic in these essays. One of the two epigraphs to the book, 'But every pleasure hath a payne, they say', from George Chapman, alerts the reader to their structure. The sting in the tail of each essay, the pain in the pleasure, seems striven for. Alice Bensen talks of the 'peril of mandarinism' that appears now and again in these essays, but makes the point that as war approached the preciousness of style disappeared and Rose began to use her writing for public ends.

The two conflicting movements in Rose's life in the 1930s – the movement out into the world, and the movement back into history – left her little time or energy for what, in the previous decade, she had been so good at, and what her publishers had come to rely on: bright, witty, fictional accounts of the contemporary world. The three novels of contemporary life that were published in the 1930s, *Staying with Relations* (1930), *Going Abroad* (1934) and *I Would Be Private* (1937), are weak shadows of her 1920s fiction. Perhaps she should have written to Mr Collins as she did to Mr Cape, please don't bother me about other books. Unfortunately she had a contract with William Collins, and therefore an obligation. As so often, Rose Macaulay showed an excellent instinct for the feeling of the times: abroad was the place to be, and if you couldn't manage it in person, either as a literary traveller or courtesy of Thomas Cook, then you could do it from the comfort of your own armchair with the help of books set abroad (armchair travel appears as one of the pleasures of 'Reading' in *Personal Pleasures*). And perhaps, too, it was easier to write about 'abroad', now that her engagement with business at home meant that she could no longer play the disinterested observer as she had once done. With *Going Abroad* Rose stated she had set out to write a novel of 'unredeemed levity', and the result, as the *Times Literary Supplement* put it, was 'light and unsubstantial to the point of facetiousness'. Nonetheless it became a bestseller, suggesting that facetiousness was exactly what readers wanted.

The novel is set on the Spanish Basque coast, just over the water from France. There are two targets for the unredeemed levity: the Oxford Groupers, that is, the followers of Frank Buchman, who would later develop into the movement for Moral Rearmament, and the beauty industry. As a target for satire the latter has worn rather better than the former; doubtless there will be unscrupulous people making money out of face creams and skin lotions until the end of time. The Oxford Groupers, easy target for so many 1930s novelists, seem, now, quaint rather than anything else. Rose expressed regret later on that she had made fun of the hearty Groupers: 'I think now it is rather a *bad* joke, I mean about the Groupers; one shouldn't really make fun of people who, however aesthetically repellent to one's taste, are, after all, on the right side as between moral good and evil.' Apart from anything else she is not quite nasty enough about them to make it really funny.

The satire on the beauty industry is predicated on two girls of unutterable plainness and an older woman whose face has been ravaged by these so-called beauty products. Never for a moment, in this novel that is predominantly about physical appearance, does one believe that any of the characters actually has flesh and a body. As the plot degenerates into a silly kidnapping up in the Basque mountains, so the style becomes increasingly awkward, with a plethora of sub-clauses and awkward breaks in the sentences.

The most interesting character is Philippa Buckley, whose daughter Hero has joined the Buchmanites, and who quarrels vigorously with her disapproving son Giles because she believes that Hero must be allowed to do what she likes. The quarrel is cast in terms of a clash of values between the pre- and post-war generations in which it is the older generation that holds the liberal views:

The representatives of two generations looked at one another with that half-irritated, half-baffled recognition of a point of view alien and opposed which so frequently divides families. Philippa Buckley, born in 1890, brought up on principles the most liberal, the most libertarian, the most humane, to view compulsion, whether that of state or individual, as the last outrage on adult humanity, brought up, in fact, a late Victorian liberal individualist, looked across a gulf at a new generation, born about the same time as the Great War, which seemed to share the harshness, the reckless compulsions, the ardent belief in regimentation, of that dire and ruthless event. Fascist and Communist, the young, illiberal, regimented world split into these two camps, mutually fearing and loathing one another, but reserving their contempt for such as her, for the drifting individualists who uttered the foolish cry of 'Liberty'.

Within the edifice of phrases and sub-clauses in that paragraph is a picture of a 'late Victorian liberal individualist', a creature not very different from Rose Macaulay herself, a creature that has survived one world war but will not survive another.

The premise for Rose's next novel, *I Would Be Private*, was the highly publicised birth of quintuplets to a couple in Canada. In the novel Rose gives the quins to a Scottish-born London policeman and his wife, who flee to a Caribbean island for privacy. The failure to find it is both predictable and tiresomely unfunny.

She amused herself by writing a 'fake paragraph' for the epigraph, with which, she proudly told John Hayward, she had 'teased a few Americans' who had written to enquire about it. It comes from a work entitled *Roger Rampole's Cheaping*: 'Press me not, throng me not, by your leave I would be private. Jupiter Ammon, is a man then not free? What a pox, may he not choose his road, is he to be bethronged, beset, commanded, as he were a beast in a drover's herd, or a zany in a fairman's show? Stand back, you knaves, you buzzing flap-dragons, give me leave to be private, by Cock's death I'll walk free, or I'll not walk at all.'

She had had the satisfaction, she wrote, 'of seeing it quoted in some one's detective novel, as from that well-known work, Roger Rampole's Cheaping'. The first line at least seems to have echoes of the opening of the late sixteenth/early seventeenth-century poet Michael Drayton's *Idea's Mirrour*.

> You not alone, when you are alone,
> O God, from you that I could private be!

which does indeed appear in 'someone's detective novel': a good two years before Rose's pastiche. Harriet Vane, in Dorothy L. Sayers's *Gaudy Night*, says it to herself when she is feeling 'pressed upon and bullied by reality'.

I Would Be Private was not a success. William Collins was displeased, and wrote to Rose's agent, reminding him of the last contract signed with Collins in 1929,

> a time when Miss Macaulay was writing novels regularly at two-yearly intervals and when her sales were steady in the neighbourhood of 15,000 . . . There have, however, been longer and longer intervals between each of Miss Macaulay's novels, as she has been spending much of her time in doing other work, and . . . she [has] kept finding it difficult to think out plots for new novels. One of the results of the long intervals between her books and of her difficulties over plots has been that her sales have suffered a very considerable drop. *I Would Be Private* sold just over 8,000 copies . . . in the original (Home) edition, representing a drop of almost 50%, and leaving us with an unearned royalty of £465, a considerable loss on any book.

Rose had been living on royalties and the proceeds of her journalism since the early 1920s. To publish a book that failed to earn its advance was a serious matter. But in December 1937, when Reginald Heber Macaulay, her last surviving uncle, died, he left her £10,000. He had come to her rescue again, for she was the only one of his nieces to whom he made a bequest (four of his nephews, including his only Macaulay nephew, Will, also received £10,000 each). Rose invested her legacy, and the results freed her from dependence on royalties.

The Writings of E. M. Forster was the last book of Rose's to be published before the outbreak of war. It came out just over a year after the publication of his collection of essays, *Abinger Harvest*. Forster was two years older than Rose. His first novel, *Where Angels Fear to Tread*, was published in 1905, the year before *Abbots Verney* came out. But where Rose had not achieved wide success until the 1920s, which, later, was often seen as the beginning of her career, Edwin Morgan Forster had published his last and final novel, *A Passage to India*, in 1924. He had been involved with the Woolfs and the Hogarth Press since its inception, and was an established member of the Bloomsbury group in a way that Rose herself never was. *The Writings of E. M. Forster*, commissioned by Leonard Woolf for the Hogarth Press, was the first full-length critical book on Forster's work.

Rose Macaulay's overall reading of his work is sharp but sympathetic. There were parallels not just between some of her novels and his – their common interest, for example, in the English abroad – but also between her life and his. Looking at E. M. Forster was a way of looking at herself. Forster's antecedents, the 'liberal bourgeois culture' from which he comes, are very similar to her own, and the picture that she draws of his early and mid-Victorian forebears is a portrait of her own ancestry: 'Gentle, intelligent, high-minded, high-browed, these ancestors of ours look down on us from drawings and paintings on our walls, faintly coloured in their gold frames, their minds set on freeing West Indian slaves, on lightening child labour, on attending Evangelical conferences, on reading good books; whatsoever things are pure, lovely, of good intent, they think, we may be sure, on these things . . .' There is a faintly mocking tone here, which surfaces at other moments throughout the book. You hear it when she talks about Forster's response to the Great War and to his nostalgia for a past age; you hear it when she talks about his claims to a passionate love of liberty. She calls this his 'libertolatry'. Forster fancied himself as a great liberal. Which he was, but he was also a great pronouncer, and Rose Macaulay recognised this.

'Piety is a handicap,' she wrote of his biography of his mentor

Goldsworthy Lowes Dickinson, which was 'first and last, and with all its various side lines . . . the life of one member of King's College, Cambridge [both had been Fellows], by another.' It was with a cool eye that she looked at Forster, and with a cool eye that, through him, she looked at herself. Piety is not a handicap to Rose Macaulay the biographer, especially when it comes to Forster's obsession with public schools ('this public school business is rather perplexing') and with his penchant for generalisations about the English character. She notes his love affair with Cambridge and how it permeates all his writing. She knew about the privileges of a male English middle-class education from close observation, and quietly points out the limitations of its understanding, as in, for example, the importance of Greek mythology in his early stories and articles, through which 'move noiselessly those invisible, immortal Greek creatures, dryads, oreads, fauns, Pan, who haunt (or haunted then) the imaginative twilight of the British classic-nurtured mind, though, it is said, few other minds . . .'

But she admired his grace, his wit, his kindness, his hatred of bullies, intellectual or otherwise, his hatred of pretentiousness, and his commitment to an idea of the truth. These were qualities that she valued, and that she strived to nourish in herself.

Although she maintained that theories about fiction bored her – she considered the subject of Forster's 1927 Clark lectures at Cambridge, published in 1927 as *Aspects of the Novel*, to be a 'rather tedious topic' – she could theorise sharply enough when she wanted. Of the characters in *Howards End* she says that they seem contrived, because they appear to have become other people, which is what people may do in real life, 'but art is different, art has a compulsion that life has not to make the strange natural'. The particular criticisms that she makes of Forster's novels have over the years become generally accepted by later critics: that, for example, Agnes in *The Longest Journey* is over-drawn and Philip is unreal, and that Philip's 'maidish disgust' at his half-brother's illegitimacy is a flaw in the book; that the credibility of the relationship between Helen Schlegel and Leonard Bast in *Howards End* leaves much to be desired (although here Rose was not the first to express incredulity: Katherine Mansfield asked if we were meant to believe that Helen was impregnated by Leonard Bast's umbrella). She suggested that the problem of Helen was that she 'represents a point of view that Mr Forster needed for the thesis of his work'. Rose herself was not above using characters in her fiction to represent a point of view needed for a thesis; it was a failure of the imagination that she recognised in herself. The ludicrous behaviour of Cecil Vyse in *A Room with a View* when he first brings himself to kiss Lucy she wittily compares to the behaviour of a young man in Charlotte Yonge's *The Daisy Chain*,

> who proposes to a young lady whom he loves while on a walk with her, and is accepted, after which, much embarrassed, they walk home on opposite sides of the road, a scene which my mother, reading this admirable book aloud to us in my childhood, assured us out of her riper experience was improbable. We did not care. We had no desire that Norman, whom we admired, should demean himself and make himself soppy kissing a girl. Norman was meant for better things; he was, in fact, to be a missionary to the heathen. By all means let him keep on the far side of the road, and not let himself get what it was our habit to call 'kissy'. Cecil, though he was not to be a missionary, suffered from the same inhibitions . . .

But her criticisms are minor ones, and she is generous in her praise of Forster's wit, irony and 'felicities of style'. She also valued what she called the 'reticent' nature of his biography of Dickinson. Rose Macaulay was reticent about herself. It was part of her upbringing, and part of the times as well. It was probably not only that homosexual activity between men was a criminal offence that stopped Rose Macaulay mentioning Forster's homosexuality in her book (although that was a factor in all books before the law was changed), but a strongly held belief that a private life was a private life. Her analysis of all the characters in Forster's early novels, of the way that his inexperience of heterosexual love permeates the love affairs they have, and in particular her drawing-out of the strongly anti-marriage views expressed throughout *A Passage to India*, suggest that she was perfectly well aware of his sexual orientation.

The sharpness of Rose's critique of Forster comes from recognition of the similarity, despite the differences, of their positions. She explored herself and her own work in her analysis of his work. In the same way as she had seen her own contradictory desires and disputatiousness reflected in her portrait of John Milton, so, reflected in this analysis of the work of her friend and contemporary, she saw her own Englishness, her own relation to the late nineteenth-century world in which they had both grown up, and her own position on the edge of the literary mainstream. His homosexuality allowed him, as her gender and her temperament allowed her, the cool, ironic, sideways glance at the English establishment, even if he didn't always choose to use it.

E. M. Forster did not like Rose's book.

'I have just finished Rose's book,' he wrote to Leonard Woolf, who had sent him an advance copy. 'It is most considerate and tactful, gratifying, and in a sense intelligent, but tamely conceived and badly written, especially towards the close. Not a good book I am afraid. And as you say, no conclusion is reached. What very odd things people do!'

The conclusion that Rose reached was that there was no novelist better equipped than Forster to capture the 'flickering aspect' of English contemporary life before the 'next great cataclysm'. Nearly twenty years had passed since Forster had last published a novel: that must have been a conclusion he did not want to hear.

'Rose Macaulay is a wise guide,' Forster wrote of Rose's description of the inter-war years in *Life Among the English*, 'tolerant, generous-minded, liberal, courageous, cheerful, and her judgments of society and social values are always sound.' It was through the biographies and her historical novel (also a biography) of the 1930s that Rose had begun to explore her own position as a woman writer, and her position within an English literary tradition. She had had a decade of happiness with her lover. She would need her courage and her cheerfulness during the years of the 'next great cataclysm'.

Chapter Nine

In Ruins

Miss Anstruther, whose life had been cut in two on the night of May 10th, 1941, so that she now felt herself a ghost, without attachments or habitation, neither of which she any longer desired, sat alone in the bed-sitting-room she had taken, a small room, littered with the grimy, broken and useless objects which she had salvaged from the burnt-out ruin round the corner. It was one of the many burnt-out ruins of that wild night when high explosives and incendiaries had rained on London and the water had run short: it was now a gaunt and roofless tomb, a pile of ashes and rubble and burnt, smashed beams. Where the floors of twelve flats had been there was empty space. Miss Anstruther had for the first few days climbed up to what had been her flat, on what had been the third floor, swarming up pendent fragments of beams and broken girders, searching and scrabbling among ashes and rubble, but not finding what she sought, only here a pot, there a pan, sheltered from destruction by an overhanging slant of ceiling. Her marmalade for May had been there, and a little sugar and tea . . .

'Miss Anstruther's Letters'

In 2001 the A686 road from Penrith in Cumbria to Corbridge in Northumberland was declared by the Automobile Association to be one of the world's greatest drives. The road snakes up the North Pennine Scarp 2,000 feet to the Hartside Pass. Here you can look north across the Solway Firth to

Scotland and west across the whole of Cumbria to the peaks of
Helvellyn, Great Gable and Skiddaw. On this road, approaching
Hartside Pass, Rose Macaulay collided with an oncoming car on
26 June 1939, causing her passenger to suffer a concussion. Her
passenger was Gerald O'Donovan. He was sixty-eight, and the
concussion was undoubtedly implicated in the stroke he suffered soon after.

The O'Donovan family knew that Rose and Gerald were
away together in the Lake District; they were playing the 'Rose
Macaulay is an old friend of the family' game. (Gerald had
asked his daughter Brigid to drive him round the Lake
District, and when she couldn't, or wouldn't, Rose was asked
instead.) Beryl preferred to see it that way; Rose knew that
other people would not accept such a fabrication, and was as
careful as ever to keep Gerald completely hidden from others'
view. They had stayed in separate hotels in Keswick, and the
notice in the local press that 'Miss Rose Macaulay, the well-
known novelist' was staying at the Waverley Hotel implied
that she was travelling alone. For some time Rose had been
working with Daniel George on another anthology, a bestiary
('my great Life-Work', she called it to Walter de la Mare: 'The
Characters of Animals in Literature'); they were in touch over
this or that detail and her postcards to him – cows at
Derwentwater was one – suggest a quiet holiday on her own.
Such minor deceptions had been going on for twenty years,
allowing the inference to be drawn by the recipients of her
cheerful cards that she was alone when she was in fact with
Gerald. This would be the last such deception. Rose and
Gerald never went away together again; by the time he recovered from the stroke brought on by the accident, he was
suffering from the cancer that would kill him.

Casual postcards continued to be dispatched after the accident, showing Rose's steely resolve to betray nothing of what
had happened. In the middle of July, before she returned north
for the court case, Rose told Daniel George she would be away

for a week or so, and on the postcard wrote of nothing more personal than a bad review she had seen of her *Milton*. When she appeared at Penrith Police Court in the third week of July to face the charge of driving without due care and attention she presented herself as Emily Macaulay, and no connection was made between her and the well-known novelist who had been sojourning in the Lake District the previous month. The case was reported in the *Cumberland and Westmorland Herald* under the heading 'Woman Motorist Whose Attention was Diverted': the Bench was told that 'her passenger diverted her attention from the road and she apparently swerved, colliding with an approaching car'. The approaching car was the materialisation of what she had so light-heartedly described in her personal pleasure of driving as 'the serpent in this Eden, the canker in this lovely bloom of speed'. There she had complained of how 'the other vehicles in our road' tend so irritatingly to hog the middle of it.

The defending solicitor submitted Emily Macaulay's membership of the Women's Voluntary Ambulance Service, which Rose had joined in the spring, as special circumstances which would justify the non-endorsement of her licence. The Bench were not impressed. Rose was fined £2, with £1 6s. 3d. costs, and the Chairman of the Bench remarked 'that they did not see any reason why the licence should not be endorsed as in any other case'.

That autumn Rose thought that Gerald might die. She wrote to her sister Jean, who had just returned, reluctantly, to England after three years working in a mission hospital in South Africa; she was now a district nurse in Romford, where she had settled with her friend Nancy Willetts. Rose's letters are uncharacteristically depressed in tone, quite unlike her earlier correspondence. There are no more bright, glancing asides on this or that topic, as in the last letter she had written to Jean before Jean went abroad: 'I am asked to sign a petition for voluntary euthanasia. Is this right? No hurry; send a p.c. sometime, yes or no.' It wasn't just the anxiety about Gerald that depressed her. Nine weeks after the accident on Hartside Britain declared war on Germany.

At this stage Rose was passionately against going to war. She believed, as did many others, that it would be possible to negotiate with Hitler; the war, she wrote to Jean, 'would settle nothing', there would now be 'war after war'. Her letters of this time are full of references to life being 'like a bad dream', and visions of a 'world gone crazy'. She was depressed by what she saw as liberals and intellectuals being pro-war and failing to take into account the potentially disastrous effects of a war economy on the lives of ordinary working people.

Her state of mind is reflected in the pages of the novel she was struggling to finish, *And No Man's Wit*. 'The Sun is lost, and th'earth, and no mans wit/Can well direct him where to looke for it.' The poem from which title and epigraph to the book are taken, John Donne's 'An Anatomie of the World', goes on: ' 'Tis all in peeces, all coherence gone;/All just supply, and all relation . . .' Chosen by Rose as appropriate for the subject of the novel, the Spanish Civil War, it became equally appropriate to her own state of mind as she moved down into a deep depression after the car accident and, by the time the book was finished in early 1940, to the increasing European war; 'apt to the moment', as she put it to Daniel George.

'I am dead sick of my novel,' she had written to him in October, 'but must push on. I'd so much rather get on to my beasts.' The effort that went into the finishing of this novel is echoed in the effortful trudging to and fro across the dry Spanish hinterland her characters undertake as they search, fruitlessly, for a young Englishman who has come out to support the Republicans and has gone missing. It is a trudge; but it is redeemed by a fantastical strand of the story which allows one of the characters to be half-mermaid. Through Ellen, the merwoman, we escape from the contemporary events of this rigid and unhappy novel into lighter times of fable and legend. She prompts an inspired retelling of the mermaid-from-the-sea folk tale which Rose Macaulay imagined, thanks to the Conybeare rector in Devonshire who 'married a mermaid, tho it doesn't seem to have got into the family records', to be part of her personal family history. Ellen's story ends tragically. The sea offers more than escape: it drowns identity.

A couple of years later *Life Among the English* was published, one of the 'Britain in Pictures' series of short illustrated books by eminent writers intended to boost pride in a nation at war. The series included companion volumes by Graham Greene on British dramatists and Vita Sackville-West on English country houses. Rose Macaulay described that period at the end of the 1930s when everyone was at loggerheads: 'During those stormy years the Spanish *pronunciamento* split the British public; the fashionable continental tour was to government or rebel Spain, according to the tourist's political colour. Tempers ran still higher over the desirability or otherwise of observing international obligations by defending Czechoslovakia.'

She went on to write about those months of what was called the 'phoney war', beginning with a wonderfully sly metaphor of frightened middle-class Londoners as foxes:

Britain became bomb-conscious: trenches were dug; many Londoners went to earth in the country; hardly had the trenches become water-logged and the earths abandoned than it was all to do again. After that many new fashions came in; windows were criss-crossed with tape; gas masks were carried about and left in cinemas and on blackberry bushes, bags of sand lay on pavements, rotted, sprouted and burst asunder; through Cimmerian blackness torches were flashed, annoying drivers; women went into trousers, civilians into fire, ambulance and wardens' stations, older men into the Home Guard; young men and women were put into the forces and factories, enemy aliens (hostile and friendly) into camps, British Fascists and others into gaol, policemen into tin hats.

Her take on the social changes wrought by war was hardly tub-thumping – but it expressed a note of cool scepticism which perhaps was not quite what the editors had intended.

She described the breakdown of class distinctions in the early years of the war and wondered how permanent such changes would be: 'English social life is, in these curious, dark, troubled years, moving a few steps nearer that democracy for which we say we are fighting and have never yet had. Only a few steps; and whether these will be retraced or continued when the solvent furnace of war dies down, and we are left to grope a way through wreckage and smouldering ashes, we cannot yet know.'

By the middle of 1940 the tone of Rose's letters had changed. There was no more uncertainty over the war. The fall of France in June had confirmed what had been becoming increasingly obvious: there could be no peace with Hitler, not even what she had half-jokingly called 'peace with ignominy'. Whereas at the end of 1939 Rose had supported Lloyd George's call for a con-ference of nations to discuss and negotiate a planned peace with Hitler, six months later it was clear that the plan uppermost in Hitler's mind was the invasion of England. In June 1940 Rose wrote to Jean that she regretted not having stuck up for France more in the early months of the year. To make up for her, and her country's, failings, she applied to the French Red Cross for a job as an ambulance driver in France. She would have to improve her mechanical knowledge, she told Jean. However, as her application was unsuccessful, it never was improved.

By then Gerald had recovered from his stroke, and the cancer, although diagnosed, did not yet have him in its grip. Rose was no longer depressed by the ambivalence she had felt about the prosecution of war. For the next six months, the months of the Blitz, Rose Macaulay was active, energetic and purposeful; she regained her gaiety and her insouciance. She made regular visits to the O'Donovan house in Surrey. It was a short period of stout-hearted living amongst the falling bombs.

Rose stayed in London and applied her driving skills to getting to hospital people dug out from the ruins of their houses. In September she described to Jean a hit in Camden Town:

> two fallen houses, a great pile of ruins, with all the inhabitants buried deep. The demolition men worked and hacked away very skilfully and patiently, and we all encouraged the people inside, telling them they would be out in a short time, but of course they weren't. There was a mother and a crying baby, who were rescued at 10.0 next morning after I had gone. I drove to hospital another mother, who had left two small children under the ruins. I told her they would be out very soon – but they never were, they were killed. The demolition men are splendid – we passed milk down to the baby, and water for the others, and the men kept saying to them 'It'll be all right, dear. Don't you worry.' . . . They are, of course, so used to the job (every night) that they can throw it off when they are relieved, and think about other things – I suppose it is all in the night's work to them. Perhaps it will be to me sometime, but I am still an amateur at it and it rather gets one down. One wonders all the time how many people are at the moment alive under some ruin, and how much they are suffering in body and mind. But it doesn't do to think much in these days, or to start wondering what 'There were a few casualties' covers.

She is imaginatively sympathetic, but she has yet to experience, herself, the full force of loss and ruins. And although she feels for the victims of the Blitz, she is also energised by it. She arranged for her shifts to end at 3 a.m., so that she could get a few hours' sleep and thus be able to work during the day. Staying out in the country, at Liss in Hampshire with Margaret, was lovely, but she was always keen to get back to London. When there weren't people to be rescued, and when she wasn't having to think of dead children buried beneath the rubble, she was writing articles, broadcasting, thinking, and making jokes. Oxford Street was bombed in October and half the big shops

were hit. 'What will Aunt Mary do?' Rose asked Jean. She tack-
led Middleton Murry on his pacifism: 'I shall get out of him his
alternative to war or surrender, if he has one,' she told Jean. 'But
he is too snakey to be pinned down, I think.' London was devastated, but Rose still bicycled to Soho, past fresh ruined
buildings, weaving her way between craters and ropes, to lunch
with Gilbert Murray, or Harold Nicolson, or H. G. Wells. Rose
had met the Greek scholar Gilbert Murray briefly at the end of
the First World War (her cousin Jean Smith was working as his
secretary); now a close friendship developed that was based on
their mutual interest in both the League of Nations and classical scholarship. She described one lunch with him that autumn
and how he brought sugar – already heavily rationed – with him
in a lozenge box for them to have on their apple tart.

Luxborough House was almost hit twice. Fifteen people were
killed at the beginning of December when a land-mine was
dropped 200 yards from Rose's flat, on a block of flats in
Marylebone High Street. The shops in the street, where Rose
did her regular household shopping, were smashed up, and part
of the wall between the sitting-room and the spare bedroom
came down, where it had been cracked by an earlier bomb.
'Luxborough and Paddington Streets looked like a scene out of
Things to Come . . .' she wrote. When things got bad she took her
lilo, acquired through an extraordinary stroke of luck from a
bombed-out part of Selfridge's, and which she had to blow up by
mouth, there being no pumps to be had for love nor money, and
put it in the passage under the stairs of Luxborough House.
Briefly, she had anxiety about being buried alive ('induced by
seeing too many ruins') but it was only a 'passing disease'. She
cycled through London during the day, and drove her Morris for
the ambulance service at night. In September, writing of Vita
Sackville-West driving an ambulance around Sissinghurst,
Virginia Woolf wrote: 'Rose M. is doing the same in London. I
admire that very much.'

In October that year Rose wrote to Virginia Woolf saying

how sorry she was that they hadn't seen each other since the Woolfs' house in Mecklenburgh Square had been bombed. She wanted to talk to Virginia about a novel she had in mind about a descendant of Coleridge's, a girl who would be his great-great-grandchild, 'the fruit of mild and rural sin' who would take after him. 'I suppose she would be a very odd girl, wouldn't she – opium, metaphysics, flow of talk, cadging on friends, even poetry, but it needn't be as good as his.' She went on to say that she didn't know when she would write about this girl, or indeed if she ever would, as even her Animals – her bestiary animals – were languishing. 'I expect this war is thoroughly demoralizing,' she wrote, but Rose herself did not sound demoralised. Far from it. 'I have always said I will not be buried alive but cremated instead, and shall feel it unjust if these orders are disregarded by God,' she wrote combatively. 'I like my ambulance colleagues, male and female,' she went on, and then in what can only be an outburst of fancifulness: 'You would too, I think. They teach me to knit, and are not unduly cast down by what they have to see and to do.' The image of Virginia Woolf enjoying the company of some knitting ambulance men and women does not come from a depressed imagination.

And No Man's Wit was selling well. Rose, as was her habit, managed to find an excuse for this: 'I expect it scores from so few novels coming out just now; so has fewer competitors.' At the same time she was corresponding with Penguin Books over their publication of *Told by an Idiot* and *Orphan Island*. Two of her novels were already Penguin books: *Dangerous Ages* had come out in 1937, as Penguin number 76, and *Crewe Train* (number 175) the following year. She asked them to change the biographical note on the reprint of *Told by an Idiot*, to cut out the 'remarks of a complimentary nature'. 'Probably the wittiest writer of the age . . . has held her position unchallenged with a succession of brilliantly witty stories . . .' and so on, had appeared on the first Penguin publications. No wonder the reticent Rose raised objections; nonetheless it is an indication of the high esteem in which she was held at the beginning of the war years.

In the first week of January 1941 Rose gave a broadcast talk to America on 'Consolations of the War'. 'I am mentioning ruin-seeing,' she wrote to Jean the day before, 'the beauty of the black nights and the moonlit ones, the romantic scenes during raids (fire lighting the sky, etc) increased companionableness, shelter life, the pleasure of waking up still alive each day . . .' Such robustness under fire could not last; and Rose was soon hit by a series of heavy blows against which the 'consolations of the war' offered little protection.

That same month Margaret was operated on for cancer. The operation was not successful, and she returned home 'hideously ill'. Margaret's house was full of women, whom Rose found uncongenial. Rose wrote to Sylvia Lynd in February: 'Last week she was supposed to be going to die . . . I am here with the day nurse, the night nurse, and a foolish companion of my sister's'. Tempestuous dark-haired Margaret, with whom she had swum in the River Ystwyth, climbed trees in Great Shelford, and adventured round America, had always been Rose's favourite sister. Now she was dying and the doctor refused Rose's request for a swift release from the pain. She died on 1 March, just before her sixty-first birthday. Rose had to sort out Margaret's belongings and arrange to sell the house. She complained to Sylvia about having to deal with the finicking cousins who wanted to buy it and bombarded her with letters about the fixtures and fittings, and then one of them suddenly died and the sale fell through. Two more deaths followed in quick succession.

First came news of Virginia Woolf's suicide. Rose and she had never been close, but Rose admired and esteemed her fine intelligence, her perspicacity and her wit. They had recognised each other as writers with serious intent. In an obituary in the *Spectator* Rose praised the 'interflow of the outward and the inward' in her work and compared her imaginative re-creation of the people in her life to her work as a writer: 'it amused her to embellish, fantasticate and ironise her friends, as she embellished and fantasticated and ironised all she wrote of – a room, a lighthouse, a frozen river, a paper flower, life flowing by; nothing that she touched stayed dull'. It is perhaps not so comfortable to feel oneself embellished, fantasticated and ironised by someone you know, especially if that person has become a powerful figure in the literary world you move in; but they are writerly qualities that Rose Macaulay appreciated. She herself, in different ways, embellished, fantasticated and ironised. If it had amused Virginia Woolf to sometimes make fun of Rose Macaulay, well, Rose was generous enough to admit that she wasn't made dull by it.

Virginia Woolf walked into the River Ouse at the end of March. On 18 April Leonard Woolf identified her body, and the same day Mary O'Donovan, the youngest of Gerald and Beryl's three children, died of septicaemia having swallowed an open safety pin ten days before. 'Such a wretched way to lose someone – much worse than enemy action, which would seem normal,' Rose wrote to Sylvia.

Rose struggled on with organising the disposal of the Liss house, and on 11 May came up to London with a removals van containing what she was going to keep of Margaret's. The previous night the Germans made their last bombing raid of the Blitz on London. The House of Commons was hit, Westminster Hall and the British Museum. Luxborough House also took a direct hit from a high explosive bomb. Rose arrived to find the building in ruins.

She was devastated. She wrote on a scrap of paper to Daniel George, on her way to take temporary refuge with Jean in Romford, 'House no more – bombed and burned out of existence, and *nothing* saved. I am bookless, homeless, sans everything but my eyes to weep with. *All* my (and your) notes on animals gone – I shall never write that book now.' In her next letter to him, ten days later, she wrote, 'It would have been less

trouble to have been bombed myself.' All her books were
destroyed: the red morocco-bound thirteen-volume edition of
James Murray's *Oxford English Dictionary* that her father had
collected as it came out year by year from 1884 (Murray had got
up to T by the time he died in 1915, the same year as George
Macaulay); her father's 1845 edition of Milton that she had
used when writing her own book; all the books that were, as she
wrote to Gilbert Murray, 'the heritage of four generations of
book-lovers, besides my own collection'. Scrabbling around in
the ruins she found her May and June marmalade ration, a few
bits of glass and china, a little tea, some whiskey, and her old
silver mug. She wrote to Storm Jameson of the 'gaping wound in
my heart and mind' left by the loss of her books, 'my lovely seventeenth century books, my Aubrey, my Pliny, my Topsell,
Sylvester, Drayton, all the poets – lots of lovely queer unknown
writers, too – and Sir T. Browne and my Oxford Dictionary'.
There was a partly written new novel, but, 'I don't mind that so
much, nearly. The Animal Book was my heart's blood – it was to
have been such a nice book! And all my seventeenth century
travellers – Purchas and the rest . . .'

In the short story commissioned by Storm Jameson that she
wrote the next year, 'Miss Anstruther's Letters', we see Miss
Anstruther as a ghost, cut off at a single stroke from her past and
uprooted from her history, when her flat is bombed to bits in the
Blitz. Miss Anstruther manages to save a few books at first:
'Herodotus' (doubtless the Macaulay edition), 'Mathematical
Magick, some of the twenty volumes of Purchas his Pilgrimes,
the eight little volumes of Walpole's letters, Trivia, Curiosities of
Literature, the six volumes of Boswell . . .' These were some of
the volumes that Rose herself had lost. Miss Anstruther then
jettisons the Boswell to make room in the suitcase for 'a china
cow, a tiny walnut shell with tiny Mexicans behind glass, a box
with a mechanical bird that jumped out and sang, and a fountain
pen'. But then the suitcase vanishes from the pavement, so all is
lost anyway.

Like Miss Anstruther, Rose Macaulay haunted the ruins of Luxborough House. 'I have been up alone,' she told Sylvia Lynd on 12 May, 'climbing somewhat precariously (stairs all gone) and mocked by the charred pages of my books . . . I have lost my current novel, and all ms notes for all books. And my typewriter, wireless, everything. It seems to mean a clean break with my whole past, and I am still dizzy with it.' She accepted with gratitude Sylvia's generous present of four pairs of stockings, but she refused all offers of places to stay, and took a bed-sitting room nearby, in Manchester Street, returning day after day to sift through the rubble.

The books were gone, and the work was gone. She never took up the bestiary again, but by the time she found somewhere else to live, round the corner in Hinde Street, some at least of her books began to be replaced. Ruth and Victor Gollancz, 'darling Ruth and Victor', gave her a set of the *Oxford English Dictionary* 'in the same vestage and habit as I have always known it', which let her imagine the shelves in her new flat 'abloom' with it; Helen Waddell, Gilbert Murray and her old friend S. C. Roberts from Cambridge University Press provided her with volumes from their own libraries; and some of her own books came back to her as they had been on loan to Logan Pearsall Smith at the time of the bombing. Ruth Gollancz dug out her original design for the dolphin book-plate, and printed up a new set of them.

Rose was frank about the desolating loss of her books. She wrote about it in the *Spectator* soon after it had happened, and again in 1949. Her friends rallied to her support, and she herself soon began searching the London bookstalls and antiquarian and second-hand bookshops for replacements. But in 'Miss Anstruther's Letters' she writes about another loss: the loss of her lover's letters. The story is crafted as fiction: Miss Anstruther's lover is dead. In the moment of panic when the bomb hits, Miss Anstruther takes from the flat trivial things, and not what is most important to her. When she returns to the ruins of the flat her lover's letters – the written record of their enduring love – are just a mass of burnt ashes, except for one tiny scrap: 'you don't care twopence'. There are many levels of pain and self-blame and regret here.

Gerald was the 'best-kept secret in London', according to Victor Gollancz, who thought no more than half a dozen people knew about him (Ruth put the number a little higher). If there were letters from Gerald in Rose's flat when it was destroyed, that was not something she could say to anyone; they were her secret, hidden in her heart and not to be spoken of.

Rose Macaulay wrote 'Miss Anstruther's Letters' while Gerald was dying. In the story Miss Anstruther's lover is recently dead, and she has not yet re-read his letters because of the rawness of her grief. She had been saving them as a solace for when she would be able to read them without unendurable weeping. Miss Anstruther's lover's handwriting is like Gerald's, with lines 'running small and close and neat down the page, difficult to decipher, with the o's and a's never closed at the top', which now have 'run into a flaming void and would never be deciphered more'. While the letters, with their cryptic references to an earlier betrayal, are a record of anguish and regret, they are also a celebration of their lives together and especially of their 'secret stolen travels of twenty years'. 'Miss Anstruther's Letters' is an elegy for the world that Rose and Gerald had created together, the world of abroad and elsewhere and being together, just the two of them, outside marriage and friends. But it is also a dark meditation on memory and the mutability of what has been. For the past is destroyed by the scrap of writing that remains, the 'line and a half of close small writing, the o's and the a's open at the top', words which, when she looks at them, 'seemed to darken and obliterate a little more of the twenty years that had followed them'. The words are fragments of two sentences: 'leave it at that. I know now that you don't care twopence; if you did you would . . .'

It is impossible to say whether Miss Anstruther's belief – that her failure in caring twenty years before is compounded by her failure to rescue her lover's letters – is an exact replication of a belief of Rose's. 'I did care twopence,' says Miss Anstruther, into the emptiness, 'I did.' Who can doubt her, and who can doubt Rose Macaulay? Surely Gerald, for whom she gave up so much, could not have doubted her.

But in this story all the years of passion and love become 'a drift of grey ashes that once were fire', and Miss Anstruther is turned into 'a drifting ghost too'.

After the publication of *And No Man's Wit*, 'Miss Anstruther's Letters' was the only fiction that Rose Macaulay wrote for almost ten years. It is packed with enough regret and loss and grief for a whole decade and more. When she came back to fiction with *The World My Wilderness* it was after a long journey through loneliness and despair, and she was able, then, to do something quite different with the ruins of the world around her.

Storm Jameson, then president of PEN, saw Rose at the PEN London Congress of Writers in the autumn of 1941, some months after the bombing of her flat. Gerald's cancer was by now far advanced. Rose had always seemed to Storm unchanged and unchangeable since her first kindness to her at one of the Thursday evening gatherings in Naomi's flat in Prince's Gardens in the early 1920s. Storm wrote:

> Now, listening to her rapid talk, watching the movements of her small head and abrupt flickering smile, I thought that in some persons age makes a sudden leap; overnight the flesh shrinks from the bones and hidden lines rise to the surface. But age did not account for a trace of sadness, or lassitude, given away by her voice, for all its liveliness.

Could the loss of her books and manuscript and most of her belongings five months previously account for this change? Storm wondered.

'Something sharper was biting her. I thought: I shall never know.'
One day that autumn, when Rose had been visiting Storm in her
top floor flat in Portland Place (it was a cheap flat because of its
proximity to Broadcasting House, considered a prime German
target),

> she stood for several minutes, still talking, on the stairs leading
> down to the lift. I looked at her, profiled on the wall, narrow
> shoulders, delicate arched nose.
>
> 'You're very tired,' I said.
>
> She moved down a step, paused, and looked back at me.
> 'Margaret [Margaret was S.J.'s first name] you don't know what
> it's like to watch the person you love dying.'

Gerald died the next year, on 26 July 1942. According to his
daughter Brigid, he had not suffered intense pain but had slowly,
after an operation for his rectal cancer, starved to death. Rose
had somehow found, despite rationing, enough petrol to get her
out to the O'Donovan household two or three times a week
during the last weeks of his life. Marjorie Grant Cook was
invited by Beryl to nurse him through the final weeks. One can
only guess at the levels of repressed emotion in the household as
Gerald lay dying.

A brief death notice appeared in *The Times* on 27 July. Then
on 10 August 'a friend' wrote that he was best known as a writer
by his first novel, *Father Ralph*, which, like his later ones, was 'a
careful, able, documentary, and in parts brilliant presentment of
Irish life'. The obituary then gave a few facts on his professional
life and ended, 'As a friend he never failed; his wise judgment
and unstinting interest were always on tap behind his reserve
and behind the sometimes sardonic wit that was his Irish heritage. To know him was to love him.' A handful of people only
would have known that Gerald O'Donovan's obituarist was his
fellow writer and long-term lover, Rose Macaulay.

Rose now entered a period of grief and mourning in which

the articulation of her loss was forbidden. To some of her friends, such as Storm Jameson, she said that a person she loved had died. To Daniel George, with whom she had worked so closely for the past five years, it was 'a very close friend', and she went on, 'but must get over this. Perhaps Portugal will help.' To Rosamond Lehmann she wrote more confidentially, but nonetheless suggested that she would and could get over her loss:

He died on July 26th. I had spent the day before with him, and he knew me and talked to me, and had been asking for me, but was only partly there. Then, late in the evening, he became unconscious and died next morning. I wasn't there then, but didn't want to be. I feel empty and dead, and without purpose. I'd like to get right away – to Portugal if I could – but must wait till I feel better; I expect Portuguese food wouldn't be the right thing for a gastric ulcer! (I *hope*, however, that won't develop again.) I think an entire change of scene would help me begin life again. For himself, of course, I am thankful he didn't linger on in pain. Isn't it odd, with all this dying, so inevitable, we haven't yet learned to accept it. We are unadaptable about that. It still comes as a shock. It's all this loving we do. Worthwhile, but it doesn't fit us for losing each other.

He was the dearest companion, you know. And had such a fine, brilliant mind. His grasp of things was so masterly – he would have been such a good statesman ... Well, it's over if things are ever over ...

And to Sylvia Lynd:

The story has been a good one, it might have ended worse – perhaps in weariness, faithlessness, or nothingness, or a mere lessening of love. It never did – of course it never had the strain of years of constant household use: the gilt stayed on the gingerbread. Is this the reward of sin? One of its rewards? Perhaps

our love would have survived intact; it might, I think, because
there was such a fundamental oneness – but who knows? . . . We
did have the best of it. Twenty four years of companionship,
unspoilt . . . I would like to have had a child or two of his. But it
would have made complications. Now I feel a kind of empty
ache of sadness and missing; but that will pass in time.

She went on to describe a ghastly event that had taken place the
previous evening on her return to her flat after Gerald's funeral,
when her old acquaintance Jack Squire, already well into the
long years of his decline, had drunkenly turned up in a taxi to
call on her, had enquired after his old colleague Rose's cousin,
Donald Macaulay, and on hearing that he had died months
since, broke down and wept inconsolably, 'Though I felt actually,' said Rose, 'it was me to cry and I could have.' But of course
she didn't and instead she called on all her reserves of strength to
calm him down and get him down the stairs and back into his
waiting taxi.

The next year, on 27 July 1943, a year and a day after Gerald
died, and the anniversary of his burial, Rose was having dinner
with Una Pope-Hennessy. Was it out of a well-meaning but
clumsily executed desire to keep Rose's mind off the anniversary
of Gerald's death that she also invited James Lees-Milne? He
had met Rose for the first time in January that year, in James
Pope-Hennessy's flat, and recorded the meeting in his diary: 'I
brought some of my photographs of manoeline architecture to
show Rose Macaulay, who is shortly going to Portugal to write
a book for the Ministry of Information. My first impression
was of a very thin, desiccated figure in a masculine tam'o'shanter,
briskly entering the room. James says she is like Voltaire to look
at. Actually her profile is less sharp than her full face, and is
handsome. She talks too fast and too much.' Lees-Milne was a
witty and observant chronicler of other people's weaknesses.
That evening in 1943, on 27 July, he wrote: 'I dined with Dame

Una. Only Rose Macaulay there. She was dry and twitchy . . .
She said some silly things . . .' Rose, full of unspoken grief but as
sharp as ever, must have been only too aware of her own twitch-
iness and garrulousness; and only too aware that it would be
faithfully and mercilessly recorded by James Lees-Milne.

There were parties and meetings and people to see, but
London was a desolate place. The ruined buildings and bomb
craters and piles of rubble were no longer part of the romance of
war – let alone of its consolations – but the incontrovertible
material evidence of Rose's break with the past, of her own
ruination. She was tired, she was ill, she was useless; she was, as
she had foreseen in her creation of Miss Anstruther, a drifting
ghost.

Rose went abroad.

In March 1943 she went to Portugal. Portugal was neutral: it
was one of the few places in Europe that you could go to at that
time, flying in a small plane with blacked-out windows. She
spent two months in Lisbon doing the preliminary research for
what would become *They Went to Portugal*. To say that it is a collection of essays on the many English visitors to Portugal from
the crusaders in the twelfth century to the tourists and merchants of the eighteenth and nineteenth centuries does not do
justice to a book that is part vivid history, part travel book, part
social and cultural history, and is unfailingly racy with a depth of
scholarship displayed lightly on every page. In Portugal she
could hardly have had a moment to dwell on her own grief, so
busy was she with lives of other people, so concerned to tease out
a sense of how history is made up of each generation's view of
the past, and of how cultures define themselves in opposition to
other cultures. Each essay is a few pages long: there are no footnotes; it is altogether too fast-paced for footnotes despite the
wide range of sources on which Rose was drawing.

On top of everything else, she had not been well. In
November 1941 she had ended up in hospital with a gastric
ulcer, and the ulcers recurred. The writer Norman Douglas,

seeing her just before she went to Portugal, described her as looking 'frail'. And in Portugal she suffered some kind of a heart seizure in May while bathing at Foz de Arelho with David Ley, a lecturer at the British Institute in Lisbon. Ley wrote to his father that she was 'in a dreadful state'. She returned to England the following day, 7 May, but there was further trouble that summer and she was again in hospital. But no sooner was she out than she was back in the London Library continuing her research. And the British Museum Reading Room, and the Public Records Office. For the rest of the war she was immersed in her work for *They Went to Portugal*. It had replaced the massive undertaking of the book of beasts that had been destroyed in 1941.

The book grew and grew. When she finally delivered the manuscript to William Collins in March 1945 they took one look, said it was too long, and then unkindly used her self-deprecation against her: 'You have always said we would not want to publish it, and I am afraid we are not too happy about it.' Paper was still rationed. But Daniel George was now working as a reader for Jonathan Cape, and a few weeks later Cape agreed to take it, on the condition that Rose made substantial cuts. Fifteen years after Jonathan Cape had written to Rose Macaulay asking her for a book, and she had politely put him off, she gave him *They Went to Portugal*, a book quite different from her novels of contemporary life of the 1920s, a great big generous book, over 400 pages long even after it had been cut, full of wit and stories and expertise in the use of the semicolon. There are delights on every page. Here, for example, she is on Richard Flecknoe, the 'mediocre poet' who became famous more for being lampooned by Dryden and Marvell than for his own work: 'He was scarcely worth it; he wrote much, but it did not matter; he said himself, "There is none that prints more nor publishes less than I, for I print only for myself and private friends."' On his poem in praise of the house of Mr Muley, an English Catholic merchant, she says, 'It is a pity that it was not

Marvell who stayed at Mr Muley's quinta; we should have had a better poem.' And on his return to England in 1650: 'He settled down to versifying, play-writing, and miscellaneous compositions; they included, as was common form, an appreciation of the Lord Protector at his death and another of King Charles II at his Restoration.'

The jostling cast of characters in *They Went to Portugal* left little room for its author to meditate on her loss and on the past. But it enabled her to carry on living and working. During her research in Portugal she made some good new friends: David Ley, who helped her with the reading of Portuguese texts, and Susan and Luis Marques, another family in whose small children she would gain much delight.

Work had kept the sense of loss at bay, but there was another blow to come. The war ended, but in November came news from Canada of Will's death from a heart attack. There had been only three of the Five on the romantic, hilarious, lovely trip down the Pacific Highway, and now both those companions of her youth were dead. Like Aulay so many years before, Will – little Will on whom Rose had doted, with the sweet smile and the curly hair – had died far from family and his original home.

Rose was profoundly unhappy. She knew she needed to work but knew too that she was not capable of writing a novel. In this period she bought a picture called *The Coffin House*. It was by the young artist and writer Denton Welch, to whom in a letter which he copied into his diary she described her response to it:

> The detail is so exquisitely mortal and corrupt, the robin singing against it with such brave, larger-than-life protest. I especially like the blind white hare pawing the toadstool; and the clawing tree-trunks, like dendrofied [*sic*] ghosts or dragons reaching for their prey . . . The picture almost smells of fungus and a damp wood; I know the smell so well . . . There is some poem of de la Mare's about a wood, that your picture suggests to me . . . it is precise yet ghostly, like an odd and beautiful and frightening dream . . .

Of all Rose's pictures this is the only one that is brooding, sinister and redolent of death and decay. It spoke to her at the lowest, darkest moment in her life.

Then the publisher Hamish Hamilton asked if she would be interested in the idea of a Spanish travel book. She grasped at the chance: travel, research work, abroad. There was a lot of preliminary organisation required to travel in the immediate post-war years, but in the summer of 1947 Rose got out her old Morris from the garage where it had been mouldering and set out, alone, with the back seat weighed down with ancient and contemporary travellers' tales, and drove down the Mediterranean coast of Spain round to Cape Vincent on the south-western tip of Portugal.

There were no tourists in Spain; hardly anyone else on the roads. Rose would drive for miles and pass only a donkey under a load of wood being driven by an old man along the road, or further south, in Valencia, a donkey piled high with panniers full of oranges and a tiny boy perched on top. The signs of the Civil War – the razed churches and broken bridges and piles of rubble – were all around: Franco's victory had not brought prosperity. Spain was starving and backward and empty of visitors. In many parts a woman had never before been seen driving a car; indeed a woman alone seemed to the Spanish 'at once entertaining, exciting and remarkable, as if a chimpanzee strayed unleashed about the streets'.

As with *They Went to Portugal*, *Fabled Shore* (1949) is not a book that can easily be classified: it is part travel, part history, part quest. It is full of voices from the past, those voices to which she had learned to attune her ears when at the end of the 1920s she had first turned to writing books of history. Romans, Goths and Carthaginians whisper in its pages, the voices of soldiers and princes, architects and builders, and the voices of long-vanished farmers and fishermen and merchants. While *They Went to Portugal* was crowded with other people's lives, in *Fabled Shore* there are echoes of the travels Rose had undertaken with Gerald over the last twenty years. She was lonely in Spain, her solitariness accentuated by the ghost of the companion who was no longer there. And in the lapping of the waters of the Mediterranean on the fabled shore you can also faintly hear the lapping of those other Mediterranean waves on the Ligurian shore fifty or more years earlier, when the Five had swum and sailed the *Argo*.

It is an enchanting book, of high intelligence, Elizabeth Bowen said, and second sight. It is a meditation on time and history and the movement of peoples. Through it runs the sense that a personal journey is being undertaken, that this solitary drive south is paralleled by a solitary journey back through the author's life, a feeling that gets stronger the further south she gets. There is the suggestion of more than one ending when she reaches Cape Vincent, where Prince Henry the Navigator had built a town and fortress in the fifteenth century. Rose Macaulay drives amongst the rocks and the shaggy goats, amongst the familiar smells of thyme and the sea. Her journey ends on 'a windswept cape at the end of the inhabited world, among the dark and ghost-trodden ruins of Prince Henry's town'. There was no inn, so 'I made my bed in the roofless apse of what must have been once a chapel; all night the wind whispered and moaned coldly about the Sacred Cape; the long beams of the lighthouse, and of that of Sagres, speared and shafted the desolate wastes of the sea which bounds the known world.' This looks ahead to *The World My Wilderness*, which she would start almost immediately she had finished writing *Fabled Shore*, with its epigraph from T. S. Eliot's *The Waste Land*:

> . . . the grass is singing
> Over the tumbled graves, about the chapel
> There is the empty chapel, only the wind's home.
> It has no windows, and the door swings . . .

'My journey was over,' Rose wrote at the end of *Fabled Shore*. She had made some kind of peace with the ghosts of her past;

she had regained the strength she needed to re-enter the inner world out of which she created her fiction.

By the end of 1947, as she was finishing writing up her journey down the fabled shore, Rose Macaulay seemed to have re-engaged with the world. In the 1947 *BBC Yearbook*, she set out a wide-ranging remit for radio broadcasting in 'If I Were Head of the Third Programme'. She called for both historical music and contemporary music from round the world (what would nowadays be called world music, introduced on to Radio Three schedules a mere fifty years after Rose suggested it); and for contemporary drama, suggesting as an example a dramatisation of one of Ivy Compton-Burnett's novels, so notable for their 'plot, conversation and subtlety'. Returning to an old enthusiasm she said that more controversy on all subjects was desirable, and even that 'disputes from the past might be re-hotted'. Unaware, of course, how popular alternative history in books and films would later become, she suggested a series of talks on 'What if . . .?' (Napoleon had won, for example). And for more entertainment on that rather serious programme, the Third, she demanded a serialisation of comic novels, such as Evelyn Waugh's *Black Mischief* and *Scoop*, or Anthony Powell's *Venusberg*. Such a wide-ranging agenda – bearing in mind that 'if I were' fantasies promote exactly that – shows Rose Macaulay in her late sixties as critically appreciative of the work of her contemporaries, as imaginative and speculative about both literary content and genre, and as having revived in herself an enthusiasm for the past and her own past pleasures, that, after the death of Gerald, she seemed for a time to have lost.

The next year, 1948, Rose returned to Spain. This time she went with Gerald's son Dermod and his wife Muriel. They were the parents of her and Marjorie's god-daughters, Gerald's granddaughters. She spent a happy month with them on the coast at Denia, the place where on her solitary journey she had stopped and listened to the voices of the English raisin merchants who once had lived and worked there, and now were buried in the

English cemetery by the sea. She had been conducting a dialogue with the ghosts of her own dead.

There was still one more journey she needed to make. Already she had started to write fiction again when, in the summer of 1949, she visited Loughrea in the west of Ireland, where her fellow-novelist, beloved companion and lover, Gerald O'Donovan, had spent the years of his young manhood as Father Jeremiah. This was where he had struggled to put into practice his passionately held social, educational and political ideals, and where, although he had been personally defeated by the Catholic episcopacy, he had helped create, in the decorations of St Brendan's Cathedral, an enduring tribute to Irish art and culture. She was accompanied by Marjorie Grant Cook who, of all Rose's friends who knew Gerald, had known him best and closest.

CHAPTER TEN

Pleasures

I started dreaming of Caucasian mountains, over which Tartars gal-
loped upside down on long-tailed ponies, shouting horribly, wild
mares with their koumiss foaming into green pitchers, sledges and
droshkys speeding over the steppes fraught with fur-capped men and
Circassian slaves and pursued by wolves, who, every mile or so, were
thrown a Circassian slave to delay them, but, never having enough,
took up the chase again, till at last they had devoured all the
Circassian slaves, the horses, and the fur-capped men. I dreamed too
of the Crimea, of crumbling palaces decaying among orchards by the
sea, of onion domes, of chanting priests with buns . . .

Laurie in *The Towers of Trebizond*

i

At the end of the 1940s Rose Macaulay was settled in Hinde
House, Hinde Street, W1, a short street parallel to and just north
of Wigmore Street and a few blocks south of Luxborough Street
where she had once lived. At its western end Hinde Street opens
into tree-filled Manchester Square. Here she would stay until her
death in 1958. (A blue commemorative plaque was put into the
wall of Hinde House in the early 1990s.) From here she would
venture regularly abroad, as she had used to do in the 1920s and
1930s.

There are a number of photographs of Rose in this flat, type-writer on lap, with her books, once again, behind and around her. One of these photographs hangs on a wall in the London Library, above a red leather armchair and another plaque, a small brass one, that says 'Rose Macaulay: This corner of the Reading Room has been furnished in her memory by her friends.' Rose was about to enter on a period of great creative productivity despite increasingly frequent bouts of bronchitis, continuing gastric problems and regular fevers that were described as 'undulant fever', which was probably brucellosis, a bacterial disease caught from unpasteurised milk. She would lose weight during the bouts of fever, dropping from nearly eight stone to just over seven stone, an astonishingly low weight for someone five foot eight inches tall.

Rose never complained.

Her recovery from the dark years after Gerald's death came through facing and exploring the very representations of that death-in-life period. She began to think about and to work with the subject of ruins. First she dealt with ruins as a novelist, in *The World My Wilderness*, which she began to write in 1948, and she then began work, even before the novel was published in 1950, on her great discursive tract on ruins, in which she picked apart the multifarious cultural and emotional strands entwining, like ivy, the very object of her study, and refashioned ruins in celebration of their continuing hold on the human imagination.

Ruins dominate *The World My Wilderness*. At the heart of the book, both emotionally and topographically, lie the bombed churches and guildhalls and merchants' houses of the City of London, already overgrown in 1946, when the novel is set, by fireweed and willow herb and bracken and bramble, and now the haunt of army deserters and petty criminals. For the seventeen-year-old protagonist Barbary and her stepbrother Raoul this waste land of ruins is both more real and more natural than the solid, improbable rest of the world, with its houses and streets, rules and conventions. Barbary and Raoul have come to London

from the *maquis* of southern France, which is shown in the novel
as another kind of ruination: one in which ties of friendship,
community and even kinship have been destroyed, irremediably
it seems, first by the German occupation, then by the actions of
collaborators, and finally by members of the Resistance seeking
revenge.

T. S. Eliot's defining voice is used as a refrain throughout.
One of the epigraphs to the book consists of the ten lines from
The Waste Land following '. . . bats with baby faces in the violet
light/Whistled . . .' with the upside-down towers, exhausted
wells, tumbled graves and the empty chapel. The other epigraph
is three lines from a poem by 'Anon.', or rather by Rose Macaulay
herself as she later admitted:

> The world my wilderness, its caves my home,
> Its weedy wastes the garden where I roam,
> Its chasm'd cliffs my castle and my tomb . . .

Barbary seems to hear the brambled wilderness of the City
speaking to her, saying that it 'is the maquis that lies about the
margins of the wrecked world', asking, in the words of *The Waste
Land*, 'What are the roots that clutch, what branches grow/Out
of this stony rubbish?' and answering for her: '. . . it is you yourself, your own roots, that clutch the stony rubbish, the branches
of your own being that grow from it and from nowhere else'. Her
elder brother Richie, who has returned from three years' barbarism of war, is given the last words spoken in the novel. He
shudders at the thought of universal doom and murmurs a line
from Eliot's poem: 'I think we are in rats' alley/Where the dead
men lost their bones,' before taking a track across the wilderness
towards St Paul's. Rose Macaulay had first read *The Waste Land*
as a vision that was not specific to any particular age. Now she
used its portrayal of the end of one war to enrich her representation of the end of another.

Roots and rats and stones and bones are not the only powerful images from Eliot's *The Waste Land* transposed by Rose Macaulay into 1940s London. The novel's young protagonist Barbary is yet another in the long line of Macaulay girls and women who display androgynous qualities and attempt to resist any sexual activity that might define them as feminine. Here, amidst the overt and conscious references to *The Waste Land*, Barbary is more than just another tomboy; rather, and especially with the hints of her involvement in murder, she reflects Tiresias in Part III of Eliot's poem, the old man with wrinkled female breasts, the man/woman and blind seer who sat outside the walls of Thebes while the House of Atreus fell apart within, and in the poem appears in the violet hour, the hour between day and night, which looks forward to the violet light of Part V, when the bats with baby faces are crawling down a blackened wall.

The World My Wilderness has been read as part of an increasing dialogue engaged in by Rose Macaulay with matters theological. This is not altogether surprising. The book is packed with churches: lists of the ruined City of London churches are repeated as a kind of litany throughout. In the middle of the novel there is a vivid, melodramatic scene with a mad priest who comes into the ruined church of St Giles where Barbary and Raoul are performing a mildly trangressive religious ceremony of their own with jazz playing on a portable radio and a black kitten for a symbolic sacrifice, and tries to hold his own mass, crying out, 'This is hell, hell, hell'. Rose Macaulay's return to the Anglican Church in the last decade of her life featured prominently in appraisals of her after her death, and there has been a tendency to interpret her last two novels, this one and *The Towers of Trebizond*, in the light of that return. But the Church receives short shrift in this novel. In both its Roman Catholic and its Anglican manifestations, it is represented as a snobbish institution, as a refuge for the privileged few from the post-war world of 'pre-fabs for the multitude . . . a thin, weak, tainted mass culture'. War-weary Richie is in flight from barbarism, both wartime and post-war, and while he recognises that Roman Catholicism might be a 'stronghold' against the gates of hell of this new world, he realises it is too alien for him. Anglicanism, he knows, 'would go better with his father, suggesting to him college chapels, good glass windows, Byrd anthems, Gothic cathedrals, the Temple church, the benchers at lunch on Sundays at Lincoln's Inn . . .' This is a sharper view of the Anglican Church as the Church of the Father than is found in many of Rose Macaulay's earlier novels.

The morality examined in the novel has little to do with theology or with religious doctrine. Two sorts of morality, the private and the public, are explored, and the interaction between them. The personal, private nature of sin and forgiveness is set against the background of good and evil within the context of warfare and its social consequences.

In this novel more than in any of her previous ones Rose polarises father-law and mother-love. Questions of sin and forgiveness are most insistently explored in the differences of character of Barbary and Richie's father, the KC Sir Gulliver Deniston, and of their mother Helen, his first wife. (Barbary's sin of complicity in the murder by drowning of her French stepfather doesn't fully convince.) Helen is hedonistic, adulterous and lazy. She is negligent of her adoring daughter and profligate in her love of men. Sir Gulliver is correct, conventional and has only ever loved Helen but is now married to Pamela, who is 'upright and Roedean'. Sir Gulliver's honour, of which he is over-fond, is maladapted to the new, post-war world. He cannot allow himself either to love or to be loved. Pamela is what Sir Gulliver deserves, and what he gets. Rose Macaulay's vote goes to Helen, even though she has lived with a collaborationist, deceived her husband, neglected her daughter, and indulged in some major forgery of twelfth-century Provençal poetry. Helen Deniston sees herself as, amongst other things, one in a long line of playful if not crooked scholars; it is not hard to imagine that Rose Macaulay, with her 'seventeenth-century' epigraphs and poems, enjoyed thinking of herself as one such too.

Helen lives and lets live. Her capacity to give and to inspire sexual love is shown as a life force amidst a ruined world. *The World My Wilderness* is a precursor to *The Towers of Trebizond* in its exploration of the nature and power of sexual love.

But it doesn't quite work as a novel. The reader can hear the author's discomfort with the form. There is too much argument; the very name of the central character, Barbary, is symptomatic of the overdetermination of the images to the theme of a world in ruins. What we get is not the vision of a hunted, vulnerable, needy seventeen-year-old. It is Rose Macaulay's vision; and it is her meditation, not Barbary's, on the significance of the ruins around her. It is as if the very form of the novel is a straitjacket, against the constraints of which the author struggles. Perhaps it is the largeness of the themes of the novel that creates the problem. For the themes she is dealing with – love, betrayal, sin and forgiveness – are larger themes than those of her novels of the 1920s and, with the exception of *They Were Defeated*, the 1930s. This kind of novel, with its thin story and its handful of invented characters, is perhaps not best suited for the exploration of such themes, at least not by Rose Macaulay.

The vision that haunts the reader long after the book is closed is that of the jungle encroaching on the ruined churches of the City of London. These are some of the finest sections in the novel, with their lists of saints' names of vanished churches: 'St Vedast's, St Alban's, St Anne's and St Agnes', St Giles Cripplegate, its tower high above the rest, the ghosts of churches burnt in an earlier fire, St Olave's and St John Zachary's, haunting the green-flowered churchyards that bore their names . . .', and their recreation of an old world of commerce and trade, of 'wrecked guild halls that had belonged to saddlers, merchant tailors, haberdashers, waxchandlers, barbers, brewers, coopers and coachmakers . . .' These images have become part of many people's visual memory of post-war London, whether they have read the novel or not. So detailed an account did Rose Macaulay give of the area of little streets around St Paul's that when

Penguin reprinted *The World My Wilderness* in 1958 they found themselves caught up in a libel action brought against them by someone who claimed that the 'dubious merchant from Japan' could be recognised, by the specificity of the description of the building, as the firm of which he was managing director.

The World My Wilderness came out in May 1950. Reviews were mixed. Some people liked it very much, responding doubtless to the ambition of its themes and to its vivid picture of post-war London. William Plomer praised it highly in a radio review. In her thank-you note Rose displayed a hypersensitivity to the novel's critical reception. She listed some of the people who liked it – many of whom were friends they had in common, such as Joe Ackerley, E. M. Forster, Raymond Mortimer, V. S. Pritchett, John Betjeman and Elizabeth Bowen; this, she said, consoled her for the 'abuse' it had received elsewhere. It is an anxious, insecure letter. One critic, she worries, had told her he liked it 'as if he meant it' but 'didn't even mention it' in the list of good books he had recently compiled for the National Book League journal.

The World My Wilderness was her first novel for ten years. No wonder she was anxious. But, anxieties expressed, she ended the letter cheerfully: 'I am digging away at Ruins, and diving into the Serpentine (alternately).'

Pleasure of Ruins had started out as 'The Pleasures of Looking at Ruins', a short book of 40,000 words contracted by Weidenfeld and Nicolson to be part of their 'Pleasures and Treasures' series. Rose began it in 1949, as soon as she had finished work on *The World My Wilderness*. She went ruin-hunting in Ireland, and then in Wales with Jean and the next summer she spent a month viewing Italian ruins. On her return from this trip she found a letter waiting for her from Father Hamilton Johnson, the Anglican priest whom she had met briefly thirty-five years previously and with whose support she would now find her way back into the Anglican Church.

It soon became obvious that the ruins book would turn out to be no slim volume. But unlike William Collins, who had turned down *They Went to Portugal* in fright at its size, Weidenfeld and Nicolson made a virtue of the extent of the ruins book by deciding to publish it outside the series. Nigel Nicolson (the son of Rose's old friend Harold) said: 'It soon became clear that it would be a pity to throw away Rose and the subject on such a trivial production, so the book grew. From time to time, when I saw her, she would apologise for the fact that the book was expanding far beyond the first concept, and of course we were only too delighted.'

The pleasures of looking at ruins, which she lists in the book's introduction, include morbid pleasure in decay, righteous pleasure in retribution, mystical pleasure in the contemplation of the vanity of things sublunary and the eternity of the kingdom of God, egotistic pleasure of the survivor and a 'dozen other entwined threads of pleasurable and melancholy emotion'. Rose had considered using Henry James's descriptive phrase about ruin-seeking as 'a heartless pastime' as the title of her book. It would not have been appropriate, for her heart is obviously engaged in this pastime in many different ways. It is the human element of ruin-contemplation that is what she enjoys and gets most fun from: the stout American woman, for example, who rushes up the hillside past her at Delos, calling to her tardy daughter, 'Alice, Alice! Come and see the house where Apollo lived!', thus confounding Baedeker, Rose notes with pleasure, who maintained that Delos was of interest only to archaeologists. Under the 'host of minor pleasures' touched on in the introduction we find 'looting' and 'carrying away fragments (a treat enjoyed by great looters and small, from Lord Elgin and the Renaissance nobles and popes to the tourist pocketing stone eggs from fallen Corinthian capitals)'. There is a family connection, too, in the figure of her maternal grandfather, the Reverend W. J. Conybeare (he who wrote the mid-Victorian triple-decker *Perversion*), who with J. S. Howson, 'roamed about and found their own ruins' in the course of researches for *The*

Life and Epistles of St Paul. Herodotus – familiar to Rose since those long walks with her father and brothers and sisters over the Ligurian hills in the 1890s, when George would recount the tales of ancient history from Herodotus he was then working on – is of course a reference in *Pleasure of Ruins*. And she brings in her great-great-uncle Bishop Heber, who, visiting the ancient Great Stupa at Sanchi in Central India and climbing up towards the Lingam shrine with its stone doorkeepers, said that he was reminded, by the path winding prettily through the woods, 'of his Hodnet rectory home'. These sometimes eccentric forebears were family connections that Rose increasingly liked to recall.

This was a research-intensive book. She went to see as many ruins as she could, either alone or with willing friends. The rest she read about. Gilbert Murray now became her close intellectual companion and occasional guide in her researches into the classical world. Rose visited him regularly in Oxford, and lunched with him at the Athenaeum when he was in London. The London Library became her haunt; her bicycle, with ROSE MACAULAY written on the frame in white paint, a familiar sight leaning against the railings outside. C. V. Wedgwood describes Rose in the London Library in this period:

> Turning a dark corner among the bookstacks, one would come suddenly upon Rose squatting – an awkward position for one so tall, but squat she certainly did – in a narrow cleft between the shelves with an enormous tome open upon her knees. She liked to fetch her own books, however remote or unreachable. In one part of the library precipitous ladders provided a short-cut from one floor to the next. Notices attached to them directed members to the stairs and informed them that they used the ladders at their own risk. Perhaps the idea of risk appealed to that streak of romantic daring in Rose's nature, or perhaps she just wanted to get to the books by the quickest possible route: whatever the reason she was forever up and down those ladders like a chamois,

until the library suppressed them – possibly, as I have always suspected, out of anxiety for the safety of one of their most distinguished members.

As with her 1940s books on Spain and Portugal, *Pleasure of Ruins* defies classification into a single genre. It includes history, mythology, travel writing, anthropology and art history. An academic historian might find the anecdotal nature of the narrative of history offputting, but throughout the book runs a strong sense, just as it did in *They Went to Portugal*, of the modern notion that history is constantly being re-created by each generation, who study, write and fashion it. The story Rose Macaulay relates of Troy and its visitors, for example, shows generations of people all creating images of themselves framed in their versions of the past, such as Thomas Coryat who in 1612 had himself dubbed 'the first English Knight of Troy' and drew an admonitory parallel between Troy before its ruination and the City of London 'being as much poluted with extravagant lusts as ever was the old Troy'. Of J. T. Wood and his discoveries at Ephesus in 1877 we read: 'His own excavations added to the grandeur of the scene; in one of his illustrations a majestic rubble of drums, capitals and walls strews the mountain-surrounded site, on which Mr Wood, in tail-coat and fine beard, Mrs Wood and two other ladies in bonnets and pelisses, and a few Turks, stand with satisfaction among the noble débris.'

While Rose Macaulay was researching and writing and 'finishing' *Ruins* she wrote a short story for Cynthia Asquith's *Second Ghost Book*, published in 1952. This was only her third short story and like her first one, 'The Empty Berth', forty years previously, was a contemporary ghost story with a classical background. It takes up and plays with this central theme of *Pleasure of Ruins*, the theme of the reinvention of the past. It is called 'Whitewash' and offers a critical response to writers who romanticise and sanitise the past, in this case Axel Munthe and his portrayal of Timberio (Emperor Tiberius) in his best-selling

memoir of Capri, *The Story of San Michele*, published in 1929.
There is a prototypical Aunt Dot figure, who wears a scarlet
burnous and is forthright in her opinion that, 'Most of us are
more sinning than sinned against; why should monsters be
exceptions?' The narrator of the story has been reading *The Story
of San Michele*, and has been persuaded that Tiberius was an
excellent man, but then, alone in one of the sea-caves, just manages to escape being eaten by a shark called up by the ghost of the
emperor. The narrator hears the splash and the screams of those
that were pushed into the water, and into the jaws of the shark;
but the terror comes as much from the 'enjoying chuckle' of the
sadistic emperor. It is a short and intense study of the pleasures of
sadism.

The span of *Pleasure of Ruins* is wide, covering ruins and their
significance from as far back as imperial China and pharaonic
Egypt up to the newly created ruins of post-war London and
Coventry painted by John Piper. She moves from Grecian to
Gothic, from sentimental traveller in search of visions of antiquity to country house owners building their own antique ruins,
such as William Beckford's Fonthill Abbey, or Ralph Allen's
Sham Castle outside Bath, which Rose visited in October 1950.
It could be argued that the pleasure of ruins is one particular
strand in the complex weave of the pleasure of abroad for English
men and women.

Instead of using Henry James's phrase, 'a heartless pastime', as
the title of her book, Rose Macaulay chose instead to use as her
epigraph the whole sentence from which that phrase comes. 'To
delight in the aspects of sentient ruin might appear a heartless
pastime,' wrote Henry James in *Italian Hours*, 'and the pleasure,
I confess, shows a note of perversity.' Where was the pleasure for
Rose Macaulay in ruins, how far was that pleasure perverse, and,
indeed, how heartless was the delight?

Rose's interest in ruins goes back as far as *Staying with
Relations*, her American novel where the heroine Catherine gets
lost in the jungle and wanders into the middle of some ancient

ruins. Catherine is like Barbary, determined to deny the sexuality of her almost-adult body. It is as if in these novels, separated as they are by twenty years, there is a similar movement, a displacement, from a body that stays youthful and asexual to a ruined building. Ruins are an important part of the three last works: *The World My Wilderness*, *Pleasure of Ruins* and *The Towers of Trebizond*. Each book casts them in a different light; a light that reflects changes in Rose herself.

In 'Miss Anstruther's Letters', the story that Rose wrote in 1942 that describes the bombing of her flat and the dying of her lover, she makes a powerful elision of the wreckage of the flat and the wreckage not just of Miss Anstruther's memories but of her physical self. Having scrabbled vainly in the rubble to recover what is precious, Miss Anstruther ends as 'a drifting ghost', outside time and place, without even a body. A decade later and Rose Macaulay is still exploring the past. There is something perverse about the contemplation of the ruin and decay of buildings, the ossification of love and desire. But, just as she shows us how a romantic or sentimental vision of the past gives some of the people she writes about in *Pleasure of Ruins* a stronger sense of their identity in the present, so her own contemplation of all these ruins and representations of ruins becomes a reparative and restorative act. With *Pleasure of Ruins* Rose Macaulay placed herself once more inside history, and recreated her own sense of self just as the travellers she describes refashion themselves within their ideas of the past. The voice is confident and scholarly. Whereas in *The World My Wilderness* she was drawing on Eliotesque images of rats and bones and dry wells and empty cisterns to illustrate the crumbling of civilisation, here one can hear the echo of the line at the end of *The Waste Land*: 'These fragments I have shored against my ruins'; and an echo too of a passage in her early novel *The Valley Captives*: 'On ruins one can begin to build. Anyhow, looking out from ruins one clearly sees; there are no obstructing walls.'

Perhaps Barbary was too young and unformed to bear the significance of all that destruction in *The World My Wilderness*. In *The Towers of Trebizond* the ruins of the Byzantine Empire would be the subject of contemplation, and it would be in a ruined palace that Laurie, the narrator, who is a good ten years older than Barbary, will sit. Meanwhile, 'in ruined palaces there lies peculiar pleasure', Rose Macaulay wrote in the section of *Pleasure of Ruins* entitled 'Pleasures and Palaces'. The peculiar, or perverse, pleasure lies in all the life that has gone on in them. The life is no longer there, but the history of that life is there; through *Pleasure of Ruins* Rose Macaulay rediscovered that history for herself. History is no longer 'a drift of grey ashes' as it was at the end of 'Miss Anstruther's Letters'.

It had been some time since Rose Macaulay had allowed herself to contemplate pleasures. Nearly two decades had passed since her *Minor Pleasures* and her *Personal Pleasures*. Was Rose's pleasure in pleasure another paradox in this paradoxical woman, who wrote more than twenty novels and didn't believe she was a novelist; who was both an insider and an outsider in British intellectual life; this English Rose who was most at home abroad? Harold Nicolson described her as being a 'combination of opposites', which well describes her pleasure-seeking and ascetic selves. Many of the earlier pleasures of the two 1930s anthologies are the pleasures of, if not an ascetic life, then at least a solitary one: staying in bed, reading, driving along empty roads; pursuing, in other words, one's own, solitary, joy. But party-going features in *Personal Pleasures*, along with other social activities. Although Rose always enjoyed parties and conversation, the other sensual pleasures often associated with gregariousness left her cold. She could hardly have been less interested in food and drink; she never lost her long-limbed leanness, the lean sheepdog look, as Virginia Woolf so accurately described it.

'Pleasure is good,' Rose wrote in 1954 in a critical review of a book that suggested people feared pleasure, 'and if the nations did not waste their substance on war preparations there would be much more of it.' There are many accounts of Rose's pleasures, descriptions of her swimming, driving, talking, listening and laughing. Rosamond Lehmann, who used to swim with her in the art deco subterranean swimming pool of the Lansdowne Club, describes her jumping in from the high diving-board, then clambering up on to the lilo she had brought with her and stretching her 'peeled-wand limbs full length' and letting Rosamond tow her up and down the pool. 'Almost dreamily – for her prim, somehow practical academic accents had too much wit and crackle ever to sound dreamy – she ejaculates: "Oh, Rosamond dear, this is extraordinarily pleasant! I feel like Cleopatra in her barge."' Rosamond also describes being caught in a fearful traffic jam one day, caused by an enormous lorry blocking the junction. 'Suddenly, rapidly, from behind its inert and monstrous bulk, an unostentatious saloon model car emerged. Forward it darted headlong into non-space: then, as rapidly, reversed itself, withdrew behind the lorry, once more into non-space. A hush fell. Clearly no-one could believe their eyes. When finally, somehow, we disembroiled ourselves and I was able to crawl on, I turned to scrutinise the (doubtless abashed) perpetrator of this outrage. It could only be Rose at the wheel; and Rose it was, in a characteristic hat, passing equably to her destination, superlatively unembarrassed.'

In this decade Rose found again that sense of pleasure and gaiety that she had lost when Gerald died. She also found a growing intellectual confidence that can be heard in the tone of *Pleasure of Ruins*. On 5 June 1951 she was awarded a Litt. D. by the University of Cambridge. The Public Orator of the university, orating in Latin, placed her in the context of her Macaulay, Conybeare and Herrick Cambridge connections. Rose, now an honoured member of a cultural and intellectual institution which had educated and nourished her male forebears for generations, processed down King's Parade in a scarlet robe. Cambridge, she felt, was her intellectual home. How different was this ending to the story of her relationship with Cambridge to that of the story of Julian Conybeare, the young woman poet of *They Were Defeated*.

Confident of her scholarship she was, but she was still as hopeless as ever with the business of deadlines and the day to day organisation a writer's life requires. That summer she was 'finishing' *Ruins* and so could not go abroad. She 'finished Babylon' and was 'on to Mycenae' before going to the Isle of Wight with Jean and Nancy Willetts, Jean's companion of thirty years, for a few days in August. In the summer of the next year she was still 'finishing' *Ruins*. *Ruins* was eventually delivered to Weidenfeld and Nicolson in May 1953 with one chapter still to be written.

What many of Rose's friends didn't realise was how the ascetic style of her daily living increased in the 1950s with her return to the Anglican Church. She attended mass every morning at 8.15 or 8.30, worrying to her sister Jean that maybe she should attend the 7.30 mass during Lent, and an hour of every day was set aside for devotional reading and prayer. The pages of her green-covered prayer book, which she called her Preces Privatae – Private Prayers – are worn with use.

Rose's re-entry into the Anglican communion meant that once again she could be close to her 'twin' Jean, closer perhaps than she had ever been. Eleanor had died in Ranchi in India in 1952. Now there was only Jean and Rose left. Rose went out to Romford every Friday to visit Jean and Nancy; she spent Christmases with them, and most years would spend at least a few days with them in the summer on the Isle of Wight, which she loved for its genteel Victorian charm, even though the bathing was a bit shallow.

She had new enthusiasms to share with Jean: intercommunion was one; mocking Roman Catholics for their rigid opposition to intercommunion was another. Rose's Anglicanism was less about faith and belief than about goodness, order and virtue. 'She was, I think, quite devoid of the gift of faith,' said Evelyn Waugh with some perspicacity. Rose's intolerance of Roman Catholics sprang from her perception that their notion of sin was unrelated to a moral code. She also particularly disliked the way that educated Roman Catholics would dismiss some of their beliefs as being only for simple, or uneducated fellow-Catholics. The very last letter she wrote to her sister, on 27 October 1958, brims with laughter over the election of Pope John XXIII. 'The white smoke has gone up!' she wrote. 'Several cardinals have died of excitement since the conclave began. Now the news is announced, and none of the favourites have won. I expect the younger ones all voted for one of 76 in hopes their turn would come in 2 or 3 years. I know nothing about him, but hope he is rather mad and will utter strange things.'

Rose did not reveal her return to the Church to most of her friends until after the publication of *Pleasure of Ruins* at the end of 1953. Some took it in their stride. She remained a close friend of Elizabeth Bowen, Rosamond Lehmann, and even Ivy Compton-Burnett despite her not understanding why Rose couldn't remain 'a perfectly sound agnostic like everyone else'. But she grew away from Victor and Ruth Gollancz. He later blamed her turn to religion, but it is quite as likely that it was to do with her cool reception of his Judaeo-Christian anthology, *A Year of Grace*.

But just as in the past she had compartmentalised the areas of her life, to protect one from another – keeping herself and Gerald away from her literary friends in the 1920s and 1930s, or protecting one part of herself from another, her feminine self from her writing self, for example – so she did not allow her re-entry into the Church to necessarily modify her old friendships. Throughout these years she would regularly spend weekends or longer at Raymond Mortimer's country house, Long Crichel, near Wimborne in Dorset, where a group of disputatious friends gathered and which she described one winter as 'cold without, cosy within . . . always entertaining'. Being in the Church did not mean any abatement of the dialogues and disputes that continued late into the nights.

New friends were made and new closenesses forged through her involvement with the Church. Rose's favourite church soon became Grosvenor Chapel in South Audley Street, a quiet, elegant eighteenth-century building which allowed her to worship in the way she liked, that is, with the poetry and the passion of the liturgy but without the distractions of the very high Anglican churches. She sat in the back pew on the left of the entrance, unobtrusive, distant, but with an uninterrupted view of the altar. John Betjeman worshipped here; what had been an acquaintanceship developed into a friendship. Here she met a younger woman, Susan Lister, a lecturer in theology at King's College, to whom she dedicated *The Towers of Trebizond*. Rose would often go for a swim in the Serpentine straight after mass. In May 1951 she wrote:

> It is lovely there in the mornings at nine; very empty, and smooth and green – and rather cool, of course. The shadows of the may-green trees shine in the water, and the cuckoos cry, and the smaller birds warble, and all is peace and joy . . . Grosvenor Chapel is just about half-way between Hinde Street and the Serpentine, so it is very convenient. A kind of shining peace prevails in both places.

This is reminiscent of the picture of the ideal church she imagined back in 1929, a mobile church that travels the countryside and opens its doors and windows to the presence of the sacred in the natural world. She goes on: 'I felt this particularly yesterday morning, which was Corpus Christi; it seemed possible the *sacra mysteria venerari* [sacred mysteries to reverence] in the Serpentine as well as in church.' A return to the Church gave her back a sense of the sacredness of nature that dated from her childhood.

To restrict herself to attendance at only one church didn't suit Rose's restless nature. The advantages and disadvantages of the various Anglican churches within a five-mile radius of Hinde

Father Jeremiah O'Donovan,
c. 1897

Gerald O'Donovan, c. 1920

Rose planting geraniums, St Andrew's Mansions, 1920s

Rose in the 1920s

Marjorie Grant Cook, 1924

Elizabeth Bowen, 1947

Virginia Woolf, c. 1932, photographed by Lenese

'having a hilarious time': Rose and Margaret in Will's Essex, Pacific Highway, 1929

Rose with the publisher
Hamish Hamilton and his
Klemm monoplane, c. 1934

Ivy Compton-Burnett in the summer of 1929, photographed by Claude Harris

Rose, an amused observer, at Brimpton, 1930s, photographed by Stefan Lorant

E.M. Forster, June 1938

Rosamond Lehmann, 1944

Sylvia Lynd, 1946, in a portrait by
L. Anning-Bell

Storm Jameson, May 1940

Rose in the 1950s

Rose in her flat in Hinde House, in 1950, on publication of *The World My Wilderness*. This photograph hangs as a memorial to Rose in a corner of the Reading Room of the London Library

'Oh, me? I'm just on my way to the Black Sea.' Rose Macaulay in 1958, photographed by Victor Glasstone

Dame Rose Macaulay, 1958, photographed by Cecil Beaton

Rose Macaulay in the early
1920s, photographed by
Howard Instead

English Heritage blue plaque
outside Hinde House,
Hinde Street, London W1

House was a constant topic of correspondence between Rose and Father Hamilton Johnson: one place would have intelligent priests, another would be convenient for her to get to, yet another might, with its vestments and processions, be a little too close for comfortableness to Rome. Her intellectual curiosity sent her out here and there from the calm centre that was Grosvenor Chapel. At St Thomas's Regent Street she met a young priest called Gerard Irvine, who became a friend and a ruin-visiting companion. Through him and Father Patrick McLaughlin, also of St Thomas's, she became involved in St Anne's House, Soho, a meeting place for intellectuals of any or no religious persuasion where they could argue to their hearts' content. Here, at last, she met Dorothy L. Sayers.

Meanwhile there was still, importantly, the O'Donovan connection. With her return to the Church Rose began to take seriously her godmotherly responsibilities. Every so often she would report to Father Hamilton Johnson on the progress of Mary Anne O'Donovan and her sister, how she would take them to church, listen to them reading the lesson and so on. *Parvulae* – little girls – she called them, or *parvulae indoctae* – unlearned little girls – or when she was feeling less Latinate, 'my two little girls'. In the summer of 1955 she spent a week with them at Butlin's in Skegness, 'rather like a visit to the moon, quite out of this world'. It was at Butlin's that she first saw television, which she 'didn't think much of'. Coincidentally, one of the programmes she watched was a literary quiz game, on which something she herself had written provided one of the questions. Who wrote, the panel was asked, 'it is to the eccentrics that the world owes most of its knowledge'? No one knew, but when the truth or otherwise of the statement was discussed, she was pleased that they seemed to be mainly in agreement with her.

Throughout the 1950s Rose's voice was regularly heard on BBC radio as a panellist on 'The Critics' and as a contributor to a variety of programmes put out by the 'Talks' department. Listening to some of those recordings fifty years later one is taken back to a different world. Broadcasting conventions had barely changed since the early days of the 1920s: everyone on air sounded as if they had been to public school and as if they were wearing evening dress, as indeed most of them were. Rose sounds like the rest of them: upper class and chattery, with her high-pitched voice, slight lisp on the 's's, words tumbling over themselves as they come out. It wasn't until the 1960s that broadcasting would be transformed in the technological, commercial and cultural revolution of that decade. The wireless would be ousted by the transistor radio, the BBC challenged by pirate and other commercial radio stations and the voice of the Oxbridge-educated broadcaster begin to be displaced by more varied, demotic voices. Rose became increasingly keen on the medium of broadcasting. Upper class though she sounds, she was as icono-clastic as ever when the mood took her. Elizabeth Bowen remembered how in 1953 she and Rose and C. V. Wedgwood were invited to do a talk each on the coronation: Rose's was too 'naughty' to be broadcast.

One day in July that year Rose's wireless went up in flames, and in the resulting fire she lost her father's old bookcase which had come to her after Margaret died. The fire in the wireless was perhaps a symbolic precursor of the change from old to new ways of broadcasting; and it prompted in Rose an entirely new interest in interior decorating. She had the sitting-room redeco-rated, and then because the bedroom looked shabby in contrast, she had it painted blue, 'wth scarlet door & cupboard & new red velvet curtains', she told her friend Gerard Irvine. 'It looks lovely, so does the many-coloured tinsel-strip counterpane I've made, & I am being given a new blue bed-head lamp with red border.' The next thing was a scarlet oilcloth for the kitchen table.

She was giving talks: 'Men's Women and Women's Men in Literature' to the Oxford Literary Society in 1952; continuing to write reviews and articles for the *New Statesman and Nation*, the *Spectator*, *Time and Tide* and the *Times Literary Supplement*. She was reading, researching and partying. Mark Bonham-Carter, her editor at William Collins, said that she came to every Collins party, arriving at six and staying until the end, and that she was at every other literary party that he attended. Gerard Irvine's sister Rosemary recalled being given a lift by Rose from one party to another. There was a short cut down a one-way street, going the wrong way. Rose took it. She was stopped by a policeman, who, solicitous of the apparently frail elderly woman at the wheel of the car, led her carefully to the end of the street. No sooner had he turned away than Rose's foot was down on the accelerator and they raced off to the party. Rose's friend Una Pope-Hennessy had died in 1949, but she remained friends with Una's sons. James described looking out of his window and seeing her arrive for one of his dinner parties: 'Rose in her scooting little old car, rushing past the windows and stopping with a jolt.' James was thirty-four, Rose sixty-nine. 'I like Rose so very much,' he wrote.

And still there was abroad. In May 1953 Rose travelled alone to Cyprus, then to Palestine, Israel, the Lebanon and back to Rhodes. Part of this journey would appear in *Towers*. Before she went to Turkey Rose had been wondering whether to accept an invitation to visit Russia in a party in honour of Chekhov, and had consulted Stephen Spender on the propriety of accepting the offer. He had assured her it would be all right, but when she realised she would have to look at 'a few tiresome things such as schools, hospitals, maternity homes and factories', she decided to go to Turkey instead. She went alone, visiting Trabzon (Trebizond), Antioch, Alexandretta and then Istanbul. When she wasn't actually travelling – and now, in her seventies, she sometimes had to cancel or delay her trips because she was not well enough – she was imagining travelling. Tonga was one destination: she hoped Jean might come too. 'You nurse and I preach,' she wrote (Anglicanism, naturally: she would convert Queen Salote of Tonga who was, apparently, a Wesleyan Methodist), 'and both of us eat sucking-pigs and yams with our fingers; which Nancy would cook for us.'

In 1955 Rose wrote to Jean that she had 'an intuition that I shall die in 3 years, ie in 1958, so must bustle about and do a lot of things in the time.' She had by then already started *The Towers of Trebizond*, her last, triumphant, novel.

ii

'"Take my camel, dear," said my aunt Dot, as she climbed down from this animal on her return from High Mass.' Thus begins *The Towers of Trebizond*, published in September 1956. It has become as famous an opening line as any in a twentieth-century novel: familiar, as these quotations become, to a much wider circle of people than those who have actually read the book.

The Towers of Trebizond is a novel, a travel book, a history book, the story of a quest; it explores and celebrates and despairs over the power of sexual love; it is a story of love and adultery that revels in digressions and discursions into church history, evolutionary theory and comparative religion. It is about sin and guilt and remorse; it is about English literary life in the 1950s and louche young men and women who write up their travels; it has real people in it, like Joe Ackerley, then literary editor of the *Listener*, with whom Rose had gone to a gathering of Billy Graham's at the Harringey Stadium in April 1954, and the travel writer Patrick Kinross, who had been in Trabzon in 1952, a couple of years before Rose; and in Aunt Dot (inspired partly by Dorothy L. Sayers, Barbara Reynolds convincingly suggests) and Father Hugh Chantry-Pigg it has characters whose fame soon became greater than that of the real people in the book. It is about the Cold War, and about spying in the Middle East, with the two British physicists 'got up as yachtsmen' who sail off with 'Albanians got up as Greek fishermen', only the first of a stream of people pretending to be other people; and, with the newspaper reports of the disappearance of Aunt Dot and Father Chantry-Pigg behind the Iron Curtain, it is wonderfully funny about Cold War prejudices and the unscrupulousness of the popular press.

Rose Macaulay was seventy-two when she was in Trabzon in 1954, complaining of the muffled-up women and the fearful heat. Trabzon has changed little in half a century. The women are less muffled up, but the majority of them, being Muslims, still wear headscarves, except for the schoolgirls – legacy of Atatürk – who look bold and healthy and of whom there are a large number. The Yessilyurt Hotel is still there, where Laurie stayed in *Towers* and found in her bedside drawer a manuscript written by Charles that was then plagiarised by his friend David, and where, thinking she was saying 'I'm sorry, I don't understand Turkish' she was in fact saying 'Please to call at once to Mr Yorum', which the management duly did. You can sit in the public gardens in the square in front of the Yessilyurt and sip Turkish tea, just as Rose Macaulay did, and where she had Father Chantry-Pigg process on the feast of Corpus Christi and exchange angry words with the local imam. And in the ancient citadel, although some of the ruined battlements have been patched up with breeze-blocks and concrete, the money has not lasted to make a thorough job of it, and so that too has been left, and you can still see the pointed arches of what Laurie in the novel claims is the Comnenus banqueting hall. The ground inside the ruined palace is exactly as it is described in *Towers*: there are fig trees and hazelnut trees and brambles; hovels and lean-tos are built into and against the ruined walls, and hens scratch the ground in ramshackle pens.

The Towers of Trebizond is informed by Rose Macaulay's own experience but tempting though it is to see Laurie's story as Rose's story, and to hear Rose's voice in Laurie's voice, that would be to refuse to recognise it as a novel. Here, for the first time since *Potterism*, Rose Macaulay used a first person narrator. All her other novels are told in the third person; and there are three separate first person narratives in *Potterism*. Many have double or multiple protagonists: the brother/sister pairs of early books such as *The Furnace*, *The Valley Captives* and *Views and Vagabonds*; the three generations of women in *Dangerous Ages*, and the five siblings and their offspring of *Told by an Idiot*. In *Keeping Up*

Appearances Rose Macaulay experimented, in Daisy and Daphne, with a single protagonist split into two subjectivities. In *The Towers of Trebizond* Laurie is unequivocally the singular subject. The 'I' with which she speaks is utterly convincing. It is not surprising then that there were some readers who wanted to read into this novel about estrangement and exile the story of Rose Macaulay's return to the Church. But the ending of *Towers* is unambiguous. Trebizond, 'the ideal and romantic and nostalgic vision of the Church which haunts the person who narrates the story', as Rose wrote to Hamilton Johnson before the book came out, remains unattainable. This is not a book that ends with a return to the Church. 'Still the towers of Trebizond,' says Laurie at the very end, 'the fabled city, shimmer on a far horizon, gated and walled and held in a luminous enchantment. It seems that for me, and however much I must stand outside them, this must for ever be. But at the city's heart lie the pattern and the hard core, and these I can never make my own: they are too far outside my range. The pattern should perhaps be easier, the core less hard.' The novel ends, like so many other novels of the mid-twentieth century, with its protagonist in exile, not in a place of belonging. And in this ending there emerges a theme that has occurred throughout Rose Macaulay's fiction: as well as exile, failure.

Rose realised the pitfalls of a first person narration. 'I adopted for Laurie,' she wrote to Hamilton Johnson on hearing from him that his copy of *Towers* had just arrived, 'a rather goofy, rambling prose style, to put the story at one remove from myself.' This wasn't entirely successful, as a 'rambling prose style' (maybe not 'goofy'), or what could be called a digressive style, was precisely what she was known for in her journalism. Part of the pleasure of the Macaulay essay lies in the digression, or the rambling. Another much-discussed aspect of the novel, along with the Laurie/Rose identification, is the lack of personal pronouns that identify Laurie as a woman and Vere, her lover, as a man. 'You probably also by now know the sex of Laurie,' she wrote in the same letter to Father Johnson. 'I saw no need to stress it, since so much of life is common to both sexes; but of course I mention it near the end, and most people discerned it early.' The commonality of experience to both sexes was a favourite theme of Rose Macaulay's. Of her hallucinatory dreams of Jason and the Argonauts, Laurie says, 'I did not know if I was a hero or one of their mistresses'. However, it is possible to interpret the playful withholding of assigned gender to Laurie and to Vere in *Towers* as another distancing technique. While the reader puzzles over whether Laurie is a young woman or a young man, she, or possibly he, will be less likely to be wondering how close is the 'I' voice to the author herself.

Vere remains a shadowy figure, appearing briefly at the end of Laurie's time in Turkey and later, back in England, reappearing at the end only to say the final words that Laurie will ever hear him say, before he is killed as a result of her impatience, rage and lack of judgement exacerbated by the 'euphoria pill' that she has taken. Vere is well connected, smart, powerful, sailing round the Aegean on the yacht of his friend the press lord. With his 'wit and brains and prestige', he is given all the trappings of worldly success that Gerald O'Donovan did not have but which Rose thought he deserved.

As in any novel, the author can be found here and there amongst the characters; she is in Aunt Dot, she is there even in the figure of the 'ancient bigot' Father Hugh Chantry-Pigg, who warns Laurie as they sail along the Black Sea shore of the dangers of her soul growing blind and deaf and paralysed. Rose drew on recent events in her own life for some of the adventures in *Towers*. At the novel's opening, on Aunt Dot's return from High Mass, Laurie stables the camel in a shed that it shares with her Austin, and, until lately, with Aunt Dot's Morris, which 'had been stolen from her by some Anglican bishop from outside the Athenaeum annexe while she was dining there one evening with Professor Gilbert Murray and Archbishop David Mathew'. The absent-minded (to be charitable) Anglican bishop may have been an invention, but it was Rose Macaulay's own Morris that had been stolen from outside the Athenaeum while she was inside dining with her two old friends. That was in January 1955, and the consequence was not camel-riding, but, almost as alarming in the opinion of various of her friends, reverting with enthusiasm to her wartime penchant for cycling.

Aunt Dot's forthright views on the oppression of Turkish women were views expressed by Rose Macaulay after the month she spent in Turkey in 1954, when she went to Trabzon, Antioch, Alexandretta and Istanbul, the journey taken by Laurie in *Towers*. She was on her own, it was hot (she was there in midsummer), many of the rooms weren't fit to keep a goat in, she complained, and always the women 'in their hot muffling clothes', as she put it to her sister, had to walk behind their menfolk and were not allowed to talk in public.

The year after Rose had been to Trabzon, and while she was engaged in writing *The Towers of Trebizond*, she had a poem published in the *Times Literary Supplement*, 'Dirge for Trebizond'. The title itself is enough to make one fear the worst, and the poem has little to recommend it beyond providing an example of how the material, in this case the fall of the Byzantine Empire to the Ottomans, can be so utterly transformed when reworked in a different literary form. In the novel the theme is subtle, comic, tragic and allusive. Not so in the poem. The press attaché, a Mr Pamir, from the Turkish Embassy in London did not take kindly to Miss Macaulay's characterisation of Turks in the 'Dirge' as 'the barbarians' who 'Howl round the walls like the sea . . .' and wrote to correct her:

> May we remind Miss Macaulay through your columns that the people she characterizes as 'barbarians' had benevolently granted religious freedom to the Christians after the conquest of Istanbul by Mahomet the Conqueror in 1453? This wide tolerance in religious matters was strictly observed in subsequent expansions of the Ottoman Empire, at a time when religious persecutions

prevailed in the west. Indeed many Christians fled to Istanbul during the reign of Suleiman the Magnificent in the sixteenth century to take refuge from persecution. One is tempted to wonder whether one of Miss Macaulay's ancestors may not have been among them . . .

Miss Macaulay's reply, printed below the press attaché's letter, was disingenuous. She justified her characterisation of Turks as 'barbarians' by claiming that that was how Byzantines, the 'imagined ghosts' of her poem, would have seen them; furthermore, she informed Mr Pamir, Greeks had used to refer to all non-Greeks, even Romans, as 'barbarians'. This is not exactly borne out by stanza 4 of the poem, which starts 'But barbarians will always stay./Five slow centuries they still are here . . .' and goes on to upbraid those 'muffled women' again. Even the sea seems to have been ruined by the Turks, for where once 'rich merchant cargoes' sailed up and down from the Golden Horn to Trebizond, it is now the 'inhospitable Euxine'.

Possibly Rose felt she had not responded with strict honesty, for in *The Towers of Trebizond* she makes amends. It is intolerant, unsympathetic Father Chantry-Pigg who is determined that the Turks are barbarians, while sympathetic, intelligent, anxious Dr Halide defends Suleiman the Magnificent, repeating the words of the Turkish attaché as they appeared in the *Times Literary Supplement*: '"So much more tolerant was he than the West," she said, "that no doubt some of your ancestors fled to Istanbul to escape from persecution at home."' Laurie, full of the beauty and romance of Istanbul, thinks this would have been a very wise move on the part of her ancestors. Dr Halide goes on to admit that 'neither Islam nor Christianity had exercised a very moderating influence on cruelty down the ages, in fact, both had seemed to heighten it, though she did not think it had been worse in the east than in the west at the same period, when all was shocking, and look at the Crusaders'. It would be nice to think of the Turkish attaché reading this and perhaps being a little mollified.

The novel may appear to follow Laurie's ramblings here and there, but there is a careful structure built around the narrative of the journeying. Comedy is balanced against tragedy, hilarity with grief. And although it is a book that is centrally concerned with questions of right and wrong, of sin and of virtue, it refuses to be moralistic. Only one judgement is made, and that is of Father Chantry-Pigg: 'He was better at condemning than at loving; Aunt Dot used to wonder what Christ would have said to him.'

The many different aspects are held together by the central theme of the virtue of love. Laurie says that she cannot unravel the pattern at the secret heart of Trebizond, nor make the hard core her own, and it is the nature of love and loving that is the hard core of the novel. Rose put her own story, that of over-whelming love and grief at its ending, into her novel.

Towers was an immediate success. As it was Rose Macaulay's first novel since her return to the Church of England, and as a central part of the story is about exile from that Church, theo-logical interpretations were many and varied. Rose greatly enjoyed the game of interpretation. In November she wrote to William Plomer of a letter she had received about *Towers* from a 'convert acquaintance': 'She thinks my camel stands for "the Catholic Church", exclusive and sneering, and the ape for the C of E, "aping Rome, but never getting to it" . . . What odd notions they do have.' Her favourite headline was: 'Mad camel plays a big part in unusual book.'

To one correspondent Rose would suggest one angle, to another, another. Jean was sensitive to what she saw as criticism or mockery of the Church (even of the Roman Catholic Church), and to her Rose said: 'I didn't mean it to be mainly funny; though no doubt a few jokes got in as I wrote.' In the early stages of writing it, in April 1955, she had described it to Hamilton Johnson as a 'rather foolish and frivolous novel'; on its publication, she was more nervous about that folly and frivolity, writing to him in August 1956: 'Don't think my jokes, comments, speculations on religion etc, flippant, will you . . . It is fundamentally a serious book, particularly the religious side of it . . .'

Telling Hamilton Johnson about some of the responses she had received, Rose wrote, in October 1956, that she didn't feel she deserved the praise, 'But something in the book which was part of my own most poignant experience has somehow got across to people and moved them, and of course I am glad of that.'

To her friend William Plomer she elucidated further the differences between Laurie's experiences and her own. 'I too had hoped for an Anglican victory at the book's end; but it ended too soon for that.' (William Plomer's letter to which this was a response did not survive, but we can infer from Rose's what he said he had hoped for.) 'It took me nine years to come back after the relevant death, and that death wasn't caused by me, which would make another barrier. So I had to leave Laurie in the wilderness, though she would little by little get nearer what was for her the inevitable destination, as I suppose it was for me: – if destination isn't too static a word for this disturbingly unsteady caravanserai (I mean, one is unsteady in it, not that it is unsteady itself, tho' indeed it rather is.) An Anglo-agnostic well inside the walls, instead of outside, that is the difference . . .'

To Plomer she wrote about the Church. To her friend Rosamond Lehmann, who knew about these things, she wrote about love and grief:

It's a book I have had in mind to write for a long time and writing it, like that, at a remove from myself, in an idiom not normally my own, and in a lot of circumstances that I enjoyed making up, but still the heart of the matter being my own story – writing it did sublimate and clarify life for me a little. I never, thank God, killed my lover; I don't have that to bear; I only watched him die of cancer, and couldn't often be with him during his illness. And for years after he died, I felt starved – a ghost, as Laurie did. But less hard than what happened to you; death is not a poison, only a knock-out blow.

Looking back now I am getting old, I can't not be glad of the past, in spite of knowing I behaved dishonestly and selfishly for so long. Love is so odd. It can't help being everything at the time.

The Towers of Trebizond won Rose Macaulay a new audience. She boasted of the number of bishops she had 'bagged' with it, but was especially pleased when non-Anglicans liked and understood it; she joked about waiting to hear that the Pope had read it; she reported to various people that Princess Margaret had been reading it while on board the yacht *Britannia* on her way to Africa, and 'read aloud the bits she most enjoyed, which were about adultery, and induced all the officers to read it too!'

In February 1957 it won the James Tait Black Memorial Prize. In May 1957 she went to Venice. 'I have been having a marvellous time . . . I am by no means alone, as Venice seems full of my acquaintances, some of whom have motor launches, others gondolas. Mrs Guggenheim, who has a palazzo quite near this pensione, filled with awe-inspiring works of extremely modern sculpture etc, is taking me out in her launch this afternoon, to San Lazzaro, the island with an Armenian convent where Byron spent so much time in 1816. Then my friend Victor Cunard lives in 3 noble and beautiful rooms in the Casa Foscali . . . met the Graham Sutherlands . . . I am gondoling with tomow [*sic*], up and down the small canals, to see out of the way churches etc . . .' Rose began to think about a new novel to be set partly in Venice.

At the end of the year she was invited to become a Dame of the British Empire in acknowledgement of her services to literature. The prospect of such an accolade raised old anxieties about the public gaze. But she was supported by old friends such as E. M. Forster, who encouraged her to accept by appealing to her as a member of the community of writers: there were few enough DBEs for literature, he pointed out. She made jokes about pantomime dames, and hoped that she wouldn't be addressed as 'Dame' on envelopes. 'I prefer "Miss", that has served me all these years, and why should I desert it in my old age?'

On 11 February 1958 Rose Macaulay was made Dame of the British Empire at Buckingham Palace. A week later she was dining with the Queen and Prince Philip (perhaps it was just as well that the BBC hadn't broadcast Rose's coronation talk). At the beginning of April, coming out of St Anne's House, Soho, in the middle of a fierce theological argument, she turned back to make a further point and stepped backwards as if she was on the ground, rather than at the top of a flight of stairs. She fell down to the pavement, breaking her right wrist and femur, and spent two weeks in Charing Cross Hospital on the fracture ward and a further four weeks on a private ward in University College Hospital. The thigh bone was pinned together and she was hobbling round the ward with a stick after three weeks. 'Now I find that hip-breaking has been lately quite an epidemic, & am gratfied [*sic*] to notice that some people who fell much earlier than I are less advanced in recovery & still walk with sticks.' But the wrist, being what the surgeon called 'a great ugly brute of a fracture', took longer. She enjoyed the public ward: 'John Betjeman came to see me at Charing X, to the delight of the ward, all of whom saw him often on T.V. I also had a bishop, two vicars, & other priests, including the Prior of the Dominican Priory at Hampstead, as well as my more secular friends, so I was very sociable.'

Typing a letter with her left hand to William Plomer at the end of May she remarked, regarding her indecipherable handwriting, that her loss was her correspondents' gain, but said that she could now drive again, and had driven out to visit John Lehmann in Crawley on Whit Sunday. If she could neither write nor type with her right hand, her driving must have been even more erratic than usual.

In August 1958 she returned to Venice and, writing to Jean, indulged in fantasies, yet again, of Anglican conversions: 'If I was a clergyman I would live in Venice, try and get the job of regular chaplain to the English church, and spend the week trying to convert the natives, tempting them with clouds of incense and a great number of images and processions . . . I should quietly seduce some Italians, perhaps with little presents . . .'

This time Rose bumped into Anthony Powell, who was in Venice for an international writers' conference. He reported the meeting as if it came straight from the pages of *A Dance to the Music of Time*:

> 'What on earth are *you* doing here?'
>   'I might well ask you the same question.'
>   'Oh, me?' she said, 'I'm just on my way to the Black Sea.'

Such a Powellian exchange seems appropriate for a writer who had weaved her way in and out of the dance of English letters for half a century; and who had so often in the past adopted a persona not unlike that of Powell's alter ego, his detached and amused observer of the dance, Nicholas Jenkins. But Rose by the end of her life had entered the swim of things. From Venice she embarked on a cruise of the Aegean and the Black Sea with a group of like-minded intellectuals and classicists. They stopped at Skyros, where Rupert Brooke was buried. Trebizond was 'like coming home'. On her return she wrote up the trip in an article called 'The New Argonauts', recalling, even if it was only for herself and Jean, the last two of 'the Five', those early seagoing adventures on the Mediterranean waves.

It is tempting to a writer of biography when arriving at the death of the subject to draw a satisfying conclusion, to pull together previously disparate strands, and tie the life up neatly. All writers make patterns with their material; perhaps biographers more than others, for they have their subject's life before them, that journey from the cradle to the grave. There is a strong desire to sum up. To what extent should that be resisted? Rose Macaulay died at the end of a long and varied and successful life. She had, in her last decade, made peace with parts of herself. Yet it was the contradictions of her character, the battling lizards in her nature, that made her the writer that she was.

In 1955 she had been right about having three more years to live. She died on 30 October 1958. She rang the doctor that morning and suffered a heart attack a minute or two after she had opened the door to him.

Rosamond Lehmann wrote:

She was forever in transit, physically, intellectually, spiritually; energetically not eating, not drinking or sleeping, so it seemed; yet such was her transparency and charity of spirit that she seemed universally available to her friends. She has been called child-like; but to me she suggested youth, a girl, of that pure eccentric English breed which perhaps no longer exists, sexless yet not unfeminine, naïve yet shrewd; and although romantic, stripped of all veils of self-interest and self-involvement. I cannot write of her tenderness and understanding of the grief of others, fruit of deep personal suffering triumphantly surmounted. No one had better cause than I to know and value it. Her last letter arrived the morning before the morning of her death. One of the things it discussed was 'our corrupting profession'. I was meditating on her incorruptibility when the news reached me. With the first piercing pang came the thought: But we have all just seen her, just been talking to her! How like her to slip off and run lightly, unhampered, without backward glance, straight into her death. Straight through it.

Laurie, through whom Rose Macaulay explored her own joys and griefs, looked ahead fearfully to death, and concluded that 'life, for all its agonies of despair and loss and guilt, is exciting and beautiful, amusing and artful and endearing, full of liking and of love, at times a poem and a high adventure, at times noble and at times very gay; and whatever (if anything) is to come after it, we shall not have this life again'.

Letters

Reconstructing anyone's life poses enormous difficulties, for however copious the evidence of letters, diaries, journals, and eye witness accounts, there are always the problems of interpretation, of the subjectivity of witnesses, and of the basic contradictoriness of the human being. Moods and emotions are volatile, but when recorded on the page are often forced by posterity to carry a much greater weight than was ever intended by their author. In her book on E. M. Forster, Rose Macaulay criticised his unsympathetic response to a letter of Jane Austen's. Jane Austen wrote to her sister Cassandra: 'Mrs Hall was brought to bed yesterday of a dead child, some weeks before she expected, owing to a fright. I suppose she happened unawares to look at her husband.' Forster disliked the unkindness of this, and imagined Jane and Cassandra laughing together over unfortunate Mrs Hall. But Cassandra's reaction might have been very different, Rose pointed out. She might have chided Jane for unkindness. Jane might have repented. We can never know. 'That is the worst of publishing the letters of the dead,' concluded Rose. 'They grin and stare and grimace and scowl at us, expressing for ever, in black ink on paper, moods which were scarcely even moods, so glibly did they run by, run off the pen.'

When *Letters to a Friend*, the first volume of Rose Macaulay's letters to Father Hamilton Johnson, was published in October 1961, the revelations it contained about her love affair with a married man provoked from critics and from the general public a wide range of passionate reactions. The publication also started a controversy in the press over the ethics of publishing private letters. The *Daily Mail* quoted Rebecca West saying, 'It made me want to vomit'; on the other side the Archbishop of Canterbury, choosing a rather more episcopalian mode of diction, pronounced: 'I cannot but think that good will come of the book.'

The arguments fell into two broad groups. First, the biographical argument: what were, or, depending on one's interpretation, what would have been, the wishes of the author, Rose Macaulay, regarding the publication of the letters? And what weight should be given to those expressed or imputed wishes? Secondly, the religious or ethical argument over the content of the letters: that is, Rose Macaulay's admission of adultery, her expressions of remorse, and her return to the Church. But the two arguments become inextricably entangled in the double question of what right, if any, and what need, if any, the public had to read the letters.

The huge fuss over the contents of the letters seems curiously dated. It is hard to imagine now the sense of sin which was then, in the early 1960s, a part of many people's consciousness. Since then Britain has become a largely secular society; Rose's expressions of remorse for her sin carry a historical rather than a topical interest for the reader.

The two volumes of letters to Father Hamilton Johnson the Anglican priest came out in 1961 and 1962, only three and four years, respectively, after Rose Macaulay's death. The letters were made public in a world which would soon be very different from the one in which they had been written. Already there were indications of things loosening up: in 1960 *Lady Chatterley's Lover* had been unbanned in the courts; in 1961 the contraceptive pill went on sale in Britain for the first time. By 1965, the year a woman was first appointed to be a High Court judge, an opinion poll revealed that although the majority of people in Britain still believed in God, most of them would rather watch television than go to church.

Yet the questions raised by the arguments over the private versus the public ownership of letters, diaries and journals are enduring in relation to the work of biography. How do we know what the subject would have wished? If there were written instructions, as there were in the case of Rose Macaulay's letters to Hamilton Johnson, how do we interpret those instructions? Even if we do know what the subject wished, is the biographer's duty to the subject, or to posterity?

These questions were raised by the publication of the two volumes of *Letters*; and raised again when, in 1964, a third volume of letters came out, those of Rose to her sister Jean.

The history of the *Letters* goes like this: the two volumes edited by Constance Babington Smith and published by William Collins, *Letters to a Friend* and *Last Letters to a Friend*, are selected from the letters that Rose wrote to Hamilton Johnson between late summer 1950, when he first wrote to her after reading *The Shadow Flies* (the American edition of her 1932 novel *They Were Defeated*), and her death in October 1958. The rest of the letters are in a closed box held in the library of Trinity College, Cambridge, part of the ERM archive deposited by Constance Babington Smith, and embargoed until 2012. A few, a very few of the published letters, mainly written within the first six months of the start of the correspondence, concern Rose's sense of exile from the Church of England, her love affair with a married man (Gerald O'Donovan is not named in the published letters), and her return to the Church. Early in 1951 she made a confession (to a Cowley Father in London), and took up once more the devotional practices of the Church of England. Later, she discovered that Hamilton Johnson was a distant cousin; genealogical matters then took up a considerable part of the correspondence, along with matters liturgical. Otherwise the letters chart Rose Macaulay's everyday life: they record work undertaken, people seen, book reviews read and written, time spent with friends, excoriations of individual Roman Catholics and of Roman Catholicism in general, and an almost obsessive concern with the relative speed of sea mail versus air mail.

Rose Macaulay did not appoint a literary executor, but she passed control of the copyright in her work to her only surviving sister Jean Babington Macaulay. Rose had met Constance Babington Smith, another distant cousin like Hamilton Johnson, in the 1950s at St Paul's, Knightsbridge, which Rose sometimes attended instead of Grosvenor Chapel. Constance Babington Smith had worked in photo intelligence during the war; she is especially remembered for her discovery of the V2s being manufactured at Peenemünde. Constance had written a book about her wartime work, *Evidence in Camera: The Story of Photographic Intelligence in World War II*, and a book about test flying. She had long had a passion for aircraft (Constance 'began by making smart hats,' Rose wrote to Hamilton Johnson, 'then fell in love with planes and once designed a hat made like a bomber, which she wore at an aeronautic garden party'), and after she edited the three volumes of Rose's published letters she wrote a biography of the aviator Amy Johnson. Much later, long after she had written her 1972 biography of Rose, and after many years of devout Anglicanism, she converted to the Orthodox branch of the Christian Church, of which Rose had written back in 1925 that it has 'dignity and an ancient tradition, but its clergy do not always look well-groomed. Many of them do up their hair with hair-pins. They are not allowed to worship statues, but only eikons, or images in bas-relief. The Orthodox mind sees a distinction here that no other Church has yet grasped. They keep Easter with great enthusiasm, but at the wrong time.'

When Rose died in October 1958, Constance had not met

Jean Macaulay, but soon after their first meeting a friendship
began to grow that had its roots in their shared Christian
beliefs and practices and in their devotion to the memory of
Rose. Later, after Jean's lifelong companion Nancy Willetts
had died, Constance became Jean's closest friend and carer and
the two women would regularly attend church retreats
together. Meanwhile Jean, probably because she felt she lacked
the necessary literary knowledge and sophistication, had transferred to Constance control of the copyright in all her sister
Rose's work.

On her death Rose Macaulay left instructions that all the
papers in her flat should be burned unread. This was used to
support the argument by those opposed to the publication of the
Hamilton Johnson letters that letters *from* Rose should also be
destroyed. Constance and Jean disputed the logic of this argument; they went further, and maintained that the reason that
Rose had asked for all the papers in her flat to be destroyed was
to ensure that one particular cousin, a convert to Roman
Catholicism, should not be able to go through them. Of all
Rose's prejudices her prejudice against Roman Catholics in her
latter years was one of the liveliest. Her opinion of that branch of
Christianity had not changed since she wrote of it, in the same
essay in which she had charted the eccentricities of the Orthodox
priesthood, that it 'will save you a lot of trouble in deciding for
yourself what to believe, for it knows the truth and tells you'. It is
not impossible that she said something to Jean or Constance
about her fear of this cousin going through her private papers
after her death.

In the story of these letters much hinges on the interpretation
of remarks. On the one hand a remark about a Roman Catholic
cousin which was not backed up by written evidence was used by
Constance and Jean as a guide to Rose's intentions; on the other
hand a quite specific request, in writing, to the recipient of her
letters that he burn them all, was dismissed by Constance and
Jean as a casual remark. Rose had written to Father Hamilton

Johnson on 7 September 1952: 'I'm *glad* you like to have my letters. Really 100? I think you'd better get rid of them, of any you
have kept, in that incinerator! I own I have kept yours – but that
is another matter. They are full of such good stuff – how good
you have been to me these 2 years! But I will burn them before I
die; they're not for other people to see. How I value all that liturgical world you have opened to me.' Constance called Rose's
reference to the incinerator 'flippant' (perhaps, although
Constance didn't say this, because of the exclamation mark,
perennially an unreliable indicator of tone). As Rose was not
dismayed when she discovered later that Hamilton Johnson had
ignored the instruction, Constance said it indicated that she
hadn't meant it seriously.

In a review in the *Spectator* Stevie Smith pointed out some of
the inconsistencies in the demands Rose made of Hamilton
Johnson, giving as an example the way Rose would tell
Hamilton Johnson in one letter not to bother to read one of her
books, and in the next letter want to know exactly what he
thought of it. Stevie Smith, a careful reader, said it 'makes one
wonder if, when she says, "Put these letters in your incinerator,"
she means it'. Rose's close friend the literary and music critic
Raymond Mortimer expressed even stronger doubts over Rose's
desire to have her letters destroyed, and didn't even address the
incinerator question: 'She loved to read books of good letters,'
he wrote in the *Sunday Times*, 'and I think must have guessed
that her own would be published, if she left no instructions to
the contrary, which she never did.' He believed that because
Rose herself was a writer, there was a duty to posterity to publish letters with a bearing on that writing career. How can we
understand writers, goes his argument, if we know nothing of
what moves them deeply, in this case Rose's profound feelings
of alienation and exile, her yearning to re-enter the Church of
her youth, a love affair that lasted almost a quarter-century,
and the 'supreme importance' of her devotional life in her last
eight years?

By the time the letters were published Father Hamilton Johnson, too, was dead. He and Constance Babington Smith had met in 1956 when she travelled to America and, with an introductory letter from Rose, had visited him at the Cowley Fathers Monastery in Boston. He had sent to Constance all the letters he had received from Rose. (Or not quite all: there is the mysterious missing page, 'missing when the correspondence was received', according to Constance, from Rose's fourth letter to him, dated 27 November 1950, a crucial period two months before she took the plunge and went to confession. And there are a few other deletions, marked by Constance in her preface to the first volume, made by Hamilton Johnson in four more of the published letters. Perhaps other letters, from amongst those unpublished and unseen, are wholly or partially missing.) For Constance it was important that the publication of the letters should have received Hamilton Johnson's blessing but others felt that his views, being those of the recipient rather than the author of the letters, were not relevant, and remained unimpressed when Constance made public his expressed wish that the letters should be published 'as they might be of help to many'. Some felt that not only were his views irrelevant, but that by making the letters public he had betrayed the trust Rose had placed in him.

E. M. Forster was among those who felt that way. After he had read the extracts published in the *Observer* he wrote to Constance Babington Smith that he was surprised not to have seen a statement announcing that the letters were being published by Rose's own expressed wish. He presumed there would be such a statement in the book. Of course there was no such statement, and none of Constance's considerable mollifying skills had any effect on his implacable hostility to the publication. Like all homosexuals before the Wolfenden Report of 1967, E. M. Forster had a personal stake in upholding the privacy of personal letters, for sexual revelations could brand people as criminals. But that was only one factor, and one that was not paralleled in Rose's letters to Hamilton Johnson, for she admitted to no crime, only to a 'sin'; the equivalent danger for a woman (lesbianism was never a criminal offence) would have been the revelation of having procured an abortion. But Forster's hostility to the enterprise came from a more general cultural position. Like Rose herself, he was part of a culture that valued restraint and reticence; intimate gossip among close friends was one thing, but the publication of such intimacies was beyond the pale. He may well also have felt, as many other humanist and secular friends of Rose did, a distaste for the intrusive religiosity of the correspondence. Some indeed felt a strong animosity towards Hamilton Johnson; Elizabeth Bowen referred to him as 'that rat-faced priest' and V. S. Pritchett, in the *New Statesman*, called him 'the dog-collared fan', who wasted too much of a busy writer's time in the last years of her life.

Constance was astonished by the controversy that surrounded the publication of *Letters to a Friend*. It is surely a measure of her innocence in the matter that she had chosen to end the first volume with a letter in which Rose had so specifically talked about the destruction of her letters in an incinerator. And it is perhaps a measure of the canniness of Viola Garvin, literary editor of the *Observer*, that she chose to end the first week's selected extracts from the book with it. No wonder it drew attention.

If you read the correspondence surrounding the publication of the letters it is hard to question Constance Babington Smith's honesty and good faith. She saw the story of Rose's return to the Church, as told in the *Letters*, as a 'triumphant conclusion' to the story that was begun but left unfinished in Rose's last published novel, *The Towers of Trebizond*. But her interpretation was only one of many, and the question of how to read the letters was taken out of her hands as soon as the first volume of them was published.

On publication the letters no longer belonged just to the

editor, Constance Babington Smith, nor to the late recipient, nor to the writer's surviving relatives, nor, even, to the presumed constituency of the book's readership, those wavering Christians and agnostics whom Constance Babington Smith addressed in her introduction and prefatory remarks. The serialisation of the book over two Sundays in the *Observer*, and the full-page article in the *Daily Mail*, with its headline in massive point size, 'Did this priest betray this woman?', illustrated with a full-face picture of Rose Macaulay in a beret looking – despite the fact that she was the one 'betrayed' rather than the one 'betraying' – like a Russian spy, ensured a much wider and more vociferous expression of opinion than Constance had dreamed of. In the next few months Constance and Jean – in their innocence – consoled each other with the thought that at least more people would read the book, and that when they did read it they would respond to its uplifting moral message.

In the first week of the *Observer* extracts, adultery was highlighted at the expense of liturgy, and in the second week of serialisation Rose's not altogether complimentary comments about Graham Greene were singled out and printed around a large photograph of him. Rhona Churchill in the *Daily Mail* drew attention to Constance's ownership of the copyright and suggested, to the horror and distress of both Constance and Jean, that she had published the letters for her own financial gain. It was Rhona Churchill who elicited from Rebecca West that the publication of the book made her 'want to vomit'. This provoked Raymond Mortimer, in turn, into suggesting that Dame Rebecca West was 'not well-balanced' and because of her own past, was 'specially fussed about sexual irregularity'. There were a number of other accusations like this: one correspondent in the *Observer* said that 'adulterers and adulteresses' had been 'touched on the raw' and that publication of the letters provided a posthumous recompense for the sin that in life Rose Macaulay had not been able to rectify.

Two or three weeks after publication, when emotions were

running at their highest and Constance was under attack from all sides, her brother wrote her a letter of stout support: he thought that the purpose of the book was 'to show how a great personality wrestled with temptation and sin and triumphed over it'. This is a fine example of what many people wanted the book to show, rather than what it actually did show. For the *Letters* do not chart a Dantean descent into hell; they articulate barely a nodding acquaintance with temptation and sin, let alone a wrestling with it. For much of the *Letters* Rose seems to be seeking, and thanking Father Johnson for providing, reassurance that her own type of faith, or belief, or hope, was sufficient to allow her a place within the Church. 'An active Christian,' William Plomer described her in his review of the third volume, *Letters to a Sister*, 'she may also be called an elastic one.' In the three volumes of letters a wide-ranging interest in Christianity is displayed; but there is truth in the criticism made by Marghanita Laski in the *Observer* that 'too much is churchiness rather than religion'.

And as for the nature of the sin, that too was widely interpreted. Stevie Smith drew a distinction between sinfulness and guilt, saying that in the book there was 'no sinfulness of serious sort, though she (Rose) makes much of her feelings of guilt for an old love affair'. Some correspondents maintained that there had been no sin at all; others expressed their unease at the sight of a woman of Rose Macaulay's experience and sophistication turning to a celibate man for guidance on the troubles of her sexual life.

The lack of profound spiritual or religious matter in the letters did not, however, stop Christian readers from taking passionate sides. Although in the introduction to the first volume Constance quoted a lengthy passage from a letter she had received from Hamilton Johnson in which he insisted that Rose had made no confession to him (confusing the issue by stating that it was 'as if' he had been a priest in a confessional-box listening to 'her situation' rather than her confession), a number of people nonetheless read the letters as a betrayal not just of the trust invested in a friendship, but of the seal of the confessional. Against those people, at the other extreme, were ranged the correspondents who believed that Rose had only *thought* she was going to confession but was sadly mistaken; Hamilton Johnson, they maintained, being an Anglican, was no priest at all; he was one of those men 'calling themselves priests' and 'dressing up' as priests, a fake with no spiritual authority to hear confessions anyway.

Nor was comment of a personal nature lacking from the inter-Christian contingent. Whereas both the broad-based Roman Catholic *Tablet* and the Dominican *Blackfriars* gave the book good reviews – which greatly pleased Constance and led her to express the hope, a pious hope if ever there was one, that this indicated a 'thaw' in RC/Anglican relations – it was reviewed rudely in the Anglican journal *Theology*. It was a dean who reviewed it. In no time at all he was being described as having 'only a third-class degree' and writing for an editor who was notorious for having recently 'turned queer' on a number of other issues.

The secular responses – leaving aside Rebecca West who may well have regretted what she had said once she saw it in the *Daily Mail* – included those who agreed with E. M. Forster's opinion that without Rose Macaulay's stated wish for publication no one had any business to publish the letters. Others, including Raymond Mortimer, Harold Nicolson and William Plomer, welcomed publication for the picture the letters gave of Rose's varied interests, her intellectual curiosity, her sharpness (Raymond Mortimer's only criticism was of her obsession with the faults of Roman Catholics) and, in general, her love of life. Harold Nicolson found the letters 'charming and gay', and praised them for enhancing the zest of pagans like himself. William Plomer wrote of how Rose's 'love of travel, of history, of literature and of persons coursed through her old veins and courses through these pages'. Raymond

Mortimer felt that he was 'once again listening to her deliciously pointed talk'. What these three men read into the letters was a confirmation of Rose's happiness in the last eight years of her life, and as good friends of hers they could not but be happy on her behalf. 'Her joyous faith halved half her worries and doubled all her joys,' wrote the pagan Harold Nicolson with generosity.

All three of these writers praised Constance's editing. Harold Nicolson said she brought to the task 'a charming modesty, coupled with that intense gift of perception which enabled her to detect the V2 at Peenemünde before it was launched, thus saving many thousands from destruction'.

It is as if, for her friends, reading the *Letters* brought Rose back to them. The subjectivity of their response is obvious; it is as if they can hear Rose speaking. For those who didn't know Rose so well, it was a little different, but for them too the response was subjective. Perhaps letters particularly bring out that response in readers; they are, after all, addressed to an individual 'you'. It is hard not to become, at least partly, that 'you' when you are reading.

Some people detected in the *Letters* an expression of the loneliness of old age, including two of those who wrote most perspicaciously about them, V. S. Pritchett and Marghanita Laski. Laski challenged Hamilton Johnson's statement that the letters could be 'of help to many'. 'But whom are the letters to help?' she asked, in her review of the second volume in October 1962. 'It is no help to know that in old age, in loss and loneliness, many people turn or return to the Church, for gladly or sadly, according to our bias, we knew this already.' And like others who were not sympathetic to what they read, she disliked Constance's 'assiduous annotations'. Pritchett wrote of Rose Macaulay's 'touching attempt to break out of loneliness', and expressed sorrow at the 'very familiar sight' of someone feeling guilt and being induced to believe that the anguish and pain she had suffered was all due to a 'sin'. These too are subjective and empathetic responses of writers to another writer's words.

But amongst all the letters and articles carefully kept by Constance Babington Smith, that show such a range of sympathy and antipathy, that are so revealing about the beliefs and hopes and anxieties of their writers, there is one gaping hole. No one admits to the hurt they felt when they discovered the secret that had been kept from them. Rose Macaulay loved someone in successful secrecy for a quarter of a century and hid her grief at his loss for years afterwards. How could friends and acquaintances not have been hurt by that revelation? And how could they not be further hurt when they read Raymond Mortimer saying, inaccurately, that 'the long, reciprocated love of Rose Macaulay for a married man was a fact known to a large circle', if they had counted themselves as a friend of Rose's but were not, somehow, part of this 'large circle'? Such feelings of hurt must have coloured the way that the letters were read; how many people felt this, and how deeply, is something else that will never be known.

Rose's fellow-writers may have been divided over the correctness of publishing the letters, but on the whole they agreed that the content of the letters failed to show Rose Macaulay's strengths as a writer. Stevie Smith worried that the 'dangerous charm' of the inconsequentiality of the author's voice left a 'smear of triviality' over the subjects discussed. Marghanita Laski found a 'cloying flavour of over-enthusiastic self-indulgence' in the apparent lack of spiritual austerity, self-discipline and self-sacrifice. V. S. Pritchett, while being one of those who imagined that Rose Macaulay would have been dismayed by the exploitation of her privacy, still found what he called a 'lop-sided' biographical value in the two volumes. 'They reveal a decorous mind that must be set beside the mind of the satirist and the rebel in her, which produced her best work.' While certain facts about Rose Macaulay's life – the affair, her commitment to the Church – may have come as news to readers, Pritchett was one of only a few to find himself moved to a reappraisal. For most, it was the Rose they already knew who was in the letters; or it was the Rose they already knew who had been betrayed by the publication of the letters.

So it was that the notorious Macaulay reticence became part of the weaponry in the argument over publication. Throughout her life Rose Macaulay had guarded and cherished her sense of privacy. In 1934 she was pleading with an American anthologist to remove her biographical details from his book. Later she replied angrily to a request from a researcher for *Who's Who* that it was neither coyness nor affectation that motivated her desire to deny him personal details. She wrote a novel on the subject, *I Would Be Private*. E. M. Forster was accurate in his assessment of Rose Macaulay as reticent like himself; and Rebecca West was right to talk of Rose's dignity and fastidiousness. But there were other Roses. There was Raymond Mortimer's Rose, who could be 'cavalier in her treatment of facts'; there was James Lees-Milne's Rose, who was 'unworldly, indiscreet, impulsive, but intensely lovable as well as very clever indeed'. There was even the Rose of Malcolm Muggeridge's splendidly eccentric vision, a Rose 'so earnest, so clever, so wrong!' that she becomes 'the final destroyer of the human race'.

Each reader of the *Letters* brought their own Rose to their reading; just as, finally, each biographer brings their own subject to the biography. Constance's Rose, in her edition of the *Letters*, was not, is not, and could never be, the Rose of other readers.

When the first fuss had died down, and when, a year later, Constance and Jean had weathered the publication of *Last Letters to a Friend* (which contained no further private revelations), they remained committed to their view that the books would help people and would have 'far-reaching effects' on their moral lives. By then they had received numerous letters from Christian readers that vindicated this view. Their devotion both to the

Christian Church and to the memory of Rose Macaulay is unquestionable. What Rose herself would have thought we can only speculate, as so many did on publication. It is hard not to think that she would have been a bit impatient with all the religious fan letters that so pleased her sister and her cousin. After the second volume came out Marjorie Grant Cook, who perhaps more than anyone was privy to the secrets of Rose's heart, wrote to Constance: 'I am now sure that Rose would have said, "Yes, publish after my death." And that for mixed reasons, not really missionary.' Marjorie Grant Cook was doubtless right about the mixed reasons: one of those would surely have been for the sheer pleasure in provoking such argument and controversy. Another might well have been to see the vindication of her long-held views – explored first in *Potterism*, the novel that made her a household name in 1920 – on the power and the perniciousness of the press.

What value do the letters have now? Any editor publishing letters soon after the death of the writer, and any biographer writing about a recently dead subject, is faced with decisions about what to leave out. A subject's desire for privacy, expressed or inferred, then becomes less important than the responsibility not to cause hurt or offence to living people and indeed not to lay oneself and one's publisher open to charges of libel or slander. Paradoxically, the further away in time you are from the subject, the more you are able to know about the people they moved among.

The fullness of published letters depends on whose hands they have passed through. Rose Macaulay's letters to her sister Jean were extensively edited by Jean (she told a horrified Constance that she had been reading and burning them before she passed into Constance's hands those that remained) before Constance began her own editorial process. The difference between the original and the published letters in the Hamilton Johnson correspondence won't be known until the closed box is opened in 2012, if then.

But Constance Babington Smith has left for public access the correspondence she had with people featured in all three volumes of Rose Macaulay's published letters, and it is often more revealing than what appeared in the final version. Constance was scrupulous in contacting everyone who might conceivably have been offended by Rose's comments on them. Most, but not all, felt that it was more important to have Rose's biased comments appear in print than to change what she had written.

Graham Greene was one of these, writing to Mark Bonham Carter at Collins that it was better that 'Rose's sweet inaccuracies' about himself should not be edited out. Greene being not only a novelist at a particularly prolific period of his career, but also a Roman Catholic convert, was a natural target for much of Rose's musings on other writers' follies and the peculiar and quite inexplicable follies of Roman Catholics. On *The End of the Affair* she wrote: 'The people are all rather low types, and not convincing. And the religion in it (such as it is) is brought down to a very trivial plane by two rather absurd miracles at the end, which are supposed to show the heroine's sanctity, though there are no other signs of this . . . What a mess his mind must be – nothing in it, scarcely, but religion and sex, and these all mixed up together.' And on being invited to one of his parties she wrote: 'On Tuesday I am bidden to a party at Graham Greene's. Wouldn't it be interesting if at that party I was surrounded by G.G. characters – evil men, racing touts, false clergymen, drunken priests and with G.G. in the middle of them talking about Sin . . .'

Inaccuracies whether sweet or not there were: it was a part of Rose Macaulay just as much as her scrupulous scholarly correspondence with people about seventeenth-century manuscript songs or early editions of *Paradise Lost*. Had the letters been published later than they were, they could have included more of the lively pictures of her contemporaries, such as the exchange Rose recorded between herself and William Plomer one weekend in the country when he admitted to her shyly that he had taken to going to church now and again, and Rose replied that so, too, had she. 'What *would* Morgan say if he could hear us?' asked Rose.

The passage of time has meant that E. M. Forster is no longer alive to be hurt, as William Plomer thought he might be, by two friends whispering behind his back. It has also meant that the significance of the role Gerald O'Donovan played in Rose Macaulay's life and work is what concerns readers now, not, as appears in the *Letters*, the bald fact of his existence. With hindsight, knowing much more about Gerald than was known then, one can see how enormously important the relationship was – how could it not have been? – but in the letters his existence appears as not much more than the reason for the regret and remorse that Rose Macaulay was feeling in the decade after his death, and her reason for returning to the Church. The *Letters* no longer seem particularly revelatory. Nor do they tell us a great deal about Rose Macaulay as a writer because that was not what they were primarily about. She was a prolific, but not a great, letter writer. At the time of publication Stevie Smith and Marghanita Laski criticised the letters on literary grounds, and concluded that Rose Macaulay reserved her creative power for her books. That seems, now, a fair judgement.

The legacy of the letters is that Rose Macaulay's posthumous reputation has been skewed. There were only two recipients of all her published letters: an Anglican priest to whom she wrote during and just after her return to the Church, and a sister who was a lifelong devout Christian. It is hardly surprising, then, that in the decade following her death Rose Macaulay's Anglicanism, as expressed in these three volumes, overshadowed all other views of her.

Now, over forty years later, the story of the letters seems to reveal less about Rose Macaulay than it does about that period in British history when the foundations of the post-war social construction of church-and-family were beginning to crumble. It also raises questions about biography: questions about the partial nature of all evidence, about the difficulties of interpretation and about the final mysterious unknowability of another human being.

BOOKS BY ROSE MACAULAY
(in chronological order)

Novels

Abbots Verney John Murray, 1906
The Furnace John Murray, 1907
The Secret River John Murray, 1909
The Valley Captives John Murray, 1911
Views and Vagabonds John Murray, 1912
The Lee Shore Hodder & Stoughton, 1912
The Making of a Bigot Hodder & Stoughton, 1914
Non-Combatants and Others Hodder & Stoughton, 1916
What Not: A Prophetic Comedy Constable, 1919
Potterism: A Tragi-farcical Tract Collins, 1920
Dangerous Ages Collins, 1921
Mystery at Geneva Collins, 1922
Told by an Idiot Collins, 1923
Orphan Island Collins, 1924
Crewe Train Collins, 1926
Keeping Up Appearances Collins, 1928
Staying with Relations Collins, 1930
They Were Defeated Collins, 1932
Going Abroad Collins, 1934
I Would Be Private Collins, 1937
And No Man's Wit Collins, 1940
The World My Wilderness Collins, 1950
The Towers of Trebizond Collins, 1956

Poetry
The Two Blind Countries Sidgwick & Jackson, 1914
Three Days Constable, 1919
Twenty-two Poems, The Augustan Books of English Poetry, Series 2,
    No. 6, ed. Humbert Wolfe, Ernest Benn, 1927

Essays and Criticism
A Casual Commentary Methuen, 1925
Catchwords and Claptrap Hogarth Press, 1926
Some Religious Elements in English Literature Hogarth Press, 1931
Milton Duckworth, 1934
Personal Pleasures Gollancz, 1935
An Open Letter to a Non-Pacifist Collins (for the Peace Pledge
    Union), 1937
The Writings of E. M. Forster Hogarth Press, 1938

Anthologies
The Minor Pleasures of Life Gollancz, 1934
All in a Maze Collins, 1939 (co-edited with Daniel George)

History and Travel
Life Among the English Collins, 1942
They Went to Portugal Jonathan Cape, 1946
Fabled Shore: From the Pyrenees to Portugal Hamish Hamilton,
    1949
Pleasure of Ruins Weidenfeld & Nicolson, 1953
They Went to Portugal Too Carcanet, 1990

Letters
Letters to a Friend: 1950–1952 Collins, 1961
Last Letters to a Friend Collins, 1962
Letters to a Sister Collins, 1964

Sources

Archives

BBC Written Archives, Reading

British Red Cross Archives

Jonathan Cape Archives, University of Reading

Durham University Library Archives and Special Collections

ERM Archive: material deposited by Constance Babington Smith in the Wren Library, Trinity College, Cambridge

Hogarth Archives, University of Reading

King's College Archives, Cambridge

Lynd papers: family correspondence and papers in the possession of Nancy Nichols, Bristol

Gilbert Murray Papers, Bodleian Library, Oxford

John Murray Archives, London

O'Donovan: family correspondence and papers in the possession of Dr Mary Anne O'Donovan, Cambridge

O'Donovan/Ryan: correspondence and papers relating to the O'Donovan family in the possession of John F. Ryan, Galway

Penguin Archives, University of Bristol

HRHRC, Texas: correspondence held by the Harry Ransom Humanities Research Center, University of Texas at Austin

Sidgwick & Jackson Papers, Bodleian Library, Oxford

Jacqueline Trotter papers, Hugh Walpole Collection, King's School, Canterbury

Tynan Collection, John Rylands University Library, Manchester

The main source of archival material, deposited by Rose Macaulay's first biographer, Constance Babington Smith, is in the Wren Library, Trinity College, Cambridge, in the ERM Papers; the Harry Ransom Humanities Research Centre, at The University of Texas at Austin, holds correspondence between Rose Macaulay and a number of other writers, including Elizabeth Bowen, John Lehmann and Hugh Walpole; letters to William Plomer are held in the Durham University Library Archives & Special Collections; correspondence with her first publisher is held in the John Murray Archives, London; letters to Rosamond Lehmann, John Hayward and others in the King's College Modern Archives, Cambridge; correspondence with Gilbert Murray and with Sidgwick & Jackson in the Modern Papers Reading Room, Department of Special Collections and Western manuscripts, Bodleian Library, Oxford; letters to Katharine Tynan in the Tynan Collection, John Rylands University Library, Manchester; correspondence with Penguin in the Penguin Archives, University of Bristol; correspondence with Leonard Woolf and Jonathan Cape and others in the Hogarth Archives and Jonathan Cape Archives, University of Reading; correspondence with a number of BBC producers in BBC Written Archives Centre, Reading; and with Jacqueline Trotter in the Hugh Walpole Collection, King's School, Canterbury.

Books

CBS: *Rose Macaulay* by Constance Babington Smith, Collins, 1972

Emery: *Rose Macaulay: A Writer's Life* by Jane Emery, John Murray, 1991

Letters: *Letters to a Friend 1950–1952*, ed. Constance Babington Smith, Collins, 1961

Last Letters: *Last Letters to a Friend 1952–1958*, ed. Constance Babington Smith, Collins, 1962

NOTES

Introduction

'had denied themselves the indulgence of breaking into print': 'Auto-obituary: Full Fathom Five', *Listener*, 2 September 1936. Some of her ancestors failed to see the fruits of their labours in print. Her great-grandfather, the Reverend Aulay Macaulay, son of the Reverend John Macaulay of Inveraray, struggled for years with a massive work on the German humanist Philipp Melancthon, one of the founding fathers of Protestantism, friend of Luther and co-author of the *Augsburg Confession*, before dying of apoplexy before it was finished.

'Forever in transit': Rosamond Lehmann, 'The Pleasures of Knowing Rose Macaulay', *Encounter*, March 1959. Reprinted as appendix in CBS, pp. 223–36.

three of which: *The Lee Shore* (1912) won the Hodder & Stoughton novel prize; *Dangerous Ages* (1921) won the Prix Femina-Vie Heureuse; *The Towers of Trebizond* (1956) won the James Tait Black Memorial Prize.

'Does Ancestry Matter?': *Daily Express*, 5 June 1928. *Dulce periculum*: Sweet danger.

whose two sons: The Reverend John Macaulay (Rose's great-great-grandfather) was accused by Samuel Johnson of being 'grossly innocent of human nature'. The Reverend Kenneth Macaulay appears as a 'coarse man' in Boswell's *The Journal of a Tour to the Hebrides*; Johnson had actually described him as 'the most ignorant booby and grossest bastard'. See *Boswell's Presumptuous Task* by Adam Sisman, pp. 105 and 316.

'I'm a mere battlefield': Recorded by Virginia Woolf, 9 October 1934, *Diary, Vol 4*, p. 249.

Besides the writing and reading: In *The Towers of Trebizond* Rose Macaulay gives Laurie and Aunt Dot's family a crest of 'three pikes *couchant*, with the motto *"Semper pesco"*'; Laurie, on the inherited family enthusiasm for catching fish: 'Aunt Dot maintains that this propensity is peculiarly Church of England; she has perhaps made a slight confusion between the words Anglican and angling.' *Towers*, p. 5.

'some Conybeare rector': Letter to Hamilton Johnson, 9 February 1951, *Letters*, p. 68.

Rose Macaulay's work is important: Rose Macaulay is one of the writers whose work appears in Bonnie Kime Scott's anthology *The Gender of Modernism*, where Lily Briscoe's image of a 'golden mesh' of tangled perceptions, from Virginia Woolf's *To the Lighthouse*, is used as a metaphor for the connections between the twenty-one women and five men whose work is analysed in the book. Kime Scott arranges the names of the twenty-six authors alphabetically counterclockwise, while authors and editors who are not anthologised but whose names appear in the analytic pieces and in the primary texts appear in lower case. The resulting diagram, while not definitive, illustrates some surprising literary relationships:

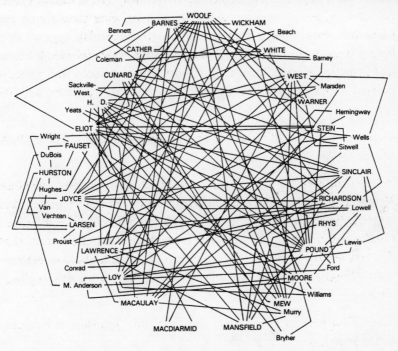

A glance at this shows the connections between Rose Macaulay and Eliot, Lawrence, Murry, Sitwell, Wells, Hemingway and Woolf.

a handful of critics: Susan Squier, in a short introductory essay to Rose Macaulay's work in *The Gender of Modernism*, suggests that the phrase 'battling lizards' 'captures Macaulay's complex relation both to the high modernist tradition and to the female modernism so profoundly shaped by Macaulay's dinner companion, Virginia Woolf'. See Susan Squier in 'Rose Macaulay', *The Gender of Modernism*, pp. 253–9. Rose would doubtless have laughed in incredulous denial; unlike Virginia Woolf she did not articulate her literary anxieties, but that is not to say they were not expressed in her work. It is the tensions and the conflicts of the battlefield that intrigue, along with that other tension, the one between what makes her say she is a 'mere battlefield' and the large volume of her published work.

For full-length works see *Rose Macaulay* by Alice Bensen; *Paradise Pursued* by Alice Crawford; *Eros and Androgyny* by Jeanette Passty. The two previous biographies are Constance Babington Smith's *Rose*

Macaulay and *Rose Macaulay: A Writer's Life* by Jane Emery. And Gloria Fromm has written persuasively of the debt Virginia Woolf owed Rose Macaulay in 'Re-inscribing *The Years*: Virginia Woolf, Rose Macaulay and the Critics', Journal of Modern Literature, 13/2, July 1986.

the glory of the bird: The tune the bird sings, transcribed by 'Miss Livia Gollancz, who patiently and skilfully took down this tune straight from the bird's beak – no easy task, with so rapid a performer', is reproduced in Victor Gollancz, *Reminiscences of Affection*, p. 67:

'very erudite': Virginia Woolf, 9 October 1934, in the same diary entry as for 'battling lizards'. Woolf concludes the entry with: 'She is a ravaged sensitive old hack – as I should be, no doubt, save for L.'

For Noel Annan, Rose was a 'fox': 'Family connections,' wrote Noel Annan, 'are part of the poetry of history.' The intertwining of the Macaulays with other nineteenth-century liberal intellectual families such as the Babingtons, the Roses, the Vaughans and the Trevelyans was the subject of his essay on 'The Intellectual Aristocracy'. He started with Rose herself, whom he knew, and, through an extended fox-hunting metaphor, worked backwards through the various writers, thinkers, historians, scientists, reformers, clergymen and scholars who appear in her genealogy, making up one of those caucuses 'of power or influence . . . which moulds the country's culture'. See Noel Annan, 'The Intellectual Aristocracy', *Studies in Social History: A Tribute to G.M. Trevelyan*, ed. J. H. Plumb.

For Gerard Irvine: Rose was delighted when Irvine suggested St Rose of Viterbo as a more suitable patron saint than St Rose of Lima. The latter was a masochist and burned her own face away with quicklime because she was too pretty. St Rose of Viterbo, however, was precociously clever; at the age of three she raised a maternal aunt from death by chanting and reciting prayers over her grave, and at twelve converted a sorceress by standing unscathed for three hours in a fire. Rose enjoyed discussing these conceits with Gerard Irvine. See correspondence, 29 and 31 August 1951. ERM archive.

Five months after Rose Macaulay's death: The contributors to 'The Pleasures of Knowing Rose Macaulay' were Rosamond Lehmann, Harold Nicolson, William Plomer, Anthony Powell, Alan Pryce-Jones, Patrick Kinross, C. V. Wedgwood, Mark Bonham Carter and Diana Cooper. Their essays are reprinted in full as an appendix in CBS.

Some years: Constance Babington Smith died in 2000.

'As she grew old': V. S. Pritchett in the *New Statesman*, 17 April 1964, in a review of *Letters to a Sister* and *Last Letters to a Friend*.

'one of the great barometers': See Alice Crawford, *Paradise Pursued*.

Chapter One: 'The Gs'

Grace Mary Conybeare's surviving diaries, for the years 1867–69, 1871–77, 1879–80, 1883, 1886–90, 1898, her letters and her anniversary book, *Morning Light*, are in the ERM archive in the Wren Library, Trinity College, Cambridge. Her brother the Reverend J. W. Edward Conybeare's diaries are in Cambridgeshire County Records Office, deposited by his granddaughter F. M. McCormick. Some of Edward's diaries have been transcribed and annotated by Jonathan Hunt, to whom I am extremely grateful. Constance Babington Smith's transcriptions of excerpts that relate to Grace, George and their family are in the ERM archive. Unless otherwise indicated, quotations throughout this chapter are from these sources.

'about 14 years older than my mother': All Rose Macaulay's comments about Edward quoted here come from two 1951 letters to Hamilton Johnson, *Letters to a Friend*, pp. 56 and 163.

Mary Barton (1848), the first novel of Elizabeth Gaskell. *Eric, or, Little by Little* by F. W. (Dean) Farrar, published 1858, when he was master at Harrow, an edifying story of school life. *Guy Mannering* (1815) and *The Antiquary* (1816), by Sir Walter Scott, were enormously popular for at least 100 years after publication; both tales deal with disinheritance, mistaken identity, and virtue and nobility finally rewarded.

Heartsease, or The Brother's Wife by 'the author of *The Heir of Redclyffe*', that is, Charlotte M. Yonge, published 1855.

She abandoned them in the 1890s: Other people besides family appear in the pages of Grace's *Morning Light*. She noted, for example, the dates of death of both Dick and Rupert Brooke; and Gerald O'Donovan's birthday.

'one of those sons of the parsonage': Letter to Hamilton Johnson, 1 March 1951, *Letters*, p. 90.

Barrington: six or seven miles south-west of Cambridge. It has the longest village green in England. The church has a memorial window to the Reverend Edward Conybeare put up by his five children 'in gratitude for our happy childhood years in the Vicarage'.

He had got into trouble: The proctor was an identifiable member of the university; there was a fuss, not on account of the style of the verses – to write bawdy Latin verses was a tradition – but because of the personal nature of the portrait, and George had to sign two public apologies. See Emery, p. 15.

a rousing poem: published in the *Spectator* in summer 1876. Entitled 'The Savage Lust of Islam', it began:

> Oh for Milton's rolling thunder, Cromwell's fiery zeal for God;
> Then should England rise to vengeance, tread the path that
> once she trod.
> Once again for sacred freedom should our hosts go forth to
> fight,
> And the battle cry for England should be 'God defend the right'.

William, closest to George in age: William Herrick Macaulay was ranked 6th Wrangler when he graduated from King's College, Cambridge in 1878. During the course of his career at King's he was at different times college lecturer, tutor, Bursar and Vice-Provost. He established the Department of Engineering at the university and was author of *The Laws of Thermodynamics* (1913) and *Solid Geometry* (1930). A portrait of him by Roger Fry hangs in the College.

George did achieve the fellowship: This was just before the Statutes of the university were changed to allow fellows to marry. Gwen Raverat, granddaughter of Charles Darwin, in *Period Piece* (1952), her memoir of a Cambridge childhood in the 1890s, writes of being one of the 'first hatchlings' of married fellows.

She had a 'gathered breast': Edward Conybeare described the wound left by the bursting of such a 'gathering' on his wife Frances's breast six months later after she gave birth to the Conybeares' last child, Dorothea. It was two and a half inches in diameter and three-quarters of an inch deep.

She was named Emilie Rose: Emily was sometimes spelled Emilie.

Grace held strong dislikes: 'Does Ancestry Matter?' in the *Daily Express*, 5 June 1928.

Another girl, Jean . . .: Jean was born on 24 July 1882. When they were adults Rose would always sign birthday letters with 'your loving twin'.

'Yesterday I did a thing': See CBS, p. 22.

Chapter Two: Amphibious Days

'hanging about the dark little shops': 'Villa Macolai', in *Little Innocents: Childhood Reminiscences*, ed. Alan Pryce-Jones, p. 48.

'full of oranges and lemons': Ibid., p. 47.

'The Mediterranean lay curved': 'In Deep and Shallow Waters', *Listener*, 30 January 1936.

'returns to me still': Letter to Father Hamilton Johnson, 8 June 1952, *Letters*, p. 324.

Perhaps it was this lack of distinction: Gwen Darwin (later Raverat), for example, born in 1885, was unusual in being allowed out on her own from quite an early age. She describes cycling home at the age of eleven down the dark Cambridge Backs, pedalling with her heart in her mouth from dim gaslight to dim gaslight, imagining mad dogs slavering at her heels and murderers lurking behind the elms. Such fearsome freedoms were not available to the cousins with whom she had been having tea. Gwen could cycle home alone only because her mother was American and full of 'notions about Independence'. But even having an American mother with notions about Independence didn't save you from the bitter lesson that if you were a woman your life would be limited and circumscribed. Gwen Darwin grew up in the belief that she couldn't be an artist in her own right. At first she yearned to be the wife of an artist, even though being Mrs Rembrandt 'seemed too tremendous even to imagine'. She went to the Slade and became a successful artist and engraver, yet never lost the sense that as a woman she couldn't be a real artist. 'Of course I wanted still more, more than anything in the world, to be a man. Then I might be a really good painter. A woman had not much chance of that. I wanted so much to be a boy that I did not dare to think about it at all, for it made me feel quite desperate to know that it was impossible to be one. But I always dreamt I was a boy. If the truth must be told, still now, in my dreams at night, I am generally a young man!' Gwen Raverat: *Period Piece* (1952).

'"Man the lifeboats," shouted the captain': Letter to Neville Braybrooke, 1 October 1958. ERM archive.

They ran around barelegged: At the end of the Victorian era the English middle classes were careful that their children's bodies should be covered up from top to toe. Nina Hamnett, one of Rose Macaulay's co-contributors in *Little Innocents*, in her essay 'What I Wore in the Nineties' described 'being forced into black woollen stockings . . . on attaining the age of four' because her grandmother thought that socks were 'indecent'. When she was six or seven she would put on her brother's sailor suit whenever she could, but of course was not allowed out of the house in it. Had she been spotted in it the whole family would have acquired the reputation of being eccentric and 'consequently immoral'.

'There it lay, in that repository': 'Hatching Eggs', in *Personal Pleasures*, p. 241.

'sitting alone in an olive tree': 'Villa Macolai', *Little Innocents*. In 1932 autobiographical writing was not in vogue in the way that it became at the end of the twentieth century: many of the contributors to Alan Pryce-Jones's collection express surprise that their reminiscences could be of interest to readers, and often provide a sense of the delicate difficulties of negotiating the treachery of memory. Rose's co-contributors include Robert Byron who writes poignantly about wanting his child to learn, as he had done, to glory in the names of plants and wild creatures (Byron was killed in the Second World War, dying before he had fathered children); John Betjeman on living in fear at school, describing the 'basket' ritual at Marlborough to which he returned in *Summoned by Bells* (1960); and Sylvia Pankhurst on the death of a baby brother.

At the age of fifteen: The poem covers two pages of Grace's 1871 diary, ending: 'And when the organ's swelling notes/Had lulled them into rest,/GOD sent his angels for their souls,/To bear them to His Breast.'

'It is impossible': 'The Free Run of the Shelves', *New Statesman and Nation*, 4 December 1948.

'above my intellectual grasp': In a review of *The Faber Book of Children's Verse*, compiled by Janet Adam Smith, *New Statesman and Nation*, November 1953. She goes on to praise Swinburne's 'magnificent swing' which 'is to the child an intoxicant', and 'the haunting tenebrous quality' of 'that exquisite, uncharacteristic Kipling, with its eerie undertones, "The way through the woods" . . .'

'since I was given the Poems': Letter to John Lehmann, 28 September 1947, John Lehmann Collection, HRHRC, Texas. 'Many a green isle needs must be' is the first line of 'Lines Written among the Euganean Hills, October, 1818':

> Many a green isle needs must be
> In the deep wide sea of misery,
> Or the mariner, worn and wan,
> Never thus could voyage on
> Day and night, and night and day,
> Drifting on his dreary way,
> With the solid darkness black
> Closing round his vessel's track . . .

'I remember sitting': *Letters*, p. 98.

'there are no other English people there': W. H. Macaulay to Roger Fry, 8 May 1891, King's College archives.

'largish, self-sufficing, and somewhat neurotic community': 'The Free Run of the Shelves', *New Statesman and Nation*, 4 December 1948.

'the lovely plaster sheep': *Letters*, p. 237.

'The *parroco* wanted one of my brothers': 'Villa Macolai' in *Little Innocents*.

'I doted on my father': *Letters*, p. 89.

'Rose was very close to her father': Jean Macaulay to Constance Babington Smith, ERM archive.

'You never knew': quoted by CBS, p. 35.

'a nurse presides': 'Fraternal', *Rose Macaulay*, p. 232.

'When I think of my childhood': 'Villa Macolai', *Little Innocents*, p. 46.

'5 elder Macaulays without a trace of Eleanor': ERM archive.

'Yes, Mother did begin to think of it': Letter to Dorothea Conybeare, 28 October 1958. ERM archive.

'and pretty dim it seemed': *Letters*, p. 89.

Chapter Three: Edwardian

When Margaret, Rose and Jean: Margaret and Rose signed up immediately to the Guild of Charity, on whose committee sat a Mrs Conybeare, the wife of a first cousin of Grace's. The Guild of Charity demanded 'self-denial for Charity's sake; self-denial in the use of money and time, in pleasures and luxuries'; members paid a subscription of 2s. 6d. minimum per annum and had to make three garments for the poor each year. They were also encouraged to make and collect toys for the poor children in London, those same London children perhaps that Grace had made them regularly put aside their pennies for when they lived in Varazze. Jean had to wait until the following year when she would be old enough to be allowed to join the Guild.

The first cousin of Grace's was Frederick Cornwallis Conybeare, 1856–1924, son of John Charles Conybeare, Fellow of University College, Oxford. He established a scholarship to Somerville College in memory of his first wife, Mary Emily Müller, who, with her sister, had been one of the first girls to enter the Oxford High School. The scholarship was withdrawn in 1914 as a result of Somerville's support for the suffrage struggle. He thought the college was being given up 'not exclusively to the educational purposes for which it was founded, but also to a propaganda which, by reason of the degradation of countless poor girls incidental to it, is abhorrent to myself and, I am sure, would have been no less abhorrent to my late wife'. Quoted in Pauline Adams, *Somerville for Women*, p. 81.

'My dog Fido': CBS, p. 40.

'Gowers lost work Speculum Homines!': John Gower was a contemporary and friend of Chaucer, and one of the dedicatees of Chaucer's *Troilus and Criseyde*. He wrote in Latin, French and English. The *Mirour de l'Omme* was written in French, in octosyllabics, and is an allegory concerning the vices and virtues of fallen man.

Thule: or Ultima Thule, most northerly land of classical antiquity.

The other three stanzas: These are:

> Tell me of what you dream,
> Ocean, fair ocean,
> As you laugh and glitter and gleam,
> Shimmering ocean!
> Perchance of the fair ships that lightly glide
> Over your waters in their grace and pride;
> Or else of the dim deep,
> Where strange sea-creatures for all ages sleep,
> Ocean,
> For ever live and sleep.
>
> Gloomy and dark and sad,
> Ocean, wild ocean,

Stormy and black and mad,
Terrible ocean!
The wild waves thunder on the wind-swept shore,
Toss angry crests, and surge and rush and roar,
Towering dark and high,
Flinging their light spray to the angry sky,
Ocean,
To the wild, sullen sky.

What wild dreams haunt you now,
Ocean, dark ocean,
Ruffling your angry brow,
Furious ocean?
Surely you dream of desperate battles gained,
Fights on your water waged to a bitter end,
Fair vessels won and lost,
And ships gone down by yonder rocky coast,
Ocean,
By yonder wind-swept coast.

Only one of Aulay's letters home: This raises the question of how the past is reconstructed through the records that survive the passage of time. This letter from Aulay is tucked into one of Grace's diaries, where it was very likely put after George and Grace had read it, safe from the eyes of the girls, and very possibly later forgotten about, when the rest of his schoolboy letters were got rid of. There is no reason to suppose that such a flamboyant suicide was anything but an extraordinary occurrence. For a vivid account of daily life at Clifton College, see *Letters between a Victorian Schoolboy and his Family, 1892–1895*, edited by David Crane. Tankred Tunstall-Behrens, author and recipient of these *Letters*, was five years older than Aulay, and had also attended the Oxford Preparatory School prior to Clifton College.

Aulay retained: Clifton provided a high proportion of officers working on the North-West Frontier in the years before the Great War.

She had passed: Her sister Jean took her Higher Certificate the following year and also won a distinction in History. Family mythology, passed from Jean to Constance Babington Smith in the early 1960s, presents a picture of Rose always, from an early age, being the clever girl, and Jean herself as slowish; school records do not back this up. Margaret's leaving school at sixteen could be taken as an indication that she lacked an academic bent. It could also be taken as an indication that Grace wanted one of her girls at home.

It had opened twenty-one years earlier: Mary Somerville was a self-taught Scot who published her first book *The Mechanism of the Heavens* at the age of fifty-one, was the mother of six children and had died as recently as 1872. She was cultivated, accomplished and sociable, and also 'a skilled needlewoman, a thrifty housewife, and a competent cook'. See Adams, *Somerville for Women*, p. 13.

Somerville had the largest library: When Rose arrived in 1900 Margery Fry, the sister of Roger Fry, had since the previous year been in charge of its 6,000 or so volumes. Somerville would be the first women's college to build its own library.

Back in 1884 John Ruskin had been totally won over by the Principal, Madeleine Shaw Lefevre, and had presented Somerville with paintings, geological specimens, a set of his own works – nineteen volumes bound in blue morocco – some of his favourite books, and a case of precious stones that unfortunately had to be returned to the diamond merchant in Soho when it was discovered that they had not been paid for. See Adams, *Somerville for Women*, p. 26.

Two lines from Dante: lines 19 and 21 from the *Inferno*, Canto XIV: '*D'anime nude vidi molte gregge/che piangean tutte assai miseramente,/a parea posta lor diversa legge.*' In Henry Wadsworth Longfellow's translation: 'Of naked souls beheld I many herds,/Who all were weeping very miserably,/And over them seemed set a law diverse.' The missing line 20 is marked in the epigraph to *Abbots Verney* with a line of asterisks. Line 19 is misquoted as '*D'anime vidi molte gregge*'. There is nothing to indicate the missing word '*nude*'. The question of whether the elision was deliberate or accidental must remain open. My thanks to Laura Salvini at the University of Rome for help with this.

Maurice Maeterlinck, 1862–1949, Belgian symbolist poet and playwright (author of *Pelléas et Mélisande*, 1892), scientific populariser (*La vie des abeilles*, 1901) and philosopher. Hermann Lotze, 1817–81,

German idealist philosopher (*Metaphysik*, 1841; *Microcosmus*, 1856–64).

'I liked Oxford': *Letters*, p. 95.

At that length: Sartorial conventions were rigidly adhered to. When, for example, everyone was obliged to be in mourning after the death of Queen Victoria in 1901, offence was caused in Oxford by 'a spot of orange in the toque worn by someone at a window in the High Street', as the crowd listened to the proclamation of Edward VII's reign. Quoted by Anne Ridler in *Olive Willis and Downe House*.

In June 1903: There is a book in the Somerville archives which has all the introductory speeches pasted into it, illustrated with watercolour pictures.

In 'Eating and Drinking': 'Eating and Drinking', in *Personal Pleasures*, p. 183. The essay concludes: 'Nevertheless, expensive, troublesome, and unwholesome though it [good eating and drinking] be, it is a pleasure by no means to be forgone.' As in so many of these essays, the balanced reversal at the end seems emptily formal. It is the three words expensive, troublesome and unwholesome that carry the ring of conviction.

'She was entirely obstinate': Olive Willis in a manuscript obituary of Rose Macaulay, quoted by Anne Ridler in *Olive Willis and Downe House*. All subsequent quotes by Olive Willis are from the same source.

'disliked the food': Lady Rhondda, *This Was My World*, quoted in Adams, *Somerville for Woman*, p. 111. Viscountess Rhondda was at Somerville (as Margaret Thomas) the year after Rose left, but only stuck it out for two terms before being driven out by the physical discomfort and general girls' school atmosphere of the place. 'Somerville smelt frousty to me. I disliked the ugliness of most of the public rooms, and I disliked the glass and the crockery and the way in which the tables were set . . . dowdiness . . . cloisterishness . . . And I disliked the slightly deprecating and dowdy, and . . . self-conscious, atmosphere of ladylike culture that hung about the dons at play.'

'I myself was Imogen': Letter to her god-daughter Emily Cain. ERM archive.

'I know something you don't': *Told by an Idiot*, pp. 194–6.

'ERM applied for an Aegrotat': Margerie Venables Taylor to Constance Babington Smith. ERM archive. Rose's sister Jean always maintained that Rose had had flu just before the examinations (see CBS, p. 43). Rose wrote to Hamilton Johnson in 1951: 'unfortunately I fell ill at the wrong time and got an Aegrotat which was disappointing'.

'The Flamingo and the Hedgehogs': ERM archive.

'a dislike of formal questions': Letter to Constance Babington Smith, quoted CBS, p. 43.

But even had she had a ranked degree: Degrees for women were not recognised by the university until 1920.

'Our house is well-sheltered': The material about Ty-Issa from Uncle Edward's diaries, George Macaulay's letters to Francis Jenkinson, and Margaret's diaries is quoted in CBS.

'most painful musically': Dorothea Conybeare to Constance Babington Smith. ERM archive.

Margaret later wrote a novel, *The Sentence Absolute*: There is no evidence of when Margaret wrote this novel. In October 1909 George Macaulay wrote to John Murray asking him to look at 'a story' by 'another' of his daughters. This might have been *The Sentence Absolute*, but there is no surviving record of John Murray's response to it, if he did read it. It was published by James Nisbet & Co. in 1914.

'It seemed that': *The Valley Captives*, p. 216.

'I tried to put some bit of you': Letter to Olive Willis (n.d.), quoted in Ridler, *Olive Willis and Downe House*. 'And of course one doesn't put people whole . . .': This is interestingly similar to what E. M. Forster said of his method, with reference to his first novel, *Where Angels Fear to Tread*, published in 1905, the year before *Abbots Verney*: 'A useful trick is to look back upon . . . a person with half-closed eyes, wilfully obscuring certain characteristics. I am then left with about 2/3 of a human being and can get to work. This is what I did with E. J. Dent, who became Philip in *Where Angels* . . .' (quoted by Oliver Stallybrass in his introduction to the 1975 Penguin edition, p. 10). Rose Macaulay worked on half a real person, E. M. Forster on two-thirds.

'One thinks one will never forget': *Abbots Verney*, p. 293.

'the business of the young': Ibid., p. 347.

'Specially the Roman part': Letter to Margerie Venables Taylor, 19 February 1907. ERM archive.

'the string of scarlet seminarists': *Abbots Verney*, p. 227.

a settlement for factory girls in Chesterfield: The Chesterfield settlement was financed by the novelist Violet Markham and run by Elsie Willis, Olive's older sister. See Ridler: 'This was not the kind of work that Rose Macaulay was cut out to do, and the girls at the Club could not understand her rapid sentences . . .'

'Publishers of course': Letter to Margerie Venables Taylor, 19 February 1907.

'I have not published': Letter to John Murray IV, 8 July 1906. John Murray archives.

The reviewers called it: in, respectively, *Review of Reviews*, *Sheffield Telegraph*, *Daily Chronicle*, the *Scotsman*, *Morning Post* and *Literary World*.

'I don't fancy': Letter to Margerie Venables Taylor, 19 February 1907.

'I was afraid': Letter to John Murray IV, n.d. John Murray archives.

'She wrote from her earliest infancy': 'Auto-obituary: Full Fathom Five', *Listener*, 2 September 1936.

'Oh dear oh dear': Letter to Frank Swinnerton, 27 August 1934. ERM archive.

'rather intelligent': *Non-Combatants and Others*, p. 178.

Like *Abbots Verney*: Alice Bensen quotes a 1958 letter from Rose Macaulay to Philip Louis Rizzo, author of 'Rose Macaulay: A Critical Survey': 'It rather interests me someone should have suggested a Jamesian influence in *The Furnace*, as I remember that I was reading him with fascination at the time I wrote it.' Bensen, *Rose Macaulay*, p. 170.

'I did my best': Letter to John Murray IV, 24 July 1907. John Murray archives.

'in a slow, winding': 'In Deep and Shallow Waters', *Listener*, 30 January 1936.

poets from Plato: Alice Crawford explores Rose Macaulay's reading behind the early novels and especially her interest in mysticism in *Paradise Pursued*. Fiona Macleod was the pseudonym of William Sharp, who was publishing Celtic faery literature throughout the 1890s.
The Secret River becomes: The law regarding marriage and divorce in England had not changed since the 1857 Divorce Bill when divorce became criminalised. A man could get rid of his wife on grounds of adultery, but a woman could only get rid of a husband if she could prove that he had engaged in the criminal practices of incest, bigamy or sodomy. In the early 1900s Lord Russell had tried and failed to get the Divorce Bill humanised, but it was not until 1909, after considerable pressure from the Divorce Law Reform Union, that a Royal Commission was set up to look into possible reforms of the marriage and divorce laws.

Meanwhile the marriage question had been debated on the stage ever since it was demanded that the public confront it by Ibsen, when *The Doll's House* was first performed in England in June 1889. Not all playwrights took a radical, or even reformist attitude towards it, and those that did were likely to fall foul of the censor. In the first years of the century there was a plethora of novels and plays about marriage and – like Arnold Bennett's harrowing *Whom God Hath Joined* (1906) – divorce.

Michael Travis is less man: Rose Macaulay's own creation of Pan-types might explain her dislike for J. M. Barrie's version, first performed in 1904 and hugely popular. Later, she would write about Pan's failure to survive the Great War, and Pan has since come to represent an age of innocence, born under King Edward in the first years of the twentieth century, and lasting during the brief Georgian period before 1914.

On 11 February 1909: The Reuters Agency report gives the date of death as 15 February, but the memorial to Aulay in the Parish Church of St Mary the Virgin, Great Shelford, gives 11 February.

'The crime was non-political': Reuters Agency report reprinted in the *Draconian*, April 1909, p. 991.

Chapter Four: Georgian

'Most of us': *The Writings of E. M. Forster*, p. 20.

'verbal haloes': *Catchwords and Claptrap*, p. 35.

Her own early poetry: The poems quoted here can be found in Naomi Royde-Smith's two anthologies, *The Westminster Problems Book* (1908) and *The Second Problems Book* (1909).

'more intellectual and less sensuous': Edward Thomas, *Bookman*, September 1914.

'Out of familiar things': *Spectator*, 11 July 1914. Her poems were not on the whole difficult, with some exceptions, such as the following, in which the question and answer form echoes traditional man/woman dialogue poems:

> 'You were like cool water on still grey days,
> Limpid and quiet, and empty of the sun.
> But in you now some new day has begun:
> I fear its strange discomfortable blaze.
> Have you found God, or has the sharp amaze
> Of a world's piteous beauty stabbed you through?'
> 'I have found nothing beneath the sun but you.
> Cover your eyes.' 'You wince to meet their gaze.
> What have you seen?' 'The dawn striking the hill.'
> 'What have you known?' 'The way the cold brooks flow
> Singing on rock . . .' 'Poor liar, you lie ill.
> I need nor lies nor you; so turn and go.
> Are you so pale? Do you fear my dead desire?'
> 'I fear your slow tears, that would drown my fire.'
>
> > (*Westminster Gazette*, 18 October 1913,
> > unsigned but attributed to Rose by her sister Jean)

Rose had been winning: In 1906 a pastiche of Tennyson's 'You ask me why, tho' ill at ease' which starts 'You ask me why, tho' ill at ease/I read this volume I despise . . .' by a certain W. B. Fish (Aged 15), shows a Brooke-ish wit and facility. In the 1908 anthology compiled by Naomi Royde-Smith, *The Westminster Problems Book*, this poem by 'W. B. Fish' is followed by Walter de la Mare's 'A Ballad of Christmas' which in turn is followed by E. R. Macaulay's 'Ballade of the Superior Person'.

Of the seven named contributors: There were two anthologies of the *Saturday Westminster Gazette* competitions: *The Westminster Problems Book: Prose and Verse* (1908) and *The Second Problems Book: Prizes and Proximes* (1909), both edited by Naomi Royde-Smith, and both including non-prize-winning contributions as well as the winners. Many of the contributors appear only under initials or obvious pseudonyms, or as 'Anon', making it impossible to give an exact number of women and men contributors, but of the named contributors in the first book twenty-four are women and twenty-six are men.

'I hate it': Quoted in Christopher Hassall, *Rupert Brooke: A Biography*, p. 171.

Rupert's brother Dick died: In his 1964 biography of Rupert Brooke Christopher Hassall describes a tea party given by Rupert Brooke at King's College in October 1907, attended by Rose Macaulay, 'just down from Somerville College, Oxford', with her mother and sister. 'Just down from Somerville College' is an inaccurate description of someone who had left Oxford four years previously. Just as inaccurate, in terms of the relationship between Rose and Rupert, is Hassall's omission of any reference to Rose's writing career. She had been published alongside Brooke in the *Saturday Westminster* throughout that year, was the author of a well-received first novel and had a second novel due out the following week. Brooke, by contrast, was barely published. Hassall was not the only one of Brooke's admirers to sideline Rose: she was written out entirely by Edward Marsh, and weirdly transformed by Keith Hale, editor of the Brooke/Strachey correspondence, into an unrequited lover.

'it was rather like versicle and response': Letter to Walter de la Mare, 7 May 1915. ERM archive.

Compared to the Oliviers: A close entanglement with Rupert Brooke was a potentially dangerous business. Denham Russell-Smith, Brooke's first lover, in October 1909, at The Orchard, died in July 1912, aged twenty-three; and the Newnham undergraduate Ka Cox was abandoned by Brooke in Germany when she became pregnant by him. See Paul Delany, *The Neo-Pagans*.

'I don't want to worry them': Quoted in CBS, p. 62.

'I have come to the conclusion': Letter to Margerie Venables Taylor, 2 June 1909. ERM archive.

Perversion: Rose's maternal grandfather was author of a *Life* of St Paul, of several series of school textbooks during his time as Principal of the Liverpool Collegiate Institution, and of one novel: *Perversion: or The Causes and Consequences of Infidelity: A Tale for the Times*, published anonymously in 1856, the year before he died. Other tortures inflicted on the protagonist and his friend include being flogged with brambles, strung up by their thumbs, having their beds filled with nettles and thistles, and being forced to eat tallow candles and wash them down with dirty water from the basins. Charles survives the bullying and goes on to encounter a variety of knaves, fools and gulls; the emotional focus is dissipated in Volumes 2 and 3 as Conybeare broadens the scope of his attack on wickedness to include Mormons, Tractarians, atheists, freethinkers, and all who stray from the narrow path of Anglican righteousness.

Conybeare was notorious for his jaundiced view of human nature, which was exemplified in his diary by comments on friends, relations and acquaintances such as that Matthew Arnold was 'a prig', Thomas Arnold 'a weak character', the Macaulays 'given to talking for effect', and bishops and deans in general 'lamentable'. Rose attributed this to his being consumptive. He had lost an eye when he was a boy at Westminster School, and perhaps this too affected his picture of school life in *Perversion*. One of his textbooks, *School Chronology, or the Great Dates of History*, was written in rhyming mnemonics. It started simply enough: 'BC: Two thousand Abraham, – Fifteen hundred Moses, – / One thousand Solomon, the triad closes,' but goes on to: '1547: To Fifteen add Four-seven, Five-three, and Five-eight, / You will Sixth Edward, Mary, Elizabeth date.'

'a slight and brief novel': 'Does Ancestry Matter?', *Daily Express*, 5 June 1928.

one of the three epigraphs: The epigraphs to Rose's novels are always a source of interest and curiosity. *The Valley Captives* has an admonition from Sir Thomas Browne which seems to be directed at the father (Oliver Vallon/George Macaulay); a critique of country living – 'tepid gales, healthy country air, and purposeless exercise' – from Charles Lamb; along with P. N. Waggett's enigmatic utterance on 'the prudence of adventure'.

'peace wrapped him round': *The Valley Captives*, p. 261.

'And will there be honey?': Ibid., p. 270.

Travelling in Germany: The place and date of composition of 'The Sentimental Exile'/'The Old Vicarage, Grantchester' is given as Café des Westens, Berlin, May 1912. See *Georgian Poetry 1911/12*, ed. Rupert Brooke and Edward Marsh, and *Poetry Review*, 1, XI, November 1912.

'twisted lips and twisted hearts': Doreen Chalmers suggests that this is a reflection of Rose's own jaundiced view of Shelfordians. See 'The Macaulays in Great Shelford', in *Great Shelford Remembered 1884–1994*.

In the various drafts: These are in the Brooke papers in King's College archives, Cambridge.

He thought her important enough: The other poets in the first Georgian anthology (published in October 1912), besides Rupert Brooke (with five poems), were Lascelles Abercrombie, Gordon Bottomley, G. K. Chesterton, W. H. Davies, Walter de la Mare (also with five, including 'The Listeners'), John Drinkwater, James Elroy Flecker, Wilfrid Gibson, D. H. Lawrence, John Masefield, Harold Monro, T. Sturge Moore, Ronald Ross, Edmund Beale Sargent, James Stephens and R. C. Trevelyan.

No women were included in the first three Georgian anthologies. Edward Marsh wanted a female contributor for the fourth volume, and chose Fredegond Shove (daffodils, cows, sheep and Jesus) over the other three women suggested to him: Rose Macaulay, Charlotte Mew and Edith Sitwell. In the fifth and final volume two women appeared: Alice Meynell and Vita Sackville-West.

comparable to those of Walter de la Mare: Alice Bensen discusses how both Walter de la Mare and Rose Macaulay were experimenting with syncopated counterpointing, with anticipations and delayed stresses.

'I often wonder': Letter to Roger Senhouse, 24 October 1946. ERM archive. Rose might well have been wrong about Brooke becoming 'an outmoded elderly poet'. His poetry might have been transformed by his experience of war, as was the work of other Georgian poets, such as Siegfried Sassoon (who was a contributor to Volumes 3 and 4 of *Georgian Poetry*).

Rupert light-heartedly asked Cathleen: See Theresa Whistler, *Walter de la Mare: The Imagination of the Heart*, for a description of this scene. Rupert Brooke's bequest of his royalties to Walter de la Mare, Lascelles Abercrombie and Wilfrid Gibson gave them financial freedom for the rest of their lives. A hundred years later the deleterious effect on artistic creativity of domestic worries and responsibilities – as Cyril Connolly put it, the pram in the hall being the enemy of promise – has become a truism. It was not so then.

to a living poet: Rose's poem was addressed to the new Kennedy Professor of Latin, A. E. Housman.

'He is a delightful person': Quoted by Rose Macaulay in her contribution to *Coming to London*, ed. John Lehmann. Other contributors to this anthology were William Plomer, Leonard Woolf, V. S. Pritchett, George Barker, J. B. Priestley, Elizabeth Bowen, Geoffrey Grigson, John Middleton Murry, Christopher Isherwood, Alan Pryce-Jones, William Sansom, Jocelyn Brooke and Edith Sitwell.

'I sometimes went up': This and the following descriptions of London are all from *Coming to London*, pp. 155–66.

Rose had recently finished writing *The Towers of Trebizond* when she contributed this memoir of Rupert Brooke to *Coming to London* in 1957. In *Towers* the camel stands out from the other animals 'looking tall and white and distinguished'. Aunt Dot believes that 'there is something . . . about a white camel that gives prestige'; Rupert too has 'prestige', wearing his plaid rug and his golden hair rather as the camel wears its 'white ostrich plumes tossing on its head'.

Storm Jameson, who would meet Rose ten years later, recalled the London of 1912 in *Journey from the North*: 'Where is Appenrodt's

Lager Hall, where is Maxim's? Where is the sixpenny gallery in the Coliseum from which we watched Reinhardt's *Scheherazade*, Polaire of the fifteen-inch waist, Florrie Forde, the ageing Bernhardt, the ageless Marie Lloyd? And those ladies with magnificent poops, navigating, with a wake of powerful scent, a far less crowded Leicester Square and Piccadilly? Where is the Vienna Café? At Maxim's, near the corner of Gerrard Street, the five-course dinner cost half-a-crown, at the smaller Boulogne next door, one and sixpence. The Vienna Café, in New Oxford Street, with its red plush benches and incomparable coffee and brioches, pleasures of a poor intellectual, has been replaced by a bank. A bank, God help us all!' Vol. 1, pp. 62–3.

'He was very beautiful': *Coming to London.*

Rose would have liked to: It would have been most unusual if George Macaulay had allowed his daughter, irrespective of her age, to go off *à deux* with Rupert Brooke, for he was becoming notorious in Cambridge for sexual licence. Gwen Darwin, in her twenties, was similarly forbidden to accept an invitation from him.

exercising his paternal authority: Both of Rose's previous biographers, Constance Babington Smith and Jane Emery, interpret the following passage in *Views and Vagabonds* as a rebuke to George Macaulay for his lack of faith in her: 'One understands that it is rather outré to travel alone with a cousin of the opposite sex in a van, even with the most fraternal feelings. Whoever lays down the law on these and similar principles of conduct would appear to have laid that one quite firmly. Of course the sensible plan is tranquilly to ignore the law, if one wishes to do so; the best people always do that with laws.'

Despite the fierceness: The epigraph to *Views and Vagabonds* is taken from G. Lowes Dickinson's *A Modern Symposium*, and expresses praise of life itself, the actual, the thing, in contrast to ideals which 'are so empty . . . they don't exist'.

'I am extremely delighted': Letter to S. C. Roberts, 4 August 1912. HRHRC, Texas.

The novelist Beatrice Harraden: She was a supporter of the struggle for women's suffrage, wrote pamphlets for the WSPU, and was an active campaigner against censorship in the theatre. Her novels include *Ships that Pass in the Night* (1893), *Hilda Strafford* (1897), *The Fowler* (1899), *Katharine Frensham* (1903), *The Scholar's Daughter* (1906) and *Interplay* (1908).

The countless sects and groupings: During the years of Rose's childhood, the closing decades of the nineteenth century, various movements had arisen that offered alternatives to what Samuel Hynes has called 'the mechanistic world that triumphant Darwinism had made'. Victorian materialism, he suggests, can be interpreted in two ways: as a belief in a physical explanation of phenomena, and an exclusive concern for material things. Edwardian thinkers reacted against that Victorian materialism, and Edwardian scientists struggled to restore metaphysics to the human world. See Samuel Hynes, *The Edwardian Turn of Mind*, p. 136.

In the early 1900s there was a flowering of the radical-eccentric activity that had begun in the 1880s and 1890s: socialism, anarchism, vegetarianism, spiritualism, psychology and sexuality were all part of an anti-Victorian restlessness, a restlessness that affected Rose even though she was still at home and loath to give up the safety of her childhood world. But she had an intellectual curiosity that had been stimulated by her three years at Somerville, and it was through the intellect that she first approached the outside world. Metaphysics interested her, especially in their relationship to the natural world. Like E. M. Forster, who had published his first novel in 1905, and like Rupert Brooke before he discovered Fabianism, she was attracted by animistic, supernatural ideas.

'And your Peter': Letter to Hugh Walpole, 13 February 1913. HRHRC, Texas.

'Money *is* nice to have': Letter to Katharine Tynan, 6 May 1913. Tynan Collection, University of Manchester.

Katharine Tynan (1861–1931), Irish poet and novelist, was author of over 100 novels and a central figure in the Irish Literary Revival. She edited the four-volume *Cabinet of Irish Literature*.

Rose went to the neighbouring village: A reredos was commissioned as a memorial to Aulay for the Parish Church of St Mary the Virgin in Great Shelford, although the memorial service was held in the more strongly Anglo-Catholic church at Sawston, a few miles away. In the parish church the triptych, installed in 1911 or 1912, darkly dominates the north-east chapel, showing the centurion at the Crucifixion against a bare landscape in dark blues and purples, flanked by the two soldier saints St Alban with his round shield, and St Martin slicing his scarlet cape with his sword. 'Truly this was the SON of GOD,' appears in large Gothic letters in gold beneath the central painting, and beneath that, also gold and Gothic, 'To the glory of God and in loving memory of Aulay Ferguson Macaulay Lieutenant Royal Engineers/Killed on Duty on the North West Frontier of India February XI MDCCCCIX aged twenty-five years/Thou therefore endure hardness as a good soldier of JESUS CHRIST'.

'Mrs Macaulay led her daughters': Doreen Chalmers, *Great Shelford Remembered*, p. 117.

'The Empty Berth': *Cornhill Magazine*, December 1913.

'One is sure': *Saturday Review*, 21 March 1914.

'Behind all the talking': *Coming to London*, p. 165.

Chapter Five: Non-Combatants

'Many Sisters to Many Brothers': *Poems of Today*, 1915.

A lot of women: The novelist May Sinclair was desperate to go to the Front and managed two and a half weeks in Belgium with a medical team, even though she was over fifty.

Pro Patria et Rege: Rose's poems were regularly anthologised, and she was a frequent contributor to the charity anthologies that had their inception with the Great War. She and Rupert Brooke (through Edward Marsh) were two of the twelve contributors to *Selection of Poems*, the royalties of which were converted to War Savings Certificates and sent to the British Red Cross Society. See Sidgwick & Jackson papers, February 1917, Bodleian. Proceeds from *Valour and Vision* (compiled by Jacqueline Trotter in 1920) in which Rose had two poems, one of which was 'Many Sisters', went to the Incorporated Soldiers and Sailors Help Society. In correspondence with Jacqueline Trotter regarding the second edition of this anthology in 1923, Rose expressed anxiety over the 'militant' tone of 'Many Sisters'. (See correspondence in the Hugh Walpole Collection, King's School, Canterbury.)

Gardens and flowers: Rose's 'Many Sisters' was number 18 in *Poems of Today*; Brooke's 'The Dead' and 'The Soldier' were numbers 20 and 21 respectively. See Paul Fussell's fascinating if male-dominated *The Great War and Modern Memory* for a discussion of nature imagery in the poetry of the Great War, and in particular the imagery of dawns and sunsets.

In May 1915: Mount Blow was a Red Cross auxiliary hospital. Nursing members were given a fortnight's probation, followed by an initial contract for three months. (In the military hospitals there was a month's probation, and an initial six-month contract.) Rose was not officially discharged until November 1916.

Rose 'was not very successful': Chalmers, 'The Macaulays in Great Shelford', *Great Shelford Remembered*, p. 117.

'a mad choice': Letter from Jean to Constance Babington Smith, quoted in CBS, p. 78.

'the wild things from without': 'Trinity Sunday', in *The Two Blind Countries*, pp. 3–4.

Non-Combatants and Others: This novel pre-dated by more than ten years the works that have since been granted canonical status as novels and memoirs of the Great War: Edmund Blunden's *Undertones of War* (1928), Siegfried Sassoon's *Memoirs of a Fox-Hunting Man* (1928), Erich Maria Remarque's *All Quiet on the Western Front* (1929), Robert Graves's *Goodbye to All That* (1929) and Richard Aldington's *Death of a Hero* (1929).

'You'll never be any use . . .': *Non-Combatants*, p 19.

'What was it': Ibid., p. 21.

'The thing is': Ibid., p. 102.

'I looked at him': Vera Brittain, *Testament of Youth*, p. 442. It wasn't until many years after the war, and only because of her determination to elucidate the uncertainties in the reporting of her brother Edward's death, that Vera Brittain discovered that Edward, like Alix's Paul, had perhaps been courting death. Evidence of Edward's homosexuality (a loving letter) had fallen into the hands of the authorities. He knew he was likely to face a court martial.

Siegfried Sassoon's poem 'The Hero': See *The War Poems of Siegfried Sassoon*, ed. Rupert Hart-Davis, p. 49. And see Paul Fussell's *The Great War and Modern Memory*, p. 7. Where Rose Macaulay and Vera Brittain show us sisters in their dramatic reconstructions of receiving news of death in action, Sassoon, like most male poets who wrote about such scenes, gives us a mother. She is an idealised mother, white-haired, gentle, proud of her boy, and she doesn't for a moment believe that she's being lied to. Rose Macaulay's Alix Sandomir and Vera Brittain herself, because of their strongly sympathetic identification with their brothers, realise all too quickly that they are being lied to over the circumstances of their brothers' deaths. Perhaps the male war poets and novelists wrote more about mothers than sisters because they found it hard to imagine a non-combatant who identified with the men in the trenches.

'To have one's friends': *Non-Combatants*, p. 144.

The *Englishwoman*: Unsigned review of *Non-Combatants*, 22 May 1916.

The *Times Literary Supplement*: *TLS*, 31 August 1916. The reviewer was Alice Sedgwick.

'It seems all alive': Letter to Walter de la Mare, 7 May 1915, ERM archive. Alfred, the third and last of the Brooke boys, died in France two months after Rupert, in June 1915.

Rupert Brooke's death: Some critics have suggested that the wounded artist Basil Doye in *Non-Combatants* is a portrait of Rupert Brooke, but there is little to support this. Basil rejects Alix's offer of love in favour of the beautiful but shallow Evie. Alix lies in order to turn Evie against him, illustrating Rose's point that non-combatants are as corrupted and spoiled by war as are the combatants.

Rose and her mother Grace: See CBS, p. 78. 'Their mother was completely incapacitated by grief, and Rose herself was likewise unable to face appearing in public.'

'a slave to her mother': Chalmers, 'The Macaulays in Great Shelford', *Great Shelford Remembered*, p. 117.

'how a young lady': From a letter from Father Hamilton Johnson to Constance Babington Smith, 6 August 1959, quoted in her introduction to *Letters*, p. 17.

'A kind little mediocrity': *Non-Combatants*, p. 151.

Grace arranged: Southernwood was sold in June 1918, save for the land that went down to the river; this was sold three years later to the Parish Council for a recreation ground.

'the peacefullest': Letter to Walter de la Mare, 24 April 1918, ERM archive.

The war poems: See also *Scars Upon my Heart: Women's Poetry and Verse of the First World War*, edited by Catherine Reilly. Describing in the preface (p. xv) her response to the collection, the poet Judith Kazantzis talks specifically of her reading of Rose Macaulay's poem 'The Shadow' and its resonance with the other poems: 'The voices of despair and endurance and anger are quiet, yet they mount steadily into a cumulative effect. Always behind them I am aware of the fraught gigantic backdrop of the War, the reality of "The Shadow" of Rose Macaulay's poem. Against this looming "Fear" and "Pain" and "Hell", where the young men are submerged, the woman's voice, as Catherine Reilly names it, becomes a tragic one, in several senses. From her uneasy position on the "Rim of the shadow of the Hell" Rose Macaulay speaks sometimes with angry brilliance, sometimes with grateful idealism; there sounds under both a plain forlorn note.'

'The dark lantern': Humbert Wolfe, introduction to *Augustan Poets*, second series.

The final entry: Rose's manuscript poetry book is in the ERM archive.

'Miss Macaulay': *Athenaeum*, 26 December 1919.

'She had been having tea': *Non-Combatants*, p. 133.

Chapter Six: Gerald

I am indebted to Dr Mary Anne O'Donovan for her generous help and for allowing me access to the family papers in her possession (afterwards referred to as the O'Donovan papers).

I am indebted to John F. Ryan's work on Gerald O'Donovan for much of the material in this chapter, especially his MA thesis: 'Gerald O'Donovan, Priest, Novelist and Intellectual: A Forgotten Leader of the Irish Revival', published as 'Gerald O'Donovan: Priest, Novelist and Irish Revivalist' in the *Journal of the Galway Archaeological and Historical Society*, 48, 1996. See also his introduction to *Father Ralph* by Gerald O'Donovan (Brandon Books, 1993). I am also indebted to him for allowing me access to the papers in his possession (afterwards referred to as O'Donovan/Ryan).

Much later John Betjeman: O'Donovan papers. Betjeman's plan didn't work.

'a bitter': *Times Literary Supplement*, 30 April 1914.

The seven years: For a full account of O'Donovan's work in Loughrea, see Ryan, 'Gerald O'Donovan'.

'in deadly earnest': Review by Professor Stanley Edward Lane-Poole, *TLS*, 8 May 1913.

'He searched her face': *Father Ralph*, p. 330. Gerald may have put his Irish childhood behind him, but he named his children after Irish saints and heroes. Brigid for Ireland's major saint, Dermod for legendary Diarmuid the lover of Grainne, and Mary for the Blessed Virgin. John Ryan has noted that O'Donovan's younger sister was called Brigid.

twenty-four banners: See Joan Hardwick, *The Yeats Sisters: A Biography of Susan and Elizabeth Yeats* (Pandora Press, 1996), for details of the various difficulties and disagreements surrounding the design of the banners. W. B. Yeats thought that his brother Jack's designs were 'too fanciful and modern' for a Catholic cathedral, and informed his sisters that Father O'Donovan had 'expressed his dislike' of the St Patrick banner. Whether he was indeed unhappy, or whether W. B. was indulging in some sibling troublemaking, is not clear. Father

O'Donovan and W. B. Yeats were fellow-passengers on a boat to America in 1903 on a visit to promote, respectively, the co-operative movement and the literary revival. It seems there was a temporary coolness between the two men, which may well have been a consequence of the poet's involvement in the matter of the banners.

'The Cathedral': *Father Ralph*, p. 244.

'It is the bringing': Father Jeremiah O'Donovan, 'Is Ireland Doomed?', *New Ireland Review*, May 1899, quoted in Ryan, 'Gerald O'Donovan', p. 11.

The question of why he left Loughrea: John Ryan cites the signs throughout O'Donovan's life of his inability to see through to the end the projects that he had begun. Father Geraghty, parochial administrator and commissioner of artworks for the Cathedral a hundred years after Father O'Donovan, suggests that O'Donovan had been unhappy for some considerable time, and it was that unhappiness that sent him off here and there on lecture tours and to conferences.

Conflicting stories about Father O'Donovan and the reasons for his departure still circulate in Loughrea. Stories current in 2002 included: (1) the younger clergy in the diocese wanted him as bishop after the departure of John Healy and as a result his position became untenable; (2) the other clergy were jealous of his popularity with the people, and the people expressed such sorrow at his going because they hated all the other clergy so much; (3) the massive farewell party at the station was fuelled by everyone's delight at seeing the back of him because he had been so neglectful of them. In 1988 in 'A Light Across the Path', a radio programme on Gerald O'Donovan written by John Ryan, one of the inhabitants of Loughrea, Mrs Conlon, remembered Father O'Donovan from her girlhood for his good looks and his lively face and insisted: 'He was loved and liked in this town and why wouldn't they for what he done in this town?'

This was the Bishop O'Dea: Augustus John, *Chiaroscuro*, p. 73.

Horace Plunkett noted: Quoted in Ryan, 'Gerald O'Donovan', p. 35.

'valuable services'; 'no wish or prayer': Bishop Thomas O'Dea to Gerald O'Donovan, 22 and 26 September 1904, O'Donovan papers.

'Long before the train': *Western News*, 22 October 1904, quoted in Ryan, 'Gerald O'Donovan', p. 36.

'Cut off by his family': *Father Ralph*, p. 375. The elisions are in the original text.

only six or seven years later: This picture is in the possession of Norman Morgan, of Loughrea Printing Works.

Ten years on Jack Yeats painted: My thanks to John Ryan for pointing out that the Yeats painting was one of a series of twelve illustrations commissioned by Irish novelist George A. Birmingham for his book *Irishmen All* (1913). He – John Ryan – does not agree that the priest resembles Father O'Donovan.

'Was the writer merely stupid?': *Father Ralph*, p. 203.

Gerald O'Donovan . . . proposed marriage: This and the following quotes from Beryl O'Donovan are taken from her unpublished memoir, *Locusts Food*, O'Donovan papers.

'O'Donovan without a job': Horace Plunkett, Diary, 9 August 1911, quoted in John Ryan's MA thesis, p. 177.

No wonder it took him: For some people in Ireland Gerald's marriage was the last nail in the coffin of his reputation, but the great majority of his friends, and very many of his old parishioners, were delighted that he should at last have found happiness, and wrote to tell him so. There are many letters from well-wishers on the occasion of his marriage in the O'Donovan papers.

'invalided out': John Ryan's quotation marks.

How They Did It: On the original dust jacket Methuen printed: 'This is a racy exposure of war muddling at home. It records the ease with which the ambitious and cunning schemer could, in those breathless days, rise to eminence and power, and it shows how vain were the efforts of honest individuals to check the progress of the machinery of carelessness and waste.'

In 1917 . . . William Collins: See David Keir's *The House of Collins*. Beryl O'Donovan felt that Keir had not given due prominence to

Gerald's role in setting up the London base, and that he had glossed over the reasons for Gerald's leaving the firm. She wrote to David Keir: 'my husband felt that the way certain authors were treated reflected on his own good faith'. In a further letter, on one of the rare occasions when she mentioned Rose's name: 'Rose Macaulay, Brett Young, Wells etc. were all intimate personal friends and frequent visitors at our house' (O'Donovan papers). In a letter to Tim Foley of 28 January 1975, Collins Publishers provided him with the following reference from a 'former Manager': 'Messrs. Collins had as their first readers two well-known authors, Gerald O'Donovan and J. D. Beresford, and taking a survey of the books published since 1917 one is impressed with the high average of the work selected.' In a further letter the following month they sent a list of books 'that it is believed that O'Donovan may have edited': Henry James's posthumously published *The Ivory Tower* (1917), *The Sense of the Past* (1917), *The Middle Years* (1917), *Within the Rim* (1918); Mrs Humphry Ward's *Missing* (1917); six titles by Francis Brett Young (1917 through to 1922), and six by Rose Macaulay (from *Potterism* through to *Crewe Train*). (O'Donovan/Ryan.)

It was in the course of: My thanks to John Ryan for showing me a letter from Gerald to Beryl, 2 June 1917, in which, while describing some of his Collins work, he refers to Marjorie Grant Cook's *Verdun Days in Paris*: 'Miss Hamilton was very interesting about France – she was an administrator at that School hospital at Rayonnant which I had a book about' (O'Donovan/Ryan).

'By June, 1890': *Told by an Idiot*, pp. 70 and 71.

'He drew her up': Ibid., p. 73.

He managed to antagonise: See John Ryan's 'Gerald O'Donovan', pp. 39–41, for a detailed account of this episode, and the hostile reactions of many diplomats to the sending of 'an unfrocked priest and his wife' on such a delicate mission to Italy.

Harold Nicolson: Quoted in Emery, p. 163; John Ryan refers to FO Minute 371/3228, 127213, Public Record Office, London.

'We could wish': Letters to Rose Macaulay 11 October and 14 October 1918. Sidgwick & Jackson papers, Bodleian, Oxford.

Rose was never good at handling publishers, and was cavalier with her publishers' rights in her work. Three years after failing to give Sidgwick & Jackson a look at her second collection, she gave an anthologist permission to reprint three poems from *The Two Blind Countries* without consulting the publishers, eliciting an annoyed letter when they found out. Six months later, in 1922, Rose asked them for a reprint of *The Two Blind Countries*. It 'would not be a profitable venture,' was the reply, 'especially as we have no other work of yours to help its sale' (27 September 1921 and 14 June 1922, Sidgwick & Jackson papers).

another nervous breakdown: See CBS, p. 93, where Constance Babington Smith suggests a variety of reasons: 'the long-drawn-out agony of the war, the hard labour of her various jobs, the uncertainties of her writing (*What Not* had a mediocre press), the grind of commuting between Beaconsfield and London, the strain of living with her mother, her distress on account of Will, who was severely wounded only a few weeks before the war ended, and besides all this, of course, the anguish of conscience caused by the fact that she was in love with a married man'.

Marjorie Grant Cook's novel: Both *Verdun Days* and *Latchkey Ladies* were published under the name Marjorie Grant; her third novel, *Another Way of Love* (1923), under the name Marjorie Grant Cook; and all her later novels, post-1930, under the name Caroline Seaford. *Latchkey Ladies* was praised in the *Times Literary Supplement* (the reviewer was Miss A. M. Champneys) for the 'fundamental serenity and candour which characterise the author's outlook' and for her 'discerning, unprejudiced treatment of events and persons' (*TLS*, 27 October 1921).

The only real baby: Mary died in 1941, ten days after her twenty-third birthday, of internal complications following the swallowing of an open safety pin. Not surprisingly, the circumstances surrounding such a ghastly event are not exactly clear.

the last novel that Gerald wrote: After his first two novels had been published by Macmillan, Gerald had had a different publisher for each of the others. *The Holy Tree* was published by Heinemann, who had published Marjorie Grant's *Latchkey Ladies* the previous year.

'To me his real work': Letter to Rosamond Lehmann, 20 August 1942, King's College Archives, Cambridge. In the same letter she described *Writing* and *Conquest* as 'political' novels. 'The *people* aren't real,' she wrote, a criticism that could be levelled at some of her own novels. '*Vocation* is better and brilliant in bits. The Irish life in all of them is excellent, of course.' Yeats's lines about the holy tree come from 'The Two Trees', in *The Rose*, 1893.

'Among the most prolific': See the *Times Literary Supplement* Centenary Archive: online, at www.tls.psmedia.com, compiled and introduced by Dr Deborah McVea and Professor Jeremy Treglown.

Chapter Seven: An Earnest, Grown-up Working Woman

For some of the material in this and subsequent chapters I am grateful to Nancy Nichols for allowing me access to the private papers of her grandparents Sylvia and Robert Lynd, hereinafter referred to as the Lynd papers.

'a sad tragedy': Jean Macaulay to Constance Babington Smith, 18 August 1960. ERM archive.

'The twenties were': *Life Among the English*, p. 90.

'Here was the landscape': In 'The First Impact of *The Waste Land*', in *T. S. Eliot: A Symposium for his 70th Birthday*, ed. Rupert Hart-Davis, pp. 29–31.

'life deliberately seen': H. H. Child reviewing *A Casual Commentary* in the *Times Literary Supplement*, 10 December 1925.

'found the world': Alice Bensen, *Rose Macaulay*, p. 65.

'Rose Macaulay dined': Virginia Woolf, 18 February 1921, *Diary Vol. 2*, p. 93.

'usually considered': Letter of 13 January 1923, to unknown correspondent requesting photo. HRHRC, Texas.

'the riff raff': See letter from Virginia Woolf to Vanessa Bell, 25 May 1928, *Letters, Vol 3*, p. 501.

'With energy and wholeheartedness': *Potterism*, p. 30. Rose was possibly thinking of Hilaire Belloc as one of the correspondents who wrote home rejoicing from the front line. He is one of the few named people whom she criticises in her journalism of the 1920s. For his role as 'war correspondent' see Paul Fussell, *The Great War and Modern Memory*.

'Every profiteer': *Potterism*, p. 246.

The 'mystery part': Letter on 1917 Club notepaper to 'Irena', whose identity I have not been able to uncover, 22 June 1920. HRHRC, Texas.

'Then Rose – too chattery chittery': Virginia Woolf, 24 February 1926, *Diary Vol. 3*, pp. 60–2.
Iolo Williams: Literary journalist on the *London Mercury*.
Jack Squire: J. C. Squire, founder and editor of the *London Mercury*.

'had so much fun': Letter to Father Hamilton Johnson, 15 January 1954, *Last Letters*, p. 141.

'Naomi I found': Storm Jameson, *Journey from the North*, p. 160.

There were weekly lunches: These are described in Agnes Hamilton's *Remembering My Good Friends*, p. 133.

'Lunched and razzled around': Dorothy Brooke, 13 April 1923. ERM archive.

'Jerry O'Donovan was reading': Letter to Sylvia Lynd, 8 December 1920. Lynd papers.

Her husband Robert: Thirty books of Robert Lynd's essays were published between 1908 and 1945: for an account of Lynd's background and journalism see Sean McMahon's introduction to *Galway at the Races: Selected Essays*, ed. Sean McMahon.

'I expect you'll meet': Letter to Sylvia Lynd, 22 November 1921. Lynd papers.

'There were 10 second rate writers': Virginia Woolf, Saturday, 27 March 1926, *Diary, Vol. 3*, pp. 70–1.

'a ghastly party': Virginia Woolf to Vita Sackville-West, 29 March 1926, *Letters, Vol. 3*, p. 251.

'I fear that this means': Letter to Sylvia Lynd, 26 October 1926. Lynd papers.

who began publishing: Naomi Royde-Smith's novels include *Skin-Deep* (in which an ageing beauty desperately seeks the lotions and potions that will restore her youthful beauty), *Jake* and *The Bridge*.

She thought of Rose and Marjorie: Brigid O'Donovan, in 'A Light Across the Path'.

But she recalled: 'Miss Anstruther's Letters', first published in America in *London Calling* (ed. Storm Jameson, 1942), and in Britain in Constance Babington Smith's biography.

'The beginning of my life': Elizabeth Bowen in *Coming to London*, pp. 74–81.

'I have been talking': Letter to Elizabeth Bowen, 3 November 1925. HRHRC, Texas.

'In the end the bazaar proved': Vera Brittain, *Testament of Youth*, (Virago edn, 1978), pp. 544–5.

the Prix Femina-Vie Heureuse: A literary prize for women established in 1904.

'What she really thought': Brittain, *Testament of Youth*, pp. 595–6.

'why should we tell?': Letter to St John Ervine, who in an article for *Good Housekeeping* had accused reticent writers of coyness. Rose replied: 'I don't refrain from telling the public that I am the daughter of a Cambridge professor of English literature, & live at the above address, etc., from coyness, but merely because I feel it is no-one's business but my own, & because I dislike the whole publicity business that surrounds writers, about whom nothing is required to be known but their books (if that). Curmudgeonly if you like, but not "coy".' 18 December 1936. HRHRC, Texas.

Vera Brittain was notorious: Deborah Gorham gives the following detail of the friendship between Winifred Holtby and Vera Brittain:

their early private name for Brittain was 'very small very dear love', which Brittain abbreviated to 'vsvdl' when signing her letters to Holtby. No wonder Rose would come to dislike her. See *Vera Brittain: A Feminist Life*, p. 218. She also quotes Vera's letter to Winifred that Vera refers to in *Testament*: 'Winifred, I am terrified of that woman – terrified of meeting her on the 7th of Dec – terrified she'll see me for the egotistical *poseuse* I know I am so often. Above all, I am terrified of writing a book she may someday review' (Gorham, p. 169).

When we see Neville: Some critics have suggested that *Dangerous Ages* was written as a response to *The Dangerous Age* (1912) by Karin Michaëlis, widely read in translation. Michaëlis's novel is a powerfully written but ultimately depressing story of a woman's fear of growing old and losing her sexual powers. Rose may well have read it. Rose wrote a review of her own novel in *Time and Tide* (3 June 1921), comparing it sardonically to 'an earnest, emotional, original and uncommon book' by Romer Wilson, also out that week:

> *Dangerous Ages* is, on the other hand, an ordinary novel about ordinary people behaving in ordinary ways. The theme is the reaction of a group of people to their ages, which range from 84 to 20. There is so much to say on this theme that volumes would not exhaust it. *Dangerous Ages* is a slight study enough. One feels that it would be better for more body, that it is a little thin in parts. There is even, here and there, a rather glib facility of thought and method. But it aims at being a careful record of different characters and the psychology of their different ages. Of course the worst of it is that age has really very little to do with psychology. One has to exaggerate these things for fictional purposes. It may be added that there is no moral to this tale, and that it gives a painstaking account of psychoanalysis, bathing, love and family life. Some people may like it, others had better not try.

'one of the few hopes': In the same letter to an unidentified recipient in which she discusses *Potterism*.

'the delight of the book': H. H. Child in the *Times Literary Supplement*, 2 November 1922.

'might be used as a textbook': *New Republic*, 16 April 1924.

'a sympathetic': Marjorie Grant Cook's review appeared in the *TLS* on 1 November 1923. In his introduction to the 1982 Virago edition of *Told by an Idiot*, the novelist A. N. Wilson wrote of how he first thought *Told* owed a considerable debt to Virginia Woolf's *Orlando*. He had been struck by how close to the ideas in *Orlando* was this description of Rome: 'In 1790, 1690, 1590 and back through every decade of every century, there have been Rome Gardens, fastidious, mondaine, urbane, lettered, critical, amused, sceptical and what was called in 1890 *fin de siècle*'. Other points of comparison can be drawn between the androgynous quality of some of the characters in *Told* and the gender-changing manifestations of Orlando. But Wilson's theory of the debt owed by Rose Macaulay to Virginia Woolf collapsed, he recounted, when he checked the dates of publication and found that *Told by an Idiot* had been published in 1923, five years prior to the publication of *Orlando*. Recounting this in a lecture some years later he said, 'If there is kinship between the two books – and I think there quite demonstrably is – then it was Mrs Woolf who owed a debt to Miss Macaulay and not the other way about.' See his Introduction, pp. vii–ix, and 'Rose Macaulay' in *Founders and Followers*. See also Gloria G. Fromm, 'Re-inscribing *The Years*, Virginia Woolf, Rose Macaulay, and the Critics' for the relationship between *Told by an Idiot* and *The Years*. And see Alice Bensen's *Rose Macaulay* for a discussion of similarities between *Dangerous Ages* and *To the Lighthouse*.

'represents the spirit': Alice Bensen, *Rose Macaulay*, p. 82.

'to see how far': *TLS*, 27 November 1924.

'It was the one': Letter of 18 January 1951, *Letters*, p. 59.

Bunkum: Unpublished. ERM archive.

'What else would one do?': Recorded by Virginia Woolf, 22 July 1926, *Diary, Vol. 3*, p. 96.

'How to Choose a Religion': *A Casual Commentary*, pp. 5–13.

'Problems of Social Life': Ibid., p. 64–70.

'At the worst': Ibid., p. 82.

'There is a good deal': H. H. Child in the *TLS*, 10 December 1925.

'The only real crime': 'On Living Life to the Full', *A Casual Commentary*, pp. 173–8.

'That has wrought': Ibid., p. 95.

'bread and circuses': Ibid., p. 209.

'Into Human Speech': Ibid., pp. 101–6.

'Rather wonderful': *Crewe Train*, p. 65.

'This high, happy hum': Ibid., p. 68.

a Sudanese dancing troupe: An accurate reflection of the mid-1920s vogue for all things Black, such as Nancy Cunard's Black lover, and her anthology *Negro*. 'I liked doing the Williams-Ellis party,' said Rose of the party scene in *Crewe Train*, admitting thereby that at least some of the novel is a *roman-à-clef*, 'and adding on Fuzzies to it.' Letter to Sylvia Lynd, 21 October 1926. Lynd papers.

'There has always': Dudley Carew, *Times Literary Supplement*, 28 October 1926.

'realism is tinged': Patrick Braybrooke in *Some Goddesses of the Pen*, p. 45.

In October that year: Mentioned in letter to Elizabeth Bowen, 27 October 1926, HRHRC, Texas.

'is at her best': Professor Alan Francis Clutton-Brock, *TLS*, 25 November 1926.

'had its genesis': Letter to Father Hamilton Johnson, 1 April 1952, *Letters*, p. 299.

'If *Summer's Over*': *Keeping Up Appearances*, p. 132.

'haven't written any': From correspondence in BBC written archives, Reading.

'About work': Virginia Woolf, 31 May 1928, *Diary, Vol. 3*, p. 185.

'down the slender stalk': *Keeping Up Appearances*, pp. 240–1.

'Everyone is very much interested': Letter to Jean Macaulay, 8 December 1929, *Sister*, p. 52.

'The specialist': Letter to Jean Macaulay, 5 May 1929, *Sister*, p. 49.

Chapter Eight: Histories and Biographies

'Rose adored parties': This and following quotes are taken from the chapter 'Rose Macaulay: And Others' in *Reminiscences of Affection* by Victor Gollancz, pp. 63–93.

Sylvia described: Sylvia Lynd's unpublished diaries, Lynd papers.

A. P. Herbert, novelist, journalist, poet and campaigner for many causes, notably divorce reform and improving authors' rights, MP for Oxford University 1935–50. Frank Kermode wrote of him: 'Long ago A. P. Herbert proposed a great extension of the copyright privilege to as many as forty libraries – a notion very disagreeable to publishers, who dislike being compelled to surrender even six copies of each book and would rather see the privilege abolished than enlarged. Herbert got the divorce laws changed, but he failed in this attempt to defeat southern prejudice.' (The six copyright libraries are in Wales, Scotland, Dublin, London, Oxford and Cambridge.) See Frank Kermode, *Not Entitled: A Memoir* (HarperCollins, 1996).

Max Beerbohm, author of *Zuleika Dobson* (1911) and cartoonist.

Bryan Guiness, poet and novelist, later Lord Moyne. He was divorced from Diana Mitford in 1934.

Alan Thomas, novelist.

Lionel Hale, playwright and theatre critic.

Victor Gollancz gives a lively account of various parties at Keats Grove:

> Rose [Macaulay] and Jack Priestley were marvellous, on one occasion, in a charade, but I have forgotten everything about it except that they were marvellous . . . The two stars I remember were Max Beerbohm and James Joyce. Humbert [Wolfe] and I were lucky enough to please Max Beerbohm with a little dialogue in our best Jewish accents that ran like this:
> What sort of composer was Mozart?

Mozart? *Mozart?* Rotten! Why, he wrote Faust.

No, he didn't.

What, he didn't *even* write Faust? Didn't I say he was a rotten composer?

And:

James Joyce [was] a connoisseur of fine singing . . . 'You will agree,' exclaimed Joyce, 'that the really important thing about a tenor is that he should sing *loud*' . . . But Sylvia interrupted us, and ordered him, clearly by arrangement, to the piano . . . Against his own low accompaniment he recited, though that is not the word, *Anna Livia Plurabel*. He neither spoke it nor sang it: he used something like the *sprechstimme*, or pitch-controlled speech, familiar from *Moses and Aaron* and other works by Schoenberg. And the sound of it was lovely beyond description.

Reminiscences of Affection, pp. 89–90.

a new car: Rose kept her old car, also a Morris but bigger and noisier, acquired after the American adventure, for Will to use on his trips to England.

'several hundred miles an hour': Gollancz, *Reminiscences*.

'London burbles on': Letter to Sylvia Lynd, 18 July 1936. Lynd papers.

'A line to bless you!': Quoted by Ruth Dudley Edwards in *Victor Gollancz: A Biography*, p. 205.

'My books won't live': Quoted by Hilary Spurling in *Ivy: The Life of Ivy Compton-Burnett*, p. 377. (Conversation reported by Cecil Gould.)

'I don't take my novels seriously': Letter to Hugh Walpole, 1932, n.d. (probably early June), HRHRC, Texas. Rose was trying to scotch a rumour that she had been annoyed on hearing that Clemence Dane, on the Book Society Committee with Hugh Walpole, had turned down one of her books. Hugh Walpole (1884–1941) was a bestselling novelist of the 1920s and 1930s, probably remembered now for *Mr Perrin and Mr Traill* (1911) and for *Rogue Herries* (1930) and its sequels. He worried about being an old-fashioned sort of novelist and wished he could be more like Virginia Woolf. Like Rose Macaulay he was very encouraging towards younger writers. He and Rose were godparents to one of J. B. Priestley's children. Hugh Walpole dedicated his story collection *All Souls' Night* (1934): 'FOR TWO WISE WOMEN / SYLVIA LYND / ROSE MACAULAY'. This is very possibly a pun: Robert Lynd, because of his weekly articles signed 'Y.Y.', was known as 'Two Ys'. Walpole was a regular visitor at Keats Grove.

Ivy had a whole clutch: One brother, Guy, died in 1905. The other, Noel, whom she adored, had gone up to King's the same year as Rupert Brooke, 1907, and used to go out riding with Rose's uncle W. H. Macaulay. He was killed in France in July 1915.

'neutrals': See Spurling, *Ivy*. Elizabeth Sprigge in *The Life of Ivy Compton-Burnett* quotes the word used as 'neuters'. She suggests that Margaret Jourdain's denial of ever feeling any sexual feelings was related to a fear of disease, which haunted the Jourdain family. One can imagine that Ivy Compton-Burnett's bizarre childhood and her disastrous family relationships (described in both these biographies and in other accounts) might well have had an influence on later sexual orientation or lack of one.

Una Pope-Hennessy: Her books include a biography of Madame Roland, and a biography of Charles Dickens. In 1929 she had published an entertaining account of America and Americanness seen through the eyes of three visiting English women between 1826 and 1836: Fanny Trollope, Fanny Kemble and Harriet Martineau. Accounts of English travellers of the past provided the organising theme behind two travel books of the 1940s: Rose's own *They Went to Portugal*, and *West Indian Summer* by Una's younger son, James Pope-Hennessy. John Pope-Hennessy later became Director of the V & A, and James literary editor of the *Spectator*.

Leonard Woolf had asked her: His original suggestion was 'Letter Writing as an Art'. She would find Letter Writing, Rose replied, 'too vast a business', and asked whether she might write instead on 'a subject that rather interests me, the supernatural element in literature', which would deal 'both with religion and other forms of supernaturalism'.

An amicable wrangle developed over the next few months: Rose thought the word 'religious' would 'limit the scope' of the book, and wanted 'supernatural' (as including religious); Leonard thought that 'supernatural' would limit the scope in the other direction. The view of the publisher prevailed, as views of publishers tend to do, but one wonders whether he was right. It is hard to think of a less exciting title than 'Some Religious Elements in English Literature'.

Some Religious Elements in English Literature was number 14 in the series, which included Harold Nicolson on biography, Rose's friend Humbert Wolfe on English verse satire, Edmund Blunden on nature and Herbert Read on English poetry. The introductory volume, *A Lecture on Lectures*, was written by 'Q', Sir Arthur Quiller-Couch, at that time King Edward VII Professor of English Literature at Cambridge. Quotations are from the correspondence in the Hogarth files at the University of Reading archives.

'It is not a question of what books': Letter to Jonathan Cape, Cape archive, University of Reading.

When *Some Religious Elements* came out: It was described as 'lively and stimulating' in the *Times Literary Supplement*, whose reviewer enjoyed the author's 'attitude of ironical detachment'. He assumed Miss Macaulay's interest in religion 'to be a purely intellectual one'. Eric Batterham in the *Times Literary Supplement*, 6 August 1931.

'the son of an Elizabethan schoolmaster': Letter to Hamilton Johnson, 27 November 1950, *Letters*, p. 35.

'It is part of her boldness': Cyril Bentham Falls in the *Times Literary Supplement*, 20 October 1932.

'*They Were Defeated* is what it is about': Letter to Hamilton Johnson, 30 August 1950, *Letters*, p. 27. It was Hamilton Johnson's reading of *They Were Defeated* that sparked off the correspondence between them which was published in two volumes edited by Constance Babington Smith. Hamilton Johnson was a Cowley Father in Massachusetts, and had read an American edition of the novel, published under the title *The Shadow Flies*. In this, her first letter to Hamilton Johnson, Rose explained: 'Its real name (as published here) was *They Were Defeated*, but the American publishers didn't like the word "defeated" (I think they were just emerging from a slump!) so called it *The Shadow Flies*, taking the words of course from the poem I quote. Rather foolish of them, I thought. *They Were Defeated* is what it is about . . .'

Rose was widely praised: In the *Sunday Times* Ralph Strauss wrote: 'I know of no other work of fiction which gives such a well-balanced and intimate picture of those curious days or conveys more admirably to us the real excitement of the times. Here, indeed, is that England of long ago' (16 October 1932). In the *Spectator* Rose Macaulay was praised for making her historical characters 'integral and proportionate parts of the whole . . . perhaps the rarest achievement of the historical writer' (L. A. G. Strong, 22 October 1932).

'Julian's story and end': Letter to Helen Waddell, 1 November 1932. ERM archive.

Helen Waddell: medieval scholar and translator. Author of *The Wandering Scholars* (1927), *Mediaeval Latin Lyrics* (1929) and *Lyrics from the Chinese* (1913). Her historical novel, *Peter Abelard*, came out the year after *They Were Defeated*.

'I've just been distempering': Letter to Sylvia Lynd, 1932, n.d. Lynd papers.

Fumifugium: Or the Inconvenience of the Aer, and Smoake of London Dissipated together with some Remedies humbly proposed: Part of the attraction for Rose of John Evelyn's pamphlet was his utopian vision of orchards of apple trees in the Strand, and fields of rosemary and other sweet-smelling herbs surrounding London so that it 'would be sensible of the sweet and ravishing varieties of the perfumes'; but it was also Evelyn's time and place that attracted her, and his idealism, which was like that of Julian Conybeare; undoubtedly, the very hopelessness of that idealism was part of the appeal. She neatly described the defeat of John Evelyn's hopes in the opening paragraph: 'Writing, hopeful man, in 1661, before that prince who was "resolv'd to be a father to his country" and who "studied only the publick good" had adorned the throne long enough to be found out, he believed that King Charles and his parliament would pass an Act to abate smoke. Alas, they passed no Act; the thoughts of Charles, the thoughts of his parliament, were elsewhere.' This is Rose Macaulay the historian, measured, distant, and impartial, carefully weighing her clauses, balancing hopes against realities with a grave humour. Nothing was done: John Evelyn's remedies were not adopted, orchards and herbiferous fields were not planted, nor were noisome tradesmen, the brewers, dyers, soap and salt-boilers, nor the lime-burners, removed from the city, 'so great was the sordid and accursed avarice of the men of the age, of men,' as Rose Macaulay the historian believed, 'of all ages.' See *Fumifugium*, reprinted by the National Smoke Abatement Society, 1933.

'has an odd look of Rose': Virginia Woolf to Maynard Keynes, 23 December 1937, *Collected Letters, Vol. 6*. Thomas Babington (Lord) Macaulay was the son of Zachary Macaulay, Rose's great-great-uncle on her father's side, great-great-great-uncle on her mother's side.

'As for Mr Milton, I adore him myself': Letter to Helen Waddell, 1 November 1932. ERM archive.

'I think he was rather of my father's breed': Ibid.

'in the Strachey style': Basil de Selincourt, *Observer*, 28 January 1934.

'The League of Nations do publish': Letter to Jean, 9 December 1934, *Sister*, p. 62.

'I am all for Socialism later': Letter to Jean, 10 November 1935, ibid., p. 70.

'Will suggests that everyone should draw lots': Letter to Jean, 15 September 1935, ibid., p. 66.

'Everyone is delighted that Hoare': Letter to Jean, 15 December 1935, ibid., p. 70.

'The Cabinet are now longing': Letter to Jean, 17 June 1936, ibid., p. 79.

Victor and Ruth Gollancz at Brimpton: See thank-you letter from Ras Tafari, Emperor Haile Selassie in exile from Abyssinia, in Ruth Dudley Edwards's *Victor Gollancz: A Biography*, p. 205.

She became a sponsor: Storm Jameson and Aldous Huxley were also sponsors of the P.P.U.

An Open Letter to a Non-Pacifist: This was published in 1937 by William Collins for the Peace Pledge Union.

'I refrained from reading this opus': Gollancz, *Reminiscences*, p. 82.

' . . . the meeting is of distinguished': Letter to Hugh Walpole, 31 May 1938. HRHRC, Texas.

'Our P.M. seems to have saved the world!': Postcard to Daniel George (Bunting), 15 September 1938. ERM archive.

passports as a symptom: Before the Great War, a British traveller had no need of a passport. They were introduced in 1915 under section 14c of DORA (Defence of the Realm Act), and along with other emergency measures (such as licensing hours) became normalised after the war: an encroachment on the life of the 'liberal individualist' that became not just a part of accepted life, but with the identifying photograph and demand for 'identifying characteristics' a central symbol, as Paul Fussell describes it, of the modern sensibility in its anxious relationship with the self. See Paul Fussell in *Abroad*, especially Chapter 4, 'The Passport Nuisance'.

It must have introduced another, and more practical cause for anxiety, for a woman travelling abroad with a man who was not her husband.

E. M. Forster complained: 'We cannot go where we like. Escape is impossible. We can only get out of England on a ticket of leave, issued if our conduct is satisfactory . . . This ticket of leave is called a passport'. Quoted by Francis King in *E.M.Forster*.

' . . . what did his counsel mean?': Letter to Jean, 18 December 1935, *Sister*, p. 72.

a 'bird in the box': See introduction.

'Her *Minor Pleasures* is remembered': Anthony Burgess, *Spectator*, 2 July 1965. The companion volume was *The Major Pleasures of Life* by Martin Armstrong.

'The fact is': Letter to John Hayward, 14 January 1944. King's College Archives.

' . . . the Girles of Artemis . . .': Jeanette Passty reads this as a lesbian poem and an illustration of Rose's profoundly androgynous nature. See her *Eros and Androgyny*. The goddess Artemis is however celibate rather than lesbian.

Flying: Rose had had the 'thrilling experience' of first going up in a plane in 1932, accompanied by Margaret and Eleanor, who was back on leave. Two or three years later she went up in the publisher Hamish Hamilton's Klemm monoplane. Constance Babington Smith, herself a keen flyer and expert on aeronautics, describes it:

> The passenger's seat had a stick and after a while Rose was allowed to take over. Hamish Hamilton can still remember what happened when he told her to push the stick forward. 'Usually when I told my passengers to do this and we started to move rapidly towards the earth they would scream. Not Rose. She merely did what she was told, banking steeply as well, and enjoyed every moment of it.' He also recalls the following incident during the flight: 'The telephone connecting the pilot's seat with that of the passenger was never particularly effective, and Rose's rapid and not very clear diction didn't help matters. Accordingly, when she asked me an urgent but inaudible question I landed and said "What *were* you saying, Rose?" "I was asking," she replied, "if you could make it stand still in the air."' CBS, pp. 134–5.

Logan Pearsall Smith (1865–1946): essayist, man of letters, author of *Trivia* (1902). He was fond of playing practical jokes. Rose liked him, and was an admirer of his writing. His essays are now largely unread.

'What is that you say you have done?': In 'Showing Off', *Personal Pleasures*, p. 333. The writer Antonia White was a frequent guest at 'boasting' parties and according to her biographer Jane Dunn claimed that she had been married twice and had a certificate from the Pope vouching for her virginity, 'beating Eddy Gathorne-Hardy's declaration that he had contracted ringworm from the Archbishop of Canterbury into second place.' See Jane Dunn's *Antonia White*.

'Reading': *Personal Pleasures*, pp. 317–24.

There are some fine parodies: Her prose submission to the little magazines is in the style of Hemingway: 'She was a grand girl. You're drunk, she said. But I wasn't so drunk, either. I mean, I'd had a few, but I could see straight; and I could hold the wheel. I had the headlights on, too. To hell with those lamps, she said, and switched them down.

Do you want to dazzle everything on the road, she said, so it rushes into us? You're nuts . . . There was the hell of a mess on the road. One of those little Austins, it was, and all crumpled up, and a man and a girl all crumpled up too. There was blood and glass and things around. But my Buick had only buckled a wing . . .' 'Following the Fashion', *Personal Pleasures*, pp. 223–7.

'peril of mandarinism': Alice Bensen highlights the intense interest that Rose Macaulay shows in etymology, quoting appositely from a section on words in the pleasure of 'Writing': 'How charmingly they flit before me, heavy laden with their honey like bees, yet light on the wing . . . I trace back their ancestry, noting their diverse uses, modes, offspring, kin, trans-formations, transplantations, somersaults, spellings, dignities, degradations, lines and phrases which have enambered them for ever, phrases and lines which they have themselves immortally enkindled . . . to arrange them in juxtaposition, to entertain oneself with curious tropes, with meiosis, litotes, hyperbole, pleonasms, pedanticisms, to measure the words fitly to the thought, to be by turns bombastic, magniloquent, terse, flamboyant, minishing, to use Latinisms, Gallicisms, Hellenisms, Saxonisms, every ism in turn, to scatter our native riches like a spend-thrift tossing gold – this is the pleasure of writing.' To which a reader might respond: yes, the pleasure of writing rather than the pleasure of reading. 'Writing', *Personal Pleasures*, pp. 377–81.

'light and unsubstantial': R. A. Gallop, *Times Literary Supplement*, 5 July 1934.

'I think now it is rather a *bad* joke': Letter to Hamilton Johnson, 9 January 1951, *Letters*, p. 50.

'teased a few Americans': Letter to John Hayward, 18 January 1944, King's College Archives.

'a time when Miss Macaulay was writing novels': Correspondence with William Collins quoted in CBS, p. 128.

Reginald Heber Macaulay: Rose and her siblings had spent many hol-idays at Kirnan, Uncle Regi's house in Argyll, where he developed a famous rock garden and bred a hybrid violet that bears his name, *Gentiana Macaulayi*.

his last, and final novel, *A Passage to India*, in 1924: Forster's *Maurice*, written in 1913, was posthumously published in 1972.

There were parallels: Rose's ghost story 'The Empty Berth' (1913) can be read as a homage to E. M. Forster's own tourists-in-the-Aegean ghost story, 'Cnidus' (1904).

'Gentle, intelligent, high-minded, high-browed': *The Writings of E. M. Forster*, p. 9.

suggest that she was perfectly well aware of his sexual orientation: Unlike his next critic, the American Lionel Trilling, to whom it later came as something of a shock.

'I have just finished Rose's book': Forster to Leonard Woolf, 10 January 1938, *Selected Letters of E. M. Forster*, p. 155.

'Rose Macaulay is a wise guide': Forster, *Two Cheers for Democracy* pp. 266–7.

Chapter Nine: In Ruins

'my great Life-Work': Letter to Walter de la Mare, 4 December 1939. ERM archive.

'Woman Motorist Whose Attention was Diverted': *Cumberland and Westmorland Herald*, 22 July 1939.

'the serpent in this Eden': 'Driving a Car', *Personal Pleasures*, pp. 167–9. Even death is sunny and bright in this fantasy. 'As it is,' she concludes, 'when our time comes to go, when we fall in turn to the juggernaut, we may hope to be translated to some paradise traversed by great fair roads, to each soul a road to herself, along which her car shall dash at some supramundane speed, hugging (for souls shall be made perfect) the near border of thymey Elysian grass.'
    It is odd that here, where 'itself' could be used without strain instead of 'herself', Rose Macaulay chose, uncharacteristically, to speak as a woman. Driving was close to her heart.

'I am dead sick of my novel': Letter to Daniel George, 5 October 1939. ERM archive.

'married a mermaid': Letter to Hamilton Johnson, *Letters*, p. 68.

'two fallen houses, a great pile of ruins': Letter to Jean Macaulay, 28 September 1940, *Sister*, p. 114.

'I shall get out of him his alternative to war or surrender': Letter to Jean, 8 September 1940, ibid., p. 110.

Gilbert Murray (1866–1957), Regius Professor of Greek at Oxford, 1908–36 and Chairman of the League of Nations Union, 1928–40.

'Luxborough and Paddington Streets looked like a scene out of *Things to Come*': Letter to Jean, 11 December 1940, *Sister*, p. 120.

'Rose M. is doing the same in London. I admire that very much': Virginia Woolf to Ethel Smyth, 11 September 1940.

'I suppose she would be a very odd girl, wouldn't she': Letter to Virginia Woolf, October 1940. ERM archive.

'I expect it scores from so few novels coming out just now; so has fewer competitors': Letter to Jean, 21 June 1940, *Sister*, p. 102.

'remarks of a complimentary': See correspondence in the Penguin archives, University of Bristol.

'I am mentioning ruin-seeing': Letter to Jean, 4 January 1941, ibid., p. 121. Rose did not broadcast again for some time after this. Along with E. M. Forster and Ralph Vaughan Williams she went on strike to protest against the BBC's policy of banning from broadcasting people 'who have taken part in public agitation against the war effort', as Duff Cooper, Minister for Information, described the victims of the BBC ban (in the House of Commons on 12 March 1941). The bans were aimed particularly at pacifists and those who had attended or sub-scribed to the 'People's Convention' in January 1941. See *Forster, Selected Letters*, pp. 191–3 for details.

'Last week she was supposed to be going to die': Letter to Sylvia Lynd, 13 February 1941, Lynd papers.

Now she was dying and the doctor refused: See Emery, p. 267.

'it amused her to embellish, fantasticate and ironise her friends': *Spectator*, 11 April 1941.

'Such a wretched way to lose someone': Letter to Sylvia Lynd, 23 April 1941. Lynd papers.

'House no more': Letter to Daniel George, 12 May 1941. ERM archive.

'gaping wound in my heart and mind': Quoted by Storm Jameson in *Journey from the North*, p. 112.

four pairs of stockings: This would have cost eight clothing coupons.

'in the same vestage and habit': Letter to Ruth and Victor Gollancz, 28 May 1941. ERM archive. 'The O.D. was my Bible, my staff, my entertainer, my help in work & my recreation in leisure'.

'the best-kept secret in London': Victor Gollancz in *Reminiscences*, p. 83. Who else knew? The Lynds, the Brookes, Ivy Compton-Burnett, Una Pope-Hennessy, Rosamond Lehmann and possibly one or two others.

'Now, listening to her rapid talk': Storm Jameson, *Journey from the North*, p. 113.

Marjorie Grant Cook was invited: In a strange reprise of a scene in *Latchkey Ladies*, her novel of twenty years before, when Anne comes to the house where her lover Philip Dampier is dying, but is kept out of the room by his wife, Rose.

'As a friend he never failed': *The Times*, 10 August 1942.

'He died on July 26th': Letter to Rosamond Lehmann, 20 August 1942, King's College Archives.

'The story has been a good one': Letter to Sylvia Lynd, 30 July 1942, Lynd papers.

'I brought some of my photographs': James Lees-Milne, 20 January 1943, *Ancestral Voices*, pp. 132–3. In 1936 James Lees-Milne became secretary to the Country Houses (to become Historic Buildings) Committee of the National Trust. He took up his old position after the war, in 1942.

'I dined with Dame Una': Lees-Milne, 27 July 1943. *Ancestral Voices*, p. 194.

wide range of sources: This is what she used for her essay on Henry Fielding, who ' 'neath the green Estrella trees/Sleeps with the alien Portuguese':

> *The Journal of a Voyage to Lisbon*, Henry Fielding (1755)
> *The History of Henry Fielding*, Wilbur L. Cross (1918)
> *A Fielding Find*, Austin Dobson (1912)
> *Travels in Portugal in 1789 and 1790*, James Murphy (1795)
> *Historical Memoirs*, Sir Nathaniel William Wraxall (1815)
> *Travels through Spain and Portugal in 1772 and 1773*, Richard Twiss (1775)
> *Journal of a few Months Residence in Portugal*, Dora Quillinan (1847)
> *The Public Advertiser* (16 October 1754)

Even the sources are brought to life. Here, in the essay on Henry Fielding, Rose draws the reader's attention to the difference in powers of observation between the two 'tourists' Richard Twiss and Nathaniel William Wraxall (Twiss was the closer observer); and quotes Mrs Quillinan, Wordsworth's daughter, on Fielding's burial spot: 'His monument, a huge ungainly thing, is on a spot selected by *guess*. The bones it covers may possibly have belonged to an idiot.' Rose suggests that Fielding himself would have enjoyed such a robust comment on his final resting-place.

The writer Norman Douglas: Novelist and travel-writer. His novel *South Wind* (1917) was a bestseller.

The Coffin House: A pen and ink drawing, coloured with a light wash. Denton Welch had always intended to be a painter but in 1935, at the age of twenty, and while still an art student, he was knocked off his bicycle by a motorist and received such severe internal injuries that he was an invalid for the rest of his life. During the long periods that he had to spend in bed he started to write. His works are mainly autobiographical, and include *Maiden Voyage* and *In Youth is Pleasure*. His diaries are marvellously vivid. Many people, Rose included, thought him a more accomplished writer than painter. He died in 1948. See James Methuen Campbell's *Denton Welch: Writer and Artist* (pp. 169–70) for a detailed description of *The Coffin House*. It was reproduced in Denton Welch's posthumously published collection of poems, *A Last Sheaf.* Welch copied extracts from the two letters Rose wrote to him about the picture into his journal on 13 February 1947: see *The Journals of Denton Welch*, p. 321. On the publication of Denton Welch's journals some years after he died, Rose wrote to her friend Gerard Irvine: 'I am glad that he liked the letter I wrote about his picture enough to copy it into his diary.' Letter to Gerard Irvine, 29 January 1954. ERM archive.

'at once entertaining': *Fabled Shore*, p. 51.

She was lonely in Spain: 'It was my first European travel since the war, and in a way lonely, because I used in old days to travel about Europe with a companion who liked all I liked and knew much more about it.' Letter to Hamilton Johnson, 27 March 1951, *Letters*, p. 105.

'a windswept cape': *Fabled Shore*, p. 246.

'If I Were Head of the Third Programme': BBC Written Archives, Reading.

She was accompanied by Marjorie Grant Cook: After twenty years of anonymous reviewing of other people's books for the *Times Literary Supplement*, she had now reinvented herself as the novelist Caroline Seaford. Her attitude to her own writing was not dissimilar to Rose's. In 1946 she wrote to her publisher Mr Cape, long-suffering recipient of eccentric letters: 'I think you did very well with that deadly book [she must be referring to *They Grew in Beauty*], which I now detest and despise. It really is frightful. How clever of you to sell so many copies. As you say there are a few odd ones left, I may as well have two or three as missiles for my least liked acquaintances, what time I have to give them an embarrassing present.'

There are some discrepancies in the accounts of the trip to Ireland. Constance Babington Smith says there was one trip, Jane Emery that there were two. In July Rose and Marjorie stayed with Elizabeth Bowen at Bowen's Court in County Cork. The house is no longer in existence, but it is memorialised in Elizabeth Bowen's book, *Bowen's Court* (1942). Brigid O'Donovan joined them for a time in Ireland.

Chapter Ten: Pleasures

'dubious merchant from Japan': *The World My Wilderness*, p. 181. See Penguin Archives, University of Bristol Library.

In her thank-you note: Letter to William Plomer, 10 June 1950. Durham University Library.

She went ruin-hunting: In Wales she included Portmeirion, which Clough Williams-Ellis had begun to build in 1925; it was made famous by its use in the 1960s TV series *The Prisoner*.

'It soon became clear': Quoted in CBS, p. 186.

'Turning a dark corner among the bookstacks': C. V. Wedgwood, in 'The Pleasures of Knowing Rose Macaulay', *Encounter*, March 1959. See CBS, p. 230.

 ' . . . she was forever up and down those ladders like a chamois': Evelyn Waugh compared her to a monkey rather than a chamois, but to similar effect, describing an occasion after a lunch with Patrick Kinross when various of the guests went to investigate the problem of Rose being without water at her flat: 'When we got to Dame Rose's flat we found the cistern was on the roof approached by a rather steep iron ladder. Dame R shinned up it like a monkey'. Letter to Patrick Kinross, 31 December 1958, *The Letters of Evelyn Waugh*, p. 516. Rosamond Lehmann, on Rose's swift ascent of a ladder at the Lansdowne Club swimming pool, wrote: 'she has scampered up, up, out, to the outermost verge of the high-diving board'. Possibly such skill on ladders had its basis in early tree-climbing days; something one doesn't forget, like how to ride a bicycle.

his portrayal of Timberio (Emperor Tiberius): Rose was fascinated by Tiberius's cruelty, and by his homosexuality. He had thirteen palaces on the island of Capri, and enjoyed making his victims jump to their deaths off the high cliffs of the island. Rose published a poem, 'Pleasures of Tiberius', in the *Times Literary Supplement*, 21 December 1951. Tiberius dreams of being a dolphin:

> (He would dive with his riders to deep cool grottos [*sic*],
> Play with them there, the pretty grotteschi,
> Keep them for ever in swaying twilight . . .
> . . .

Dolphin and urchins, emperor and putti, . . .
Sporting and frisking in Baiae's bays –
So dreamed Tiberius through the August days.
There lie his cellars, where the sea-fern sways.)

the pleasure of ruins is one particular strand: Christopher Wordsworth's *In Ruins*, published in 2001 and accompanied by an exhibition of paintings, is another stitch in that strand. Rose Macaulay is sensitive to that complex weave explored by many of her contemporaries, referencing amongst others George Gissing, *By the Ionian Sea* (1901); Gertrude Bell, *The Desert and the Sown* (1907); E. M. Forster, *Alexandria* (1938); Robert Byron, *The Road to Oxiana* (1939); Osbert Sitwell, *Escape With Me* (1939); Sacheverell Sitwell, *Mauretania* (1940); Robin Fedden, *Syria* (1946) and Robert Payne, *Journey to Persia* (1951).

'On ruins one can begin to build': *The Valley Captives*, p. 219.

'combination of opposites': In 'Pleasures of Knowing Rose Macaulay', CBS, p. 223.

'Pleasure is good': *Times Literary Supplement*, 22 January 1954.

Rosamond Lehmann, who used to swim with her: This is described affectionately and hilariously in 'Pleasures of Knowing Rose Macaulay', CBS, pp. 224–6:

> Presently Rose emerges from her canvas tentings, voluble, in a one-piece striped exiguous bathing suit, her nose, mouth, chin severe, her brow, her ice-blue eyes obliterated beneath a black diving helmet some sizes too large for her. She carries an inflated rubber mattress, and as we advance towards the brink, casts it upon the waters with business-like despatch. The moment after, I am standing alone; she has vanished. Another moment, and her brisk commentary is rattling down as it were from ceiling-level: she has scampered up, up, out, to the outer-most verge of the high-diving board. There I still see her figure indomitably poised: androgynous tall figure, flat as a shape cut out in white paper and blacked in to knees and shoulders; gaunt, comical, adorable – heroically topped with an antique martial casque . . .

Meanwhile their shared publisher, Mark Bonham Carter, swims 'noiseless, watchful, amused, at a discreet distance'.

'Suddenly, rapidly': 'Pleasures of Knowing', ibid., p. 225.

'She was, I think, quite devoid of the gift of faith': Letter to Patrick Kinross, 31 December 1958, *Letters of Evelyn Waugh*, p. 516.

'The white smoke has gone up!': *Sister*, p. 296.

'a perfectly sound agnostic like everyone else': As reported by the novelist Elizabeth Taylor, autumn 1962. See Spurling, *Ivy*, p. 509.

Raymond Mortimer's country house: Raymond Mortimer was literary editor of the *New Statesman* 1935–47. He shared Long Crichel with the musicologist Eddy Sackville-West, the critic Desmond Shawe-Taylor; and Eardley Knollys, a painter and colleague of James Lees-Milne at the National Trust.

'It is lovely there in the mornings at nine.': Letter to Hamilton Johnson, *Letters*, pp. 134–5.

the ideal church she imagined back in 1929: Typescript, ERM archive. *St Paul's Review* (London Diocesan Quarterly), 1 (1).

Here, at last, she met Dorothy L. Sayers: When Dorothy L. Sayers died in 1956 Rose was one of the small circle invited to the ceremony of burying her ashes under the tower of St Anne's. My thanks to Barbara Reynolds, biographer and god-daughter of D. L. Sayers, for this information. Barbara Reynolds was one of those present.

'rather like a visit to the moon': Letter to Hamilton Johnson, 25 September 1955, *Last Letters*, pp. 208–9.

'wth scarlet door & cupboard': Letter to Gerard Irvine, 13 December 1953. ERM archive.

'Rose in her scooting little old car': James Pope-Hennessy, Diary entry, 1 June 1950, *A Lonely Business*.

'a few tiresome things such as schools': Letter to Jean, 9 March 1954, *Sister*, pp. 161–2.

'You nurse and I preach': Letter to Jean, 28 December 1953, ibid., pp. 155–6.

'an intuition that I shall die': Letter to Jean, 22 March 1955, ibid., p. 174.

'the ideal and romantic and nostalgic vision': Letter to Hamilton Johnson, 6 February 1956, *Last Letters*, p. 219.

'I adopted for Laurie': Letter to Hamilton Johnson, 24 September 1956, *Last Letters*, pp. 229–32.

'Dirge for Trebizond': *Times Literary Supplement*, 24 June 1955.

'She thinks my camel stands for "the Catholic Church"': Letter to William Plomer, 6 November 1956. Durham University.

'Mad camel plays a big part in unusual book': Letter to Jean, 24 September 1956, *Sister*, p. 203.

'I didn't mean it to be mainly funny': Letter to Jean, 28 August 1956, ibid., p 199.

'Don't think my jokes': Letter to Hamilton Johnson, 18 August 1956, *Last Letters*, p. 227.

'But something in the book': Letter to Hamilton Johnson, 14 October 1956, ibid., p. 238.

'I too had hoped for an Anglican victory': Letter to William Plomer, 31 October 1956. Durham University.

'It's a book I have had in mind to write for a long time': Letter to Rosamond Lehmann, 11 September 1956, King's College Archives.

'read aloud the bits she most enjoyed': Letter to William Plomer, 31 October 1956. Durham University.

James Tait Black Memorial Prize: Ivy Compton-Burnett was especially pleased as her own novel *Mother and Son* had won the previous year.

'I have been having a marvellous time': Letter to David Ley, 27 May 1957. ERM archive.

'I prefer "Miss"': Letter to E. M. Forster, 8 January 1958, ERM archive.

'Now I find that hip-breaking has been lately quite an epidemic': Letter to William Plomer, 28 May 1958. Durham University.

'John Betjeman came to see me at Charing X': Letter to David Ley, 12 May 1958. ERM archive.

'If I was a clergyman I would live in Venice': Letter to Jean, 22 September 1958, *Sister*, p. 287.

'What on earth are *you* doing here?': Anthony Powell, 'Pleasures of Knowing Rose Macaulay', CBS, p. 233.

Trebizond was 'like coming home': Letter to Jean, 14 September 1958, *Sister*, p. 287.

'The New Argonauts': *Queen*, 30 September 1958.

She died on 30 October 1958: Rose's estate at her death was valued at just over £84,000.

'She was forever in transit': Rosamond Lehmann, 'Pleasures of Knowing Rose Macaulay', CBS, pp. 225–6.

Epilogue: Letters

Unless otherwise stated all quotations are from letters, documents and newspaper cuttings in the ERM archive, Boxes 9, 10, 11, 13 and 14, in Trinity College, Cambridge, deposited by Constance Babington Smith.

'That is the worst': *The Writings of E. M. Forster*, p. 251.

In 1960 *Lady Chatterley's Lover* had been unbanned: Rose was not a fan of D. H. Lawrence's work: 'so tiresome about sex and so often a bore,' she had written of him to Jocelyn Brooke, Christmas Day 1955. HRHRC, Texas.

third volume of letters: *Letters to a Sister*, edited by Constance Babington Smith (1964).

Her love affair with a married man: One or two people pointed out that the few references to the married man in the *Letters* have attention drawn to them by Constance Babington Smith in her introduction; they suggested it was not unlike the commentaries in school editions of Latin verse where the editor gives full details in the annotations of all the naughty bits in the text that he felt obliged to leave out.

'began by making smart hats': Letter to Hamilton Johnson, *Last Letters*, p. 258.

'dignity and an ancient tradition': 'How to Choose a Religion', in *A Casual Commentary*, pp. 5–13.

Constance and Jean disputed the logic: Rose wrote: '. . . Destroy all papers unread and in bulk. I do not want letters and papers sorted and gone through. Please do not let any relations or friends go to the flat to help.' ERM archive.

'that rat-faced priest': Quoted by A. N. Wilson in his lecture on Rose Macaulay published in *Founders and Followers*, p. 147.

James Lees-Milne's Rose: 30 September 1972, in *A Mingled Measure, Diaries 1953–1972*, p. 287. This summing-up of Rose comes at the end of a somewhat embellished version of the Rose/Gerald story as recounted by the archaeologist Joan Evans, who told him 'the whole story of Rose Macaulay's love affair with Gerald O'Donovan. He was a renegade priest who ran away from the Beda College in Rome to marry Beryl Verschoyle . . . He met Rose during the first war and they had a passionate and lasting affair. The story in the *Sunday Times* of the flat being bombed and all the lover's letters being destroyed was entirely autobiographical.' [The *Sunday Times* ran 'Miss Anstruther's Letters', which had been published for the first time in England as an appendix to Constance Babington Smith's biography.]

Malcolm Muggeridge's splendidly eccentric vision: Muggeridge's review of *Letters to a Sister* in the *Evening Standard* began: 'I have often thought of writing a story about the end of the world in which the final destroyer of the human race would be not some power-drunk dictator armed with nuclear or bacteriological weapons, but a frail, kindly spinster lady of impeccable morals, humane sentiments and enlightened views living respectably and abstemiously in London, W.1. Searching around among my acquaintances for someone who would fill the part, none seemed more suitable than the late Dame Rose Macaulay.'

On *The End of the Affair.* See *Letters to a Friend*, pp. 196 and 343–4.

ACKNOWLEDGEMENTS

The author gratefully acknowledges financial assistance from the Society of Authors and from the Arts Council of Great Britain, without whose help this book could not have been written.

I would like to thank the following for their careful readings of all or parts of the manuscript: Lennie Goodings, Diana Hendry, Judith Murray, Jenny Newman and Michèle Roberts.

I would also like to thank the following for help given to me in all sorts of different ways: Pauline Adams, Gabriele Annan, John and Diana Ashby, Patricia Babington Smith, Veronica Babington Smith, Pat Baker, Henriette van Berkel, Michael Bott, Sabina Bowler-Reed, John Breakell, Doreen Chalmers, Alexander LeFanu Collins, Christopher Collins, HoneyBee LeFanu Collins, Ismay LeFanu Collins, Charles Colquhoun, Caroline Dawnay, Ann Ferguson, John Ferguson, Rowena Fowler, Polly Gaster, Cathal Geraghty, Helen Gillon, Awen Hamilton, Tessa Hargreaves, Peter Henderson, David Hopkins, Barbara Huelin, Jonathan Hunt, Gerard Irvine, Rosemary Irvine, Hannah Kanter, Francis King, Wai Kirkpatrick, Ann Le Fanu, Richard Le Fanu, Ian Lightbody, Rusty MacLean, Monica McLean, Rosalind Moad, Ann Mossman, Virginia Murray, Jill Nicholls, Nancy Nichols, Mary Anne O'Donovan, Christopher Phipps, Philippa Pearce, David Punter, Barbara Reynolds, Andrew Roberts, Terry Rogers, John Ryan, Laura Salvini, Sheila Stern, Muriel Thomas, Lisa Tuttle, Harriet Harvey Wood.

I am very grateful to the following for allowing me to consult private papers in their possession: Nancy Nichols, Dr Mary Anne O'Donovan and John F. Ryan.

I am especially grateful to the staff of the Wren Library, Trinity College, Cambridge, the staff of Bristol Central Library, and would like to express thanks to those who run the invaluable service of interlibrary loan.

The author and publisher gratefully acknowledge the following for permission to quote:

Rose Macaulay by permission of PFD on behalf of the Estate of Rose Macaulay and also the Master and Fellows of Trinity College Cambridge;

V.S. Pritchett reproduced by permission of PFD on behalf of the Estate of V. S. Pritchett;

Rosamond Lehmann by permission of the Society of Authors on behalf of the Estate of Rosamond Lehmann;

E. M. Forster by permission of the Provost and Scholars of King's College Cambridge and the Society of Authors on behalf of the Estate of E. M. Forster;

Rupert Brooke unpublished material by permission of Jon Stallworthy on behalf of the Estate of Rupert Brooke;

Extracts from the *Diaries of Virginia Woolf* by Virginia Woolf published by Hogarth Press, used by permission of the executors of the Virginia Woolf Estate and the Random House Group Ltd;

Extracts from the *Letters of Virginia Woolf* by Virginia Woolf published by Hogarth Press, used by permission of the executors of the Virginia Woolf Estate and the Random House Group Ltd;

Victor Gollancz by permission of Victor Gollancz Ltd;

Pauline Adams by permission of Pauline Adams and Oxford University Press;

Malcolm Muggeridge by permission of David Higham Associates on behalf of the Estate of Malcolm Muggeridge;

Evelyn Waugh by permission of PFD on behalf of the Estate of Evelyn Waugh;

James Pope-Hennessy by permission of PFD on behalf of the Estate of James Pope-Hennessy;

Storm Jameson by permission of PFD on behalf of the Estate of Storm Jameson;

Quotations from Vera Brittain are included by permission of her literary executors, Mark Bostridge and Rebecca Williams;

Judith Kazantzis by permission of Judith Kazantzis from her introduction to *Scars Upon my Heart: Women's Poetry and Verse of the First World War*, ed. Catherine Reilly;

Elizabeth Bowen by permission of Curtis Brown Group Ltd. on behalf of the Estate of Elizabeth Bowen, copyright © Elizabeth Bowen 1956.

Diagram of 'A Tangled Mesh of Modernists' by permission of Bonnie Kime Scott;

James Lees-Milne by permission of David Higham Associates;

C. V. Wedgwood by permission of the Principal and Fellows of Lady Margaret Hall, Oxford;

Anthony Powell: by permission of John and Tristram Powell on behalf of the Estate of Anthony Powell;

Extracts from *Olive Willis and Downe House: An Adventure in Education* by Anne Ridler reproduced with permission of John Murray Ltd.;

Excerpts from the 1903 Somerville Going-Down Play reproduced with permission of the Principal and Fellows of Somerville College, Oxford;

Correspondence with William Plomer reproduced by courtesy of Durham University Library Archives & Special Collections;

Correspondence with Katharine Tynan reproduced by courtesy of the Director and Librarian, The John Rylands University Library of Manchester;

Correspondence from the John Murray Archives by courtesy of John Murray Ltd;

Correspondence from the Jonathan Cape and Hogarth Press Archives by permission of the Random House Group.

The author and publisher would like to thank the following for permission to reproduce illustrations in this book:

Veronica Babington Smith p.1 bottom right; p.2 bottom; p.3 top left; p.8 bottom; p.20 top left and top right; p.11 middle and bottom; p.14 bottom; p.15 top and bottom; Cambridgeshire Collection, Cambridge Central Library p.8 top; English Heritage NMR p.16 bottom; Victor Gollancz Ltd p.12 middle; Hulton Getty p.5 bottom left; p.11 top; Master and Fellows of Trinity College Cambridge and the Rose Macaulay Estate p.1 top left; top right and bottom left; p.2 top left; middle and right left; p.3 top right and bottom right; Nancy Nichols p.13 top right; The National Portrait Gallery, London p.4 top; p.12 bottom; p.13 top left and bottom; p.16 top; Dr Mary Anne O'Donovan p.9 bottom; p.10 bottom left; Principal and Fellows of Somerville College Oxford p.3 bottom left; Private Collection p.5 bottom right; John Ryan endpapers; Timepix p.10 bottom right.

Every effort has been made to trace the copyright holders of the copyright material in this book and to provide the correct details of copyright. Virago and the author regret any oversight and upon written notification will rectify any omission in future reprints or editions.

BIBLIOGRAPHY

Books and articles about Rose Macaulay

Annan, Noel, 'The Intellectual Aristocracy', in *Studies in Social History: A Tribute to G. M. Trevelyan*, ed J. H. Plumb, Longmans, Green, 1955

Bensen, Alice, *Rose Macaulay*, Twayne English Authors Series No 85, Twayne, 1969

Chalmers, Doreen, 'The Macaulays in Great Shelford', in *Great Shelford Remembered 1884–1994*, privately printed by Great Shelford Parish Council, 1994

Crawford, Alice, *Paradise Pursued: The Novels of Rose Macaulay*, Associated University Press, 1995 (this contains an extensive selected bibliography of articles and reviews by Rose Macaulay, and of reviews of her work)

Emery, Jane, *Rose Macaulay: A Writer's Life*, John Murray, 1991

Fitzgerald, Penelope, introduction to *The World My Wilderness*, Virago, 1982

Fromm, Gloria, 'Re-inscribing *The Years:* Virginia Woolf, Rose Macaulay and the critics', *Journal of Modern Literature*, 13/2, July 1986

Howatch, Susan, introduction to *They Were Defeated*, Oxford University Press, 1981

Passty, Jeanette, *Eros and Androgyny: The Legacy of Rose Macaulay*, Associated University Press, 1988

Pryce-Jones, Alan, introduction to *Orphan Island*, Collins, 1960

Smith, Constance Babington, *Rose Macaulay*, Collins, 1972

Squier, Susan, 'Rose Macaulay', in *The Gender of Modernism*, ed Bonnie Kime Scott, Indiana University Press, 1990

Wedgwood, C. V., introduction to *They Were Defeated*, Collins, 1960

Wilson, A. N., 'Rose Macaulay', *Founders and Followers: Literary Lectures given on the occasion of the 150th Anniversary of the Founding of The London Library*, Sinclair-Stevenson, 1992

—— introduction to *Told by an Idiot*, Virago, 1982

Selected background reading

Adams, Pauline, *Somerville for Women*, Oxford University Press, 1996

Berry, Paul and Bostridge, Mark, *Vera Brittain: A Life*, Chatto & Windus, 1995

Bowen, Elizabeth, *Collected Impressions*, Longmans Green, 1950

—— 'Coming to London' in *Coming to London*, ed. John Lehmann

Braybrooke, Patrick, *Some Goddesses of the Pen*, C. W. Daniel Co, 1927

Brittain, Vera, *Testament of Youth*, Victor Gollancz Ltd, 1933

—— *The Women at Oxford: A Fragment of History*, Harrap, 1960

Brooke, Rupert, *The Collected Poems of Rupert Brooke, with a Memoir by Edward Marsh*, Sidgwick & Jackson, 1918

Brooke, Rupert, *The Letters of Rupert Brooke*, ed. Geoffrey Keynes, Faber, 1968

Campbell, James Methuen, *Denton Welch: Writer and Artist*, Tartarus, 2002

Connolly, Cyril, *The Condemned Playground, Essays 1927–1944*, Routledge, 1945

Crane, David (ed.), *Letters between a Victorian Schoolboy and his Family, 1892–1895*, privately printed, 1999

Cunningham, Valentine, *British Writers of the Thirties*, Oxford University Press, 1988

Delany, Paul, *The Neo-Pagans: Rupert Brooke and the Ordeal of Youth*, Free Press, 1987

Dick, Kay, *Ivy and Stevie: Conversations and Reflections*, Duckworth, 1971

Dudley Edwards, Ruth, *Victor Gollancz: A Biography*, Victor Gollancz, 1987

Dunn, Jane, *Antonia White: A Life*, Jonathan Cape, 1998

Eksteins, Modris, *Rites of Spring: The Great War and the Birth of the Modern Age*, Bantam, 1989

Forster, E. M., *Selected Letters Vol II 1921–1970*, eds. Mary Lago and P. N. Furbank, Collins, 1985

———— *Two Cheers for Democracy*, Edward Arnold, 1951

———— *Abinger Harvest*, Edward Arnold, 1936

Fussell, Paul, *Abroad: British Literary Travelling between the Wars*, Oxford University Press, 1980

———— *The Great War and Modern Memory*, Oxford University Press, 1975

Gilbert, Sandra M. and Gubar, Susan, *No Man's Land: The Place of the Woman Writer in the Twentieth Century, Vols 1, 2 & 3*, Yale University Press, 1987, 1989, 1994

Glendinning, Victoria, *Elizabeth Bowen: Portrait of a Writer*, Weidenfeld & Nicolson, 1977

Gollancz, Victor, *Reminiscences of Affection*, Victor Gollancz, 1968

Gorham, Deborah, *Vera Brittain: A Feminist Life*, Blackwell, 1996

Grant Cook, Marjorie, (in order of publication), *Verdun Days in Paris*, (as Marjorie Grant), Collins, 1918

———— *Latchkey Ladies* (as M. Grant), Heinemann, 1921

———— *Another Way of Love*, Heinemann, 1923

———— *Glory Jam* (as Caroline Seaford), Gollancz, 1934

———— *More Than Kind* (as Caroline Seaford), Gollancz, 1935

———— *The Velvet Deer* (as Caroline Seaford), Lovat Dickson, 1937

———— *Dear Family* (as Caroline Seaford), Gollancz, 1938

———— *They Grew in Beauty* (as Caroline Seaford), Jonathan Cape, 1946

Gretton, R. H., *Modern History of the English People 1880–1922*, Secker, 1930

Hamilton, Agnes, *Remembering My Good Friends*, Jonathan Cape, 1944

Hardwick, Joan, *The Yeats Sisters: A Biography of Susan and Elizabeth Yeats*, Pandora Press, 1996

Hart-Davis, Rupert, (ed.), *T. S. Eliot: A Symposium for his 70th Birthday*, 1958

Hassall, Christopher, *Rupert Brooke: A Biography*, 1964

Hynes, Samuel, *The Edwardian Turn of Mind*, Oxford University Press, 1968

Jameson, Storm, *Journey from the North, Vols 1 & 2*, Collins and Harvill, 1969, 1970

John, Augustus, *Chiaroscuro: Fragments of Autobiography*, Jonathan Cape, 1952

Keir, David, *The House of Collins*, Collins, 1952

King, Francis, *E. M. Forster and His World*, Thames & Hudson, 1978

Lee, Hermione, *Virginia Woolf*, Chatto & Windus, 1996

Lees-Milne, James, *Diaries: Ancestral Voices & Prophesying Peace 1942–45*, Chatto & Windus 1975 & 1977; John Murray 1995

———— *Caves of Ice & Midway on the Waves 1946–49*, Chatto & Windus 1983 & Faber 1985; John Murray 1996

———— *A Mingled Measure 1953–1972*, John Murray, 1994

Lehmann, John, *The Whispering Gallery: Autobiography I*, Longmans, Green, 1955

———— *I Am My Brother, Autobiography II*, Longmans, Green, 1960

———— *The Ample Proposition, Autobiography III*, Eyre & Spottiswoode, 1966

———— *Coming to London*, (ed.), Phoenix House, 1957

Light, Alison, *Forever England: Femininity, Literature and Conservatism Between the Wars*, Routledge, 1991

Lynd, Robert, *Galway at the Races, Selected Essays*, ed. Sean McMahon, Lilliput Press, 1990

Lynd, Sylvia, *The Goldfinches*, Richard Cobden-Sanderson, 1920

Macaulay, Margaret, *The Sentence Absolute*, James Nisbet, 1914

Mackenzie, Compton, *My Life and Times, Octaves V – VIII*, Chatto & Windus, 1966–9

Marsh, Edward, (ed.), *Georgian Poetry (5 Vols)*, The Poetry Bookshop, 1913–22

Maslen, Elizabeth, *Political and Social Issues in British Women's Fiction 1928–1968*, Palgrave, 2001

Michaëlis, Karen, *The Dangerous Age: Letters & Fragments from a Woman's Diary*, The Bodley Head, 1912

Montefiore, Janet, *Men and Women Writers of the 1930s*, Routledge 1996

O'Donovan, Gerald, (in order of publication) *Father Ralph*, Macmillan, 1913 (Brandon, 1993);

———— *Waiting*, Macmillan, 1914

———— *How They Did It*, Methuen, 1920

—— *Conquest*, Constable, 1920

—— *Vocations*, Martin Secker, 1921

—— *The Holy Tree*, Heinemann, 1922

Plomer, William, *Double Lives: An Autobiography*, Jonathan Cape, 1943

—— *At Home: Memoirs*, Jonathan Cape, 1958

Poems of Today, Sidgwick & Jackson, 1915

Pope-Hennessy, James, *West Indian Summer: A Retrospect*, Batsford, 1943

—— *A Lonely Business*, ed. Peter Quennell, Weidenfeld & Nicolson, 1981

Pryce-Jones, Alan (ed.), *Little Innocents: Childhood Reminiscences*, Cobden-Sanderson, 1932 (reprinted Oxford University Press, 1986)

Raverat, Gwen, *Period Piece*, Faber & Faber, 1952

Reilly, Catherine (ed.), *Scars Upon my Heart: Women's Poetry and Verse of the First World War*, Virago, 1981

Rhondda, Lady, *This Was My World*, Macmillan, 1933

Ridler, Anne, *Olive Willis and Downe House: An Adventure in Education*, John Murray, 1967

Royde-Smith, N. G. (ed.), *The Westminster Problems Book: Prose and Verse*, Methuen & Co, 1908

Royde-Smith, N. G. (ed.), *The Second Problems Book: Prizes and Proximes*, Sidgwick & Jackson, 1909

   (as Naomi Royde-Smith, in order of publication)

—— *Skin-Deep*, Constable, 1927

—— *The Bridge*, Gollancz, 1932

—— *Jake*, Macmillan, 1935

Ryan, John F., 'Gerald O'Donovan: Priest, Novelist and Irish Revivalist', *Journal of the Galway Archaeological and Historical Society*, 48, 1996

—— Introduction to *Father Ralph*, Brandon 1993

Sage, Lorna (ed.), *The Cambridge Guide to Women's Writing in English*, Cambridge University Press, 1999

Sassoon, Siegfried, *The War Poems of Siegfried Sassoon*, ed Rupert Hart-Davis, Faber & Faber, 1983

Scott, Bonnie Kime, ed. *The Gender of Modernism: A Critical Anthology*, Indiana University Press, 1990

Showalter, Elaine, *A Literature of Their Own*, Virago, 1978

Sinclair, May, *The Divine Fire*, Constable, 1904

Sisman, Adam, *Boswell's Presumptuous Task*, Hamish Hamilton, 2000

Sprigge, Elizabeth, *The Life of Ivy Compton-Burnett*, Gollancz, 1973

Spurling, Hilary, *Ivy: The Life of Ivy Compton Burnett*, Richard Cohen, 1995 (*Ivy When Young*, Gollancz, 1974 / *Secrets of a Woman's Heart*, Hodder, 1984)

Trotter, Jacqueline (ed.), *Valour and Vision, Poems of the War 1914–1918*, Longmans, Green, 1920

Waugh, Evelyn, *The Letters of Evelyn Waugh*, ed. Mark Amory, Weidenfeld & Nicolson, 1980

Welch, Denton, *The Journals of Denton Welch*, ed. Michael De-La-Noy, Allison & Busby, 1984 (Abridged edition first published 1952)

────── *A Last Sheaf*, John Lehmann, 1951

Whistler, Theresa, *Walter de la Mare: The Imagination of the Heart*, Duckworth, 1993

Woolf, Leonard, *Downhill All the Way*, Hogarth, 1968

Woolf, Virginia, *The Diary of Virginia Woolf, 5 Vols*, ed. Anne Olivier Bell, Hogarth Press, 1977–84

────── *The Letters of Virginia Woolf, 6 Vols*, ed Nigel Nicolson and Joanne Trautmann, Hogarth Press, 1975–80

INDEX

Petersfield.

Dec: 26th 1920

My 🦌 Mary

Thankyou so much for the ▬ you sent me. It is a beautiful one, and will be most useful for ❓❓❓❓ or for 🖐✏️. 👁 hope 🐑 enjoyed Christmas and had lots of things in your 🧦.   I have left my 🖨, with which I usually write my letters, behind in London, so forgive this bad writing. There is a 🐕 here called Ben, and a 🐐 called Fluff, who is very